WILD
MAN OF
LETTERS

WILD MAN OF LETTERS

The Story of P. R. Stephensen

CRAIG MUNRO

MELBOURNE UNIVERSITY PRESS
1984

For Dick and Diane and family, With much love, and in special memory of three important dates — 1955 (Vancouver), 1975 (Kingston), and 1990 (Brisbane). The rest is history (and, of course, biography)!

Craig
16/10/90

First published 1984
Printed in Australia at
Griffin Press Limited for
Melbourne University Press, Carlton, Victoria 3053

This book is copyright. Apart from any fair dealing for the purposes of private study, research, criticism or review, as permitted under the Copyright Act, no part may be reproduced by any process without written permission. Enquiries should be made to the publisher.

© Craig Munro 1984

National Library of Australia Cataloguing-in-Publication entry

Munro, Craig, 1958– . *This was a publisher's error —*
Wild man of letters. *which I'll undoubtedly*
Bibliography. *come to treasure as I grow*
Includes index.
ISBN 0 522 84275 5.

1. Stephensen, P. R. (Percy Reginald), 1901-1965—Biography. I. Authors, Australian—Biography. I. Title.
A828'.209   *ever more ancient.*

Contents

	Preface	ix
	Part 1: Queensland, 1901–1924	1
1	Wartime Rebel	3
2	Students and Workers	12
	Part 2: England, 1924–1932	29
3	A Bolshevik comes to Oxford	31
4	Bloomsbury Fanfrolics	46
5	D. H. Lawrence and the Lord's Police	68
6	Mandrake, Magic and Depression	88
7	Cutting Adrift	104
	Part 3: Sydney, 1932–1942	113
8	A New Endeavour	115
9	Xavier Herbert, P. R. Stephensen & Co.	135
10	Mercurial Nationalism	150
11	War of Words	170
12	Fascism and Australia First	197
	Part 4: Liverpool, Loveday and Tatura Internment Camps, 1942–1945	221
13	Behind Barbed Wire: High Treason or Low Comedy	223
	Part 5: Victoria; Sydney, 1945–1965	249
14	Ghost in Exile	251
	Abbreviations	272
	Notes	273
	Bibliography	301
	Index	311

Illustrations

Plates

	between pages
Stephensen's grandparents	4–5
His parents on their wedding day	4–5
Henry Tardent, Stephensen's Swiss grandfather	4–5
Aged twenty months in 1903	4–5
At the age of twelve in July 1914	4–5
Maryborough Boys' Grammar School	4–5
The Rugby team	4–5
A group of St John's Collegians in 1919	4–5

	facing page
The cover design of *The Kingdom of Shylock*	20
Lieutenant Stephensen in his militia uniform	21
Leaving for England on the *Jervis Bay*	21
Queenslanders in Paris at Easter in 1925	52
Stephensen with Tom Inglis Moore and Robert Hall in Paris	52
Winifred and Inky in Oxford in May 1925	53
Their scout with Stephensen and Burton in Oxford	53

	between pages
Jack Lindsay and Stephensen in the Fanfrolico office	100–1
The title page and the last page of *The Antichrist of Nietzsche*	100–1
D. H. Lawrence in Florence in 1928	100–1
A photograph of the clay bust of Lawrence used in *Lady Chatterley's Lover*	100–1
Stephensen in 1929	100–1
Aleister Crowley in 1929	100–1
The row houses in Knockholt, Kent	100–1
Ailsa Lodge, Toys Hill, Kent	100–1

	facing page
Rosaline Stephensen riding with her brother in January 1932	148
Miles Franklin with the pet monkey	148

viii   *Illustrations*

With Norman Lindsay at Springwood, just after Stephensen's return to Australia	148
Xavier Herbert in London in 1932	149
W. J. Miles in the 1930s	149
At Gundagai in July 1939	180
Sadie and Xavier Herbert in Darwin in the 1930s	180
The September 1937 *Publicist*	181
Stephensen with his brother Eric and friend Monty Tickle	244
Stephensen in 1939	244
With Xavier Herbert and W. J. Miles	244
J. T. Patten	245
Stephensen and Winifred in 1941	245
Ian Mudie in 1941	245
A portrait painted at the Tatura internment camp in 1943	245
With Frank Clune in the late 1940s	276
Stephensen and Winifred with friends at Bethanga in 1950	276
Stephensen with Albert Namatjira in the late 1950s	277
Inky and Winifred with Jules Tardent in Sydney in 1961	277

Line Drawings

	page
The title page and the last page of *Propertius in Love*	56–7
The *Fanfrolicana* catalogue, June 1928	60
A proof copy of the first number of the *London Aphrodite*	63
One of the drawings from *The Sink of Solitude*	70
The title page and the last page of *The Paintings of D. H. Lawrence*	83
Crowley's cover design for his *Confessions*	95
The title page design for the *Confessions*	97
Norman Lindsay's *Bulletin* cartoon, 2 November 1932	118
A copy of *The Foundations of Culture in Australia*	167
Stephensen's letter to Ian Mudie, 22 March 1937	174
A copy of the special rag paper edition of *Capricornia*	182
The June 1938 *Publicist*	190–1
Stephensen's first *Publicist* editorial for 1942	214
George Finey's caricature of Stephensen in the *Sunday Telegraph*	230
The internment camp at Loveday, South Australia	237
Stephensen's letter to Ian Mudie, 10 March 1944	242

Preface

During fifty years of personal, literary and political adventures, P. R. Stephensen hoarded correspondence, books, manuscripts and a mass of other material from which, in the 1950s, he had planned to write an autobiography. Yet he got no further than a brief memoir of the Fanfrolico Press, *Kookaburras and Satyrs* (1954), some articles and other fragments.

The late Walter Stone suggested that a life of P. R. Stephensen would require three volumes at least, and the daunting prospect of this, as well as advancing age, meant that Stone himself never wrote the biography of his friend Inky Stephensen.

In the early 1970s Richard Fotheringham wrote an account of Stephensen's first thirty years, but unfortunately did not have access to the extensive collection of uncatalogued Stephensen Papers in the Mitchell Library, Sydney. These papers were, and still are, restricted but, with the support of Stephensen's stepson and literary executor, Jack Lockyer, I was granted special access to them and this formed the basis for much of my research.

For various reasons, including the nature of the material available, and the style of my own approach to history, this is not a psychologically analytical or experimental biography, but rather a chronological narrative in which the evidence is carefully sifted, arranged and presented.

I would like to take this opportunity to thank those who assisted my work. I owe a special debt to a number of Stephensen's friends, relatives and acquaintances who granted me interviews, supplied important material, and in some cases read drafts of this biography: Jack Lockyer, the late Professor Herbert Burton, Cecil Hadgraft, Lord Roberthall, Jack Lindsay, Bruce Muirden, Rosaline Stephensen, Eric Stephensen, the late Walter Stone, Arthur Dibley, Professor A. J. P. Taylor, and Professor Manning Clark. I am also indebted to Richard Fotheringham and to Dr Laurie Hergenhan for their comments on the manuscript.

My research could not have been completed without the resources and time offered by Margaret O'Hagan and the staff of the Fryer Library,

University of Queensland; Glenda Acland, the University of Queensland archivist; Shirley Humphries and other librarians at the Mitchell Library, Sydney; the Australian manuscripts section of the National Library, Canberra; and the reference section of the State Library of Queensland. I would also like to thank Caroline Creevey for transcribing research work, Sandra Gough for typing the manuscript, and Sue Munro for preparing the index.

For permission to quote from unpublished letters and other material, acknowledgement is made to: Jack Lockyer and the Mitchell Library (for the work of P. R. Stephensen); Laurence Pollinger Ltd and the Estate of Mrs Frieda Lawrence Ravagli (for the work of D. H. Lawrence); the Permanent Trustee Co. Ltd (for the work of Miles Franklin); Curtis Brown (Aust.) Pty Ltd, Janet Glad and Angus & Robertson Publishers (for the work of Norman Lindsay); Ailsa Morris Young (for the work of E. Morris Miller); A. P. Clune (for the work of Frank Clune); and Marjorie Barnard.

The Literature Board of the Australia Council generously supported and encouraged my research as did the English Department of the University of Queensland (where I held the Hayes Postgraduate Scholarship).

Craig Munro

'but heavens! how that man could talk. He electrified large meetings. He had faith—don't you see?—he had the faith. He could get himself to believe anything—anything. He would have been a splendid leader of an extreme party.' 'What party?' I asked. 'Any party,' answered the other.

                      Joseph Conrad
                      Heart of Darkness, 1902

Part One

Queensland, 1901–1924

The alternatives are fascism or proletarian dictatorship.
In any case we live in stirring times... Perhaps with Banjo
and other varsity chappies, we could make History
very interesting for a time.
                              P. R. Stephensen
                              letter, 1923

Our silly aim was to astonish the burghers.
                              P. R. Stephensen
                              Kookaburras and Satyrs, 1954

1
Wartime Rebel

In September 1944 the Bankruptcy Court in Melbourne was the scene of one of the most sensational hearings in Australian history. But this had nothing to do with bankruptcy. It was a commission of inquiry into the internment of a group suspected of plotting treason and sabotage. The leader of the group had already been imprisoned without trial for more than two and a half years, and was escorted to the inquiry each day by a uniformed soldier. When he entered the witness box his name was given as Percy Reginald Stephensen, though he was more widely known as 'Inky' or PRS. On his first day in the stand he somewhat disconcerted the court by describing himself as a 'Man of Letters'. It was a defiant but also an exact definition. Having been admired by D. H. Lawrence, parodied by Aldous Huxley, trailed by MI5, and vilified as a traitor in his own country, P. R. Stephensen was indeed one of Australia's most remarkable men of letters.

For the inquiry he had obtained a hearing aid, and he answered questions in a clear, if rather high-pitched voice, the result of many years of defective hearing though he was still in his early forties. In court he wore a double-breasted suit with the wide lapels fashionable in the 1940s. His distinguishing feature was a 'toothbrush' moustache, a characteristic he shared with Adolf Hitler and the comedian Charlie Chaplin.

Military intelligence reports read out at the inquiry made newspaper headlines, and the public gallery of the courtroom was packed with legal observers. Stephensen was cross-examined in detail about his political beliefs and about his experiences during the 1920s and 1930s as a Rhodes Scholar, writer, publisher, company director and Communist Party activist. More recently he had been both a critic and an admirer of Hitler, though it was his apparent sympathy for Germany and Japan which absorbed most of the inquiry's attention. It should have been obvious from the first words he spoke in court that he was essentially a literary man and an intellectual. But this philosophical anarchist, who numbered Gandhi among his political heroes, was too complex and volatile, too intelligent and at the same time too naïve. So the wartime commission of inquiry completed the destruction of his public reputation.

P. R. Stephensen has continued to puzzle historians, and to exasperate and intrigue those who knew him. His comet-like career blazed from one world war to the next, though he fought in neither, spending the first at boarding school and the second behind barbed wire in a concentration camp. He had been both fascinated and horrified by the 1914–18 war in which mass slaughter and political propaganda established a new religion—the sacred cult of Anzac. Yet that war was also a time of social conflict, with uprisings and revolutions in many countries. For those of Stephensen's generation and political temper, issues such as loyalty and dissent, imperialism and national liberation became increasingly important.

On the haphazard path which led to his political heresy trial in 1944, Stephensen played with the competing ideologies of the twentieth century as if they were new and dangerous toys. He was a child of the age, who became a warrior and a victim of words.

With 'Viking' Danes on his father's side and French Swiss on his mother's, he had grown up to be proud of his racial origins, for this was a time when theories of eugenics were popular. Although his flamboyant style and intellectual interests were attributable to his mother's family, equally important to his sense of identity was his father's pioneering background in Queensland.[1]

His Danish grandfather, Jens Christian Julius Steffensen, had arrived in Maryborough by sailing ship in the 1870s with his wife and two brothers, settling at Tinana on the Mary River. The Steffensen family had left Denmark during a time of widespread hardship following Bismarck's invasion of the country on the now familiar pretext of a German population there. On arrival in Australia the family changed their religious affiliation from Danish Lutheran to the Church of England and Anglicized their name to Stephensen. Their first child, a girl, had been born in Denmark, and the first of eight sons, Christian Julius, was born at Tinana in 1878. A few years later, when the railway line moved west from Maryborough to Brooweena and Degilbo, Jens had the contract to supply stores to the construction teams. One of the staging places on the coach route to Gayndah had been Baxter's Live and Let Live Hotel on Degilbo Creek, and when the rail line came to a halt nearby, the township of Biggenden began. Jens built one of the first houses and opened a general store with a blacksmith shop at the back.

By the late 1890s his eldest son Christian was working in the Biggenden blacksmith shop where he became a qualified wheelwright. It was still a small bush township of fewer than two hundred people so Chris also shod horses and even made coffins. He never spoke Danish and was proud of being Australian born. In 1898 the Swiss Henry Tardent arrived with his family in Biggenden to establish an experimental state farm, having managed a similar farm at Westbrook near Toowoomba. Within a couple of

Stephensen's grandparents, Jens Christian Julius and Sedsel Christina Stephensen

His parents, Chris and Marie Stephensen, on their wedding day in 1900 (photograph by courtesy of Rosaline Stephensen)

Stephensen's Swiss grandfather, Henry Tardent, in 1923

Stephensen at twenty months, in 1903

Stephensen at the age of twelve in July 1914, a month before World War I began; with him are his sister Rosaline, nine, and baby sister Violet

Maryborough Boys' Grammar School (photograph by courtesy of Maryborough State High School)

MBGS rugby team, with Stephensen holding the ball; the controversial headmaster, J. T. Noble Wallace, is on the right

A group of St John's collegians in 1919; Fred Paterson is on the left of the front row, behind him in the second row are Herbert Burton (left) and Robert Hall, while Stephensen is in the back row on the right

years his teenage daughter Marie-Louise married the twenty-two-year-old Chris Stephensen. Henry Tardent was a significant influence on his son-in-law and an even more important influence on his first grandson, Percy Reginald Stephensen, who was born in the year of Australian Federation, 1901. For patriots like Chris Stephensen and Henry Tardent the coincidence must have seemed propitious.

Like the Steffensens, Henri Alexis Tardent had Anglicized his name to Henry on coming to Queensland. He was an ardent Australian nationalist though he maintained links with the Continent as a correspondent for French and Swiss publications. A former teacher of languages in Europe, Tardent had arrived in Queensland in 1887 and established a winery at Roma on the Darling Downs. In many respects he was the prototype for P. R. Stephensen. A brilliant linguist, Tardent was also a voluble and articulate public speaker who lost no time in organizing literary, debating and show societies in Biggenden. Later he was a newspaper editor in various parts of Queensland and contributed with equal enthusiasm to the fields of journalism, literature, science and politics. He was a friend of Andrew Fisher, the Labor member for Wide Bay who became prime minister in 1910, and Tardent himself stood unsuccessfully as a Labor candidate. His faith in Australian nationalism, in culture and democracy, formed a model which his grandson perhaps unconsciously strove to emulate and exceed.

The young Percy Stephensen did not have much regular contact with his Swiss grandfather, who had returned to Toowoomba in 1901, but Henry Tardent remained the family's intellectual and cultural figurehead. Stephensen's parents were no less energetic and public spirited. Only nineteen when her son Percy was born, Marie Stephensen became the Biggenden correspondent for the *Maryborough Chronicle*, and her husband Chris was secretary of the local Workers Political Organization (later the Labor Party branch). Although Chris was still working in his father's blacksmith shop, he and Marie lived on a small farm, Ivydale, just outside Biggenden. Later he took over the general store, and his seven brothers all worked in and around Biggenden or in other stores established by the pioneering Jens Stephensen. There had been an early goldrush in the district at a place called Paradise, and Jens had contracted to dismantle and move by dray a couple of buildings from this abandoned Eden to the new township of Biggenden.

Other mines were still in operation at Mount Shamrock and Mount Biggenden, and one of Percy Stephensen's boyhood memories was of driving Andrew Fisher out in a sulky to address the miners. Fisher had been a miner himself during the Gympie goldrush. With a father and a grandfather involved in politics, it was not surprising that Stephensen, even as a boy, should be fascinated by its machinery and drama. Queensland already boasted a strong tradition of labour politics, having had the first Labor government in Australia in the late 1890s, and during elections Stephensen was always among those waiting outside the Biggenden post office to observe the posting up of results.

Like all bush children he could ride practically before he could walk, and with his younger sister he went out riding and shooting, especially after the parrots which plagued the sorghum farms. His pony was called Togo after the Japanese admiral who had routed the Russians in 1905. The name was a joke but it also indicated the pervasive impact of this Asian naval victory which reawakened fears of the Yellow Peril and sustained the siege mentality of the White Australia Policy. Such unquestioned racism was as much a part of Stephensen's boyhood world as his bush adventures and his liberal democrat family. The one Chinese market gardener in the area, Willy Ah Foo, a relic of the goldrush days, was often taunted and ridiculed by the children. Aborigines had already been driven out of the area, concentrated on unfamiliar reserves and their numbers depleted by sickness as well as by violence. One boy did attend local cricket matches, travelling from the Barambah Aboriginal settlement further inland. A shadowy guilt about this genocide stayed with Stephensen and, along with theories of eugenics, formed in him a durable but also ambiguous racism.[2]

He attended the Biggenden primary school, and then, at the end of 1914, made the slow train journey down to the coast to sit for the state scholarship exam at Maryborough, staying overnight at Hansen's Coffee Palace. All students who obtained at least a 50 per cent pass were awarded scholarships, putting further strain on a school system already understaffed because of wartime recruiting. Stephensen was placed in the first hundred candidates in Queensland and won a two-year scholarship which enabled him to board at the Maryborough Boys' Grammar School.[3]

Founded in 1881 on the lines of an English public school, MBGS provided education for a privileged minority and was controlled by a board of trustees representing the Maryborough establishment. The headmaster, J. T. Noble Wallace, was a graduate of the University of London, and had taught at Maryborough since the 1880s, having married the daughter of the school's founder. The year Stephensen began there, 1915, was a significant one for the country and for the school. Not only did it witness Gallipoli and endless patriotic rallies, it was also the year T. J. Ryan's new Labor government in Queensland introduced sweeping and innovative changes. For a short time in 1898 Ryan had been a teacher at Maryborough Grammar, and one of his government's progressive measures was to replace the school's mercantile trustees with a board of Maryborough Labor supporters whom the headmaster regarded as ill-educated tradesmen and trouble-making radicals.

Maryborough was a prosperous provincial centre of five thousand people with sawmills and engineering works, and the boys' grammar school was a prominent part of the city's social hierarchy. With about thirty boarders and fewer than a hundred day boys, the school occupied a ten-acre site in central Maryborough. The main building, an imposing slab of Victorian gothic with elaborate timber arches and fretwork, accommodated classrooms and assembly hall as well as dormitories and the headmaster's residence. The school prospectus assured parents that 'every boy has a separate bed', and in the tradition of such establishments the headmaster's wife was 'mother' to the boarders.[4] The head himself was a severe disciplinarian who, along with his three assistant masters, dealt out regular doses of the cane, six 'cuts' being the favoured remedy.

Beside the main building was the gym, a high-roofed pavilion with a sawdust floor. When Stephensen began at the school the bars, rings, and vaulting horse were rusty or splintered, and the gym had become an essential part of the initiation tortures. New boys were made to perform on the horizontal bars, forced to crawl under the legs of students with belts, or packed like sardines into a box holding the cricket gear. Yet it was the most innocent seeming of these rituals which brought Stephensen down with a jolt.

Adjacent to the gym was a pole topped by a revolving plate from which radiated ropes with wooden handles. This was the giant's stride and it provided an exhilarating experience when circulated normally, each boy able to spin around with his legs momentarily off the ground. However, when a couple of the stronger boys brought their ropes under that of any particular victim the force would propel him in a terrifying arc almost horizontal to the ground. Being a cheeky initiate, Chicken—as he was soon known for the 'hen' in Stephensen—received this special treatment from two of the biggest boys in the school. Unfortunately his hands slipped on the ring and he flew off and landed heavily. Fortitude was the primary virtue encouraged by such rituals and it was three weeks before the headmaster discovered that Stephensen had broken his wrist in the fall.

The thirteen-year-old boy was promptly sent off to the local doctor, Lee Garde, but as he went unescorted Stephensen found his way instead to Garde's uncle, an eccentric surgeon known locally as Old Garde. Wearing a blood-spattered apron and swearing profusely, the Boer War veteran came out on to his front veranda to inspect the wrist. As it had set crookedly he sat down and rebroke it quickly across his knee before returning inside to attend to a more urgent patient. Half an hour later he emerged with a bandage and splints, swearing that the '(adjective) wrist' would now be stronger than before.

Although boarders were virtually imprisoned for the four terms of the school year they were sometimes allowed into town on Saturday morning in their dark serge suits and straw boaters. The central attraction was the soda fountain in the shop of Holger Fulsig who advertised himself as a 'mixologist'. As there were few motor vehicles every shop had its hitching post, and horses, buggies, sulkies and drays shared the streets with innumerable bicycles. A lamplighter toured the city on a bicycle at dusk igniting each lamp with a long rod, and street cleaners were kept busy sweeping up the manure.

About once a term the boarders were treated to a flickering silent film at Fowler's Bungalow Theatre, the first cinema in Maryborough, which had galvanized-iron walls, canvas seats and a sawdust floor. Even on the hottest nights a pieman sold his wares at interval. Most Saturday evenings the boarders' entertainment consisted of a sing-song or games in the common room. Stephensen learned to play chess and his passion for this game continued throughout his life.

Being bush bred and of athletic build Stephensen was a keen and competent sportsman, captaining the cricket and football teams, and he was always a prize-winner on the annual 'Patriotic Sports' days. The hurdles and pole jump were his specialties and he could sprint a hundred yards in under eleven seconds. English and French were his best subjects but he regularly failed mathematics. He improved sufficiently to pass the junior public exam in 1916, ensuring a two-year extension of his scholarship. The school fees for boarders were eleven guineas a term and the state scholarship reduced this to seven.[5] Stephensen's parents, now running the Biggenden store, were by no means well off and the thirty pounds a year it cost to send him to the grammar school was a heavy burden. This was increased when, towards the end of the war, his younger sister began at the girls' grammar school in Maryborough.

During Stephensen's schooldays, the war constantly intruded upon both political and personal life. One of his uncles was killed in France, and he took an enthusiastic part in the various patriotic fund-raising activities. Despite the bitter campaigns then raging over conscription, Stephensen's loyalty to the war effort was unquestioned. Cadet training was now compulsory for all boys between fourteen and eighteen, and Stephensen became the grammar school's platoon officer with the rank of cadet second lieutenant.

He was also a natural exhibitionist, willing to initiate any anarchic or foolhardy stunt. When in 1917 the wartime shortage of teaching staff became critical, some classes were without supervision for weeks at a time, and on one occasion Stephensen took charge of the chemistry laboratory. Latching the window and locking the door with the flourish of a melodrama villain, he pocketed the key and announced he would make chlorine gas, the cruel new weapon of war. Perhaps disbelieving, or too stunned to react, the class watched as Stephensen combined the necessary chemicals in a retort and warmed them over a burner. As the pungent greenish-yellow gas began to circulate Stephensen warned the others not to interfere with the experiment. But, more concerned with self-preservation than scientific observation, his classmates leapt on him and held him down, got the window open and flung the retort outside. Released, Stephensen then produced a packet of fire-crackers, lit the fuse and threw them into the shelves of chemicals. The explosions finally drew the attention of the headmaster who hauled the whole class off to his study for six of the best.

Violence was not restricted to the frontline fighting in Europe. One of the school's quainter traditions was the administration of 'thuds'—sharp blows across the skull delivered by the knuckles of a closed fist. This punishment was supposed to be the sole prerogative of prefects but was widely practised in the underworld of boarding school life. An adept at thudding, even as a junior, Stephensen celebrated his appointment as one of the school's four prefects in 1918 by lining up the entire junior school for one thud each, thus establishing his authority beyond any doubt. The motive spirit was self-promotion rather than sadism but it did indicate the authoritarian basis of his otherwise anarchic personality. Such impulses also found an outlet in aggressive political argument and debate, for which he became notorious, even as a schoolboy.

Stephensen's fourth and final year was the high point of his role in school politics and also the lowest point in the school's administrative morale. During the war years a succession of new teachers had come and gone, and in 1918 the Labor Party's state education minister appointed to the school staff two men who outraged the conservative sensibilities of the headmaster, Noble Wallace. One immediately tried to find alternative employment as a drover but the other was a real shock to the Maryborough establishment: a 'red-hot red ragger' and anti-conscriptionist, Vere Gordon Childe.[6]

The son of an Anglican rector, Childe had been a distinguished student at the University of Sydney. He had joined the Fabian Society at Oxford and was strongly opposed to both the war and conscription. Returning to Sydney in 1916, he was dismissed from St Andrew's College for addressing an anti-war meeting but found employment in Maryborough through the more sympathetic Queensland Labor government. A thin and rather wizen-faced man, though still in his twenties, Childe arrived with the reputation of a communist and pacifist, and his students treated him unmercifully. Cadet second lieutenant Stephensen was amongst his tormentors, arguing issues like conscription with the unhappy Childe. It is also possible that Childe converted the youthful rebel to the anti-conscription side, though perhaps not overnight as Stephensen later claimed.[7] Caught up in the political mood of the war and the stormy federal Labor split, and with a growing awareness of the recently achieved Russian revolution, Stephensen at some point realized that the way to rebellion in the wider field outside the school gates was being led by Bolsheviks and men like Childe. In the narrower, equally rough-and-tumble world of the school, however, Childe could not survive, and soon departed for Brisbane.

Staff appointments like Childe's and other interference by the trustees angered the headmaster who was the last barrier now to the Labor Party's plans for democratizing the school. The influx of socially less desirable scholarship boys, combined with the wartime staff difficulties, had sharpened Wallace's conservative instincts. During the second half of 1918, as war and then peace hysteria raged, friction between students and staff, and between headmaster and trustees, was such that the school became a public scandal. At one point the senior boys even threatened to 'take matters into their own hands' which was scarcely surprising as they had been managing much of their own schooling without teacher supervision. Wallace was asked by the trustees to report to them and finally in late

September 1918 he attended a humiliating board meeting at which his report was ignored. Exactly a month later, during the prolonged Armistice celebrations in the city, Wallace received a letter of dismissal.[8]

Along with some of the other seniors, Stephensen broke bounds for several nights to join in the Armistice festivities. There were processions, with singing and dancing in the streets, but in Maryborough as in other centres this was also an opportunity to vent anti-German feeling. Effigies of the Kaiser were burnt in various towns and a gang of drunken returned soldiers broke into the Maryborough Lutheran church and smashed its windows.[9] This period of intense public excitement and political intrigue at the school was also the time when Stephensen had to sit for his senior exam, but he managed enough passes to matriculate.

The final crisis at the school came on the annual speech day, 4 December 1918. This was a combined function of both the boys' and girls' grammar schools, and as a further snub to Wallace the trustees decided to hold the ceremony at the girls' school. They invited the state treasurer, the Hon. E. G. Theodore, MLA, to hand out the prizes, and demanded that Wallace submit his speech to them beforehand for approval. He refused and the trustees responded by forbidding him to attend speech day.

The headmaster informed his prefects that he would not be attending and asked them to gather the school in the assembly hall, call the roll and march the boys over to the ceremony. No other masters appeared and the roll call developed into a meeting of protest at the headmaster's dismissal. All the prefects spoke, urging a boycott of speech day, and Stephensen appeared on the platform last to make an eloquent and emotion-charged speech. After praising the headmaster and Mrs Wallace, and denouncing the trustees, Stephensen called for a democratic vote on the boycott by a show of hands. More in the style of a demagogue than a democrat, Stephensen asked the assembled school if any were in favour of attending—'And may God help any bastard who raises his hand!' None did. The senior boys decided to play cricket and others went off to the city baths. Dressed in his cricket clothes, Stephensen went over to the girls' school to inform the trustees of the boycott decision.

News of the protest created quite a storm. The chairman of trustees accused Wallace of acting like an 'overgrown schoolboy', and one of the former trustees continually interjected during the ceremony. Far from being embarrassed, the ebullient Theodore used the occasion to call for more equality of opportunity in education, claiming that it was 'only a short step to the complete nationalization of education from the earliest schools to the finished product of the universities'. One of the mothers fired off a letter to the *Maryborough Chronicle* expressing pride in the boys' 'Australian pluck', and others associated with the school held a hastily convened meeting at the Royal Hotel that evening to farewell Noble Wallace. Largely organized by former trustees, the meeting heard much invective against the new trustees and their lack of education and culture. Fighting an aggressive retreat, the supporters of Wallace also applauded the 'manly' action of the boys and assured Maryborough society that 'while they had that spirit in their midst, the Bolshevik business would have a very bad time in Queensland'.[10]

The irony of course was that the prime mover of that manly action, and the school's leading student spirit, was himself a youthful radical awaiting an appropriate spectacle on which to lavish his anarchic energies. With his Labor background and sympathies, Stephensen had been on friendly terms with the new Maryborough Grammar trustees but he chose instead to champion their arch enemy, Noble Wallace. It is more than a trifle significant therefore that Stephensen's first impulsive act of public rebellion was in support of the forces of reaction. He was, as one of his school contemporaries said of him, a rebel in search of a cause. But it had to be a cause that provided plenty of fun and allowed him to stand centre stage before as big an audience as possible.

2
Students and Workers

At the age of seventeen Stephensen enrolled in the arts faculty at the University of Queensland instead of spending a fifth year at Maryborough Grammar. The university, then not a decade old, took fewer than a hundred new undergraduates each year and was housed in the former government house, adjoining Brisbane's botanical gardens. It was a small, friendly university, and very near the centre of power and privilege in the state. Close by were parliament house and the élite Queensland Club, and also the Domain where speakers entertained Sunday crowds. The university's vice-chancellor was a member of the upper house Legislative Council and during the war had been chairman of the state recruiting committee.

When Stephensen enrolled at the beginning of first term 1919 the echoes of war still dominated life. The jubilant hysteria of the Armistice, which brought fifty thousand people out to dance in Brisbane streets, had evaporated and in its place were a world-wide influenza epidemic and the pressures of troops returning home. Australians donned white linen masks during the influenza panic and crept about 'like mimes in a dance macabre, or mutes at a funeral', Stephensen remembered.[1] Unemployment in Queensland rose to 14 per cent and the new battle for jobs increased tensions between fiercely patriotic ex-soldiers and militant unionists who had campaigned against the war.

Within the labour movement it was also a time of continuing struggle, with attempts to form the One Big Union along the lines of the International Workers of the World. Radicals were disillusioned with the mild reformism of the state Labor government and were seeking direct action instead. Intelligence agents saw Queensland as a centre for revolutionary conspiracies at a time when the allied war machine and public propaganda were being redirected against the new Bolshevik Russian state.[2] It was a 'cold war' atmosphere, and the ideological lines were drawn.

For a country boy just arrived in the state capital this was also a period of personal excitement and adventure. Stephensen signed the university's matriculation book on 18 March as did three other freshers who had also been school prefects: Robert Hall,* Herbert Burton and Edmund Dimmock. Dimmock was from north Queensland, while Hall and Burton were Ipswich Grammar old boys who had both been awarded open scholarships to the university. Hall had won the Byrnes Medal in 1916 for the best pass in the state's junior public examination. Not as gifted academically, Stephensen was a fee-paying undergraduate, his parents making further sacrifices to ensure their eldest son received what was then a rare opportunity in Australia, a university education.

Stephensen, Hall, Burton and Dimmock all lodged at St John's College and their close association became a lifelong friendship. Nicknames were part of the boisterous college spirit so Hall was 'Hoss', Dimmock 'Demon', and Burton 'Jersey' after his father's prize cows. Stephensen's habit of singing at the top of his voice snatches from the wartime favourite 'Mademoiselle from Armentieres', with its refrain 'Inky pinky parlez-vous', quickly earned him the name 'Inky'. There were several returned soldiers at the college including 'Chut' Fryer who joined Stephensen and the others, forming a push of leading university personalities. They concocted private jokes and sayings, and were soon known as the vestibularizers for their habit of congregating noisily in the entrance hall of old government house where the arts faculty now held court.[3]

St John's College was across river from the university on the clifftop of River Terrace, Kangaroo Point. The college consisted of three rambling, wide-verandahed Queensland houses in which about thirty students resided under the protection of the warden, a burly former English rugby international. The college routine was not unlike that of boarding school but less regimented, and groups of students would gather in the common room to talk and argue late into the night. Stephensen was invariably amongst these as was Fryer who entertained them with tales of soldiering. Stephensen's patriotic attitude to the war had in fact been confirmed by his close contact with Fryer and other ex-soldiers.

Stephensen was an enthusiastic rather than conscientious student and his aim was to enjoy life with his friends. He played various sports but specialized in pole vaulting, practising on a piece of lawn at the back of the college. At the Queensland amateur athletics meeting in July 1919 Stephensen even managed second place in the junior pole vault championship with a height of eight and a half feet. He told his parents he had jumped higher at Maryborough but had been disconcerted by the lack of a pit or mattress to cushion his descent.[4] Pole vaulting in fact was a sport which perfectly expressed his reckless, high-flying personality. It anticipated his Quixotic tendency to tilt at one or another phantom, and it was not the only field on which he fell heavily.

As he was still settling in at university Stephensen did not become mixed up in the violent red flag riots of late March 1919 and the loyalist, anti-Bolshevik backlash which continued throughout April. However, he undoubtedly took an interest in these events which were a prelude to his

* Hall became an economist and was later created a baron (Lord Roberthall) for services to the British government.

own political involvement. Under the federal War Precautions Act the red flag was banned, but at a procession from the Brisbane Trades Hall to the Domain on Sunday 23 March red flags, banners and other emblems were defiantly broken out and the few foot police assigned to the march were unable to hinder its progress through the city. A handful of Russians headed the procession and the stridently xenophobic and conservative *Daily Mail* warned that Queen Street had been Russianized and the revolution was at hand.[5]

The conservative reaction in fact was swift and well organized. A mob of soldiers and other loyalists broke up a meeting of the One Big Union Propaganda League at North Quay, and the following evening several thousand loyalists armed with anything from pistols to fence posts fought with police guarding the empty Russian Association rooms in South Brisbane. The Russian club was eventually wrecked as were adjoining houses and stores occupied by Russians.

Further big loyalist rallies were held, urged on by the *Daily Mail* and the *Brisbane Courier*. The left-wing *Daily Standard* deplored the violence of 'riotous ex-soldiers' who responded by marching on the newspaper's office, smashing its windows and firing off revolvers. In the aftermath of these riots loyalist leaders received only light fines while radicals were rounded up and imprisoned or deported. During May, at the height of right-wing speculation about a Bolshevik rising, a group of farmers and graziers in the upper Brisbane Valley secretly prepared a mounted force for battle. The *Daily Standard* got wind of the plan and the Home Secretary John Huxham, whose daughter was a science student and one of Stephensen's university friends, ordered police to suppress the movement.

This was the tumultuous background to Stephensen's first few weeks at university. He also met and quickly befriended Norman Lindsay's son Jack who was studying classics and sported the nickname 'Plato'. Jack's parents were separated and he lived with his mother and two younger brothers Ray and Phil in a house at Kangaroo Point. His main interest was literature and he edited the university magazine but was also closely involved with the Workers' Educational Association (WEA) and radical personalities in Brisbane.[6] Jack taught WEA classes and he introduced Stephensen to Theodore Colquhoun Witherby, an Oxford-educated Anglican priest who organized WEA teaching as the university's acting director of workers' tutorial classes. Other members of the WEA state council in 1919 included Childe, Stephensen's former Maryborough Grammar master, and Charles Schindler, Stephensen's French lecturer at university and another significant influence on him. Schindler had read law at the University of Paris and had worked as a newspaper correspondent in London before coming to Australia. Like Childe and Witherby he was politically 'advanced' and a man of culture and wide experience.[7]

By April Stephensen was regularly visiting Witherby with Lindsay, and making use of his extensive library to read the latest works on Bolshevism. A tall and gauntly dignified man, Witherby spoke with an aristocratic English drawl which he punctuated with Australian oaths to disconcert the pious. His eccentricities were legion. Jack Lindsay recalled that Witherby once got under the table at a restaurant and began reading because he was bored with the company. On another occasion, at the approach of a stuffy and unwelcome visitor, he got down on hands and knees and crouched at his gate like a dog, yelping and barking until the man walked away.[8] As well as a house in Brisbane, Witherby had a shack in the rainforest at Mount Tambourine where Stephensen, Lindsay, Childe and other WEA enthusiasts spent weekends, discussing culture and revolution.

Stephensen was also caught up in a gregarious round of other activities. During late April, while the papers were full of influenza and Bolshevik scares and lamenting the 'indignities' suffered by the Grand Duke Nicholas of Russia, Stephensen turned up regularly at Frank Thorn's gym in Ann Street for boxing lessons and, on his walks, got to know the university's Italian gardener who spoke five languages including French. In between he tinkered at the piano, played football and billiards, and saw the propaganda films *The Surrender of the German Fleet* and *The Australians in Palestine*, both of which he recommended to his parents.[9]

In fact, apart from his dalliance with WEA radicals, Stephensen was the conventional patriot for most of his first year at university. His article in the June *University Magazine* was a strong plea for the study of Australian poets and the 'fostering of a national literature', a preoccupation he would return to more zealously in later years. The war, he wrote, had invalidated the contention that Australia had no history, for 'the manhood and youth of Australia have proved their valour'. Stephensen deplored the universities' disdain for Australian literature and concluded with a cry to 'fearlessly champion the cause of our own land'.[10]

In other writing for the university magazine during 1919 Stephensen supplemented his patriotism with a playful misogyny. He was, and would remain, a man's man: an all-round chauvinist. Perhaps with tongue in cheek as well, he urged the revival of the Khayyamite Club at the university to provide 'entertainment for men only' because too much 'social intercourse with the other sex ... will ultimately destroy the manly spirit'.[11] There were cold showers at the college, even through winter, but it was social propriety which sustained his virginity during his late teens and early twenties. He certainly never avoided female company. There were river picnics by moonlight, fancy dress balls at the Women's College, and dinner dances to welcome home returned 'Varsity soldiers'.

These were standard activities for a fresher. Stephensen's only challenge to authority was a respectful rebuttal of the Catholic Archbishop Duhig who, as a member of the university senate, had addressed students on the evils of cremation. Stephensen's thoughtful and carefully researched article on this burning issue pointed out that it was the Jews through Christianity who had passed on the custom of earth-burial to the 'civilized world'. It was, he concluded, a danger to public health as well as a useless barbarity. Having thus disposed of the subject he made a present to the university library of a small collection of works on cremation.¹²

Towards the end of 1919, however, as political radicalism in Brisbane was being effectively suppressed, Stephensen's own outlook became more militant. Contact with his WEA friends was no doubt partly responsible, though he had been sampling and exchanging views with them all year. Equally important was Stephensen's friendship with another St John's collegian, Fred ('Banjo') Paterson. Like Robert Hall, Paterson was a brilliant student who had topped the state in his junior examination. He had begun an honours classics degree at the university in 1916 but had interrupted his study to enlist for overseas service in May 1918, returning to Brisbane after the Armistice. Paterson had been an Anglican Sunday school teacher and president of the Student Christian Movement, but he returned from the war more than a little disillusioned by his experiences, having taken part in strikes to secure better rations for soldiers.¹³

Although Paterson was not a committed political rebel during his final year at the University of Queensland, his increasing interest in the left helped Stephensen to define the conflict between a patriotic response to the Australian war effort and the exciting prospects of the Russian revolution. As the Brisbane riots had shown, many returned soldiers were violently opposed to radical dissent, Childe describing their assaults on the red flaggers as a pogrom.¹⁴ But in Fred Paterson Stephensen found a returned soldier who was prepared to take a new perspective on the war. Paterson shared Stephensen's growing sense of social injustice and they were involved in various student protests.

The most significant of these involved a WEA public lecture Witherby gave late in 1919 on 'Who Shall Control Industry'. In a sensational report in the *Daily Mail* under the headline 'Revolution ... What are a few thousand lives?', Witherby was quoted as saying 'I do not care a _____ whether the revolution comes about peaceably or by bloodshed'. Although Witherby claimed he had been misrepresented and parodied, he was attacked by a long and outraged *Daily Mail* editorial for disseminating 'doctrines of naked revolution' which were 'plainly treasonous'. The paper called for his suppression by the government and university. In the furore that followed, the vice-chancellor hastened to dissociate the university from the WEA and from Witherby's views, and there was a special debate on the controversial lecture in the Legislative Assembly.¹⁵ Under pressure from the university senate, Witherby resigned some months later. According to Paterson, the students' representative council was preparing to support the senate but at the council meeting both Paterson and Stephensen spoke out strongly in defence of Witherby and no motion of support for the senate materialized.¹⁶

A few weeks later Paterson was chosen as Queensland Rhodes Scholar. Before he sailed for England in early 1920 something happened which confirmed his misgivings about the war and redirected his sympathies towards communism. His friend Inky Stephensen lent him a copy of a new book, *Red Europe* by Frank Anstey, the long-time Labor member for

Bourke.[17] Anstey had spent the last months of the war in Europe and his detailed account not only exposed the role of war propaganda on both sides but also showed that in 1918 Germany and Britain had worked virtually side by side against the Russian socialist state.

The effect of this book on Stephensen was scarcely less significant. Along with the Witherby incident, it convinced him that press coverage was frequently distorted and even deliberately manufactured, especially in wartime. In his chapter 'Mass Hypnotism', Anstey blamed the atrocity campaigns of both sides for arousing the British and German people to slaughter each other. Anstey's conclusion was that the only genuine struggle was between the 'Master Class' and the 'Subject Masses', and that in the face of mounting debts the bankruptcy of capitalism was imminent. The book's final rallying cry would have appealed in particular to the youthful Stephensen: 'Capitalism listens with quaking soul to the drumbeats of the Armies of Revolution. Those beats grow louder and louder—they draw nearer and nearer'.[18]

The urgency of this call to arms and even the military imagery itself no doubt reassured Stephensen that his continued training in the part-time militia was equipping him for the social struggle ahead. His political imagination and personal confidence were such that the likely outcome of events did not interfere with a cause once it took hold of his mind and excited his mercurial spirit. Like the anarchists, Bolsheviks and 'Wobblies', he felt that once a revolution had succeeded, its ideological momentum would be sufficient to construct a new and better society.

At a time when even on the left there were 'widespread fixations upon national homogeneity and racial purity',[19] Anstey's work also indicated the strength of a popular prejudice which lay dormant in Stephensen until its resurrection almost two decades later. Anstey's previous book, which Stephensen would very likely have known, was entitled *The Kingdom of Shylock* and on the cover was a typically crude caricature of the Jew as money-lender, clasping his hands in greedy pleasure and lurking behind a window bearing the words 'Interest ish Rising ... 6 per shent to day 7 per shent to-morrow'.[20] The book was in fact a cogently argued account of the influence of international finance, with no other reference to Jews except for the symbolic spectre of the Rothschilds in an early chapter. Yet even such clichés of prejudice could arouse hate in dispossessed workers, so synonymous were Jews with financial exploitation.

A university acquaintance remembered Stephensen being antagonistic towards an elderly Jew at a Sunday afternoon tennis party in 1920, but this was possibly little more than the instinctive symbolism of the class struggle.[21] Race prejudice, xenophobia and a preoccupation with eugenics were in any case part of the dominant ideology. In Queensland, anti-Germanism and Russophobia had become highly developed, taking their place alongside recurrent fears of Asia.[22] Race pride and race guilt, with their attendant irrational prejudices, were as deeply ingrained in Stephensen as they were in the predominantly WASPish society around him. Anti-Semitism was also an instinctive part of his European heritage, and the image of the Jew as the instigator of both usury and Christianity drew together the threads of Stephensen's anti-capitalism and his questioning of religion. His grandfather Tardent had been ruined in the 1893 bank crash, and spoke of 'rich' Jews as 'narrow-minded and cunning'. From Jack Lindsay Stephensen learned that vital paganism was opposed to 'Hebrew' values.[23]

In his article in the university magazine in May 1920 Stephensen championed the idea of proletarian revolution and the role of a progressive university as a 'Power in the State'. Describing Britain as a country 'where the iniquitous Class System exists in its worst form, and where Education is a privilege of the Ruling Class', he went on to praise the Russian revolution and to call for the abolition of university fees. In the same issue of the magazine was an article on Hugh McCrae and lyric poetry in Australia. This was unsigned but written by Jack Lindsay, and it sparked a debate with Stephensen on nationalism and literature which was a prelude to their literary relationship. Compared with Stephensen's satirical doggerel which also littered the magazine's pages for several years, his subsequent tilt at Lindsay—also unsigned and entitled 'Satyrs or Kookaburras?'—showed that his true field of combat was incisive, polemical prose.[24]

Jack Lindsay's article in praise of McCrae reflected the considerable influence Norman Lindsay was now having on his son. Although Jack had not heard from his father since 1911, Norman wrote him a friendly and encouraging letter in late 1919 and sent him some drawings as well as the proofs of the forthcoming *Creative Effort*.[25] Having lost his younger brother Reg in France and his sister Ruby in the influenza epidemic, Norman tried with *Creative Effort* to transcend this nightmare world of war and decay. Inspired by Nietzsche and an increasing interest in spiritualism, he attempted to formulate a philosophy around an élite of great artists in the 'tradition of Greek blood ... setting alight a spark of genius through the centuries, and battling always with the black torrent of barbarism'.[26] For Lindsay barbarism included the wowsers who attacked his own work so vociferously. He admitted to his close friend Hugh McCrae that his creed was 'infernally aristocratic', but it was also unashamedly sexist, anti-modernist and racist, giving an early indication of Lindsay's own fantastical anti-Semitism.[27] It was, however, his classical aesthetic which won his son Jack over as a disciple.

Praising McCrae, Jack Lindsay criticized the 'absurd tradition that poetry should be national': 'We have had enough of sick stockmen and men from the Snowy River', he commented scornfully. The 'true god of Art' was Dionysus.[28] In his published response, Stephensen stressed the importance for the Greek poets of local experience. He also criticized Jack's bookishness and Europhilia, describing him with some affection as a pagan blinded by the mist of his 'impulsive radicalism'.[29] This brought a strong statement from Jack Lindsay in the form of a signed article, 'Nationality and Poetry'. He asserted that McCrae's satyrs were 'more real than kangaroos', and added to Norman's rhetoric his own mystical formulations of Art with a capital 'A'. For Jack sex was the basis of all art: 'Poetry is not written with words, but, as Nietzsche would say, it is written with blood'. For the Lindsays, the Nietzschean *Ubermensch* was the artist as persecuted hero. Turning his back on the proletariat, Jack also pronounced the 'peasants of England' to be 'not the proper material for an English poet'.[30]

Stephensen had the last word, as he always liked to, in a mock epic under the pseudonym of 'S. Currility'. He wrote himself as the character Stephanus—'With Lenin and Trotsky I agree'—who exits singing the 'Red Flag'. Jack Lindsay was Plato, declaiming that 'Art is not national, for Art is Life' and professing the 'pagan Dionysus cult' to shock the puritans.[31] Like their mutual friend Witherby, both Stephensen and Lindsay were rebelling against Australian bourgeois values. Lindsay was a long-haired, scruffily dressed scholar-poet relishing the company of revolutionaries, prostitutes and bohemian artists. Stephensen was outwardly more conventional, and his rebelliousness had in it the spirit of a new generation. He looked forward to the political future rather than back to a classical past.

His iconoclasm, however, was always liable to turn into larrikinism. After the annual Men's Club dinner at the Hotel Daniell in late November 1920, Stephensen and other undergraduates decided to invade His Majesty's Theatre where the respectable citizenry of Brisbane were enjoying a performance of *The Saving Grace*. The group stormed up and down the staircases and banged on doors before being evicted. They adjourned to the Cremorne Theatre at South Brisbane but it too locked its doors against the revellers. Returning to Queen Street, the students disrupted Saturday night traffic, dancing around the constables on point duty until four, including Stephensen, were arrested. Apologies and reprimands followed but Stephensen described the incident as a 'great joke' to his sister: 'We were not in the cells (unfortunately, as it would have been a fine experience) but were only in the office of the Chief Inspector, where we bailed ourselves out at once. The Press Reports are lies as you may well believe'.[32]

Stephensen's final year at Queensland University was his most eventful. He was teaching part-time at the Central Technical College and had acquired a 'girl-cobber', Madalen Hulbert. He took over the editorship of the university magazine which he revamped and renamed *Galmahra*, a local Aboriginal term for poet, teacher or messenger and therefore an offensively Australian retort to the University of Sydney's *Hermes* magazine. Galmahra was also the name of 'Jacky-Jacky' of the Kennedy expedition, 'the last of the great heroes amongst the primitive people that our cruelty and neglect has driven into servility and degradation in the land which was their age-old heritage'.[33] Stephensen's burgeoning concern for social oppression now included the dispossessed Aborigines though it is doubtful whether they would have regarded Jacky-Jacky as a hero; more likely a collaborator.

Thumbing his nose at the puritanical morality of 1920s Brisbane, Stephensen published in his first *Galmahra* a selection of erotic lyrics by Jack Lindsay. Having completed his classics course with first-class honours, and been passed over for a travelling scholarship to Oxford in favour of Eric Partridge, Lindsay was preparing to leave for bohemian Sydney. His poems in the May 1921 *Galmahra* therefore, along with an article deriding academics as 'dead and sexless' eunuchs, were his farewell gesture to the philistines of Brisbane. The most explicit of the verses, 'Rivals', was inspired by a Norman Lindsay etching and its climax illumined 'our nakedness/Grown one, in joy, together—breasts and hips'. This was too much for the professorial board and its chairman, a strict Presbyterian, so all unsold *Galmahras* were hastily recalled. The students' council informed Stephensen that future issues of the magazine would be censored by a 'lady' before going to press.[34]

Stephensen learned the rudiments of printing, as well as the power of scandal, from his work on the lavishly produced *Galmahra*, but his extravagant plans for the magazine were indicative of his lack of financial realism. He decided that *Galmahra* would now work strenuously for 'University extension' and formed a student sub-committee, writing to the registrar for a grant of £150 over three years. *Galmahra*'s deficit in his year as editor had already risen to nearly a hundred pounds.[35]

From Biggenden he received disquieting news that his parents' general store, a struggling concern, was now faced with competition from a newly opened co-op store. Stephensen's younger sister had been forced to finish her schooling after junior because the family could not afford her boarding fees while he was at university. Perhaps showing some guilt as well as brotherly concern, he wrote suggesting she use the Biggenden school of arts library, for reading was 'a wonderful way of educating the self'. His view of religion was now aligned with that of Marx, and he concluded his letter to his sister with a caution: 'Don't take any Religion for granted. Form your own and live by it, spurning all others. Heaven, God, Jesus, Hell and other myths are invented for the simple-minded who cannot think for themselves'.[36]

During 1921 Stephensen joined the Brisbane branch of the Communist Party of Australia as a rank-and-file member, though this did not inhibit his enjoyment of the full round of undergraduate activities. He worked on the college journal *Argo* and was on various university committees, marshalling Commemoration Day festivities with typical panache on a penny-farthing cycle. He led a debating team which showed conclusively that democracy in the modern world had proved a failure, and played Rosencrantz in a student production of Gilbert's *Rosencrantz and Guildenstern*.[37] In a satirical article in *Argo*, Stephensen was portrayed, along with other college personalities, in the imaginary future at a 1945 reunion dinner. He was now 'President of Soviet Russia' with plans for the 'regeneration of Australia'.[38]

This red-hot communist now began canvassing his most respectable acquaintances for references to help him secure a teaching post. Because of staff restrictions he missed out on a job at the Central Technical

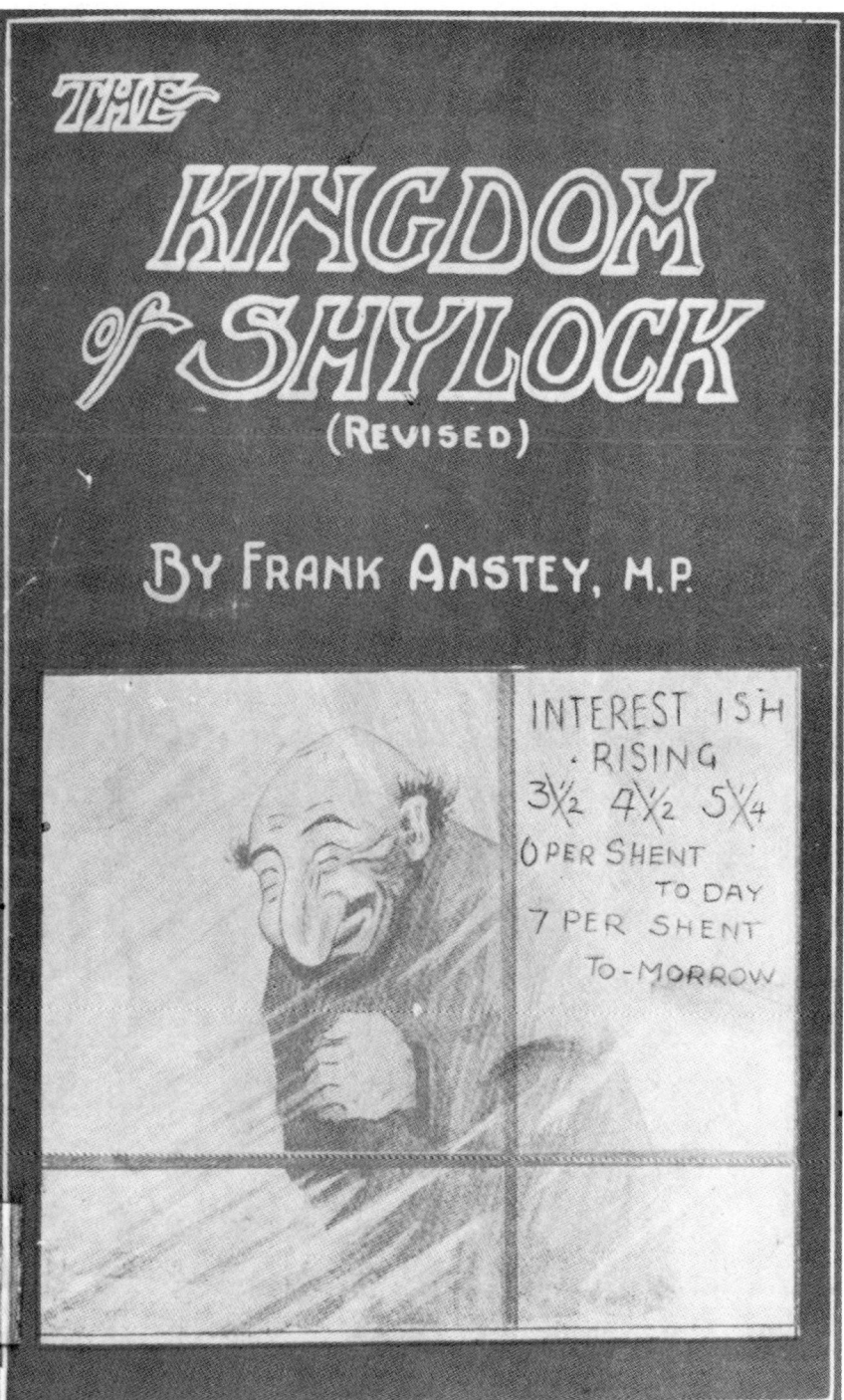

The anti-Semitic cover design of Anstey's The Kingdom of Shylock *(Melbourne, Labor Call, 1917)*

Lieutenant Stephensen in his militia uniform, Brisbane, October 1920

Leaving for England on the Jervis Bay, *August 1924*

College but was taken on as a resident master at Ipswich Boys' Grammar School, joining his friend 'Jersey' Burton there in first term 1922. He still maintained close contact with the university, writing his usual dollops of verse for *Galmahra* and coming down for evenings and weekends, but now turned more seriously to the task of political organizing. Ipswich was handy to Brisbane but it was also an ideal place to work for the proletarian revolution. At the railway workshops in North Ipswich men were facing retrenchments and a reduction in the basic wage, both measures introduced by Theodore's Labor government.

The most militant radicals were to be found in the Australian Railways Union whose Queensland journal the *Advocate* was unequivocal in its condemnation of the state Labor party. It was equally direct on racial issues. In an editorial which appeared about the same time as Stephensen was unpacking his bags in his comfortable grammar school quarters, the *Advocate* declared that the 'Ideal of a White Australia' was one of 'stern economic self-preservation'. The unrestricted entry of 'cheap Asiatic labor' would mean the end of the Australian worker's standard of living, and it was suggested instead that Northern Territory Aborigines be brought over to do the 'drudgery work'. In the same issue the Ipswich correspondent reported the scarcity of work there and the high level of unemployment. He warned unionists to 'look forward to a strenuous year' and called for the solidarity of 'one union and one voice'.[39]

Stephensen lost no time in contacting the railway workers and, with the encouragement of R. A. Kerr, his headmaster, immediately set about reviving the defunct Ipswich branch of the WEA, making it one of the most active in the state. During the year, as well as acting as energetic branch secretary and running up debts to equip the office, Stephensen led evening study circles on logic, psychology, industrial history and literature.[40]

At Ipswich Grammar he was a spirited rather than dedicated teacher, taking charge of French and continuing his military involvement as lieutenant in command of the cadet corps. There was nothing regimented, however, about his teaching methods, and his classes were noisy, especially in French where he encouraged plenty of singing. An unconventional communist, he liked nothing better than good food and wine, organizing a formal dinner with all the trappings at the Metropole Hotel in Ipswich to farewell Burton who was leaving for Oxford to take up the 1922 Rhodes Scholarship.[41] In September that year, with a party of friends, he drove out by car to a hill-top farm to view the total eclipse of the sun, a dazzling and eerie event he later described in an article for the *New Statesman*.[42]

Encouraged by Burton's success, Stephensen gathered various testimonials together and applied for the next Rhodes Scholarship, persuading his friend Robert Hall to enter for it as well. With a more distinguished academic and sporting record, Hall won the 1923 Rhodes Scholarship. He regarded Stephensen's gesture as a generous one but also as an example of not considering consequences.[43]

Early in 1923 Stephensen's 'girl cobber' left to take up a teaching position in Sydney and his friend Chut Fryer died of tuberculosis as a result of war service. In an emotional *Galmahra* obituary Stephensen wrote that he was saddened by 'the spectacle of Civilised Humanity sacrificing with cruel rites its splendid Youth on the altars of the ruthless God of War'.[44] In March his other ex-soldier comrade Fred Paterson returned from Oxford with first-hand evidence of social oppression after visits to Belfast and the East End slums of London. At Oxford he had read books on guild socialism and had met the Australian communist Esmonde Higgins, Nettie Palmer's brother. Stephensen wrote to Burton that 'Banjo' Paterson had come back 'a real rebel and an outright communist'.[45]

Stephensen introduced Paterson to WEA people like Albert Welsby in Ipswich who had a fine collection of books on Marxian economics. Paterson read the works of Marx and Lenin as well as John Reed's *Ten Days That Shook the World* and Philips Price's *Reminiscences of the Russian Revolution*. All these texts were familiar to Stephensen who encouraged Paterson to join the Communist Party soon after his return. Paterson recalled that Stephensen had a big influence on the railwaymen and was especially popular with the militants, encouraging their campaign against the Labor government which eventually culminated in the state-wide rail strike of 1925. Stephensen was one of the best 'mass speakers' Paterson ever heard, with impressive sincerity, energy and fearlessness.[46] This was high praise from the man who later became the only Communist Party representative to win a parliamentary seat in Australia.

Ipswich Grammar, however, was beginning to get Stephensen down. In a long letter to Burton in July 1923 he complained that he had no companionship at the school being the only 'smoker and boozer' there now. His only solace was in the company of some 'good blokes' at the railway workshops. Perhaps disappointed with the more moderate aims of the WEA, Stephensen had formed a Communist Association in Ipswich and he urged Burton to 'give a bit of serious thought to communism' as it was a 'world force' which would not be denied:

> I hope you will come and see me in jail when you get back. I've made my debut as a dinkum Bolshevik at last! About every fortnight I give regular lectures a la soapbox on such topics as 'The Class Struggle', 'The Dictatorship of the Proletariat', 'Defence of Terrorism', 'The Menace of Imperialism', 'The Fallacy of the God Idea', 'The Church and Superstition', and so on.[47]

Stephensen's Communist Association included Fred Paterson and a number of railway radicals among its members. To some extent all this was an outlet for Stephensen's frustrated energies, and he mused that life would be a 'slug without some such diversion'. British imperialism was his special hatred and one which stayed with him until long after he had renounced communism:

> They talk grandiloquently about 'filling up Australia's vast empty spaces' and then they dump down the scum of London here. Last batch

landed in Sydney was 75 per cent venereal. To hell with capitalism and the empire! The whole imperial scheme is a capitalist dodge to make more money and profits from the blood and sweat of the toiling masses ... We are going to build up a great revolutionary organisation here in Australia and wait till the crash comes ...[48]

Along with radicals like Welsby and Paterson, Stephensen cherished plans for an 'Australian Workers' and Farmers' Socialist Republic'. The republic's Queensland Central Congress would consist of delegates from the district soviets representing every branch of industry as well as 'housewives soviets'. The ruling body or Central Executive would be the 'commissars', department heads elected by the congress. While the ten-point plan detailed voting and organizational procedures there was no mention of how power would be seized or maintained.[49] This was indicative of the gap between reality and ideological fantasy in Stephensen's mind. To Burton, Stephensen boasted that he was now a menace to society, wickedly teaching his grammar school pupils to be 'little rebels'.[50] Despite the headmaster's liberal attitude to the WEA, he was conservative when it came to running his school and Stephensen's political extremism must have met with growing disapproval.

Through the influence of his grandfather who was the paper's agricultural writer, Stephensen began writing regularly for the *Daily Standard* towards the end of 1923. His first effort for the labour daily was a translation from Lamartine's poem *'Les Révolutions'*. Originally this had been written against the feudal despotism of the French monarchists but Stephensen now adapted it for the struggle against modern reactionaries 'striving equally in vain, to oppose the irresistible onward march of Socialism'.[51]

Stephensen once again decided to try for a Rhodes Scholarship and, to render negligible his chances for this most imperialist of honours, he wrote a couple of articles calling for the working-class control of education, something he claimed was within the power of the Queensland Labor government. A matter of days before the Rhodes selection committee met in Brisbane, Stephensen launched a broadside in the *Daily Standard* against the liberal-reformist attitude to worker education, and declared that world revolution was 'not only inevitable but imminent':

> In order to secure victory on the economic field, the working class movement must first make a smashing attack upon the reactionary ideology of the capitalist environment. This can only be done by means of independent working class education ... If the workers are apathetic, it is precisely because the cramping influence of their slavish environment has made them so. Not only are they physically benumbed in the process of their economic exploitation, but, what is worse they are mentally hypnotised by the bourgeois dope ideology disseminated unceasingly in the schools, churches, and press. It is this hypnotic spell which it is the task of working class education to break.[52]

This was left-wing rhetoric at its most eloquent, and in his Rhodes application Stephensen stated, with either defiance or disarming ingenuousness, that his plan was to study social science at Oxford 'with a view to taking part eventually in Educational Activities in Queensland'.[53] His sights were no doubt set on becoming commissar for education.

He also submitted a glowing reference from the chief inspector of schools who had been his philosophy tutor at university. In the inspector's opinion Stephensen's French lessons at Ipswich Grammar were 'brilliant applications of the "direct" method of approaching the language'.[54] A fellow teacher at the school, however, later recalled just what method Stephensen had used to impress this non-French-speaking inspector. Stephensen had arranged with his class that whenever he put a question to them in French they could answer with anything that came to mind, including phrases from songs, as long as they sounded fluent.[55]

Stephensen had not lost his flair for amusing his colleagues. When he heard that a particular businessman was on the Rhodes selection panel, he claimed he owed the man money and made a show of writing out a cheque to improve his chances.[56] To everyone's amazement, including no doubt his own, Stephensen was awarded the 1924 Queensland Rhodes Scholarship, to follow his two closest friends to Oxford.

Stephensen's welter of undergraduate activities must have caused the selection committee to overlook his revolutionary politics. Either that or they considered a dose of privileged Oxford would clear it all out of his system. In any event the poor competition for the scholarship must have left them no alternative. Like his friends Burton and Hall, Stephensen had been a leading university personality. Still, there was an element of farce about his selection which must have appealed to his sense of humour.

With his horizons suddenly expanded, he resigned from Ipswich Grammar almost straight away. He was 'thoroughly and completely disgusted with the joint', and especially with the headmaster, but the school was also undoubtedly relieved to see the last of this potential troublemaker. Replying to a toast at the university Men's Club dinner, Stephensen 'took the cap right off and called them all the god darned fools in creation', boasted that he was 'a revolutionary, an atheist and a booze expert', and advised them to 'pay no heed whatsoever to the counsel of their elders'. In a long and effervescent letter from Biggenden, where he was spending Christmas, he told his Oxford compatriots Burton and Hall that the only political alternatives were 'fascism or proletarian dictatorship'.[57]

For the time being, however, Stephensen was enjoying his rural leisure, writing book reviews for the *Standard* and buzzing round selling cars for the dealership his parents ran as part of their general store. He had decided to spend in Biggenden the months that remained till his boat left. Reflecting his own mood, the country thereabouts was 'green and smiling' and he was playing cricket with the 'pumpkinville eleven'. He was something of a celebrity in tiny Biggenden which now boasted two Rhodes scholars, one having been selected during the war. Stephensen's ebullient atheism, though, went down like a lead balloon among the district's Catholic population. They promptly took their business away from the Stephensen store, making the future even bleaker for his parents.[58]

Stephensen of course was impatient with anything but his own exciting future. He told Burton and Hall his immediate plans included putting together a book of verse, and preserving his virginity against the future prospect of 'gai Paris'. After many heartbreaking scenes, he had convinced a persistent girlfriend that marriage was out of the question although she had been prepared to 'commit a deadly mortal sin to satisfy her raging lust'. Having narrowly escaped her passion he could now 'breathe a free man'.[59]

Among his freelance writing for the *Daily Standard*, Stephensen reviewed *How Labor Governs*, Childe's critical study of the history and problems of the Australian labour movement. This book was published in 1923 after Childe's return to England to begin his notable career in European archaeology. Stephensen dismissed his former schoolmaster as a 'Guild Socialist, very theoretical and abstruse'. Childe was a 'cynical, tired philosopher' whose detached Olympian manner smacked of a 'professorial discourse on the life and customs of the ancient Hittites'. However, Stephensen was forced to admit that Childe's criticisms of the labour movement were justified, and he quoted with approval Childe's description of the 'selfish and cowardly opportunism' of Labor parliamentarians. Stephensen also introduced a two-part review by the Melbourne socialist R. S. Ross of *Kangaroo* with the comment that the novel had 'burst like a bomb' among Lawrence's critics. Foreshadowing his own keen interest in Lawrence, Stephensen commented that Australians should feel 'a little pardonable pride' in the novel's scene and treatment.[60]

In a long article for the *Standard* on the 'Enslavement of Farmers and Traders', Stephensen indirectly attacked his shopkeeper parents as 'poor deluded souls' who were 'bound in economic servitude to the capitalist class'. Exasperated and perhaps bitter at the increasingly desperate financial plight of his parents, Stephensen described in painful detail the 'whole process of the petty traders' immolation on the altars of the god capital'. Calling up the image of Shylock, Stephensen said that the self-employed often suffered worse than wage-workers from the 'machinations of the financial schemers who have secured control of the world's resources in their pudgy, grasping hands'.[61] Proud of their son as they were, Stephensen's parents also must have been relieved at his departure for England in August 1924.

Just a few weeks before his ship sailed, he could not resist getting into 'some beautiful hot water' with a strongly anti-Christian lecture for the Rationalist Association. The *Catholic Advocate* and the *Mercantile Gazette* were among those to question his selection as Rhodes scholar, but Stephensen answered his outraged critics with polemical flourish, quoting Job. 'We of the twentieth century have our special problems to face', he observed, 'and it would require more than the reproaches of ancient splenetics, or theological dogmatists, to deter us from formulating our independent solutions'. An amused friend told him he'd be sure to frizzle in hell for a thousand years.[62]

'The life of a rebel has much to commend it', he wrote off jauntily to his Oxford mates, but the rebel had to know 'how to laugh at himself, his doctrines, and, above all, at the stupid unthinking mob'.[63] As he commented to one of his WEA friends, Victor Smith, the lack of humour in the proletarian movement was the one aspect he deplored:

> There is little opportunity for hilarity and drunken irresponsibility. 'Comrades' ... are notoriously serious and humourless, almost wowsers in fact and I must have some geniality or perish! I am fundamentally a revolutionary just because modern life is so drab and colourless and if I don't look for the 'resurrection of the dead' I at least look for some LIFE in the WORLD TO COME![64]

Despite the fact that Stephensen had more or less abandoned his railway worker friends in Ipswich along with his job at the grammar school, they still respected him greatly. A few days before he sailed, a small group of them held a send-off and presented him with, of all things, a gold fob watch. Capitalist habits die hard, and the watch was inscribed as a 'token of appreciation' from the Ipswich Workers.[65]

Stephensen acknowledged that these 'Ipswich plugs' had given him more of a personal insight into the class struggle than the complete works of Marx, and two of them in particular appealed to his anarchic personality: Joe Maguire and his wife Mona. Joe was a 'bloody fucking REBEL, of the most lovable and repulsive type ... very impressive and glib though obscene in expression', and 'hating Jesus with an undying hatred'. Joe would be 'an invaluable ally in the destructive battle which we must wage against capitalism and the church'. His wife on the other hand was 'twice the man that Joe is but yet not half so picturesque'. Stephensen's regard for these people was already tempered by a disquieting and patronizing arrogance:

> I like to imagine to myself that I should mate with Mona Maguire, a real little rebel, but she looks a bit pasty and pudgy, and her work in the factory will not improve her health. Mind you, I am not at present sexually attracted by Mona, but I regard her as a possible mate at some time in the future, or at least someone of her type mentally. I should like to cross my breed with Joe's, just for the interest of the eugenic experiment. This thought I regard as a high tribute to Joe ...[66]

Stephensen hastily arranged his passport and was authorized by the editor of the *Daily Standard* to act as the paper's correspondent in Britain and Europe. His seventy-year-old Swiss grandfather was at the wharf to farewell him, and Stephensen described Tardent as an 'idealist and an intellectual' who had been his early guide and inspiration. Although Stephensen now disagreed with the old man on 'almost every point of socialist theory', he acknowledged his gratitude to the democrat's 'lofty, almost Roman spirit of work and sacrifice'. All this Stephensen unburdened to his friend Smith. His feelings towards the rest of his 'well meaning and entirely bourgeois' family were ambivalent, rendering him both callous and mawkishly sentimental. His father was 'a sterling bloke, limited only by environment and a shamefully deficient education', and rather pleased that university had not made his son 'a snob or a gentleman'. His mother on the other hand was sorry he was not more cultured. Stephensen was prepared to see them both starve 'rather than compromise in the revolutionary cause'. He had even warned his father never to expect any monetary return for the sacrifices which had made possible his education:

> I have continually treated them with contempt in the hope of turning them against me, yet they continue to manifest affection ... A curious thing is family sentiment! Yet I have gained this much, that they know me to be a revolutionary and an atheist etc., and they realise that my ambitions of fame, career etc are not the accepted comfortable ones of the ordinary bourgeois type.[67]

As the ferry moved off for the short trip down-river to the passenger liner *Jervis Bay*, Stephensen's Ipswich friends threw a symbolic barrage of red streamers. From the ferry he felt the intrusive presence of warships at anchor along the Brisbane River and he had a romantic vision of his fate at the hands of such 'armed capitalist might'. He was, he wrote at sea to Smith, not 'physically cowed by the possibility of martyrdom in "the only just war in history"'. Such portentous sentiments were a good indication that Stephensen was in fact enjoying himself immensely as he set out on his great adventure.

He travelled to England via Sydney, Melbourne, Fremantle, Colombo and the Suez Canal, and his description of the few days spent in Sydney makes them seem weeks. He called at the *Art in Australia* office in an attempt to locate Jack Lindsay who had been editing *Vision* magazine with Ken Slessor and Frank Johnson:

> Leon Gellert was there, looking very smug and unlikeable, and he told me to go to Dymock's [bookshop] and ask for Frank Johnson. This I did, but Frank Johnson had been sacked for selling a Boccaccio to a small girl, and I was at a loss for a moment until just as I was going out, I ran fair into young Philip Lindsay! We went together and got drunk, after which we went out to visit Jack at Bondi ... There was much talking, mirth, mutual admiration, profound philosophy, poetry, and Norman-worship. Jack ... has all the ingenuousness of a true poet, and his eyes are those of a visionary. I spent a great deal of time with him, read all his manuscripts, and gazed often at his fine collection of Norman's etchings ... Men such as [Jack] Lindsay can lead the moral attack on this stinking, decrepit civilisation, and their assistance to the actual revolution is enormous ... I think he will desert his wife eventually, and come over to England for a while. In that case we may be associated in some bourgeois-killing stunts.[68]

Stephensen also entertained an old girlfriend who was staying at Bondi, but once again escaped with his innocence intact. 'I refused to bang her through fear of the results, for her', he confided to Smith with a gentlemanly restraint and dignity that was not quite convincing. He called on two of the founders of the Australian Communist Party, Jock Garden and Guido Barrachi, and met 'thousands of other Sydney Communists'.[69]

In a mood of personal and political exhilaration just before the *Jervis Bay* sailed from Sydney, he penned an article which was published anonymously in the Sydney *Workers' Weekly* under the title 'Another Idol Shattered: The Yellowness of Theodore'. Attacking the Queensland Labor premier as 'a person open to the suspicion of having sold himself to the enemy', Stephensen went on to describe him as a 'feeble cardboard Mussolini' who was ignorant of the class struggle and had made Queensland an 'exploiters' paradise'. With all the stature of his twenty-two years, Stephensen accused the ex-miner of 'treacherously deserting the Australian working class' in the interests of personal ambition. 'Get out, you miserable Judas!', Stephensen flung at him from the refuge of his anonymity and his English-bound liner.[70] Puffed up by this act of bravado, he commented to his friend Smith that now he had exposed Theodore's treachery he hoped the bastard would get 'punked quick and lively'.[71] Theodore did in fact resign as state premier a few months later, but went on to become federal treasurer before allegations of shady mining deals in Queensland brought him down.

On board the *Jervis Bay* Stephensen met the Australian writer Jack McLaren and the two of them helped produce a newspaper which was distributed when the ship crossed the equator. At Port Said his pockets were picked and he was offered the obligatory dirty postcards.[72] As the ship approached England, his old college magazine *Argo* whimsically reflected that the founder of the Rhodes Scholarship might have lamented the choice of one who failed to share the great vision of a world-wide British Empire. But Rhodes himself would be converted 'could he hear "Inky" paint a word-picture of the glorious blood-besmeared victory of the Proletariat in the near future'.[73]

Part Two

England, 1924–1932

Oxford was not a place of study, but of exuberant, anarchic, fantasizing hedonism.
>Martin Green
>*Children of the Sun*, 1976

A revolutionary theory which is not going to lead to street-fighting, sooner or later, is the most ridiculous fake.
>P. R. Stephensen
>Bakunin essay, 1929

Inky was temperamentally a man to whom extreme positions seemed inherently good.
>Lord Roberthall
>memoir, 1969

He made his living, and in the process convinced himself that he was serving the arts, by printing limited and expensive editions of the more scabrous specimens of the native and foreign literatures.
>Aldous Huxley
>*Point Counter Point*, 1928

3
A Bolshevik comes to Oxford

After ploughing through fog in the English Channel the *Jervis Bay* docked at Tilbury towards the end of September 1924. Stephensen was met by his friends Burton and Hall who had waited on the wharf for ten hours. They took the excited newcomer back to the Duchess of Connaught Hostel, a Bloomsbury boarding house used by students, and from there to a cheap French restaurant near Piccadilly Circus. Walking back to the hostel that first night, intoxicated with wine and with his first taste of metropolitan Europe, Stephensen suddenly bolted from his friends and disappeared into a cab with a prostitute. Dismayed by his impetuosity, Burton and Hall could do nothing but return without him. Sexually inexperienced, with only a few shillings in his pocket, and without the address of the boarding house, Stephensen was forced to abandon both the girl and the taxi and eventually found his way back on foot some time later.[1]

Despite this false start Stephensen spent a hectic and exhilarating ten days in London. He felt he was 'truly in the centre of the world', though the silk hats and bowlers reminded him sharply of the contrast between rich and poor which the city also epitomized. The noise, speed and 'bad air' of the underground tube railway and the constant stream of traffic through the streets made him realize what a sleepy colonial backwater he had left behind. Disconcerted at first, he quickly caught up with the city's pace. He had two visiting cards printed: one with the magical name of Oxford in italics, the other in plain bold type announcing him as a representative of Brisbane's labour paper, the *Daily Standard*. With these he could secure entrée to the elevated levels of society as well as to the fringes of political dissent. Not that he needed either at speakers' corner in Hyde Park where he met some comrades and 'spoke from the stump' himself about the reprehensible Queensland Labor government.[2]

Stephensen's dual identity enabled him to socialize with members of that same government. The former home secretary, John Huxham, whose daughter Stephensen had known at university, had also arrived recently in London with his wife to take up the position of agent-general for

Queensland. Stephensen lunched with them and escorted Mrs Huxham to the British Empire Exhibition at Wembley where he was impressed with the amusement park but 'disappointed and disgusted' to find that the Empire was nothing but a 'vast trading concern'. In his report on the exhibition for the *Daily Standard*, Stephensen described the whirring machines and silent steel leviathans of the Palace of Engineering as fascinating but evil. Modern civilization was 'converting millions of human beings into mechanical slaves of these iron masters', he observed.[3]

On his tour of London, Stephensen took in Madame Tussaud's waxworks and the House of Commons, but he also attended the Labour Party conference at which Prime Minister Ramsay MacDonald announced an imminent election. This had been forced on his government by conservative reaction to Britain's closer ties with Russia. In the visitors' gallery at the conference Stephensen sat beside Lloyd George who reminded him of a 'broken down old warrior' like Billy Hughes.[4] He also visited his shipboard friends, Jack and Ada McLaren, who had moved into the basement of a boarding house in Nevern Square. In an adjoining room lived Winifred Venus, a former ballerina whose husband was in America. Stephensen made her acquaintance and through the McLarens also came in contact with writers, artists and journalists.

Burton and Hall had already returned to Oxford and Stephensen followed them several days later, in time for the start of a Michaelmas Term on Sunday 12 October. 'You are arriving at a kind of National, or International, Madhouse', the university magazine *Cherwell* warned freshmen.[5] In Stephensen's intake of 'commoners' at Queen's College were students from Madras and Mysore, from Iowa and New York and Sydney, and from English grammar schools as well as from the élite public schools like Eton and Rugby. In the college entrances book, where details of new students were noted, Stephensen's religion was given as Church of England, his future profession uncertain, his sports athletics and rugby, and his chief interest 'politics and social questions'. He had not been reticent about his radicalism, the college recording him as a 'Communist in views'. He was also listed as 'Not musical' and 'Rather deaf', a congenital affliction which worsened as he grew older.[6] Another Australian at the college was Tom Inglis Moore who had graduated from the University of Sydney with a 'triple first', winning a travelling scholarship to Oxford.

The six-hundred-year-old Queen's College was ruled over, in theory at least, by an octogenarian clergyman who had been at the college since 1864. However, the twentieth century was beginning to chip away at the medieval and neo-classical face of Oxford. In the immediate post-war years Greek had been abolished as a compulsory entrance requirement, and women 'undergraduettes' were now admitted to the university. Oxford 'bags'—baggy flannel trousers—and long winding scarves were fashionable, and in some circles so was homosexuality.

It was fifty years since the youthful Oscar Wilde had come under Walter Pater's influence at Oxford, but aestheticism was enjoying a new vogue. The leading aesthete was Harold Acton of Christ Church, a precociously cultivated and cosmopolitan Etonian. Although his family owned a magnificent Tuscan villa, his maternal grandfather had been an American and the founder of the Illinois Trust and Savings Bank. Acton firmly re-established the cult of aestheticism at Oxford and was largely the model for Anthony Blanche in Evelyn Waugh's *Brideshead Revisited*. A. J. P. Taylor remembered him as 'absolutely the dominant figure at Oxford', whose poetry was then ranked well ahead of Auden's.[7]

Stephensen did not mix with the literary dandies. His room in the college's back quadrangle, overlooking Queen's Lane and the Church of St Peter in the East, soon had a photo of Karl Marx on the wall. On the floor below he shared a sitting room with Burton. His other Queensland friend Hall was at the more fashionable Magdalen College which had its own deer park beside the River Cherwell.

Colleges were staffed by butlers, stewards and porters, and each 'stair' or group of rooms was attended by a man-servant. The 'scout' was an Oxford institution, a respected and respectful servant who called his young charges 'Sir' while they in turn addressed him by his surname. As the *Cherwell* informed freshers, the scout could 'recommend a virtue or a cobbler, warn against a vice or an advertisement with equal ease and certainty'.[8] Attended by one's scout it was possible to entertain a small group for breakfast, lunch or afternoon tea, with white linen and silver toast racks. Scorning such aristocratic rituals, Stephensen instead became friendly with Quelch, his scout, and went drinking with him, praising the brown ale as 'thick as treacle, and packed full of vitamins'.[9]

Along with other Rhodes Scholars, Stephensen joined the Colonial Club and within a few weeks he delivered a learned paper to the club in the form of an 'irreverent, obscene and even obscure' letter intercepted on its way to Allez-au-Buggahree, the Caliph of Baghdad. The author of this fabulous document purported to be Mustapha Furk, a colonial student requesting pocket money from his father. In Furk's account of university life Stephensen wittily sketched his own response to Oxford. The inhabitants of the university he found to consist of three classes: the Athletes, the Aesthetes and the Obsoletes. The Athletes were 'vast of stature and small of brain', while the Aesthetes refused to kiss maidens, and the Obsoletes were the scholars, old in mind and 'eunuchs in body'. There were also women, 'but not as we understand the term in Baghdad'.[10]

Stephensen was enrolled in the honours school known as Modern Greats, covering philosophy, politics and economics. As well as lectures his work was directed by personal tutors for whom he prepared weekly essays. Only at the end of his three years would he have to face a rigorous series of final exams. His history tutor was a member of the university Labour Club, Godfrey Elton, whom Stephensen described as 'a bit of a mild rebel himself'. They had had some 'good hot arguments', although Stephensen modestly reported to his Ipswich friends that all round 'I am teaching him more than he is teaching me!' Most of the Labour sympathizers at Oxford Stephensen found too tame, causing him to 'shove the ginger into 'em pretty hard'.[11]

There were usually a few communists in the Labour Club but dissent from Oxford's prevailing conservative ideology had always been suppressed. In 1921 the editor of a new communist journal, *Free Oxford*, had been expelled—'sent down'—by the vice-chancellor, and the journal's sub-editor 'rusticated' or banished temporarily. Even the activities of the Labour Club had been restricted, with Bertrand Russell banned from speaking there. Stephensen became a member of the Labour Club as did his contemporary, A. J. P. Taylor, and both joined the tiny Oxford branch of the Communist Party.[12]

During his first term at Oxford Stephensen competed in relay and pole vaulting events, renewed contact with Vere Gordon Childe, and sent off several long articles for the Brisbane *Daily Standard* including one on the defeat of Labour at the British election. Stephensen criticized the 'journalistic gutterlings' of the Rothermere press who had used the fake Zinovieff letter as anti-Labour propaganda just before the election.[13] Supplied with information from Australia, he wrote articles for the London *Workers' Weekly* on Australian labour issues such as the seamen's strike. During his Christmas vacation in London, he surrendered his virginity to a prostitute and attempted, without success, to broaden his journalistic contacts by submitting work to papers like the *Express*, the *Royal Magazine* and even the anti-Bolshevik *Daily Mail*. He also spent time with the McLarens and with their neighbour Winifred, the former ballerina who was also a teacher of ballet and ballroom dancing.[14]

Acting as correspondent for the *Daily Standard* took up much of his spare time, but early in 1925 he had a brief and vitriolic exchange with Harold Acton in the columns of the *Cherwell*. An apostle of modernism as well as aestheticism, Acton had scorned peasant culture as 'loutish and uncouth' and a 'triumph of the illiterate and of the unintellectual'. In response, Stephensen attacked modernism and modern life with its 'thudding machines, shrieking underground trains, pallidness, daily papers, chemical foods' and 'hideous negroid cacophony of jazz'. He also implied that Acton's modernist verse was 'chaotic' and 'crapulous'. Acton wrote to the *Cherwell* that 'Miss Stephenson' must be either a '*poseuse*, or that her libido is topsy-turvy'—'At any rate Miss Stephenson has much to learn; she must learn to refrain from indulging in cheap abuse, bad spelling, and poor arguments expressed in lamentable journalese'. Addressing Stephensen as 'Miss' was a nicely calculated insult, and the *Cherwell*'s editor had to close the correspondence after the angry Australian wrote declaring 'How altogether sapless these moderns are!'[15]

Stephensen had scarcely ruffled Acton's elegant self-possession and had revealed instead his own prejudices. Politically avant-garde, Stephensen was nevertheless culturally conservative and he did indeed have much to learn in hand-to-hand literary combat. Graham Greene's small volume of verse, *Babbling April*, was reviewed with acerbic condescension by Acton in the *Cherwell*, but Greene put up a more intelligent fight than Stephensen had against the Olympian aesthete. Acton had accused Greene of dinting the 'contaminated dusk with the slender banjo-tunes of an adolescent hysteria', and Greene replied with wit and restraint, thanking Acton for his lengthy advertisement: 'Attack by Mr. Acton is a recommendation to most readers'.[16]

Unlike Harold Acton or the imaginary student whose father was Caliph of Baghdad, Stephensen did not have a wealthy family on which to rely for unlimited pocket money. Quite the opposite in fact. The Stephensen store in Biggenden was in deep financial trouble, having made a trading loss in the second half of 1924. Stephensen's parents had begun without capital and were now heavily mortgaged with little hope of repaying debts amounting to more than £5000. They were losing the store, and the expanding family would be forced to exist on what income Stephensen's younger sister could provide. By contrast, the Rhodes Scholarship provided Stephensen with £350 a year, rising to £400 in 1925. If managed carefully this was enough to pay college and university expenses and even allowed lengthy vacations in Paris because of the favourable exchange rate. A pound sterling was converted, as if by alchemy, into well over a hundred French francs.[17]

For the Easter vacation in 1925 Stephensen crossed the Channel with Hall and Burton for his long awaited taste of Paris. The city did not disappoint him. With his friends he dallied about a month in the Latin quarter, playing chess, drinking, arguing and enjoying himself. He stayed at the Hotel de l'Univers near the Pantheon and the university where the students wore black hats, cloaks and 'marvellous beards'. Stephensen shaved off his Charlie Chaplin moustache and for a while grew his own scruffy beard. His room cost only a couple of pounds for the month, and a five-course meal with wine was less than a shilling.[18]

On the day of his arrival in Paris he witnessed a violent brawl at the university between crowds of fascist and communist sympathizers over the issue of law lectures by a socialist. In his article for the *Standard*, Stephensen compared the significance of this political conflict with the irrelevance of the Oxford-Cambridge boat race, being held the same day in England. Patriotic fascist students sang the *Marseillaise* in the 'historic battleground' of the Place de Pantheon, while the communists gathering in the narrow cobbled streets responded with the red flag and the *Internationale*. Despite police sulphur bombs and baton charges the battle continued all afternoon, and there were demonstrations and counter-demonstrations for a week in the Latin quarter. After the harmless student rags in Brisbane and the aristocratic torpor of Oxford, Stephensen found Paris exciting as well as dangerous. Stores and cafés were open all night, and the Parisian chorus girls danced with nothing on. By comparison London was 'as gloomy as the backyard of hell'.[19]

With his fluent French, his status as a newspaper correspondent and his membership of the Communist Party of Great Britain, Stephensen made many friends in Paris among students and communists. He attended a huge rally of the 'Worker-Peasant Bloc' at the Luna Park skating rink in a working-class suburb on the outskirts of the city. The crowds marching to the rally sang the inevitable *Internationale*, and Stephensen's reportage account for the *Standard* expressed his own excitement at the spectacle:

> As I joined one of these marching columns I suddenly realised just what is meant by the word 'Proletariat'. These thousands of workers, ruggedly picturesque in velveteen trousers and jackets, in loose-fitting jeans and sweaters, in pointed shining caps and coloured neckcloths, heavy-footed in their wooden shoes (sabots), singing as they marched the song of the oppressed and exploited of the earth... These, I realised, represented the Proletariat, actively class-conscious, an ever-growing menace to the peace and comfort of the privileged class.[20]

Yet Stephensen's viewpoint remained that of an outsider. As his friend Robert Hall has commented, it was the revolutionary fervour which appealed to Stephensen rather than the brotherhood of man.[21]

From the evidence of letters to his radical friends in Queensland, Stephensen was expecting a second proletarian revolution, this time in France. 'Before not so very long things will happen here which will shake the foundations of Europe', he wrote to Bevil Molesworth. Australia would then have to establish a 'Workers' and Farmers' Socialist Republic' or 'become an American dependency for a few decades'. Showing how shrewd and even prophetic his political judgement could be, Stephensen added that, without a strong Australian Communist Party, 'it will be the latter alternative, I fear'.[22] He was also impatient at the weakness of the British party, and wrote to Victor Smith that 'I intend to stick to the CP and fight to the last ditch along straight-out revolutionary principles'. He was disappointed, he claimed, at not having enough money to spend the Easter vacation 'touring the Clyde, South Wales and Ireland', but Paris was a far more congenial place for someone of his temperament, and he continued 'blowing froth in the Café du Panthéon' with his Australian friends Hall, Burton and Tom Inglis Moore.[23]

He also met, drank and talked revolution with a Russian *émigré*, Michel Zipine. Stephensen had plans for a pilgrimage to Russia that summer so he arranged to teach Zipine English while learning Russian in return. Their common language was French. In an unpublished, autobiographical novel Stephensen described Michel as an employee at the Soviet Commercial Agency in Paris who introduced him to a 'score of jolly Russians' including Bolsheviks and sons of 'White' Russian exiles. Elsewhere he remembered Zipine as a Russian Jew and a student at the Sorbonne.[24]

Winifred Venus, the dancing teacher, happened also to be staying in Paris and, with Stephensen and his friends, toured the nightclubs of Montparnasse and the Latin quarter. In smoke-stifled underground clubs with names like Le Jockey and Noctambules, they drank and danced till dawn to the music of guitarists, accordion players and Negro jazz bands. At one such subterranean tavern, frequented by a larrikin tribe calling themselves Apaches, there was an argument and one man was 'stuck with a knife'. Stephensen took Winifred to a performance of Wagner's *Tannhäuser* at the Opéra and on a steamer trip down the Seine followed by dinner on the terrace of a village café.[25]

The trip to Russia did not eventuate, possibly for lack of funds, and instead Stephensen hired a punt with Burton for the summer term to enjoy the languid streams which meander through Oxford. He invited Winifred up for 'Eights Week' in May, '*the* social event of the year at Oxford', he told her, 'when all the mothers, sisters and aunts etc of the young bloods come up to get punted around on the river'. Against a background of spring weather and rowing races, he and Winifred spent an idyllic couple of days picnicking, punting and walking. He knew Winifred was older—she had a son away at boarding school—but he never knew quite how much, for she was slightly built, with the grace of a ballerina.[26]

Winifred was in fact old enough to be his aunt. She had been born Winifred Lockyer in England in 1886 but her parents separated and she followed her father to Melbourne about 1900. Ever since childhood her life had been unsettled. She had set up a dancing studio in Melbourne and, about 1910, she went to England and then America as a dancer. She was in the chorus in New York musicals and joined a touring variety act as a ballerina. In 1912 she married and had a son, continuing to dance under various stage names. At the end of the war she became ill and returned to Australia with her son. Hoping to renew contact with her husband she went to England in 1922 but their separation continued and she had to support herself and her son by giving dancing lessons in London. Her precarious situation was relieved to some extent by an Australian friend who paid for her son to be educated at boarding school.[27]

The unexpected entry of Stephensen caused her happiness, but also anxiety on account of their age difference. She found him entertaining and lively, and he enjoyed the company of an unusual and talented woman who had travelled and experienced so much. To her, Stephensen seemed a young man with a future. An Oxford degree would virtually guarantee him a respectable career and he had the energy and ability to succeed at anything. His own special devil, however, was driving him into less conventional territory.

To be a communist at Oxford was unusual as well as risky, and in Stephensen's time the university branch of the party had only four or five active members, including A. J. P. Taylor and Tom Driberg, a homosexual, who was possibly working as an undercover agent for the British secret service (MI5). Graham Greene, another undergraduate, had been a German agent before he joined the Oxford Communist Party. However, he was just after a free trip to Russia, a mercenary motive Stephensen had seen through almost at once. Another and more serious party member, the Welsh student Ieuan Thomas, had his room at Merton College repeatedly wrecked and his books and furniture burnt, and was subjected to physical intimidation and assault.[28]

The Communist Party of Great Britain, like its Australian counterpart, had been formed about 1920 from a number of small left-wing groups and was weakened by sectionalism. When Stephensen joined, the party was under increasing pressure not just from the conservative Baldwin government but also from Soviet Russia which provided the party with funds. By a Comintern edict, the British party was responsible for communist propaganda throughout the Empire, so a 'Colonial Department' was formed and special agents were sent to India where membership of the Communist Party was illegal. The 'Colonial Department' at the party's Covent Garden headquarters also decided to recruit agents from amongst the Indian students at Oxford, so Stephensen and Ieuan Thomas were instructed to contact Indians and make a report. As the India Office also had its own spies at Oxford, Stephensen and Thomas were entering a complex network of intrigue.[29]

Early in June 1925 they sent party headquarters a summary of the political inclinations of the sixty Indians in the university's Majlis club, describing in detail half a dozen likely individuals who were returning to India at the end of term. Some were already socialists and communists, others fiercely nationalist. One, the president of the Majlis, believed in non-violence but felt that India would be 'compelled to free herself by violence'. Stephensen and Thomas suggested that 'Comrade Saklatvala', a Parsee from Bombay and the Communist MP for North Battersea, should interview these Indians as soon as possible. Thomas passed their reports on to London headquarters and received in exchange a supply of propaganda literature to be 'judiciously' distributed amongst the Indians.[30]

As he had done in Ipswich, Stephensen also made contact with local railwaymen and helped produce *The Searchlight*, a workers' paper printed on a duplicating machine and 'privately circulating' among Oxford railway militants. The first number declared that sooner or later the workers of Britain would clear out the 'whole rotten gang' of 'capitalist class parasites' and take direct control. Stephensen sent a copy of the paper to his Ipswich communist friends, telling them that unemployment was getting worse and a 'big fighting alliance' of miners, railwaymen, dockers and others was being formed: 'I believe I shall see the revolution begin over here before another two years are up, but if it happens I don't know whether the Communist Party will be strong enough to control the situation'.[31]

At the end of the summer term Stephensen's philosophy tutor reported that he was 'one of the most promising men of the year', and his economics tutor said his work was 'remarkable for the tenacity with which he has maintained a point of view which is not that held by most modern Economists'. Nevertheless Stephensen was one of his best pupils, who 'reads more Economics, thinks more Economics, and talks more Economics than any other working under my direction'. Earlier, Stephensen had written asking Molesworth to send over his Brisbane WEA lectures on Marxian economics to help in the 'admirable business of flooring tutors'.[32]

In a paper on modern imperialism read to the Queen's College Historical Society, Stephensen said that, during World War I, the lives of ten million men had been laid down in the cause of imperial trade rivalry.

Free competition had almost disappeared in this new age of 'steel and finance capitalism' ruled by a dictatorship of banks and trusts. Showing sympathy for Germany, he spoke of the cynical financiers who had 'settled like vultures to the task of dismembering the corpse of Germany', and concluded prophetically: 'I believe that the history of the remainder of the twentieth century will be that of wars of revolts of colonial peoples against imperialist exploitation and economic domination'. This argument is central to an understanding of his later support for nationalism and even fascism. His racism and fear of non-whites was also evident. World socialism alone, he wrote in another article, could prevent the 'rising tide of colour' from swamping white civilization.[33]

For the 1925 summer vacation he returned to Paris and attended an eight-day school arranged by the French Communist Party. He played chess with Hall, 'talked endlessly', and again took with enthusiasm to the life of the cafés, *quais*, parks and boulevards. He renewed his friendship with Michel Zipine who helped him translate Mayakovsky's long poem 'The Death of Lenin'. Their translation appeared a few months later in the *Communist Review* under the initials 'P.R.S. and M.Z.' While in Paris Stephensen also translated Lenin's *Imperialism* from the French version and began translating another Lenin work, *On the Road to Insurrection*. Both were published by the Communist Party of Great Britain the following year.[34]

During autumn 1925 there was an increased campaign within the conservative government, especially by the home secretary Joynson-Hicks, to expose the 'red menace'. Another ardent anti-Bolshevik was Lord Birkenhead, the secretary of state for India, who was equally determined to fight Soviet subversion and propaganda. The general mood of the country was summed up by D. H. Lawrence who revisited England early in October: 'There's a million and a quarter unemployed, receiving that wretched dole ... They look for a revolution of some sort: I don't quite see anything violent, but added to the fog, it's horribly depressing'.[35]

A few days later Scotland Yard's Special Branch raided the Communist Party and several members of the party executive were arrested, charged with sedition under the Incitement to Mutiny Act of 1797. In all, twelve men were found guilty by a jury, and those with previous convictions were sentenced to a year's imprisonment. The judge offered the others good behaviour bonds if they promised to have nothing more to do with the Communist Party 'or the doctrines which it preaches', but they refused and were gaoled for six months.[36]

Meanwhile the party's publications manager wrote to Stephensen urging further instalments of the Lenin translations and apologizing for the delay with *Imperialism* which was 'out on proof with a comrade for correction against the Russian text for political values'. It was no joke, he told Stephensen, expecting a van from Scotland Yard to carry away party literature as soon as it was printed.[37] The crisis in the mining industry was worsening and, with a general strike feared, an Organisation for the Maintenance of Supplies was formed. The *Cherwell* warned in November that such a catastrophic strike 'would reduce this country to the condition of Bolshevik Russia'.[38] Even the Labour Party conference had turned against the communists, prohibiting their affiliation.

In the midst of this bleak winter Stephensen took a flat in Chelsea for the Christmas vacation with Hall and another Queensland friend. On 9 December *The Times* ran a short article under the headline 'Communists at Oxford' which clearly indicated that Joynson-Hicks's raiders had found the reports compiled by Stephensen and Thomas. Within a week Sir Arthur Hirtzel, Birkenhead's under-secretary of state for India, had sent photographs of 'certain documents' implicating Stephensen to the pro-provost of his Oxford college, the Rev. E. M. Walker. Walker thought Stephensen should be expelled, and immediately passed these 'very shocking' documents on to the Rhodes secretary who was responsible for Stephensen's scholarship.[39]

Tipped off by *The Times*, Stephensen had organized Hall and another student to go carefully through his college room and remove anything that looked compromising. They had found a pamphlet giving ten good reasons why the ALP should exclude communists, and thought it might be amusing to leave that as conspicuous evidence of his moderate views. They took away papers, files and boxes, however, and stored them in another room. Apart from this precaution Stephensen was not overly concerned. His name had not been mentioned, and Joynson-Hicks parried a question about the affair in the Commons.[40]

Stephensen invited Winifred and her son over for Christmas dinner, and early in the new year he went off to Leeds for a few days to attend a conference of the University Labour Federation. He wrote to Winifred that he was 'fed up to the teeth with university socialists' who were ignorant of the real struggle of the working class. Perhaps unaware of the irony, he added that he had chummed up with a 'nice fellow' who was a 'peer of the realm from Cambridge'. Still, Inky had made some 'fiery speeches', including one reported by *The Times* on expropriating the property-owning class. 'Before we contemplate nationalization as a practical programme', he had told the conference, 'we must have the will to set up a dictatorship of the people'.[41] Such sentiments were hardly likely to endear him further to the Oxford authorities.

As soon as he returned to college in mid-January for the beginning of first term 1926 he was told by Walker to attend an interview with the university vice-chancellor, Dr Wells, and the proctors—officers responsible for discipline. Along with the other communist Thomas, he was given twenty-four hours to sign a promise to 'hold no communication, direct or indirect, with any organised Communist association' and 'not endeavour to propagate Communist views'. Threatened with immediate expulsion, both agreed to sign but Stephensen sent his letter back the same day with two provisos added: that he retain financial membership of the Communist Party, and that he be allowed to take part in 'public debate or discussion on theoretical Communism'. The vice-chancellor politely agreed to the former but refused the latter as inconsistent with the promise not to propagate communist views.[42]

Stephensen had a busy few days. At 2 a.m. he penned Winifred a note asking her to personally deliver to Communist Party headquarters a letter explaining his predicament. In effect he had already broken his promise hours after making it. Stephensen wrote to the party secretary that he genuinely desired to continue his studies and would be 'entirely destitute and stranded far from home and friends' were he deprived of his scholarship. With the collapse of his parents' business he was indeed dependent on his own resources, but he went on to claim that the party would not have gained had he chosen the 'martyr's crown'.[43] Yet he had also saved his skin, and his chances of a career, by rejecting the path Shelley had taken a century before at Oxford.

It is unlikely that Stephensen's plaintive arguments would have convinced his party leaders who, just a few weeks before, had themselves gone to prison rather than disown their party. Whether or not Stephensen admitted it to himself, his credibility as a proletarian revolutionary was now in some doubt. With the party in disarray and its executive behind bars, the 'acting general secretary' acknowledged Stephensen's letter and expressed regret but not surprise at the incident. Giving away perhaps more than he intended, he said he 'condoned' Stephensen's attitude and hoped this 'little lesson of class tactics' would be of use to Stephensen in the future.[44]

To the Rhodes secretary, in effect his paymaster, Stephensen betrayed his radical beliefs even more shamelessly, though he did choose his words with legalistic precision: 'I do think that this drastic action has been taken under a certain amount of misapprehension', he wrote, 'as I regard myself primarily as a student, and I have none other than a theoretical interest in politics while in that status'. The Rhodes officials knew very well his interest was more than theoretical but accepted his promise, later noting in their records that he was 'rather wild in his politics, but sincere' and had 'won respect along with criticism'.[45]

The conservative press in Britain was undoubtedly aware of Stephensen's status as a Rhodes Scholar but such details were notably absent in the controversy which followed his suppression. Only in the Brisbane press were there sensational headlines about the 'Queensland Rhodes Scholar on the Carpet'. Several months earlier, Stephensen had sent home the tutors' reports for his first year and his grandfather Henry Tardent now distributed copies for publication in the local papers. Stephensen's WEA friend Victor Smith wrote to both the Brisbane *Telegraph* and *Daily Mail* vigorously protesting at Stephensen's persecution. He compared Stephensen's predicament with that of Shelley ('whose first name also happened to be Percy') and, somewhat more incongruously, with that of Jesus. This was too much for the religious sensitivities of the *Daily Mail* whose editor deleted the reference.[46]

Criticism of Stephensen, however, continued in Australia and he later sent an article, 'Must Rhodes Scholars Be Imperialists?', to the Brisbane

Daily Standard. Although on firm ground as a victimized intellectual, he weakened his case rather alarmingly by claiming that if Cecil Rhodes were alive the man might conceivably be a member of the Communist International. He also praised the secretary of the Rhodes Trust, F. J. Wylie, claiming Wylie had declined his offer to resign the scholarship.[47]

Rumours circulated in Oxford about the roles of Lord Birkenhead, the vice-chancellor Dr Wells, and Queen's College's ancient and invisible provost the Rev. Magrath who had been a student of John Stuart Mill; but one thing is certain: encouraged by the government and the media, Britain was in an advanced state of paranoia about Bolshevism. On the same Saturday Stephensen was hauled before the vice-chancellor, the Catholic priest and writer Ronald Knox broadcast a satirical 'news bulletin' from an Edinburgh radio station announcing that a cabinet minister had been hanged from a lamp-post, that Big Ben and the Savoy Hotel had been blown up and an irate mob was marching on the BBC. More than a decade before Orson Welles's famous hoax in New York, thousands of listeners in Britain were 'thrown into a panic by the thought that a revolution had broken out in the metropolis'.[48] It was a joke Stephensen no doubt appreciated greatly, though there was little joy for him in the manner of his suppression.

Hoping that the episode was now concluded, Wells the vice-chancellor wrote a brief letter to *The Times* to put on public record the students' promise. One acquaintance of Stephensen's in particular, however, would not let the matter rest: Frank Lee of Balliol College, a former trade unionist and now chairman of the university Labour Club. The club unanimously passed a motion condemning the vice-chancellor's action, and at a 'private business meeting' of the Oxford Union on 11 February Lee put another motion censuring Wells which was finally carried by 215 votes to 92. He also requested that this be put to a formal poll of the whole society. Conservative country clergy and dons flocked to vote and the motion was narrowly defeated by 403 votes to 367. Decency having thereby prevailed, *The Times* pontificated in an editorial that if any charge was to be framed against the university authorities it was one of 'excessive tolerance' not repression, considering the poison and perversion spread by students who had 'dishonestly' accepted scholarships.[49]

Stephensen was not altogether silenced. The *Communist Review* which appeared that month had an article on the Australian labour movement by 'P.R.S.' in which he urged the antipodean masses to rally under the slogan of the Australian Workers' and Farmers' Socialist Republic. Thumbing his nose at the university authorities with the same cavalier sense of discretion he had always displayed, Stephensen attended the annual dinner of the Oxford Majlis and souvenired a menu on which his signature appeared with those of a couple of dozen Indians.[50]

There can be little doubt, though, that the previous few months had shaken Stephensen's confidence, if not his faith, in the Communist Party, and vice versa. Anticipating a general strike, militant conservatives like Joynson-Hicks had been able to suppress the leadership of a party whose influence in any case was never very significant. Moscow knew this only too well, as did Stephensen.[51] Jack Lindsay, who had suddenly turned up in London, wrote to him in jocular fashion that communists were either 'in chase of the silliest of delusions or a lot of personal amusement and "sense of power" '. He knew Stephensen belonged to the class in search of power and amusement.[52]

Stephensen had gone over to Paris at the end of March 1926 for the Easter vacation, and Lindsay's letter was forwarded on from Oxford. Stephensen wrote back enthusiastically that he would show him Paris and Lindsay went straight over by train:

> P.R.S. met me at the Gare du Norde, running along the platform with his usual zest, chattering in argot to grumpy porters and carrying me off under his arm to the nearest café for *vin rouge*. Norsely fair, clearly handsome, athletic and bristling with a compact energy, he was able to stamp any moment with a casual effect of historic importance.

Installing Lindsay at his favourite left bank hotel, Stephensen was soon hauling him out again 'with brisk hilarious gestures'. Lindsay recalled Stephensen's commentary on the street scene, and his 'impressario generosity as if he himself had invented it all only the day before for my special benefit'.[53]

Winifred was also there, and Lindsay described her in his autobiography as 'incredibly finely-bodied and gracefully slight' with a 'soft small big-eyed face'. She was 'as strong and steady as her dance-image was light and swan-gliding', but privately Lindsay was also struck by how much older than Stephensen she was. Lindsay thought their relationship was a mixture of 'devotion and aloofness', and that Winifred was a stabilizing influence, an 'amiable kind aunt'. With them, and also with Robert Hall, Lindsay roamed the Latin quarter. Then, in the company of Michel Zipine and other Russians, Stephensen took him on a tour of the Paris underworld:

> We visited bars and cellars thick with smoke where throaty singers bawled witty songs of which I couldn't follow a word, and then took a look at cheap dimly-lit brothels where stolid workers sipped bocks at splintery tables from the corners of which a huge swarthy tart picked up coins with an unlikely part of her anatomy.[54]

Literary ambition had driven Lindsay to England, and he infected Stephensen with something of his artistic self-confidence. In many ways Stephensen was a frustrated literary man. He had penned some rather banal satirical and polemical verse at Oxford, though there was one lively pattern poem depicting a 'Charles/toning/flap/per/as/viewed from the rear...'[55] In prose his touch was surer. The *New Statesman*[56] published his brief, evocative account of the eclipse he had witnessed in Ipswich, and there was a considerable amount of stimulating left-wing journalism. His enthusiasm for literary culture had had little outlet since his *Galmahra* days, and the Paris holiday with Jack Lindsay reminded him that it was possible to *épater le bourgeois* with literary as well as political warfare.

Returned to Oxford for the new term, however, it was the revolutionary possibility of the general strike which occupied Stephensen's attention. The strike was not masterminded by radicals but brought on by the increasingly desperate plight of the mining industry. Coal had been one of Britain's great export industries in the nineteenth century but it was now a costly and inefficient nightmare, heavily subsidized by the government. A commission of inquiry into the coal industry suggested numerous reforms in March 1926 but also called for the abandonment of subsidies. Miners would have to choose either a longer workday or reduced wages, though the best paid received barely half Stephensen's scholarship allowance. Their employers the mine owners wanted both heavy reductions in pay and an extension of working hours. In response the Miners' Federation dug in behind the slogan 'Not a penny off the pay, not a second on the day', and a general strike began at midnight on Monday 3 May, involving more than three million miners, transport workers, dockers, industrial workers and printers.[57]

Most members of the Oxford Labour Club, including Stephensen's comrade Ieuan Thomas, gathered during the strike at the house of G. D. H. and Margaret Cole, compiling and printing strike literature. Stephensen, though, headed straight for the Oxford Trades and Labour Council. On the Saturday the strike was planned he had joined the Oxford branch of the Transport and General Workers' Union and from all accounts, including his own, played a leading role in the Oxford area, among other things helping to prepare the daily *Oxford Workers' Strike Bulletin*. A. J. P. Taylor said Stephensen impressed the railway workers as a potential leader of the working class. Taylor also remembered Stephensen's striking personality: confident, romantic, and full of recollections of his own past victories. He had made much of his militant labour experience in Australia and 'spoke with all the authority of a real Wobbly'.[58]

An hour after the strike officially began, Stephensen wrote to Winifred before dropping exhausted into bed:

> Impossible for me to leave Oxford, as I hold a key position here for a very large area and the work I am doing is *vital*. The Workers are winning all along the line, darling, and everything is going magnificently for us. Do not be frightened by any rumours. This will be a peaceful victory.[59]

His promise to the vice-chancellor all but forgotten, Stephensen felt he was witnessing the beginning of the revolution at last. His room mate at Queen's College, Tom Inglis Moore, himself working for the Trades Union Congress (TUC) in London, also had the exciting feeling that history was being made.[60] In what was possibly a speech to striking workers, Stephensen denied that communists were advocating 'armed insurrection in England', just 'the most desperate resistance'.[61]

With printers on strike, the government issued its own daily propaganda paper, the *British Gazette*, which quoted patriotic verses from Kipling and Tennyson, and ran reassuring headlines like 'NATION CALM AND CONFIDENT'. The TUC's own propaganda organ, the *British Worker*, also stressed this with headlines like 'Paralysis but Peace in Midlands'. The opposing forces therefore both professed calm while fully expecting chaos.[62]

At Oxford University there was a rumour that undergraduates would be conscripted as strike breakers but such a move was unnecessary. With the vice-chancellor's permission, students were given leave of absence by their colleges and more than a thousand volunteered to drive cars, buses and trains, and move food on the docks. A few women students tried to persuade an Oxford bus driver and conductor to go on strike, calling them 'Blacklegs' and 'Rotters' when they refused, but for most undergraduates the strike meant volunteering for novel and adventurous strike-breaking work. One student who had driven some volunteers to Hull docks was set upon by a 'mob of rowdies' who kicked him in the knee and spat on him with amazing accuracy 'from six yards' range'. Some of the 'hooligans' even used marbles in catapults; but it was an 'exciting adventure' and he was proud of having motored '400 miles in 18 hours'.[63] Stephensen's *Oxford Workers' Strike Bulletin* was not immune to frivolity either, nor to racism. From Southampton it was rumoured that shipowners were 'endeavouring to introduce NEGROES and LASCARS', and this appeared under the heading 'Black Legs'.[64]

Despite the hopes and fears of the various participants, nothing like a revolution occurred. After ten days the TUC capitulated and called off the strike, allowing the conservative government and press to claim a victory. Stephensen and other militants were disillusioned and angry with the union leadership, for the capitulation had killed any hope of a widespread revolutionary movement. Instead greater political surveillance and suppression would follow. Stephensen wrote to Winifred that hundreds of communists all over the country had been gaoled, and he warned her not to include her address when writing to him. This was a wise precaution. The secret service, possibly through Tom Driberg, now monitored his activities, keeping the university informed and also corresponding with the Australian government for further information about him.[65]

A few days after the end of the strike, Stephensen returned to his frustratingly theoretical studies at Oxford, writing a philosophy essay on Hegel and social Darwinism in which he praised Nietzsche (misspelling it 'Neitzsche') for reformulating the doctrine of Plato. Nietzsche had 'glimpsed the task before mankind' with his philosophy of the '*dominant will*'.[66] It is significant that Stephensen was reading and absorbing Nietzsche, the evangelist of individualism, in the wake of the failure of mass consciousness to bring about a proletarian revolution. Stephensen retained communist sympathies for a number of years, but after his Oxford suppression and the abortive general strike his rebellious spirit found new creative outlets. Midway through his final year at Oxford he even allowed his financial membership of the Communist Party to lapse.[67]

4

Bloomsbury Fanfrolics

With the cloud of his final examinations on the horizon, Stephensen became increasingly frustrated with university life. He was formally banned from political work and during his last year at Oxford his optimism and *joie de vivre* were only sustained by his closer relationship with Jack Lindsay.

Since their Brisbane days Lindsay had become a bohemian intellectual and poet. He had published a book of poems and a translation of Aristophanes' *Lysistrata*, both illustrated by his father Norman. During the five years he spent in Sydney, Jack had drawn inspiration and guidance from direct contact with his father. They had both written for *Vision* magazine and for *Art in Australia*, then a quarterly devoted to art, literature, music and architecture. As early as 1904 A. G. Stephens had ironically compared Norman Lindsay's anti-Christian moralizing with the 'reforming zeal' of Lindsay's grandfather who was a Wesleyan missionary in Fiji. Norman's obsession with classical form and Nietzschean philosophy had certainly taken on a religious intensity, and Jack was one of the few disciples of this tiny cult, echoing and refining his father's doctrine.[1]

Jack had come to England with his publisher John Kirtley who had worked at that philistine institution, the Sydney Stock Exchange. A keen book collector, Kirtley had become involved in fine printing when he published Jack's first book, *Fauns and Ladies*, on his 'Hand Press of J. T. Kirtley' in 1923. Discussing at Springwood the production details for the forthcoming *Lysistrata*, Norman Lindsay had shown his son and Kirtley an album of private erotica he had written and illustrated. This was a sequence of tales about the imaginary court of the Duke of Fanfrolico, a name suggested by Rabelais' *fanfreluche*. Because of his position with a respectable stockbroking firm, Kirtley was anxious to avoid publishing *Lysistrata* under his own name so the 'Fanfrolico Press' was chosen instead.[2]

This was an appropriate title, for Norman Lindsay was the Dionysian spirit behind the new enterprise just as he had been the visionary of the earlier *Vision* magazine. He not only suggested a philosophical basis for the Fanfrolico Press but also supplied the press's most saleable commodity, his illustrations. The philosophy was pagan, anti-modernist, neoclassical, transcendental; and when there were plans to transfer the Fanfrolico Press to London his drawings were packed with Jack's luggage. Reluctant to see his son go, Norman nevertheless remained the press's spiritual and financial patron, paying Jack's fare to England and buying him a new suit for the adventure.

On arrival Kirtley and Lindsay had rented a house in St John's Wood, and while Kirtley explored printing facilities Lindsay made use of his father's letters of introduction. This was not a success and he was patronized as a 'rash raw colonial' by the editor of the influential *London Mercury*, J. C. Squire.[3] Although he resolved to avoid family contacts in future, Lindsay remained in the shadow of his distant father. His attempt to establish a creative identity first had to come to terms with Norman who had ranged himself alongside the somewhat daunting genius of Plato, Praxiteles, Shakespeare and Beethoven. Although Jack's talents in poetry and classical scholarship were different from his father's, he had carried to England a heavy psychological burden as well as his father's artwork. Norman had conceived him out of wedlock, as Jack lightly mentioned to Stephensen, and then had deserted him during childhood.[4]

After the Easter reunion with Inky in Paris, Lindsay went to visit him at Oxford for 'three very wonderful and crowded days', drinking at various pubs and swaggering into places forbidden by university edict.[5] Contact with someone as vital and outgoing as Stephensen was a tonic for Lindsay, and they were both intoxicated with the *vie de bohème*. To be drunk and penniless, to belong to extreme and unlikely movements, and above all to shock the bourgeois, this was the spirit of their London adventures. In common with their decade they were enjoying the last years of their boisterous twenties.

Their friendship was also strengthened by Winifred. At her Chelsea flat Lindsay met Jack McLaren and through him Thomas Burke and other London literati. Winifred's parties also introduced him to the unhappy Elza de Locre. Just before moving into a basement flat with Lindsay she had tried to commit suicide by slashing her wrists, and she became fiercely possessive of him.

During the summer vacation in 1926, Stephensen turned up at their basement 'full of adventurous spirits' and suggested a holiday in Brittany. They got out a map and Lindsay narrowed their selection to the tiny Ile de Bréhat by shutting his eyes and jabbing a pin at the Brittany coast. They wanted somewhere remote from civilization and Bréhat seemed ideal. So along with Winifred and her son, on holiday from boarding school, they took the ferry across the Channel to St Malo. Before leaving, Lindsay used his last shillings to cable his father for £50.[6]

The island of Bréhat was a 'perfect miniature', with cafés, cottages, vegetable plots and grazing goats. The village 'square' in the centre was not square at all but oblong and bounded by stones like a primitive ceremonial ground. Here, under the trees, fishermen and other locals danced and imbibed Brittany's traditional strong cider. The two couples stayed together at a boarding house for about three weeks, exploring the island, drinking and playing chess. Lindsay resumed writing, and Stephensen celebrated the island in a ditty entitled 'Rus Insula' which he issued in a strictly limited edition of one copy, handwritten, as from the Apple Press, Bréhat. Girls and goats and cider formed the theme—drink and sex being inextricably combined in his rumbustious philosophy. As he had versified to Lindsay from Oxford: 'the beer's in the glass and the sun's on the river/And many a heaving arse is a-quiver'.[7] However, Stephensen viewed Elza as another of Jack's obsessions, bringing him not satisfaction but her own kind of introspective despair.

Stephensen and Winifred left the island in September but Jack and Elza stayed on Bréhat for a further three months. Meanwhile Kirtley had found and office for the Fanfrolico Press at the corner of Bloomsbury Square, giving the press a stylish address. The reactionary Lindsay aesthetic could now be launched from inside enemy territory since Bloomsbury was synonymous with literary culture and sophisticated modernism. Kirtley took a conspicuous double-column advertisement in the *Times Literary Supplement* announcing the publication of a series of 'fine books of interest to collectors and readers'. The first three titles would be a new edition of Lindsay's translation of *Lysistrata*, Kenneth Slessor's *Earth-Visitors*, and Lindsay's own verse play, *Marino Faliero*. Kirtley had found a sympathetic printer in the Chiswick Press and spared no expense on paper, type, ink, binding, or promotion, spending £50 on advertisements alone.[8]

As Kirtley realized, it was the lavishly printed classics, illustrated by Norman Lindsay's sensuous drawings, which would attract buyers and assure the success of the Fanfrolico venture. By October 1926 Kirtley had already drummed up advance orders for 135 copies of *Lysistrata* compared with 35 for the Slessor volume and only 17 for *Marino Faliero*. Kirtley was investing, or had borrowed, about a thousand pounds to establish the Fanfrolico in London so it was not surprising he was anxious to produce books that would sell.[9] In any case, he prized a book for its physical elegance whereas Jack Lindsay was more concerned with the philosophical, intellectual and literary content.

Kirtley therefore preferred Jack's translations which avoided becoming tangled up with Norman's philosophy, 'cunt' propaganda and the desire to be 'daring'. Though he admitted to ignorance of Greek, Kirtley told Stephensen he would wager his 'bollocks' Jack's version of the *Lysistrata* was better than the original. The Fanfrolico's star item was to be an edition of Petronius, translated by Jack and illustrated with the pen drawings Norman had done for an earlier London private edition. Kirtley planned to bind it in full vellum, and his excitement was obvious. It would be a 'grand book', he told Stephensen.[10]

Feeling pinned down at Oxford for the autumn term, Stephensen began to share this excitement over the new publishing venture. He also began acting as a double agent, for a personal rather than political cause. He became the confidant of both Jacks—Lindsay and Kirtley—as each poured out his frustration with the other, and with life in general. Trying to organize a publishing company single-handed, Kirtley was suffering from nervous indigestion and the depressing climate. He was womanless in England, and resented Lindsay's escapade with Elza, claiming to Stephensen that it was the 'talk of the typographical world'.[11]

Stephensen's role in this quarrel by proxy was not exactly that of peacemaker. At Oxford he patiently received all Kirtley's deflected frustration and abuse, and promptly passed on the gist of it to Lindsay still languishing in creative exile on Bréhat. Wedged between them, Stephensen began to see a place for himself in the Fanfrolico universe and wrote to Lindsay in October 1926 that he planned to join the new press. Lindsay was filled with 'unholy joy', and implored Stephensen to hang on to the decision and not let it be 'merely one of your delirious ideas'. With Stephensen's political weapons added to Norman's philosophical armoury, they would carry out some 'literary terrorism in England's black and unpleasant land'.[12]

Stephensen had moved out of college into 'digs', a room in an Oxford house, and was undergoing private traumas about his own future. His gesture of commitment to the Fanfrolico Press was a folly in his last and most important year at university. This doubt was compounded by uncertainties about his relationship with Winifred who was sick and gloomy throughout the autumn. Unknown to Stephensen, she had turned forty in September, and wondered how long her affair with this twenty-five-year-old student could last. At Oxford he too felt caught in 'closed circles of futility', as he wrote to her in October:

> I'm still floating around in the quiet whirlpool here and there like a water insect vainly hoping for something not quite within reach. This is a most important period for me, dear. I am trying, trying to get straightened out on big things so that little things won't matter any more...

His concern for social justice was now tinged with an aesthetic element derived from the Lindsays:

> There is too much trouble in the world, too much weariness and strain of mind and body. The clear, shining image of beauty is dragged into mud. Nothing simple or partial can restore it, only great strenuous actions, rough and terrible doings can shake weary mankind to arise for one more effort towards freedom and beauty.

He was assailed by a romantic vision of his future. 'I shall go out on the ramparts', he told her, 'stamping my feet, shaking my hair in the great winds of the earth. My love shall destroy not comfort. I challenge life or I shall die'.[13]

During November, as the publication of the first Fanfrolico books approached, Kirtley wrote to Stephensen that advance sales were good and he was so excited it was interfering with his sleep. Stephensen had hinted to Kirtley about delays but Kirtley protested that it was impossible to rush a printer on a fine press job. The *Lysistrata* had to be proofed as many as four times, and only a handful of printers could manage the technical subtleties required to produce Norman Lindsay's line drawings in the text. Kirtley had also cut the opening paragraph of the foreword, commenting that Jack was obsessed with 'naked kisses', Christ and the academic mind.[14]

Preparing to return to London, Lindsay wrote to Stephensen from Bréhat that he was 'bloody annoyed' Kirtley had tampered with the foreword: 'I am also bloody annoyed that anyone who depends on fixing his fortune by the Lysistrata and Petronius should speak of the cuntliness of my work'. For the sake of harmony, and Stephensen's Machiavellian schemes, Lindsay said he would be discreet with Kirtley though he was in the mood to let Kirtley 'blow up his couple of balloons of Lysis. and Petronius and then explode'. Lindsay was only sustained by the thought that he and Stephensen would soon be drinking together again, a far more significant event than the 'birth, stillbirth, or abortion' of the Fanfrolico Press.[15]

Lindsay had been depending on his Oxford friend for more than moral and psychological support: Stephensen had in fact been sending money to him in France. Because of this and payments to help Winifred, Stephensen himself got into debt and had to ask the Rhodes secretary for several advances on his scholarship allowance. He also assisted with Fanfrolico publicity, arranging for Tom Driberg to write a *Cherwell* feature on the new press just a couple of days before the *Lysistrata* was published in mid-December 1926. Comparing the Fanfrolico with two other small presses, the Nonesuch and the Pleiad, Driberg thought the newcomer the most interesting. Norman Lindsay's 'extremely carnal' illustrations were true to the genius of Aristrophanes and more successful, in Driberg's opinion, than Beardsley's. Although he could not divulge the name, Driberg reported that one of the 'three young partners' in the Fanfrolico Press was an Oxford undergraduate.[16]

This was Stephensen's version, for when the company was formally registered several weeks later Kirtley listed himself as sole proprietor. His two young 'partners', however, were manoeuvring to take advantage of his disillusionment with England. In the depths of winter Kirtley described the country to Stephensen as a 'death trap' to an Australian —physically, mentally, and financially—and resolved to return to Australia. Winifred had found a large flat in South Kensington, and Kirtley, after a drunken few days with Stephensen at Oxford, moved into one of her spare rooms. This was a cosy arrangement in view of Stephensen's machinations, and he even asked Winifred to keep an eye on Kirtley.[17]

With his Oxford finals just three months away, however, Stephensen was becoming exasperated by the antics of the Fanfrolico triangle, and he complained to Winifred that Kirtley was trying to double-cross him. Kirtley had told Lindsay Stephensen was not a good businessman which was both a vindictive and a perceptive observation. Concerned that these distractions would affect Stephensen's exam results, Winifred urged him to *work*, for 'success in your exams will be like a large bank account that you need not touch unless necessary'.[18] An Oxford degree promised a future security which Winifred herself had never known.

Yet Stephensen continued to be embroiled in scheme and counter-scheme as Lindsay and Kirtley maintained a transparent fiction of amiable relations. Lindsay was receiving five pounds a week from Kirtley as an advance on royalties and felt unable to assert himself. Privately he assured Stephensen that the game was to 'get rid of K on any pretences whatever and you and I to obtain the hegemony of the Press'. To resolve the crisis before the Fanfrolico evaporated into thin air, Stephensen descended temporarily from Oxford and helped draft agreements for a transfer of ownership. Kirtley would leave after June, the month of Stephensen's finals, and Lindsay and Stephensen would take over the Fanfrolico Press in July. Technically the ownership would pass to Jack Lindsay, with his father Norman entitled to a half share of any profits.[19]

On his sister's birthday Stephensen wrote home to his family from London with the news. It was the Easter vacation and he was impatient to quit Oxford. He assured his parents that the Fanfrolico Press had good credit and connections, but when he told them there was £500 in capital he was rather colouring the picture for his own, as well as for their, psychological benefit. The profits from titles like *Lysistrata* were quickly absorbed, and disappeared altogether with poor sellers like *Marino Faliero*. Kirtley was also naturally reluctant to hand over any of the surplus from books he had worked for a year to produce.

Stephensen, though, did sound one note of caution. 'I am to be manager on a salary', he told his family. 'This leaves me free of all risk of bankruptcy, etc also of all ultimate responsibility.' He had no immediate plans of returning to the fold. 'Australia is a back-water; also a back-number in many ways', he observed, 'and London is the place to make good if a man is really ambitious in my line'. Under pressure to help support his impoverished family, he claimed he would be more useful to them in England: 'It is better for me to make good here and send you a bit of financial assistance than to come home and disgrace you all by Bolshevik activities. I love Australia too much to go and live there quietly under the rule of the banks'. To his sister Stephensen wrote in even stronger terms that Australia did not want men of intelligence or ability. 'I'm staying away till I've earned some cash', he told her, 'then I can go back to the country I love and the people I hate'.[20]

Meanwhile, another of Stephensen's undergraduate acquaintances, Eric Partridge, who was lecturing in London, wanted to invest money in the press for the publication of his selection of the work of Robert Eyres Landor. Kirtley wanted the £200, but it was Stephensen who handled the negotiations with Partridge to ensure he did not regard his cash guarantee as a partnerhip in the Fanfrolico Press, and later the same year Partridge founded his own private press, the Scholartis.[21]

Before his final exams Stephensen helped his communist friend Driberg and other students stage a 'Homage to Beethoven', to mock the endless series of performances commemorating the centenary of the composer's death. Driberg wrote the words and another the music for a Dadaist concerto featuring typewriters and an extended megaphone solo. The students then hired a hall and lured a capacity audience of unsuspecting elderly dons and their wives. As Driberg described it, the air was 'thick with the aroma of moth-balls'. After assailing the audience with experimental cacophony, the orchestra suddenly and solemnly stood to attention, drums rolled and into the ensuing silence cascaded the loud flush from a w.c. just offstage followed by a door slamming. Lifting his megaphone once more, Driberg loudly advised the audience to 'Please adjust your dress before leaving'. Lindsay asked when he heard Stephensen's report of this sophisticated prank, 'Was the chain-pulling finale intended as a criticism of the performance that preceded it?'[22]

By a coincidence, Lindsay not long after welcomed the first unsolicited manuscript submitted to the Fanfrolico Press: a transcription of an Elizabethan text on 'shithouses', *New Discourse of a Stale Subject*, by Sir John Harrington, the inventor of the water closet. This learned and amusing treatise had been ferreted out of the British Museum by Philip Heseltine, a composer and Elizabethan expert who had adopted the pseudonym Peter Warlock.[23] He and Lindsay quickly became friends, and Lindsay was encouraged to explore for further antiquarian treasures in the British Museum.

Although Stephensen's decision to enter the bizarre world of Fanfrolico had rather sidelined his political ambitions, he had joined the advisory committee of the newly formed Workers' Theatre Movement (WTM) in London, and wrote at least two satirical workers' plays.[24] He also helped out on the *Sunday Worker* which provided the WTM with a base. The failure of the 1926 General Strike had given radicals the incentive to organize a 'propaganda theatre', committed to agitation rather than entertainment, and Stephensen had written his first political sketch within a month or two of the strike. Entitled *Stanley's Pipe Dream* ('A Workers' Play'), it was set during an imaginary cabinet meeting in Stanley Baldwin's 'smoking-room' at 10 Downing Street, and featured the chief anti-communist militants Sir William Joynson-Hicks ('Jix'), Winston Churchill and Lord Birkenhead. The play was a mixture of traditional vaudeville and Russian agitprop, and at its conclusion a 'Voice of the Workers' is heard castigating the conservatives:

> Revolution is in the air
> Gentlemen beware beware!
> The fire will burn if you only poke it
> Put that in your pipe and smoke it!

Although Stephensen wrote the play under the name 'Peter Stephens', the British secret service, possibly through an informer like Tom Driberg, knew the identity of the author and planned to bring Stephensen's WTM and other communist activities to the attention of the Rhodes Trust because of his promise to refrain from such activities while at Oxford.[25]

Queenslanders in Paris at Easter, 1925; from left: H. E. Roberts, Hall, Burton, Stephensen, and an unidentified companion

Stephensen (left), Tom Inglis Moore and Hall relaxing over their beers at a Paris sidewalk café, Easter 1925

Winifred and Inky, 'Eights Week', Oxford, May 1925

Stephensen (right) with Burton and their scout Bill Quelch, Oxford, May 1925

Nothing came of this, however, and during March 1927 *Stanley's Pipe Dream* was staged at the Progressive Club, North Camberwell, along with two other strike plays. Then, a matter of days before his Oxford finals, Stephensen read a paper on 'The Essentials of Revolutionary Drama' to the WTM general meeting in London. He claimed to have had the 'privilege' of being brought up in a 'worker's home', and suggested that WTM plays should be written by committees of workers, acting the material as it was written to achieve spontaneity. He may not have been aware that Erwin Piscator had formed just such a writing collective in Germany which included Bertolt Brecht.

Stephensen faced his final examinations in the 'Honour School of Philosophy, Politics, and Economics' about the middle of June 1927, with ten three-hour papers in the space of a week. Although he felt that much of his study had been irrelevant, he was nevertheless disappointed when he missed out on first-class honours, being awarded second-class along with the majority of candidates. Not that he had the inclination or temperament to join his friend Robert Hall in an academic career. Stephensen did not even bother to pay the fees to collect his Oxford B.A. degree (which could then have been converted into an M.A. later after the payment of a further sum). For one thing he could not afford to do so, and as it was he went down from Oxford owing money.[26]

Stephensen's world was changing. He now had to pay his own way in England and was taking on a ready-made family as well. He and Winifred had decided to live together as husband and wife, and moved into a small flat just north of Bloomsbury. They were unable to marry because her husband refused all pleas for a divorce. Kirtley left for America on his way back to Australia, and the second-floor office at 5 Bloomsbury Square became Stephensen's province as manager. Although he continued to write for the *Sunday Worker*, and took Lindsay along to see WTM plays and Eisenstein films in the East End, Stephensen's allegiances were moving west into bohemian Bloomsbury, and the unlikely creed of Fanfrolicanism was to be an alternative to communism.

Just before they combined forces at Bloomsbury Square, Lindsay wrote to Stephensen: 'We shall then see if the Fanfrolico aesthetic moves in this barbarous country; if not we shall go to Moscow and become Lunachasky's lieutenants—if necessary assassinating him . . .'[27] In his joking reference about turning to communism, Jack Lindsay prefigured his actual course during the 1930s. As Inky Stephensen was beginning to fade out of communism Jack was fading in, the Fanfrolico Press being the point at which their images briefly overlapped. Ironically, it was Stephensen who receded further in the direction of Norman Lindsay.

About the time Stephensen took over managing the Fanfrolico Press, Norman sent him from Springwood a thundering epistle of praise and encouragement. Hailing Stephensen as another 'voyager from Olympus to earth', Norman was convinced of a 'contact with your identity and my own—contact already established in time and space'. With Stephensen's roistering love of beer and wine, his masculine vitality and optimism, he was surely the man of action Norman had claimed in *Creative Effort* was so necessary to the 'mission of regeneration'.[28] Norman had never actually met Stephensen, but his son Philip had based the hero of an unpublished novel on the legendary Inky. Jack Lindsay felt his business partner was thus 'strangely twisted' into his destiny,[29] and though Norman felt likewise he was by no means uncritical of Stephensen's politics:

> Bolshevism in the terms of your announcement I heartily endorse—I translate them into my own idiom as satanism and laughter ... But alas your Bolshevist is too apt to assume the garb of saviour; to become an earnest-eyed official jotting down statistics all day long in a government office and striving to reduce life to a reasonable, rational and well-fed process; in short the ideal of the shopkeeper once again.

This last disparaging reference had a special meaning for Stephensen whose own parents were failed shopkeepers. Norman went on to say he was altogether of opinion with the 'inimitable' Bakunin, one of Stephensen's heroes: 'The thing is rotten, destroy it. Don't talk nonsense about reconstructing it'.[30]

Norman also elaborated on the fanatical theories he had already sketched in *Creative Effort*. Jews, not capitalism, were the real enemy, he told Stephensen:

> It seems to me that the coin is only a surface factor in the real area of spiritual destructiveness, which is based purely in the Semitic. Of the four racial divisions of man, black and yellow are negative; ... white (the Greek and Roman) constructive, and red (Semitic) purely destructive ... I believe the Semitic, by the racial genesis of what is now the North American Indian, to have been the prime factor in the excessive wars that finally smashed the whole Atlantean effort ...

Lindsay displayed all the symptoms of classical anti-Semitism: the Jew was rapacious, a 'thumbless creature' who made nothing; in short the Jew was a universal pariah and the devil behind both capitalism and communism. There was only one thing, Lindsay said, the Semitic could not destroy—'a created form image'.[31] Crude folk theories of the stake and the vampire could not have been more fantastic.

Receiving this tirade a couple of months later in England (sea mail only being available), Stephensen typed a reply but did not send it. He was forced on the defensive about his politics, saying he did not want to discuss Bolshevism but pointing out that 'the artist under Communism could not possibly be more suppressed than he is in commercial society'. He drafted the letter after coming home tired and hungry from the Fanfrolico office where he had been dispatching circulars 'into the gaping void'. He had 'almost nothing' to add to Norman's philosophical synthesis and accepted it 'not provisionally, but wholly'. Then, contradicting himself, he said he would abandon the 'incidental gesture of working-class revolution' for the time being to push Norman's cause, but if this failed, 'back I go to Bolshevik philosophy' to see whether the 'vast groping paws of the working class cannot fashion a form image that shall signify love and laughter on earth'.[32]

That Stephensen failed to post this letter suggests he had not properly digested, or more likely could not quite swallow, Norman's philosophical stew. The reply he finally did send was a more businesslike and pessimistic account of books published and general progress at Bloomsbury Square. He characterized their efforts as an 'absurd adventure', and said the problem was to get money in quickly enough to 'stave off the howling creditors':

> The whole enterprise has been a ridiculous venture of faith as we have simply launched out without any capital save the small sums we were able to wrench from Kirtley by threats. We are proceeding now flatly against all commercial principles and nothing but the interposition of the Gods can enable us to pay off our debts to printers etc. If we sell our editions quickly all will be well, but if even one of them falls flat, we are done.

Stepping around any doubts he might have about Norman's ideas, Stephensen felt it was better to 'leave philosophy alone than to abstract the creative principle as a theory'. He acknowledged that one of the aims of the Fanfrolico Press was simply to 'put Jack Lindsay on the market'.[33]

Lindsay's consuming ambition was to make his name as an original writer rather than as a translator, scholar or publisher. A number of his works had been dedicated to his father but he dedicated one book to Norman Douglas, whom he had never met, and the next, his essay on Blake, to Walter de la Mare whom he had encountered only once in his awkward first months in England. It had been Kirtley's opinion that introducing a new author with elaborate limited editions was a 'short cut to success',[34] but he did not really understand the literary scene, still less that of England. Lindsay was on firmer ground with attempts to broaden his contacts through dedications and the like, but it was not easy to make a name as a poet, especially since he was a 'colonial' writing in a classical style at a time when the hard-edged modernism of T. S. Eliot was fashionable. Fanfrolico books were noticed in reviews, but it was Lindsay's translations which attracted favourable comment.[35]

The press was relatively secure, as Kirtley had realized, only while it continued to produce illustrated classics and reprints in sumptuous editions. The title pages and elegant colophons of the *Lysistrata*, *Petronius* and *Propertius* were works of art in themselves, lent their special style by Norman Lindsay's drawings and Kirtley's careful choice of type. The *Propertius in Love*, for example, was designed by Kirtley as his swansong, in an extremely limited edition of sixty copies at fifteen guineas each. Printed on Van Gelder hand-made paper, the book was bound in goat vellum and encased in a special folder within a leather-edged box. Although Lindsay later questioned the story, Kirtley claimed he sold the whole edition in advance by calling a meeting of major booksellers, providing them with refreshments and offering them the whole edition which

PROPERTIUS IN LOVE
DONE INTO ENGLISH VERSE FROM THE LATIN BY JACK LINDSAY WITH XVIII ILLUSTRATIONS BY NORMAN LINDSAY

FOR SUBSCRIBERS ONLY
FROM THE OFFICE OF THE FANFROLICO PRESS
FIVE BLOOMSBURY SQUARE LONDON MCMXXVII

HERE END THE LOVE AFFAIRS OF SEXTUS PROPERTIUS ILLUS‑
TRATED BY NORMAN LINDSAY & DONE INTO ENGLISH VERSE
BY JACK LINDSAY FROM THE ORIGINAL EMBRACES & LATIN
BY A METHOD OF SELECTION WHICH OMITS THE AETIOLOGICAL
ELEMENT ACCENTUATES THE CHARACTER OF PROPERTIUS AS
LOVER RATHER THAN AS DOCTUS POETA & THUS SEEKS TO
ACHIEVE A LIVING & COHERENT PICTURE OF A PERSONALITY
AMIABLE AMOROUS AND BRAVELY AT THE MERCY OF HIS
INSTINCTS
PRINTED AT THE CHISWICK PRESS IN BLADO ITALIC
WITH POLIPHILUS ROMAN CAPITALS ON VAN
GELDER HANDMADE PAPER BOUND IN
GOAT VELLUM & PUBLISHED BY
THE FANFROLICO PRESS
IN LONDON

Facing page and above:
The title page and the last page of *Propertius in Love* (Fanfrolico Press, 1927)

they promptly bought. Whatever the means, it was certainly one of the very few Fanfrolico titles to be fully subscribed on publication.[36] The book was not actually printed until after Kirtley's departure, and he later complained that his type specifications for the text were altered, ruining its appearance. Not that Kirtley was blameless. Before handing over the press he had gone round to the Chiswick Press and warned the printers that Lindsay had no capital and was a heavy risk.[37]

Towards the end of July 1927 Stephensen returned to Oxford to be best man for Tom Inglis Moore at the Church of St Peter in the East which their Queen's College rooms had overlooked. Moore was marrying an Australian chemist, Peace Little, who had a twin sister called Mercy. When the engagement was announced Stephensen had chaffed him with an appropriate couplet from Blake which Lindsay had quoted in an essay, and which Stephensen later also used in his introduction to the *Antichrist*:

> Misery's increase
> Is Mercy, Pity, Peace.

Tongue in cheek about his own quasi-married state, he read Moore the dictum: 'When should a man marry? A young man not yet; an older man, not at all'. For a wedding gift Inky presented the Fanfrolico *Lysistrata* with its comic vision of feminine supremacy.[38]

Stephensen's life in London was becoming centred on the Fanfrolico office and, to Winifred's increasing irritation, on Bloomsbury's nearby bohemian watering holes like the Plough Inn in Museum Street. As well as after-work chats with Lindsay over a pint, there were some sustained drinking sessions with writers, editors and artists, their emulators and sycophants. The Irish novelist Liam O'Flaherty was among those who shared the Australians' love of bawdy and booze, and Lindsay recalled him sitting in the Plough or the teashop close to the office 'telling long tales of the Troubles in his persuasive voice, with his blue eyes flashing'.[39]

O'Flaherty and Stephensen in particular were kindred spirits. The Irishman too had been involved with Bolshevism and revolution, and prided himself on his wild, Celtic ancestry. He had served in the Irish Guards during the war and been wounded in France. Invalided out of the army suffering from shell shock, he was awarded a special bachelor's degree (War) from University College, Dublin, and was involved with the Industrial Workers of the World in Canada before returning to support the Irish Republicans. During January 1922 he had helped seize the Rotunda in Dublin for a few days, raising the red flag in a gesture of defiance.

When Stephensen met him he was thirty years old and had already published four novels and a couple of story collections, establishing his reputation as one of Ireland's leading writers along with Joyce and O'Casey. Like Stephensen he was a rebellious spirit, but O'Flaherty was also a restless outsider whose fits of depression were frequently occasions for heavy drinking. Stephensen toasted their favourite Plough Inn with a parody of Gray's 'Elegy written in a Country Churchyard' in which 'Irishmen and Bolsheviks combat'. This depicted O'Flaherty and Inky Stephensen himself, no doubt entertaining his friends with tales of past political adventures. Stephensen's patronage of another Bloomsbury haunt, the Fitzroy Tavern in Windmill Street, is recorded by his ditty on a Christmas card printed by the pub's Jewish proprietor. A speciality of the Fitzroy was a concoction called Jerusalem brandy which Lindsay described as throat-rasping and which Stephensen rhymed as so over-proof it hit the roof.[40]

Despite the time spent in such recreation, both the Fanfrolico partners worked hard to get the business on its feet. From autumn 1927 through to the following spring the Fanfrolico Press issued a wide range of reprints and translations as well as more verse plays by Lindsay and a collection of Hugh McCrae's poetry, 'illustrated and decorated' by his friend Norman Lindsay. The title *Satyrs and Sunlight* was taken from McCrae's first book of verse and was indicative of the conscious attempt by the Lindsay group to weld classical mythology on to what they saw as the physical vitality of sunlit Australia. Paradoxically, the movement was both nationalist and anti-nationalist in character, though its cultural emphasis was European. The Fanfrolico Press was also sponsoring a reactionary anti-modernism. Thomas Earp's introduction to *Satyrs and Sunlight*, for example, criticized the 'technical rebellion' of modern poetry, dividing this into 'the primitive, the negro, and the French' fallacies.[41]

The Fanfrolico partners went to extraordinary trouble to match style and content, and as a result each production of the press was unique; sometimes whimsically so. McCrae's *Satyrs and Sunlight* was bound in stained sheepskin with a shagreen finish, and a reprint of Skelton's rollicking *Tunning of Elynour Rumming*, featuring four-colour illustrations of the low-life debauches, had a sacking cover crudely embellished with three Xs and a tankard. The *Homage to Sappho*, published in May 1928 and the most expensive book produced by the press, must have been an attempt to outdo Kirtley's fifteen-guinea *Propertius*. Only seventy copies of the *Sappho* were offered for sale at the astonishing price of £31 10s each, and the whole book was printed on Japanese vellum. It was also bound in full vellum, the exquisite cover having the texture of engraved marble. Like the *Propertius*, it was sold out before publication.

In April 1928 Stephensen sent his sister eight of the Fanfrolico books which he said had a 'terrific high price' and, being illustrated by Norman Lindsay, were not for Methodists. Stephensen denied that their publications were bawdy but was careful not to send home *Lysistrata* or the *Satyricon* of Petronius. He said they had hired an office girl at £2 a week (he and Lindsay were each drawing £5 in salary), so the press in effect now had a staff of four including a sales 'traveller' who worked on commission and had been recruited originally by Kirtley.[42]

Another reason for the Fanfrolico Press's deceptive stability was an injection of £200 sent over by Norman Lindsay.[43] Although almost half of the press's first ten titles had sold out, the available cash was limited. A Maori friend of Heseltine/Warlock's, Hal Collins, who had illustrated the Elizabethan reprint, *Parlement of Pratlers*, refused to sign copies of the special edition in April unless his fee was paid.[44] Towards the middle of 1928, with a Fanfrolico magazine planned as well, the press was again in difficulties. Lindsay was now spending three days a week in London, dividing his time between the press and a cottage in Essex where he lived with the reclusive Elza. He dropped Stephensen a note that the publishing list for the rest of the year was 'hopelessly inadequate'. He went on: 'I don't know how you work out our debts at £250. They are well over £500 surely, and by the time the magazine is added they will be over £600, while all that is definitely due fairly soon is some £500 ...'[45]

In May, Lindsay trimmed his beard and put on a suit and tie for a publicity photograph of the two proprietors sitting at a desk in the Bloomsbury Square office beside an impressive stack of their publications. For the summer they issued not just a catalogue but a 'Bibliography' entitled *Fanfrolicana*, complete with specimen passages and illustrations and a 'statement of the aims of the Fanfrolico Press both typographical

FANFROLICANA

JUNE 1928

BEING A STATEMENT OF THE AIMS OF THE FANFROLICO PRESS BOTH TYPOGRAPHICAL AND ÆSTHETIC WITH A COMPLETE BIBLIOGRAPHY AND SPECIMEN PASSAGES AND ILLUSTRATIONS FROM THE BOOKS

THE FANFROLICO PRESS
FROM THE OFFICE AT FIVE BLOOMSBURY SQUARE LONDON

The *Fanfrolicana* catalogue, June 1928

and aesthetic'. Stephensen contributed the introductory 'Policy of a Fine Press' in which he compared a 'well-dressed book' with a 'well-dressed girl'. The press was unique among its peers in having a specific policy, and Stephensen restated their unfashionable creed: 'In the poisonous atmosphere of "modern" literary weariness, ultra-sophistication and aesthetic shallowness, a bold and by no means callow attempt is here being made, rightly or wrongly, to re-define beauty in terms of delight and to piece together the fragments of aesthetic consciousness shattered by the War'.[46]

Norman Lindsay's postwar disillusionment was shared by Stephensen, however tentative he remained about the more bizarre aspects of Norman's thinking. In a manuscript fragment on the decadent contemporary scene written about this time, Stephensen saw around him only despair and depressing self-analysis in the wake of the catastrophic world war. In literature, modernism was just one more symptom of the decline of civilization:

> Nearly ten years ago the blasted war came to an end, and for more than ten years millions of shell-shocked nerves have been turning . . . their frayed ends in an abyss of dismay, where jazz bands clang . . . adding terror to horror, voodoo to frenzy, wails to the sighing of the dead. And all the poor lost souls wander aimlessly in mists, seeking not laughters but more agony . . .
> Meanwhile the precious Sitwells piddle on harmlessly, D. H. Lawrence lubricates Lucubrites in a world of painful sex . . . Joyce sprawls faecally and raves in delirium . . .

Pound was incoherent and Stein infantile. Across the Atlantic, America was just a 'loud Blasting noise', a chaotic polyglot of jazz, puritanism, and capitalism. The iconoclastic Mencken offered nothing but 'wise-cracking sneers', while the satire of Dreiser and Sinclair Lewis was 'laborious'. Only in Russia were the 'best minds' occupied with 'social reconstruction'.[47]

Stephensen's statement in *Fanfrolicana* was both his and the Lindsays' answer to such widespread decadence and pessimism. The signature of all the Fanfrolico books, he blithely asserted, was a 'love for life'. Or as Lindsay formulated it in his poem 'Hypothesis of a Publisher':

> Our claim then is: that you may find
> Venus here tailored to your mind.

Lindsay also reproduced in *Fanfrolicana*, without approval, a letter his father had written in 1924 describing Australia as a 'moribund hole'. Norman was unhappy that the letter had been published, and he let his son know that it had caused him annoyance in the Australian press. 'You and Inky must practise a certain discretion in regard to me', he wrote, chiding them both.[48]

The magazine which began to erode the Fanfrolico's finances had been planned for more than a year. An early title proposed for it was 'Salamander',[49] but it became *The London Aphrodite* as a cheeky retort to Squire's

London Mercury. Squire had consistently rejected Lindsay's verse, and with just the slightest twitch of irony the *Mercury* glanced sideways at the appearance of its unlikely rival: 'The Fanfrolico Press, 5 Bloomsbury Square, W.C.1, announces for August 21st a belligerent new periodical, *The London Aphrodite*, which will appear bi-monthly for six numbers only. It is intended as "an antidote to the modern poisons of painful introspection, mere intellectual slickness, and pseudo-academic dictatorships"'.[50]

Lindsay and Stephensen shared the editorship of the new magazine. In his 'Ex Cathedra' commentary in the first number, Stephensen invited contributions from the world outside the 'lunatic asylums of the abstract'. Lindsay's editorial manifesto anticipated the outrage both of modernists like T. S. Eliot and E. E. Cummings, and of reactionaries such as Squire and the puritanical editor of the *Sunday Express*, James Douglas. It is doubtful, however, that such luminaries were in any way bothered by the upstart in their midst. Stephensen's own editorial manifesto was a typical piece of larrikinism. In a welter of anti-modernist puns and jokes he maintained that the 'emptiest moderns make most noise, owing to the Decline of the Best' (an allusion to Spengler's *Decline of the West*), and that modernity itself, like maternity, was out of date owing to 'correspondence from France'. After a pun on Kant and 'can't', Stephensen decided that 'you cannot get blood from a Stein' and that 'Freud means Joy not Joyce'.[51]

In an essay on 'The Modern Consciousness' for the first number, Lindsay attempted to develop more seriously their anti-modernist philosophy. His 'integration', however, was not wholly successful, inspiring the *Times Literary Supplement* to comment that 'Mr. Lindsay argues furiously but not intelligibly about literature and painting and music and Freud and Relativity'.[52] Lindsay praised the South African poet Roy Campbell, describing his *Flaming Terrapin* as a vital, 'swaggering fantasia', and Campbell must have souvenired the article for he later lampooned the *London Aphrodite* and its Norman Lindsay cover in his Bloomsbury mock epic *The Georgiad* (1933):

> All maids are willing in the magazines ...
> And any one who feels a trifle flighty
> Can get off in 'The London Aphrodite',
> Where upon every page, always in 'hay'
> These donkeys jack their mares the livelong day.
> Here's the first number—see, upon the cover,
> The living image of a country lover,
> In woolly underpants, a sort of Faun
> Who seems to wish he never had been drawn ...
> Upon his Clydesdale Pegasus he rocks,
> That, rearing proudly, squats upon its hocks,
> Raises, like rabbits' paws, its short fore-legs
> And for some unseen cake, or biscuit, begs.[53]

W.S.S.
A LITERARY PERIODICAL

PROOFS ONLY
Publication 25th Aug

THE LONDON APHRODITE

EDITED BY JACK LINDSAY & P. R. STEPHENSEN

NUMBER ONE

Published by
THE FANFROLICO PRESS, LONDON

A proof copy of the first number of the *London Aphrodite* showing the Norman Lindsay illustration Roy Campbell satirized

Campbell was not the only critic to be less than enthusiastic about Norman Lindsay's drawings. While the *TLS* was prepared to condone Norman's boldly erotic contributions to the *Lysistrata* it condemned his 'mildly silly illustrations' for *Satyrs and Sunlight* as 'not at all well drawn'.[54]

The first number of the *London Aphrodite* was largely Australian in authorship, with poems by Slessor and McCrae, and a story by Jack Lindsay's brother Philip. The magazine was really one more outlet for Jack's own work, and his verse, drama and prose filled nearly three-quarters of the August issue's sixty-four pages, some of it under the pseudonym 'Peter Meadows'. In this and later numbers there was also work from such writers as O'Flaherty and the Welsh novelist Rhys Davies, and even a poem from Sacheverell Sitwell. Lindsay and Stephensen had met Aldous Huxley who gave them not only a couple of sonnets for the magazine but also the dubious honour of inclusion in his new novel *Point Counter Point* (1928) as a couple of walk-on caricatures. Not that this sort of thing was unusual in the hothouse literary world. Their friend Philip Heseltine had already featured centrally in novels by both Huxley and D. H. Lawrence.[55]

In *Point Counter Point* Lindsay was the model for Willie Weaver, an erudite and self-conscious poet who 'exploited artistically that love of eloquence, that passion for the rotund and reverberating phrase with which, more than three centuries too late, he had been born'. In Shakespeare's youth, Huxley wrote, Weaver would have been a literary celebrity. But among his contemporaries his 'euphuisms only raised a laugh'.[56] Huxley's parody of Stephensen as Cuthbert Arkwright was less subtle and more malicious:

> Arkwright was the noisiest and the most drunken—on principle and for the love of art as well as for that of alcohol. He had an idea that by bawling and behaving offensively, he was defending art against the Philistines. Tipsy, he felt himself arrayed on the side of the angels, of Baudelaire, of Edgar Allan Poe, of De Quincey, against the dull unspiritual mob. And if he boasted of his fornications, it was because respectable people had thought Blake a madman, because Bowdler had edited Shakespeare, and the author of *Madame Bovary* had been prosecuted, because when one asked for the Earl of Rochester's *Sodom* at the Bodleian, the librarians wouldn't give it unless one had a certificate that one was engaged on *bona fide* literary research. He made his living, and in the process convinced himself that he was serving the arts, by printing limited and expensive editions of the more scabrous specimens of the native and foreign literatures.[57]

This was an indictment as well of the anti-wowser campaign conducted by the Fanfrolico Press and the *London Aphrodite*.

In the second number of the *Aphrodite* Stephensen summarized the reactions to the first. Reviewers had not been amused, a titled lady had cancelled her subscription, and the bookseller Charles Lahr had sold sixty copies at his shop in Red Lion Street. The magazine's reception was hardly the occasion for great celebration, but Liam O'Flaherty was momentarily flush with a cheque from a film company and he helped the editors get drunk in a cellar near the office. Among the other celebrants were Lahr, Rhys Davies, the Australian cartoonist Will Farrow, 'two roaring Irish bhoys covered in tap-room sawdust; two great policemen; and other Bloomsbury intellectuals'.[58]

This wild and memorable debauch left Lindsay with a broken thumb and bruised kidneys, as a result of which he caught a chill and his health began to suffer as the autumn closed in again. He had also begun another affair, complicating his relations with Elza. Stephensen had been making some of his vital spark available to Sadie the Jewish girl in the Fanfrolico office, and one of the Bloomsbury 'roaring girls', the Australian Anna Wickham, had attached herself to him.[59] He included her poem, 'Salut D'Amour', in the second *Aphrodite*. As she did on other occasions, Winifred discovered these infidelities.

The Fanfrolico partners therefore experienced some stormy sexual weather; not quite the Fanfrolican ideal of carefree fauns and nymphs. There was considerable friction as well between Elza and Stephensen. Each resented and disliked the other, and when Lindsay tried to put one of her poems in the *Aphrodite* Stephensen cut it out of the proofs; Lindsay put it back again and his co-editor deleted it once more. The poem was finally reinstated just before going to press, but this 'odd duel' took place without a word being spoken.[60] At this time each was struggling to find his own creative direction. Stephensen translated Nietzsche's *Antichrist* and planned works of fiction, while Lindsay was still experimenting with various modes and genres, later acknowledging that it was Stephensen who had encouraged him towards the novel.[61] Under such amorous, creative and financial pressures, Lindsay and Stephensen began to slip apart, welcoming any excuse to avoid each other's company.

Stephensen was also resisting the unbohemian prospect of settling down to a life of quiet domesticity with Winifred at a cottage they had rented in Kent. He took a small flat in London, the address of which was kept secret from her. In need of a break, he slipped across to St Malo in September 1928 with his Oxford friend Hall. They stayed a fortnight at a cheap hotel on the Brittany coast and did nothing but eat and drink, swim and sunbathe.[62] Stephensen was much restored by the holiday and suggested Lindsay should take a break as well which he did, spending a couple of weeks in Florence during October.

In November the Fanfrolico Press published two books about Friedrich Nietzsche: Lindsay's long critical essay *Dionysos: Nietzsche Contra Nietzsche*, and Stephensen's translation of *Der Antichrist*. Nietzsche had been a professor of classical philology before resigning to travel and write works of philosophy, and although his output included a volume of witty aphorisms, it was books like *Zarathustra* and especially the *Antichrist* which influenced the Lindsays and Stephensen. Written in 1888, less than a year before Nietzsche became insane, the *Antichrist* was a mixture of 'diabolic polemic and furious rhetoric'.[63] Like much of his writing it was also erratic and open to misinterpretation and distortion. For Nietzsche, as for his Australian disciple Norman Lindsay, classical Greece and Rome formed a vision of paradise lost. This was not surprising in Nietzsche's case since his academic training was classical. His anti-Christianity, however, was deliberately blasphemous and often illogical, as was his use of anti-Semitic stereotypes.

Critics of Nietzsche have maintained he was not anti-Semitic, claiming that he loathed fanatical anti-Semites such as his brother-in-law, and that he tarred self-righteous Christians with the same brush as the Jews they despised. Christianity was therefore a 'product of Jewish ways' and Christ 'remained a Jew, a god of back streets, god of dark holes and corners, god of all the world's slums!'[64] Despite the apologies of Nietzsche scholars, his *Antichrist* still reads like the virulent anti-Semitism of the *Protocols of the Elders of Zion*, the notorious forgery which Stephensen read, apparently with some credence, in the late 1920s.

For Stephensen there was another message in the *Antichrist*, about the 'socialistic rabble' who 'undermine the working-man's instincts, destroy his happiness, and his feeling of contentment with his trivial existence', making him envious and vengeful. 'There is nothing wrong with unequal rights; only in the claim to equal rights', Nietzsche concludes.[65] In spite of his humanism and his professed anti-Germanism, it is easy to see how he was later enshrined by Hitler as a Nazi demigod. Nietzsche's fascination with the idea of man as a ruthless predator may have been nothing more than an intellectual game, but in politics metaphor and symbol, fantasy and myth, can be very dangerous toys indeed.[66]

It had been Lindsay's suggestion that Stephensen prepare the *Antichrist* translation, 'to help him feel more a part of the press',[67] and Stephensen threw himself into the task with typical vigour. Not knowing German, he used a dictionary and two previous English translations, but his version nevertheless has an evocative fluency which is sometimes missing from more orthodox translations. In the prospectus, Stephensen said his version aimed to bring out the 'nervous force' of the original, although he felt the book's real strength lay in Norman Lindsay's drawings (which vividly illustrate Lindsay's own racial obsessions). Stephensen also recommended the 'beauty of format' which had 'seldom been surpassed in modern Fine book production'.[68] The type was printed in two colours, and the whole text was set in monumental sixteen-point capitals in deference to one of Nietzsche's concluding metaphors: 'I shall write upon all walls ... I have letters that will burn even upon the eyeballs of the blind'.[69]

Stephensen's introduction, set in more readable upper and lower case, was as vigorously polemical as Nietzsche's text. Like Norman Lindsay, Stephensen had lost relatives in World War I and he scourged the clergy for their role in war-mongering propaganda:

> In every country the parsons, who are by profession soaked in love, shrieked loudest for the bitterest consummation of the War in hate ...

We must not allow ourselves to forget and forgive them for their macabre visitings of women bereaved ... Could any phrase be too strong for mephitic maggots glutting themselves upon the bodies of brave men slain? Compared to such vermin the witch-doctors and rain-makers of the jungle assume a nobility ...

Stephensen was also as inconsistent as his hero. Describing Nietzsche accurately as a 'mad iconoclast', he went on to characterize the *Antichrist* as Nietzsche's 'most lucid and compact and reasoned philosophical work'. He ignored the German's patent anti-socialism with the comment that 'Karl Marx and Nietzsche will revise the Prayer Book'.

Though he remained a student of philosophy and politics, Stephensen threw himself into the campaign for more liberated sexual expression during the last months of 1928. In Florence the bookseller Pino Orioli had shown Jack Lindsay some of D. H. Lawrence's paintings, and Lindsay had casually suggested the idea of a book or 'portfolio of reproductions'.[70] Returning to London, he had thought no more about it.

In the meantime Stephensen had decided to take off again, this time to the South of France where Liam O'Flaherty was staying. 'I wish you and Jack would prowl down here at Christmas', O'Flaherty had written, towards the end of October. 'We could lower some stuff and perhaps sample some French hide.' He signed off, 'Balls to you both'.[71] O'Flaherty's offhand invitation was too much for Stephensen to resist, and the approach of another bleak London winter no doubt decided him. He might even sell some books, so he packed a trunkful of Fanfrolico titles and prepared to leave for the South of France.

5
D. H. Lawrence and the Lord's Police

About the middle of December 1928, just before his departure for France, Stephensen received a letter from Rhys Davies who was in Nice. Davies was hard up and wanted some money for his story in the October *Aphrodite*, but he wrote for another reason as well: 'I've just had a note from D. H. Lawrence who is travelling about here. He has heard that you would do a portfolio of reproductions of his paintings, and he asks me to mention it'.[1]

Davies had just spent a few days with Lawrence and Frieda at the Hotel Beau Rivage at Bandol, a Mediterranean resort where the couple were wintering. With the sun and the sea, and the wild pine forests in the hills behind, Bandol was good therapy for Lawrence's spirit as well as for his tuberculosis. Having been driven from England into years of restless exile, he was now fighting back. During the summer he and Orioli had arranged for the private printing of *Lady Chatterley's Lover* in Florence after English publishers had refused to handle it. The book had appeared about the same time as Radclyffe Hall's lesbian novel, *The Well of Loneliness*, and both had been set upon by the watchdogs of public morality during the autumn of 1928.

Customs authorities seized copies of *Lady Chatterley's Lover* entering England, and were vigorously supported by the press. Acknowledging Lawrence as a man of genius and a great artist, *John Bull* nevertheless denounced his novel as a 'Landmark in Evil', an 'abysm of filth', and 'the foulest book in English literature'.[2] As Lawrence's writing scrupulously avoided the lurid fantasies of genuine pornography, the outraged reactions to *Lady Chatterley's Lover* were an indictment of the still prevailing Victorian morality, rather than a reflection on Lawrence. Yet his supposed moral degeneration fed the prurient appetites of the popular press up and down the country.

The reception of Radclyffe Hall's novel was another example of the prevailing climate of sexual inhibition and hostility. Radclyffe Hall was herself a 'female invert', though her novel was less physically explicit than Lawrence's. It confronted readers with the taboo subject of lesbianism, and featured an introduction by Havelock Ellis, whose own pioneering study, *Sexual Inversion*, had been taken to court for obscenity in 1898. Publishers and printers operated an effective self-censorship, so the most peculiar thing about Radclyffe Hall's *Well of Loneliness* was that Jonathan Cape agreed to publish it at all.

Under siege from James Douglas, editor of the *Sunday Express*, and Joynson-Hicks, the pious home secretary, Cape withdrew his edition but secretly sent moulds of the type to Paris. There the book was reprinted and exported back to England, to run the familiar gauntlet of customs and postal officials. There was already a precedent for Cape's smart footwork: during the General Strike, Joynson-Hicks's friends at the *Daily Mail* had used the same expedient, printing their anti-strike newspaper in Paris. Joynson-Hicks was thus awake to the manoeuvre, and the French-printed *Well of Loneliness* was condemned by the chief magistrate to be burned.[3]

At a time of such puritan vigilance, the Fanfrolico Press had received many anonymous letters threatening police action over its publications. Despite Huxley's caricature of him in *Point Counter Point* as nothing more than a raucous pornographer, Stephensen had been undaunted by any threats, and instead had launched himself into the campaign against sexual and political suppression. In the October *Aphrodite* he had criticized J. C. Squire, the *Mercury* editor, for perpetuating the code of gentlemanly good manners in literary culture where 'sexual candour is tabu and abhorrent'. He also attacked James Douglas for performing a similar function in the popular press.[4]

With a few of his Bloomsbury friends, Stephensen compiled a pamphlet ridiculing Douglas and the suppression of *The Well of Loneliness*. Entitled *The Sink of Solitude*, the pamphlet was said to have caused Radclyffe Hall 'considerable pain',[5] no doubt because in his preface Stephensen dismissed the novel as silly and feeble, 'either as a work of art or as a moral argument'. Stephensen's own prejudices and polemical skills enabled him to pour even more scorn on Douglas by depreciating the whole incident as 'trivial and vulgar', involving 'pathetic post-war lesbians' and the 'sentimental scientificality of psychopaths like Havelock Ellis'. *The Sink of Solitude* consisted of a series of satirical drawings in the Beardsley manner by

> BERESFORD EGAN, *Gent*, to which is added a *Preface* by P. R. STEPHENSEN, *Gent*, and a *Verse Lampoon* composed by SEVERAL HANDS and now set forth for the first time, the whole very proper to be read both on *Family* and *Public Occasions*.

The pamphlet was issued as from the 'Hermes Press' at 34 Bloomsbury Street, and according to Jack Lindsay the lampoon was mostly Stephensen's work.[6]

Stephensen followed the *Sink of Solitude* with a bolder and better lampoon, this time on Jix, Sir William Joynson-Hicks. Entitled *Policeman of the Lord: A Political Satire*, and illustrated once again by Beresford Egan, this was issued as from the 'Sophistocles Press', Bloomsbury, and

One of Beresford Egan's drawings for *The Sink of Solitude,* showing a crucified Radclyffe Hall, with James Douglas looking on appeared either late in 1928 or early in 1929 before the general election at which Joynson-Hicks's Conservative Party was tipped out of office. In his preface Stephensen urged the home secretary's Twickenham constituents to 'Vote for Jix', since parliament 'has need of a certain amount of comic relief'. Stephensen reminded his readers that he considered *The Well of Loneliness* to be a 'dull and insipid book', and that the principle of censorship was his target, Joynson-Hicks and Radclyffe Hall being merely his weapons:

> Repression is always a boomerang. Most literate people are of the opinion that the Holy Bible is 'immoral and disgusting' in many celebrated passages; but no voice has been raised for the suppression of the Zenana Bible Mission, of which Sir William Joynson-Hicks is the Distinguished Hon. Treasurer ... Let him once begin, however, the repression of books which displease him, and who knows to what lengths a future Home Secretary, with different moral prejudices, may go?[7]

In the *Policeman of the Lord* lampoon, one of his wittiest verse creations, Stephensen compared the evangelical Joynson-Hicks with God, Jix being not only that exalted gentleman's protégé but also his charlady and 'copper'. He was 'Mussolini Jix' as well as Martin Luther reincarnate, and as the home secretary's justification was Christian morality, it was to heaven Stephensen turned for judgement:

> JIX paused. And Heaven sighed a deep 'Amen'
> (Celestial applause ironic). Then
> An impulse shuddered through the Holy Host
> And all eyes turned to MILTON'S sturdy ghost
> Sitting aloof upon a golden stool.
> JOHN MILTON rose, and spoke but one word: 'Fool!'
> Then floated off, secure in his divinity,
> To make a Foursome with the Holy Trinity.
> While Heaven's Electorate doubled up with mirth
> And flapper-angels mocked: 'Go back to Earth! ...

In his preface Stephensen affirmed that 'Works will be written dealing with sex in the frankest possible manner', and that 'a new English renaissance may even come' which 'Jix and all his policemen' would be unable to restrain.

Just such a renaissance had been proclaimed by Norman Lindsay and the Fanfrolico Press, and Stephensen started a short-lived Fanfrolico Pamphlets series with his spirited *Norman Lindsay Does Not Care*. This was printed, with a Lindsay drawing, on one sheet and sold for a farthing in the traditional pamphlet style. It was a defence of Lindsay against both the suburban philistines and the 'Official Art Mob' who put Lindsay down as imitative of Beardsley and a mere illustrator.[8] Although Stephensen never lost his respect for Lindsay's artistry, he later commented that the *Yellow Book* anti-moralism of the 1890s, which had inspired Lindsay, was out of date by the 1920s.[9] Yet that spirit was returning through the Harold

Acton-inspired aestheticism of novelists like Evelyn Waugh. Homosexuality was in the avant-garde again, as *The Well of Loneliness* had shown.[10]

When Jix's police seized the entire edition of Nora James's innocuous novel, *The Sleeveless Errand*, as soon as it was published in February 1929, Stephensen quickly penned yet another pamphlet, entitled *Well of Sleevelessness*. Illustrated by Philip Heseltine's friend Hal Collins, the pamphlet was published by the Scholartis Press of Eric Partridge who had also been the hapless publisher of *The Sleeveless Errand*.[11] It is an interesting, though perhaps irrelevant, coincidence that just at the time when all women over twenty-one were given the vote in Britain, outnumbering male voters, there was conservative rearguard harassment of two women writers, Radclyffe Hall and Nora James. On a related issue, one historian of censorship, noting the increased violence towards female characters in modern pornography, has remarked that 'As women achieved emancipation in life, they became enslaved in literature'.[12] Such degradation appalled D. H. Lawrence who was, in his own way, intensely moral and even puritanical. In his study, *Pornography and Obscenity* (1929), Lawrence commented that 'even I would censor genuine pornography, rigorously'. It was possible, Lawrence said, to recognize genuine pornography 'by the insult it offers, invariably, to sex, and to the human spirit'.[13]

Lawrence's own spirit, increasingly besieged by ill health, was turning from writing to painting with a new sense of joy and release. On his first visit to Bandol early in December 1928, Rhys Davies had found Lawrence's absorption in painting 'almost pathetic'. Yet though he considered Lawrence's canvases technically faulty as art, Davies felt that every line and every shade of colour blazed with Lawrence's 'exuberant surge of passion', achieving a primitive, barbaric life.[14]

At this time Lawrence was in a fury over the English suppression of *Lady Chatterley's Lover*. So he eagerly seized upon the possibility of publishing his paintings, a project Jack Lindsay had suggested in an offhand way to Orioli. Lawrence not only asked Davies to mention it to Stephensen, but on 14 December wrote to his London friend, S. S. Koteliansky, enclosing a letter to Lindsay offering an introductory essay on modern painting if the Fanfrolico would issue his 'pictures'.[15] Before Lawrence's letter reached England, Stephensen arrived in France with his trunk of books, putting up in fashionable Nice where he had little difficulty disposing of his expensive stock.[16]

Rhys Davies was also in Nice, and a week before Christmas 1928 Stephensen decided to travel down to Bandol with him by train, a journey of some hours, to visit Lawrence. They spent two days with Lawrence and Frieda at the Hotel Beau Rivage, and Stephensen dropped Winifred a line on hotel notepaper saying he had 'Got on wonderfully' with Lawrence.[17] For his part, Lawrence found Stephensen an attractive but overwhelming character who kept him talking late into the night. Next morning Lawrence told Davies he had not been able to sleep because 'the walls of the room still shook' after Stephensen had left him.[18]

Stephensen and Lawrence discussed everything from politics to publishing, including Joynson-Hicks, Douglas, and the whole campaign of repressive censorship. They also talked of Australia and of *Kangaroo*, which Stephensen had read with great interest when it first appeared. Stephensen agreed to publish some Russian translations by Koteliansky, but of most importance to Lawrence was the proposed paintings volume. Dorothy Warren had been holding a collection of his paintings in storage for several months at her London gallery, pending an exhibition in the new year, and Stephensen suggested that the exhibition coincide with publication of the book. He also presented seven Fanfrolico books to Lawrence who afterwards characterized them to Huxley as '*what* a waste of good printing!' But Stephensen assured Lawrence that the paintings volume would be published under a new imprint, and one which would not employ any of Norman Lindsay's artwork, for which Lawrence obviously had scant respect.[19]

The new press, which Stephensen called the Mandrake, had already been discussed with Jack Lindsay and was tentatively planned as an offshoot of the Fanfrolico. In the climate of heavy-handed censorship in which it was conceived, Stephensen's name for the press was particularly apt, 'mandrake' being a poisonous plant said to shriek when pulled up by the roots. Financial nourishment had been offered by Edward Goldston, a London book dealer who had purchased a Gutenberg Bible from a European monastery and resold it in New York for a huge profit. He had been keen to invest in the Fanfrolico Press for some time, but Lindsay had been putting him off. The Lawrence project was the catalyst for the new imprint because Lindsay was concerned about a police raid should the Fanfrolico publish Lawrence's paintings. Stephensen was already at Bandol when Lindsay wrote from London that he had seen Goldston and would draw up prospectuses for the Mandrake titles over Christmas. He urged Stephensen to see Lawrence and secure an agreement for the paintings book.[20]

This letter took a couple of days to reach Stephensen care of American Express, Nice, and in the meantime he had already become friendly with Lawrence. 'I was glad you came', Lawrence wrote to him after the Bandol visit. 'I was glad to see somebody young with a bit of energy and fearlessness. It's *most* precious ... don't rush in and squander it.' Lawrence urged him not to drink too much with the bohemian crowd since they were wasters who believed in nothing.[21]

The letter was a new rallying cry to Stephensen, and much closer to the old Bolshevik faith than Norman Lindsay's philosophical effusions. Although exhausted by the tuberculosis which would kill him fifteen months later, Lawrence could still muster enough demonic energy to defy the enemy and spur on his ally. 'I believe one must put one's fist through something much more solid and pernicious than panes of glass', he told Stephensen.

> We *must* make a hole in the bourgeois world which is the whole world of consciousness today. If your mandrake is going to grow let him shove

up under the walls of this prison-system, and bust them. But patience, patience all the time, even while one acts most strenuously, somewhere patience. I am determined, like Samson in the temple of Philistia, to pull the house down sooner or later and all I want is men to tug silently and constantly along with me. But you Australians seem to believe in squandering, which is a pity, because squandering, like drink, is only a form of evasion—mere evasion of life. To live one has to live a life-long fight.[22]

Lawrence also enclosed three 'doggerels', from his *Pansies* manuscript, for the *London Aphrodite*.[23]

Stephensen penned a reply next morning at his Nice hotel, and it too was full of fighting spirit, from the class war this time. His letter began, 'Dear DHL':

> ... How could I have expected to find my own succinct hatreds so anticipated? I have tried to hate purposively, not merely to snarl. I blush now to admit that before meeting you I did not realise how integrated your antagonisms are. It is not easy to hate to a plan, to hate synthetically as you do—pardon me, as I do also. We are to destroy the most vile conspiracy which has ever subjugated the human blood; destroy it not merely because it is powerful and established ... but because it is vile and a menace to our own pulse. It is too easy, too much like ordinary envy, to hate the ruling class as a *social* class. We must hate and destroy it as cancerous; as threatening life ...

Stephensen also felt it necessary to defend his respect for Norman Lindsay:

> I have to explain to you that my respect for Norman Lindsay has always been due to his capacity for getting under the skin of the citizens with his fat nudes—stressing femininity (buttocks and bubs) he conditions a wonderful uneasiness in the breast of the pater familias. With all the differences of method and personality this is precisely what you are doing. The process is to bring sex (balls and all) into consciousness effectively with the distinguishing subtlety of art—frankness cum delicacy more effective than say pictorial pornography. This is the first vital attack upon our citizen—to force consciousness of blood upon him—it is enough to destroy him utterly. The second attack is to pinprick him into frenzy at a million points of exposure of his hypocrisy, social, sexual-tribal, political ... He is only destroyed by looking with the mirror of consciousness—blood and balls consciousness ...

On the question of how to reproduce Lawrence's paintings, Stephensen agreed to do them in 'colour tone process'. He also assured Lawrence that he would not let drunkenness and 'pseudo-bohemianism' divert him, and welcomed the older man's warning about the discipline of patience.[24] Lawrence replied briefly that he had begun the introduction to the paintings and signed off with another reference to the Samson image: 'I feel you and I have something in the spirit in common—or uncommon—we must work in unison and plan together. I hear those pillars going crack already. Fun!'[25]

Just before Christmas Stephensen received Jack Lindsay's letter about Goldston and the advance of the new press in London, and he sensed that Lindsay was trying to oust him from the Fanfrolico. His intuition told him Elza was behind it. He also suspected, wrongly, that his partner was going ahead to form a new company without him. All the pressures which had been gradually building up between them erupted in a violent and unreasonable letter from Nice, in which Stephensen accused Lindsay of exploiting him. It angered Stephensen that Lindsay considered himself sole proprietor of the Fanfrolico Press, and Stephensen demanded recognition for helping to build up the press.[26]

Taken aback by the sudden outburst, Lindsay was forced to admit that Elza disliked Stephensen, but Jack denied the significance of this. 'As I love you very much', he wrote to his friend in Nice, 'I do not want you to feel bitterness over my treatment of you'. Lindsay said he had always thought in terms of any Fanfrolico profits being divided equally among Stephensen, Norman, and himself. He assured Stephensen he had no intention of going into the new press without him and suggested they share the Mandrake profits, though he offered, perhaps calculatingly, to stand aside: 'If you wish to push me out to compensate yourself for what you feel has been my attitude in the F.P. well and good ...' He added a plea to 'jettison all our irritations' and start again on the old friendly basis, but with a more organized approach and definite hours allocated to each press.[27]

Stephensen's anger quickly dissolved, and in a succession of letters Lindsay apologetically blamed himself for the flare-up: his kidneys had been worrying him, then he blamed his nerves, and finally the 'next drama kicking in my womb'. Knowing it would flatter and appease his friend, Lindsay likened their situation to that of Wagner and Nietzsche. Inky was the Nietzsche figure, and Jack asked him to excuse 'my Wagnerian antics'. He even offered to wire Stephensen cash if necessary, as proof of his financial good faith.[28]

Stephensen spent about a month in the South of France. He visited Liam O'Flaherty at La Colle sur Loup, where the Irishman was staying, not far from Nice. Then they dined together and drank flagons of beer at a *brasserie* in Nice where, in O'Flaherty's words, they 'heartily cursed the fecklessness of the arid high-brows'. In a letter to Stephensen from La Colle sur Loup, O'Flaherty denounced the 'salon crowd of degenerates who prefer literature to life'.[29]

Temperamentally, and by nationality, neither of them was fitted for the intellectual drawing rooms inhabited by figures like Aldous Huxley, now Lawrence's close friend and the epitome of O'Flaherty's 'arid high-brow'. In a parody of *Point Counter Point* in the December *Aphrodite*, Stephensen had accused Huxley of having been 'all round the world without quitting the stateroom of his own mind, the first-class cabin of his eremitic and privileged experience'. In the world of 'literary eunuchs, perverts, inverts, and onanists', however, Stephensen thought Huxley was 'one of the few, perhaps the last great English novelist not bogged in the mire of psycopathia sexualis ... the last heterosexual Englishman of first-grade Intelligence'.[30] As if to prove his own lack of prejudice in personal relations, Stephensen took the train into Italy towards the end of December to visit the homosexual Norman Douglas in Florence.

On New Year's Eve 1928, Stephensen wrote to Winifred that he would be leaving for England about the seventh of January, 'unless something else happens'.[31] Something did, in the form of another friendly letter from Lawrence asking Stephensen to visit again. Lawrence mentioned that Jack Lindsay had sent him *Dionysos* and Lindsay's verse play volume, *Helen Comes of Age*: ' ... oh! if you Australians didn't do it all so easy! It's as if you could eat a thousand dinners without ever swallowing one of them, or having anything on your stomachs: everything just tasty'.[32] It was a further warning to Stephensen as much as a criticism of Lindsay.

Stephensen went to Bandol again in early January and stayed for a few days with Lawrence and Frieda at the Hotel Beau Rivage. According to Frieda's daughter Barbara, who was also visiting, the 'cheerful colonial' was Lawrence's only attempt at matchmaking for her. But the visit was not a success for any of them. Barbara was in a miserable and nervous state, Lawrence was very ill, and Stephensen read them a story he had written which Lawrence immediately demolished as unconvincing. They had all been sitting in Frieda's bedroom, and Lawrence told Frieda afterwards he could not understand why everyone wanted to write when there wasn't much fun in it. He described Stephensen as a businessman rather than an artist. A young Californian, who was also there, offered a somewhat different version of the visit, with the group of them lazing comfortably on the beach in the warm sun while Stephensen read a story.[33]

Lawrence wrote to Rhys Davies that Stephensen had 'stirred us all up as usual', but that he seemed more downhearted this time and was rushing back to publishing work in London.[34] No doubt the blow-up with Lindsay had shaken him. Stephensen's plan for the paintings volume was to print five hundred copies for sale at ten pounds each, an exorbitant price. Lawrence's comments on this to friends ranged from 'Holy Lord!' and '*Dio mio!*' to '*Avanti Italiani!*' At his 'wits' end' over the proliferation of pirated editions of *Lady Chatterley's Lover* in America, Lawrence was nevertheless highly excited about the publication of his paintings.[35]

Stephensen returned to England about the second week in January, taking with him three paintings Lawrence had just completed: a small oil and two small watercolours including *Leda*, showing a naked woman raped by the fierce-eyed swan of Greek legend. Stephensen packed these in his suitcase and carried them through customs at Folkestone, innocently claiming he had 'nothing to declare'.[36] He arrived back in London to frantic activity. The rest of the Lawrence paintings, about fifteen oils and half a dozen watercolours, had to be collected from Dorothy Warren and photographed for the book. Publication was planned for March, though delays with colour proofing pushed this back to the summer. Arrangements for the new Mandrake Press had yet to be concluded, and the next number of the *London Aphrodite* was due in February.

In his discussions with Jack Lindsay, Stephensen was determined to politicize and modernize their publishing list. He had joined the Fanfrolico as a provisional disciple of Norman's creed, accepting rather than generating ideas. Since the dispute with Jack, and the re-energizing by Lawrence, Stephensen now wanted some say in the direction of the Fanfrolico Press as well as control of its offshoot, the Mandrake. He had assured Lawrence, before leaving France, that there would be no Lindsay, either father or son, in the Mandrake Press.[37]

Jack was still prepared to help with the Mandrake but candidly admitted that he needed the Fanfrolico Press to establish his literary reputation:

> The continuance of the [Fanfrolico Press] is the only possible way of (a) producing my own poetry, (b) creating an air of dignity about my poetry by producing poetry of a similar nature (i.e. the Greeks, Marlowe, Byron, etc.) ... If the F.P. continues, a powerful and immediate basis is given for my work. If it stops now I am substantially where I was in Australia, because not a single publisher in England will print my poetry ... I am ultimately a lonely Unicorn, and in Australia I was a thousand times worse than I am now.[38]

Lindsay wanted Stephensen to help lead the Fanfrolico Press out of its 'present muddle', but though he stayed on as manager for a few more months, Stephensen was preoccupied now with Lawrence and the Mandrake Press. On 19 February he went ahead and registered the name of the new company as The Mandrake Press, trading at 41 Museum Street. The partners were Stephensen, listed as a publisher's manager, and Edward Goldston, an 'oriental bookseller'. Described by Stephensen as a 'humorous Jew', Goldston specialized in art books, and his prosperity was evident from the low-slung French sporting coupé he drove. As well as boasting the Plough Inn, Museum Street in Bloomsbury was then a centre for antiquarian and secondhand bookselling, with more than a dozen shops including Goldston's.[39] Although Stephensen actually ran the Mandrake Press, from an office across the road from Goldston's shop, the bookseller contributed all the initial capital, allowing Stephensen a half share of profits.

Despite his new Jewish partner, and his old Jewish girlfriend at the Fanfrolico Press, Stephensen began to take the irrational prejudice of anti-Semitism more seriously. His grandfather had feared and despised the 'cunning' Jewish bankers, and in Lawrence's novels, *Kangaroo* and *Lady Chatterley's Lover*, there were examples of a similar anti-Semitism.[40] In fact from the far left of the ideological spectrum to the far right, from Frank Anstey the Australian socialist to Norman Lindsay the avowed élitist and D. H. Lawrence the 'spunky' instinctualist,[41] anti-Semitism was deeply ingrained.

It was about the time of his friendship with Lawrence that Stephensen read *The Protocols of the Elders of Zion*, with its sinister plans for world conquest through the subversion of modern civilization. First published in Russia just after the turn of the century, for the benefit of the fanatically anti-Semitic Czar Nicholas II, this preposterous piece of propaganda was translated and widely distributed throughout the world, appearing in Britain in 1920.[42] Since then it has remained the bible for those who are both outraged and comforted by the thought that every pernicious aspect of modern industrial society, from the gold standard to socialism, the press and pornography, must be a fiendish Jewish conspiracy. Norman Lindsay, D. H. Lawrence and, increasingly, P. R. Stephensen, all opposed the mechanization and dehumanization of industrial society. For them, World War I had hideously symbolized its destructive power, and bogeys like 'Jewish finance' promised to explain away the nightmare.

In his poem, 'Barrel-Organ Rhapsody', in the *London Aphrodite*, Stephensen added his own forthright solution to the problem of these 'bloodless conquerors' issuing 'shares for Jerusalem':

> The Middle Class is the upperclass now
>   that England's gone to seed;
> Dividend-drawers are reaping the harvest
>   sown by the bulldog breed;
> They are reaping it down in the City,
>   placid in bowler hats;
> *Les aristocrats à la lanterne* ...
>   but there ain't no aristocrats!
> The bloodless conquerors, skimming the scum,
>   with a pudgily cunning hand,
> Have issued shares for Jerusalem in
>   this green, green, pleasant land ...
> Ho! some unemployed draw dividends and
>   some unemployed draw the dole;
> And some are drawing the moral, which
>   is simple on the whole—
> That the middle class is the muddleclass now,
>   and the sensible thing to do
> Is to stick a financier in the guts
>   if he tries his finance on you.

Stephensen's sympathies were still proletarian, despite Norman Lindsay, Nietzsche, and the *Protocols*, and he concluded his poem by extolling the out-of-work workers as the new 'bulldog breed'.[43]

Receiving this issue of the *Aphrodite*, Lawrence wrote to Stephensen from Bandol that

> The bourgeois, the machine civilisation, *and* the 'Worker' (as such) all want to destroy real humanness. If Bolshevism is going to classify me as a Worker or a non-Worker, I am against it.—I *hate* our civilisation, our ideals, our money, our machines, our intellectuals, our upper classes. But I hate them because I've tried them and given them a long chance—and they're rotten. If a man has not 'risen in the world' he'll be *forced* to admit there is something 'above him'.—Many ladies nowadays, very many, have love affairs with their chauffeurs—the chauffeur is the favourite fucker. But the chauffeur stays where he is—and

is a *machine à plaisir*—and the lady stays where *she* is—and nothing is altered in the least. If Mellors [in *Lady Chatterley's Lover*] had never *found out* the upper classes, by being one of them, Connie would just have had him and put him down again—elle m'a planté là!—No, it's all much more difficult than you imagine. The working man is not much of a British Bulldog any more—he's rather a shivering cur—one has to try slowly to rouse the old spirit in him—and *definitely* disillusion him about the 'upperness'.—You see you yourself are really much more *impressed* by the 'upper' gentleman—even by Aldous [Huxley]—than ever Mellors is.

Lawrence was at his most vitriolic. He went on to criticize the whole *London Aphrodite* idea as adolescently self-indulgent: '... you'll merely be shoved aside, you Australians, you don't *bite on* hard enough. All that silly twiddling with girls!—it isn't even really sex.—I have the *Aphrodite*—and it's very much that twiddling business—sticky and feeble'.[44]

With Lawrence, Stephensen also discussed plans for *The Bushwhackers*, his dozen 'Sketches of Life in the Australian Outback', written probably between February and May 1929. Stephensen later claimed to have written them all 'during a long weekend, over the Whitsuntide holiday, in absurd haste'.[45] As the stories totalled less than 20 000 words, such a claim is implausible rather than impossible. They *were* written quickly, but Stephensen may have exaggerated his haste in order to excuse the sketchiness and incompleteness of some of the pieces. Talking with Lawrence about Australia and *Kangaroo* had undoubtedly spurred Stephensen into fiction about his native Queensland, though there was as much ideology and anger as nostalgia in *The Bushwhackers*.

'It's all very well being a bush-whacker', Lawrence wrote to him, 'but ... the business-men and intellectuals are going to whack the bushwhacker into limbo'. Two weeks later Lawrence returned to this theme, saying 'Do write your book about how the bush hit back', but warning him not to forget to include a sketch, '*The Bush in 1960*—and a concluding one: *The Bush in 2500.*—And see who gives whom the death-blow. Whack —whack—whack!'[46] Stephensen felt he was wrestling with Lawrence's *Kangaroo* for a truer interpretation of Australia, and Lawrence was surprised at Stephensen's competitive intensity:

> I shall be interested to see your *Bushwhackers*. I am puzzled that you should feel you have to conquer or contradict something of me inside yourself. *Kangaroo* was only just what I felt. You may indeed know something much deeper and more vital about Australia and the Australian future. I should be the first to admit it.[47]

When Lawrence received a copy of *Bushwhackers*, he was only able to admit what he felt, neither praising nor really denigrating the sketches of Queensland bush life, but dismissing them and Stephensen's efforts as lacking perseverance:

> I read Bush-Whackers, and it's not 'childish', it's that it's too sketchy. You won't be patient enough and go deep enough into your own scene.

You always stay at the level of the sketch, because of the hurry. If you went deeper you'd get a *real* book out of it. But you haven't the submission.[48]

In other words, Lawrence was sticking to the view he had expressed to Frieda and Barbara six months earlier: Stephensen was a businessman not an artist.

It is interesting, however, to compare Lawrence's comments with those of Miles Franklin. In 1932, as 'Brent of Bin Bin', she wrote to Stephensen:

> *Bushwhackers* . . . made a milestone day for me, one of those days when I threw up my hat because of finding a new accretion to the real Australian Literature; that which savours our unique, our inebriating, laughing, haunting, wistful, brooding, ancient, ageless, unplumbed, silent land . . . it is *Australian* writing, and that has special, I may say sacred . . . significance to me.[49]

The *Times Literary Supplement*, in a short notice, compared the book unfavourably with Henry Lawson's work, and though Nettie Palmer was kinder, she too was forced to admit that Stephensen had not benefited from the experiments already made by Lawson, Dyson and Baynton.[50]

The Bushwhackers consisted of stories or legends Stephensen remembered from his boyhood in and around Biggenden. 'Sketches' was an accurate label for them, not only because of their often simple outlines, but because Stephensen also retained the real names of places and characters in some stories. They were dashed off hastily for the Mandrake's first list, and Stephensen used exotic, even horrific episodes of bush life and death to appeal to a metropolitan English audience. Two of the most unsatisfactory and derivative stories concerned snakes, and the book's casing was decorated with a luminescent gold reptile-skin pattern.

While a number of the pieces in *Bushwhackers* did owe something to the work of Steele Rudd and Henry Lawson, the influence of O'Flaherty's Irish stories was also operating, and there was greater emphasis on history and myth than in earlier bush tales. The title story itself, though weak and unrealized as fiction, was an emphatic protest at the exploitation and erosion of the land by greedy European settlers. Stephensen in fact made ironic use of the word 'settle', with its Australian vernacular meaning of 'ruin'.[51] His polemical cast of thought and his experience in the Workers' Theatre Movement shaped his stories not so much into psychological narratives as around historical themes and social issues.

At a deeper level, Stephensen was also attempting to resolve his own ambivalence towards his native land—'the country I love and the people I hate'.[52] Yet he could not conceal his admiration and affection for the plundering pioneers who 'took whatever came to hand lightly with a laugh and a curse, and with no thought for the future, no confidence in the past'. Anticipating his later isolationist anger with Europe, Stephensen vehemently declaimed: 'These, sirs, are the Australians, and the best of them were killed in your stinking war to end war recently, and their like will not again be seen on the earth'.[53] His lament for the dispossessed Aborigines, 'Sorrow of Black Alf', though it distorted and mythologized Aboriginal history, also expressed outrage at the black genocide, and prefigured his later involvement with Xavier Herbert and the Aboriginal protest movement in the 1930s. Stephensen in fact had a fascination with racialism and race conflict. Underlying the effective comedy of 'Willy Ah Foo'—the tale of 'the last Celestial left in our district'—was a vivid analysis of Australian racial attitudes and, in particular, the formation of the White Australia Policy.

In the final story, 'Fecundity', Stephensen attempted to reconcile his carefree bush childhood with the complex heritage of European culture. The central figure was a romantic projection of his Danish grandfather, who appeared in the story as a piano virtuoso and a man who had 'never chopped a tree, or killed an animal, or even mounted a horse'. He became an ideal symbol for Stephensen: 'Nobody could have been less an Australian of that bustling generation; and yet nobody will ever live more worthily in that land than he did. That man used his Freedom, and destroyed nothing'. He had achieved a rare integration of spirit. A product of European high culture, the old man 'never once [wished] himself back in Europe from his dream-adventure', his nerves 'calmed by a flute-like calling which haloed tall trees in his mind'.[54] Such a vision of harmony and integration was forbidden the exiled Stephensen, and he continued to be tossed on the storms of ideological and personal conflict.

While he was writing *The Bushwhackers* and organizing the Mandrake Press, he found his relationship with the Fanfrolico Press becoming more and more untenable. One of the causes was Brian Penton, who had arrived in London in March 1929 to join the growing band of Fanfrolico expatriates. A friend of Philip Lindsay (soon to follow him to London), but more devious and ruthlessly ambitious than any of Norman's other supporters, Penton had letters of introduction to people like Beaverbrook. When no opportunities were forthcoming in London journalism, however, he turned to the Fanfrolico Press and took over Stephensen's role as business manager. Jack Lindsay wrote to his father on 3 April 1929: 'Brian has been working at the office for some days now and has already done invaluable work in producing order. P.R.S. fights trench after trench to keep his muddle intact ... However, order can only be achieved by his departure'.[55]

With his own role in the Fanfrolico coming to an end, Stephensen must have given Lawrence the misleading impression that the press itself was finished. Lawrence wrote to Orioli in April that 'The Fanfrolico Press has more or less dissolved', adding that the '*working* partner was always P. R. Stephensen—Lindsay was the literary side of it'.[56] Lawrence was just then arguing with the publisher Secker over the deletion of poems from his forthcoming volume *Pansies*, and he authorized the bookseller Charles Lahr not only to organize a special complete edition of *Pansies*, but also to arrange a secret London edition of *Lady Chatterley's Lover*.[57]

Stephensen's friend Lahr had been one of Lawrence's surreptitious London distributors for *Lady Chatterley's Lover*, and in January 1929 Lahr had suggested to Lawrence a plan for a German edition of the novel. The bookseller had helped keep Lawrence informed of the latest *Lady Chatterley* piracies, and the German plan, like the Paris edition in May, was an attempt to compete with the pirates. Early in the year Stephensen and Lahr must have discussed their mutual friend Lawrence and his frustration over *Lady Chatterley*, which was being brazenly pirated in America at the same time as it was ruthlessly suppressed in England. Possibly at Stephensen's suggestion, Lahr changed his mind from a German to an English edition, and he conveyed this bold plan to Lawrence who replied on 18 April 1929: 'I don't mind a bit if your friend does 500 of Our Lady. He can give me 15% on his selling price, that being the usual. Let me know'. A few weeks later, Lawrence wrote to Orioli about this secret project: 'A man in London talks of doing an edition of 500 [of *Lady Chatterley's Lover*] there—printing it himself in London, right under Jix's nose. Don't know if this will come off'.[58]

The secret London edition of *Lady Chatterley's Lover*, authorized by Lawrence but bearing a false Florence imprint, was not in fact printed until after Lawrence's death. Stephensen had some difficulty locating a printer prepared to undertake such a risky job, and eventually the novel was produced at a basement workshop near Euston Station. The very secrecy of this 'third edition' caused even Frieda to consider it a piracy, and it is still listed as such in the *Bibliography of D. H. Lawrence*.[59]

In the last year of Lawrence's life, Stephensen took many other risks for the novelist. He published Lawrence's paintings, and allowed Lahr to use 'P. R. Stephensen, 41 Museum Street' as the ostensible publisher of the complete *Pansies* which appeared a month after Secker's faint-hearted edition. Though Stephensen was not the publisher of the unexpurgated *Pansies*, except in name, he was prepared to face court action as a test case against the obscenity laws. He told a reporter from the *Manchester Guardian* that he believed Lawrence was 'a genius whose works should be available for posterity intact'.[60]

Not that Stephensen accepted the genius's ideas without question. For the second last *London Aphrodite*, in April 1929, Stephensen wrote a brief philosophical essay which marked a new synthesis for him. It showed that he had clarified his own position in relation to communism, Norman Lindsayism and D. H. Lawrence. All these influences were significant, but Nietzsche was now predominant. The essay was no doubt intended as a public/personal dialogue with Lawrence, developing some of the ideas and arguments they had exchanged in letters. It was by no means uncritical of Lawrence whom Stephensen described as a 'modern Luddite rioter', 'singing swan songs aloofly'. Praising Nietzsche's statement in *Zarathustra* that 'Blood is spirit', Stephensen added that it must be the 'delighted blood' of Dionysos, not the 'dark blood' of Lawrence.[61]

Punningly entitled 'The Whirled Around', the essay was subtitled 'Reflections upon Methuselah, Ichthyphallos, Wheels and Dionysos', and it showed that Stephensen's political emotions still lingered in Russia. In his best oratorical style he proclaimed that one soldier of the Red Army

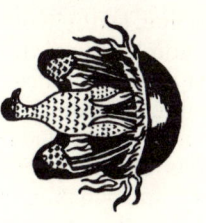

The title page and the last page of *The Paintings of D. H. Lawrence*

could bring more reality to social discussion than 'ten drawing-rooms full of daring modern novelists and playwrights':

> Therefore let us have practical Communism, world communism, quickly, ruthlessly, and efficiently. The bourgeois require shocking all will agree. Well, shock them properly. Expropriate them. They started the wheels going, now they cannot control the wheels. Expropriate them; smash them on their own wheels. Let us have proletarian ownership of the wheels, then. The axles will be better greased, the wheels will whirl more steadily...
>
> There will still be wheels. And upon the Communist wheel, revolve it ever so smoothly, there will still be individual communists; each with a pulse of blood. I speak of a rhythm uncontrollable by politics.

Stephensen hailed 'Lorenzo'[62] for affirming ego as blood, but was repelled by the death-yearning of Lawrence's 'pure emotional' ego just as he was by the Methuselah-like ego of the 'pure intellectual' Shaw. With his 'impertinent degradation of the Beyond-man in terms of intellectual super-humanity', Shaw was the 'first and worst vulgariser of Nietzsche'.

Lawrence's reaction to this philosophical *mélange* was swift but light-hearted. Stephensen sent him a copy of the April *Aphrodite*, and Lawrence replied from Mallorca that he had not inspired Stephensen to a brilliant article—'not even very estimable—but it might have been worse, like the one on poor Douglas. *Caramba*! (since we're in Spain)'.[63] This reference to Jack Lindsay's piece on Norman Douglas in the same issue allowed Lawrence to sidestep any philosophical argument with Stephensen.

But Stephensen's philosophical course was firmly set: Nietzsche remained his guiding light, his mythological identification was with Dionysos, and his political hero was the anarchist Bakunin. As the intensity of his exchange with Lawrence over *Bushwhackers* and *Kangaroo* indicated, the resolution of his Australian identity was still of vital importance to Stephensen. In England, his inferior 'colonial' status had been accentuated. He could not yet escape, as the working-class Lawrence had, by fleeing England and tossing bombs like *Lady Chatterley's Lover* back over his shoulder. As the 1920s drew to a close, Stephensen's personal exile came increasingly to resemble Lawrence's. The two men did indeed have 'something in the spirit in common', as Lawrence had told him. They were both, for example, products of class-conscious parentage, having strong-willed, bourgeois mothers and working-class fathers. It may not have been altogether a coincidence that they had developed close and sustaining relationships with women (Frieda and Winifred) who were older and already mothers.

During May 1929 Lawrence carefully checked proofs of his paintings and sent Stephensen detailed criticisms. 'I think after all it will be a lovely book', he assured Stephensen, and himself, though he found something to complain about in every proof. Lawrence scorned the prospective purchasers of his ten-guinea edition as 'ten-guinea pigs', and when advance orders came flooding in he was both excited and disgusted.[64]

Sixty orders alone had been received for the ten special vellum copies, on offer at the ridiculous price of £52 10s each. '*Figurati*', Lawrence commented to Huxley; and to Max Mohr, another friend, Lawrence criticized the 'insanity' of book collectors when a 'good author' could not even get work printed.[65] 'I hate this expensive edition business', he told Mohr, which must have been small consolation to Mohr who was then undergoing his own trials with publishers. Lawrence, after all, hated everything, and he was not about to refuse the income from this 'expensive edition business'. He did, however, encourage Stephensen to keep the plates so a 'cheaper edition' could be produced later, for which he promised a 'more popular' introduction.[66]

The Paintings of D. H. Lawrence cost about £2000 to produce, and grossed somewhat less than expected because Stephensen 'sacrificed' 150 of the ten-guinea copies at half price to an American dealer visiting London.[67] In early June, when finished copies were coming from the printer, Lawrence advised Stephensen not to announce the publication. 'Makes one sick to think the police might interfere', Lawrence commented. 'Certainly don't announce it until you've sent out all your orders ... Keep as quiet as possible for the first few weeks. And don't send out any review copies—why waste them? The book will sell of itself ...' The exhibition of Lawrence's paintings opened in mid-June at the Warren Gallery, and Lawrence, annoyed at not hearing a word from 'that wretch' Dorothy Warren, let Frieda travel to London to make sure the paintings were safely returned after the showing.[68]

Meanwhile, Stephensen had finally parted company with the Fanfrolico Press, exactly two years after supplanting Kirtley. Stephensen wrote Norman Lindsay a friendly letter, describing his experiences in the press as hard work but also great fun. He characterized his parting from Jack as amiable, and tried to be gracious about Penton but was less successful here in concealing his animosity. He described Penton as 'Full of Australian energy, soft from the sun, and full of personal literary ambitiousness'.[69] Lawrence told Stephensen that it was just as well the partnership with Jack Lindsay had been dissolved as Lindsay had 'too strong an influence over you'.[70] Lawrence had felt this all along. After his first meeting with Stephensen in December 1928 he had told Koteliansky he thought Stephensen had been 'a bit taken in by the "culture" of the other lot'—meaning the Lindsays.[71]

Towards the end of June 1929, with Frieda now in London, and the exhibition under way at the Warren Gallery, there was a renewed press campaign against Lawrence, this time focusing on his paintings. Frieda went to stay with Stephensen and Winifred for a few days at their house at Knockholt in Kent, and there was a party for her at the gallery in London on Thursday evening, 4 July. The next day two plainclothes detectives called at the gallery and asked Dorothy Warren and her husband Philip Trotter to close the exhibition. They refused, and an hour later more police arrived with a van and proceeded to take away thirteen paintings, including two that Stephensen had brought back from France.

Buttocks and breasts apparently did not offend these guardians of public morality, but any painting showing pubic hair or genitals was taken. The police also seized four copies of the Mandrake *Paintings of D. H. Lawrence*, which were on sale at the gallery, and a copy of *Ecce Homo* by the German expressionist George Grosz which was actually the Trotters' private property.[72]

Despite the loss of more than half of the Lawrence paintings, the Warren Gallery continued its exhibition for a couple of months. Although few of the paintings were actually sold, more than twelve thousand people paid a shilling each to view the controversial show, or what was left of it, netting Dorothy Warren and her husband a small fortune. They were prepared to laugh all the way to court when summonses were issued against them, under the antiquated Obscene Publications Act of 1857, by the even more antiquated 82-year-old Marlborough Street magistrate. The prosecutor was the same Herbert G. Muskett who had appeared for the police in the action against Lawrence's novel *The Rainbow* in 1915. Now, fourteen years later, Muskett fired off the charge that Lawrence's paintings were 'gross, coarse, hideous, unlovely, and obscene'.[73]

The case was adjourned till August, but the spectre of another public burning was too much for Lawrence, and he advised Dorothy Warren not to fight a protracted legal battle but to accept any compromise. 'I want you to get my pictures back', he wrote to her. 'If you have to promise never to show them again in England, I do not care.'[74] Stephensen had his own reasons to be angry with Warren, for snubbing him and Goldston, and also for allowing the police to seize one of the expensive vellum copies of the book. He wrote, or at least drafted, a letter to Lawrence, accusing Warren of greed and stupidity, and warning him not to trust her.[75]

Stephensen had expected police to raid the Mandrake Press, and he was prepared to 'make a straightforward defence' against any prosecution, over either the paintings book or the unexpurgated *Pansies* which had just been released bearing Stephensen's name and address. Both volumes, however, bore the precautionary label 'Privately Printed for subscribers only'. 'I'm ready for 'em', Stephensen wrote to Lawrence, 'without either heroics or hysteria. This fight for free expression has to be fought all over again since those blackguardly little police pimps and spies have goose-stepped into action'. Stephensen assured Lawrence that he and Goldston were not worried. 'As Goldston says, they can fine us or perhaps lock us up, but they can't put us in the family way!'[76]

At the hearing on 8 August the octogenarian magistrate agreed to a suggestion from Lawrence's solicitors that no further action be taken if the gallery returned the offensive paintings to Lawrence and agreed not to exhibit them further. The Mandrake books, including the £50 vellum copy, were destroyed. The whole episode left Lawrence 'depressed and nauseated', but the publicity gave Stephensen's Mandrake Press a sensational start.[77]

The same month Lawrence's exhibition was raided, the last issue of the *London Aphrodite* appeared, with a long essay by Stephensen on Bakunin.

Stephensen clearly identified himself with the Russian anarchist, and his essay began: 'Only one man has lived dangerously—Michael Bakunin'. He went on to criticize the British Communist Party for putting the 'soft pedal on anti-god propaganda', and D. H. Lawrence for 'muddled' and 'fake' revolutionism. The 'quasi-revolutionary thesis' of *Lady Chatterley's Lover*, Stephensen said, was mistaken both in its targets and methods, using 'sexual-social humiliation' against a gentry which had already relinquished real power to the capitalists. Communism would remain the working-class movement of the twentieth century, but when the whole world was a 'federation of working-class states', anarchism—the destruction of state power—would become 'practical revolutionary politics'. Providing a key to his own defiant spirit, Stephensen characterized the true revolutionary as possessing that 'uncompromising pugnacity in rebelliousness which marks Satan for our respect'.[78]

The devil, the anti-Christ, the eternal rebel—these formed Stephensen's unholy trinity. And he was not the only one to express respect for Satan that summer. The day his paintings book was ready, Lawrence had written to Frieda's sister in Germany: 'Yes, I am all for Lucifer, who is really the Morning Star. The real principle of Evil is not anti-Christ or anti-Jehovah, but anti-life'.[79]

About this time a man who not only admired Satan but also practised black magic approached Stephensen with a publishing proposal which more than rivalled Lawrence's paintings for daring and devilry. Stephensen took him up with characteristic enthusiasm, but the magician proved to be as dangerous to the future of the fledgeling Mandrake Press as Lawrence had been beneficial.

6

Mandrake, Magic and Depression

In the early summer of 1929 the omens were all promising for Stephensen and the new Mandrake Press. The company's first publication, *The Paintings of D. H. Lawrence*, straight away provided a couple of thousand pounds profit, and this enabled Stephensen and Goldston to expand their future list with some confidence. Between June and August contracts were signed for about twenty new titles.[1] Goldston handled all the financial dealings of the press, injecting some extra capital himself when necessary, and Stephensen was paid a weekly salary to manage the literary and production side.

Stephensen's experience with the Fanfrolico Press was reflected in the Mandrake's early list, which included a reprint of the first English edition of Boccaccio's *Amorous Fiammetta* and an anthology of writing about drunkards. The latter had been lovingly collected by a connoisseur of booze, Philip Heseltine, and it was published under the transparent pseudonym 'Rab Noolas' ('Saloon Bar' seen from the inside).

However, Stephensen wanted to balance such reprints and 'scholarly' works with contemporary fiction. The first three titles in the Mandrake Booklets series were published soon after the Lawrence paintings, and attempted to combine fine book production with an inexpensive format, appealing to the general market as well as to collectors. The dozen and more titles in this series were printed on vellum and attractively bound, yet sold for only 3s 6d each. All were produced by the Crypt House Press in a rather unusual, small squarish format with large type, so that a novella or several short stories filled over a hundred pages.

Stephensen's own *Bushwhackers* helped to launch these booklets, along with Rhys Davies's sensual and horrific story set in a Welsh mining community, *A Bed of Feathers*, and O'Flaherty's sharply satirical *A Tourist's Guide to Ireland*. Other literary friends, including Jack McLaren, Thomas Burke and Edgell Rickword, contributed stories to the series. Lawrence had promised one also, but this never materialized, and Jack Lindsay wrote some which did not appear either.[2] Although the booklets were mostly fiction—and mostly stories of violence and death—there was a sprinkling of what Stephensen described in the first Mandrake catalogue as *belles lettres*: some Dostoevsky letters translated by Lawrence's friend Koteliansky, an essay on New York by W. J. Turner, and translations from Gaelic tales by the Hon. Ruaraidh Erskine of Marr. The London *Observer* praised the series as beautiful and original, presenting a range of work 'remarkable in its catholicity'.[3]

Without Norman Lindsay's philosophy and artwork, and indeed without Jack Lindsay, Stephensen was now free to indulge his own ideas and entrepreneurial flair. What he sought was a new focus for the Mandrake Press. There was Lawrence, of course, who had provided the press's initial impetus, but he was already enmeshed in his own complex network of publishers and agents, both official and unofficial, and his health had deteriorated to such an extent that he was resorting to desperate 'cures' of arsenic and phosphorus. During the last summer of the 1920s Stephensen met the other rebel of English fiction, James Joyce, but there was even less chance of Joyce's attachment to the Mandrake Press. He had already spent several years on the project which did not appear until 1939 as *Finnegans Wake*.

Early in the summer of 1929 a gentleman walked into Stephensen's Museum Street office followed by an assistant carrying a great stack of unpublished typescripts. This was Aleister Crowley, or, as he had been baptized, Edward Alexander Crowley.[4] In his mid-fifties, Crowley was thick-set, with head shaven smooth as an egg, some said so that it resembled an enormous penis. This was appropriate, for Crowley was known to the reading public of the Sunday newspapers as the 'wickedest man in the world'.[5] He wore a musk-like scent of his own manufacture, but no underclothing since he regarded sweat as the physical basis for the 'magnetism of men and women'.[6]

Crowley was a notorious rogue and adventurer, whose life and personality had an irresistible appeal for Stephensen. Both men were by temperament Nietzschean anarchists, brashly self-confident, fiercely anti-Christian and anti-bourgeois. They shared a scorn for sexual repression, but this did not stop them exploiting images of virile masculinity and authority. Crowley considered women to be animals 'with no consciousness beyond sex', and he approved of men who were strong enough to use women as 'slaves and playthings'.[7] His message was self-control, but he could not resist controlling others.

Crowley's parents had been strict Plymouth Brethren, and his upbringing had given him not only a fascination with exotic cults and rituals, but also such a loathing for Victorian Biblical morality that he became a sex crusading satanist. He signed his name with an exaggerated phallic 'A', and adopted the identity of the beast of Revelation, with the magical number 666. Crowley was also very much in the mould of an 1890s dandy, affecting outrageous clothes and living extravagantly. As part of this style, he issued numerous privately printed volumes of his Swinburnian verse. His conceit was inseparable from an aggressive, sardonic wit. In his *Confessions*, he judged himself and Shakespeare to be England's 'two greatest poets', and described his first wife's second husband as an 'eminent masochist'.[8] As with Lawrence, his books were regularly seized by customs officials for obscenity.

Crowley's fantasies were aristocratic as well as sexual, and among his aliases were the self-proclaimed titles Lord Boleskine, Count Vladimir Svareff, Prince Chio Khan, and Alastor de Kerval. He had used part of his inheritance to purchase Boleskine Manor where he had lived for a short period in feudal splendour by the shore of Loch Ness in Scotland, practising 'magick' as well as elaborate practical jokes. Somerset Maugham, who based his early novel *The Magician* (1908) on Crowley, described the trick Crowley had of focusing his eyes so they 'seemed to look behind you'. In Maugham's opinion, Crowley was 'a fake, but not entirely a fake'.[9]

He had retained his wicked sense of humour, but by the 1920s his money had mostly run out and he was living on his wits and on the largess of his followers. After being deported from Italy and then France, he had washed up again in England, looking for a publisher for all the literary and 'magickal' works he could no longer afford to sponsor himself. Indeed, he had sold so few copies of his privately printed books that, just before his expulsion from France, he had conceived the idea of faking his own suicide to enhance the value of his stocks.[10]

When he stumbled on the Mandrake Press about June 1929, he greeted Stephensen with the sacred injunction: 'Do what thou wilt shall be the whole of the law'. Crowley claimed this had been dictated to him in Cairo in 1904 by his guardian spirit, but it was lifted from Rabelais, as was the name of his magical law, *thelema*—the Greek for 'will', and the name of Rabelais' fantastical abbey by the Loire.[11] Crowley's magical formulations combined Jewish, Egyptian and other occult mythology with eastern techniques of yoga and meditation, but sex acts were his main medium for mystical experience, referred to always as 'sex magic'.

The first contract Stephensen signed with Crowley, late in June 1929, was for a volume of short stories for the Mandrake Booklets series. A month later, after the police raid on the Lawrence exhibition, Stephensen arranged contracts for a further four Crowley titles, including the novel, *Moonchild*, and his multi-volume *Confessions*. Crowley had walked in, with his theories of sexual liberation, just at the time when Stephensen was most enthusiastically involved in the crusade against repressive censorship. So Stephensen eagerly adopted him as the Mandrake Press's centrepiece. Crowley even had enough of his own paintings to promise another controversial exhibition.

Having thus found a willing publisher, Crowley left for Germany in August to marry his most recent 'scarlet woman', Marie de Miramar of Nicaragua, returning with her to London. Jack Lindsay met them a few times in Goldston's shop:

> She was a fairly well-blown woman, oozing a helpless sexuality from every seam of her smartly cut suit, with shapely legs crossed and uncrossed, and keeping all the while a sharp glittering gaze on her swarthy and unsavoury husband... Marie spoke in various languages,

including English, which I could not understand, and [Crowley] listened attentively like a well-behaved poodle, giving an impression of uxorious dependence.[12]

Their marriage, however, lasted barely a year, which was also the span of Crowley's stormy relationship with the Mandrake Press. Although his grandiose and unscrupulous plans for self-promotion eventually drained the life blood from the Mandrake Press, it was a nice point as to who exploited whom in the Crowley-Stephensen association. They were both on the make, and neither was a novice at business dealing. Crowley arranged for a confidential credit report on the Mandrake Press before entrusting the company with his life's work.[13]

Stephensen's press had acquired a reputation for fearless, if foolish, publishing. D. H. Lawrence recommended the Mandrake to other writers, while warning Rhys Davies that its future was uncertain:

> It seems to me, that if you catch them on the rise of the wave, the Mandrake ought to serve your purpose very well. They have aroused a certain interest—and there is a big public waiting to get anything which they think is not orthodox ... And they may have a run of success—I would risk them if I were you. But I don't think they'll have a long run. Stephensen is another sort of mushroom—he grows too fast. And the big publishers, after a while, will quash them.[14]

Lawrence also warned Stephensen, with uncharacteristic restraint, of the danger of sinking the new press with too much Crowley:

> I want to write you one day about your Mandrake list. I'm a bit sorry you've got Aleister Crowley at such heavy tonnage, I feel his day is rather over. You need to be selective, not in too big a hurry with the Mandrake books, to build the thing up. You've got a good thing there, but I'm afraid you'll overload it.[15]

There was more to the Mandrake list, however, than Aleister Crowley. During the summer of 1929, with little in the way of staff, Stephensen saw through the press a number of new titles, and even installed and fed Liam O'Flaherty so he could complete a war novel Stephensen had commissioned. Stephensen hoped to capitalize on the controversy aroused by novels like *All Quiet on the Western Front*, and O'Flaherty's effort, *The Return of the Brute*, was described by the TLS as the most 'savage and hideous' war novel to appear in either England or Germany.[16] Subsequent critics of O'Flaherty's work have also objected to the novel's violence, yet *The Return of the Brute* was a pioneer in its own way, an anti-war story in which no shred of heroic sentiment was allowed to obscure its message of horror.[17]

While O'Flaherty was staying with Stephensen, James Joyce turned up at the Mandrake office to recommend the publication of Stuart Gilbert's translation of *Les Lauriers Sont Coupés* (1887), by the French symbolist writer Edouard Dujardin. It had been Dujardin's novel, with its *monologue intérieur*, which 'had stimulated [Joyce] to make the experiment of expanding a chapter of *Dubliners* into a complete book',[18] the result being

Ulysses. Joyce's enthusiasm for *Les Lauriers Sont Coupés* had brought about its republication in France in 1924, and Stephensen agreed to publish the English translation, though the Mandrake Press had withered away before it was printed.[19]

Stephensen and O'Flaherty also accompanied Joyce to Stonehenge, though their memories of the episode varied. Stephensen's version was that he drove Joyce—almost blind, and wearing three pairs of glasses—down to Stonehenge along with Mrs Joyce and their daughter. Joyce groped his way around, bringing his face up very close to the stones, saying: 'At least I've felt Stonehenge'.[20] O'Flaherty, on the other hand, made no mention of Mrs Joyce or the daughter. He claimed that a severe thunderstorm struck before they reached Stonehenge, and Joyce 'became hysterical and frightened by the thunder and lightning'.[21] Whichever anecdote was the more credible, neither O'Flaherty nor Stephensen had much taste for the literary experimentation in which Joyce was so absorbed, O'Flaherty describing his compatriot as 'quite dotty'.[22]

Inky still met Jack Lindsay for an occasional pint at their old pub, the Plough Inn, though their interests were diverging. Jack and Elza had taken a Georgian house at Hampstead, and he was now hand-printing the Fanfrolico books on his own press in the basement, with the assistance of a qualified printer. Brian and Olga Penton shared the house but soon moved out because of friction with Elza. When Jack's brother Philip arrived from Australia, he too moved in and helped with the printing and publishing work until the inevitable clash with Elza. Of the nine or ten titles produced on the Fanfrolico hand press, most were classical or Elizabethan reprints and translations. However, with the exception of *The Complete Poems of Catullus*, they were slim volumes, and the Fanfrolico Press was nearing the end of the road.[23]

Like his brother, Philip Lindsay was ambitious to make a name in London literary circles, and he frequented the Plough Inn where Stephensen and O'Flaherty regularly held court. Lindsay was particularly in awe of the Irishman whom he described as 'very vital, with the same Scandinavian look as Inky'. Although Stephensen always greeted the younger Lindsay with exuberant *bonhomie*, he would not accept any of Lindsay's work for the Mandrake Press, rejecting even the novel based on Stephensen himself.[24] Still basking in the romantic afterglow of his communist exploits, Stephensen now identified more with rogues and anarchists like Bakunin, as Philip Lindsay vividly recalled in his autobiography:

> In ... autumn, 1929, Inky was a volatile Communist, with spasms of anarchism, during which he would drink noisily to the memory of the great Bakunin, while he boasted of donnish cabals at Oxford, due to his socially heretical soap-box speeches ...
> But whatever faith Inky might accept he would accept it with such zealous excitement that it would temporarily blind him to everything else. Such was his nature, such was his charm. You heard him approaching a pub many, many minutes before he flung wide the door

and entered bellowing for drinks all round. Then would there be back-slapping, laughter, excitement that seemed to tinkle thrillingly along the very glasses on the shelves. He stirred a pub to life. Tall, fair, handsome, noisy, generous, but a trifle deaf, he was, in manner and appearance, the typical Queenslander, the Cornstalk from Banana-land, a turbulent, merry fellow, whom no one could dislike, although there were moments of despair while I sat in his office, hugging my disdained MSS., when, bitterly, I wondered if I really did like the fellow. But I had only to meet him again, to hear his loud, jovial voice, his infectious laughter, to feel the clout of his palm on my back, to know again that I was helpless, captured by his charm.[25]

The autumn of 1929, however, also brought crises which threatened Stephensen's promising career as a publisher. Towards the end of October the Wall Street crash began a chain reaction of events which made the work of specialist small presses like the Fanfrolico and Mandrake increasingly difficult. More ominous in the short term, though, was Aleister Crowley who hovered about the Mandrake Press like a vampire, amusing Stephensen but not his publishing partner Goldston. 'We folded up through lack of capital', Stephensen later recalled, 'but also because A. C. [Crowley] put the Basilisk Eye on my unfortunate co-director, "Teddy" Goldston and frightened hell out of him through sheer deviltry'. Stephensen said Goldston was an orthodox Jew and a Mason: 'I believe that the learned Dr. Cecil Roth (one of whose books we published) and several booksellers who were freemasons approached Goldston and warned him of an awful fate that would be his if he continued to be associated with that BAD MAN, THAT WICKED WICKED A.C.'[26]

This retrospective assessment absolved Stephensen of responsibility, and probably exaggerated Goldston's fear of being hexed. It was more likely that, after the initial success of the Lawrence paintings book, subsequent Mandrake titles did not bring in sufficient cash to sustain the ambitious programme Stephensen had launched. Goldston had been increasingly unhappy with Stephensen's handling of the press, though Stephensen himself voiced complaints about his partner's 'false economies' in sales and advertising.[27] After several months of dealing with Crowley, Goldston had realized what a financial liability and a pest he was. It was significant that, just after a 'General Agreement' was signed with Crowley in late October 1929, Goldston got cold feet about publishing, cut off Stephensen's salary, and temporarily closed the Mandrake office in Museum Street.

There was now nothing for Stephensen to do but retire, not so gracefully, to his 'weekend' house in Kent. His disgruntled letter to D. H. Lawrence on 31 October hinted at the crisis point the Mandrake had reached:

> I am going on a holiday from office work for the three winter months; retire to the country, and see whether anything happens to me in the way of writing a book. (Goldston of course will keep on selling the Mandrake books, and I shall come up to the office when necessary).

But I am getting heartily sick and tired of this murky London. I have been brought up in the sunlight. When Spring occurs again, I suppose the Mandrake will put forth new shoots.[28]

Never slow to interpret the signs, Lawrence wrote to Koteliansky that the Mandrake was 'as good as dead'.[29]

The book Stephensen referred to was his autobiographical novel 'Clean Earth', of which there remain only some uncompleted drafts.[30] The story traced Stephensen's experiences since leaving Australia, and the climax was provided by his communist trouble at Oxford. Winifred was 'dainty little Rosalie England', and Stephensen used fictional licence to suggest a lesbian relationship between Rosalie and her Chelsea flatmate Hilda, described as 'almost a man' and eager for Rosalie's 'wife-like kiss'. Such a relationship was no doubt suggested by Radclyffe Hall's novel *Well of Loneliness*, and may have been developed from the short story Stephensen had read to Lawrence at Bandol about 'an older woman leading a beautiful young woman astray'.[31]

While attempting to draft the novel, Stephensen was much distracted by Aleister Crowley. With his wife, and his youthful American secretary Israel Regardie, Crowley moved in virtually next door to Stephensen in the village of Knockholt, Kent. They lived in a short terrace of double-storey houses, Crowley's separated from Stephensen's by a respectable household of elderly spinsters. Inky talked at length with Crowley, played chess with him, and rummaged through his 'room full' of publications, press cuttings and manuscripts in order to compile a book about him.[32]

The result was *The Legend of Aleister Crowley*—'A Study of the Documentary Evidence Relating to a Campaign of Personal Vilification Unparalleled in Literary History'. It carried on the pamphleteering crusade Stephensen had been waging for more than a year over D. H. Lawrence and Norman Lindsay, Radclyffe Hall and Nora James. There was even an 'Epistle Dedicatory to James Douglas', editor of the *Sunday Express*, this time attacking him for using 'the dirty weapons of malice and innuendo'. However, Stephensen's prefatory broadside against Douglas lacked the wit of his earlier lampoons, and was suppressed by the printer as libellous before *The Legend of Aleister Crowley* finally appeared about mid-1930.[33]

At Knockholt, Crowley lent Stephensen his secretary, Regardie, who operated a stenotype, a shorthand typewriter which extruded a long tape. Stephensen dictated the *Legend* to Regardie who was well acquainted with Crowleyana, having been the beast's secretary in Paris. In the *Legend* Stephensen began by describing Crowley as 'a dangerously good poet both in his poetry and in his life'. With his own skill as a polemicist, Stephensen was able to applaud Crowley's 'excellent polemical style' as well as the 'vehemence of his wit', but there was a firm undercurrent of criticism. Stephensen accused Crowley of 'ninetyish romantic bravado' and of 'asking for notoriety' by baiting the philistines. He also chided Crowley for 'innocence or carelessness of results'—criticisms which applied with equal accuracy to Stephensen himself.[34]

6 Mandrake, Magic and Depression

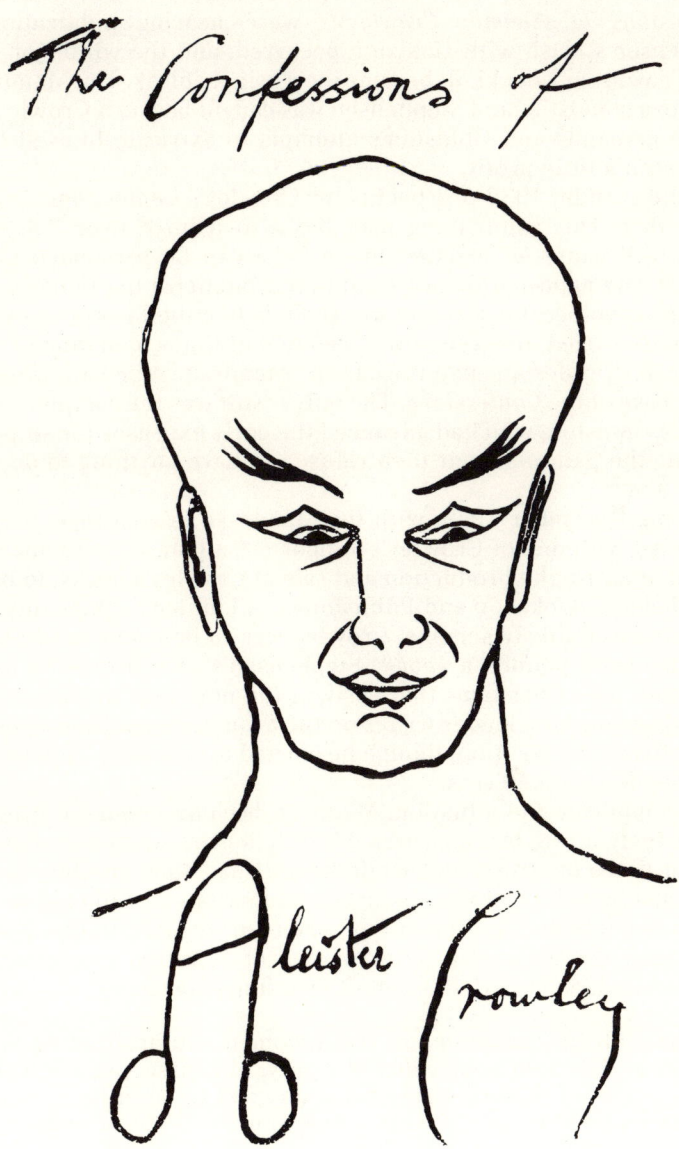

Crowley's cover design for his *Confessions*: note the phallic 'A', and the 'C' suggesting female genitalia

The first two volumes of Crowley's planned six-volume *Spirit of Solitude: An Autohagiography* (which Stephensen 'Re-Antichristened' *The Confessions of Aleister Crowley*)[35] were nearing publication when Stephensen's clash with Goldston occurred, and the winter of 1929–30 with Crowley at Knockholt became increasingly bleak. The Mandrake had come to a standstill, and Stephensen was caught between Crowley's extravagant demands and Goldston's attempts to extricate himself from the press with a little profit.

In the autumn 1929 prospectus for Crowley's *Confessions* Stephensen wrote that 'This astonishing man has also painted over 200 canvases which will cause an artistic furore if he can be persuaded to exhibit them'.[36] The expected furore would then publicize the *Confessions*, and perhaps even become a *succès de scandale* like the Lawrence exhibition. Stephensen tried unsuccessfully a couple of times to arrange a showing of Crowley's gruesome paintings in the Mandrake office, to coincide with the release of the *Confessions*. The only result was the complete estrangement of Goldston, who had advanced the early expenses for shipping and framing the paintings, but then refused to have anything to do with the exhibition.[37]

During December 1929, with the Mandrake in abeyance, Stephensen discussed with one of Crowley's supporters a plan for a financial syndicate to organize the production and sale of Crowley's books, to be named the 'Thelema Bookshop and Publishing Co. Limited'. Under this comprehensive and unlikely scheme, Crowley was to be guaranteed an income of a thousand pounds a year.[38] Stephensen's own prospects looked so uncertain over Christmas that early in the new year he answered a job advertisement for a leader writer on the *Evening News*. He may even have been offered the position, though he elected to stay with Crowley and the stranded Mandrake Press.[39]

To complicate the situation, Winifred became pregnant again, at the age of forty-three, but miscarried.[40] Stephensen was never easy to live with at times of stress, and while he still had some doubts about their relationship, Winifred was disturbed and irritated by his casual liaisons with other women. A scrap of typescript surviving from this period may have been the draft of a letter or one of Winifred's occasional diary entries in which she tried to let off emotional steam:

> I know all the symptoms of fresh women you are finding attractive, because they feed your colossal vanity, of course you are brilliant, of course lots of women would find you good to be in love with, do you think I'd love you if you were a fool, you are a fool in some ways.
> ... the reason you have done a lot is my being at your side, you'd have been a drunken sot hanging around the Plough now but for my constant opposition to the crowd you thought so wonderful, my loving care of you every weekend...[41]

Although the Mandrake Press was out of action over winter, Stephensen published under his own name the text of a Crowley lecture prepared

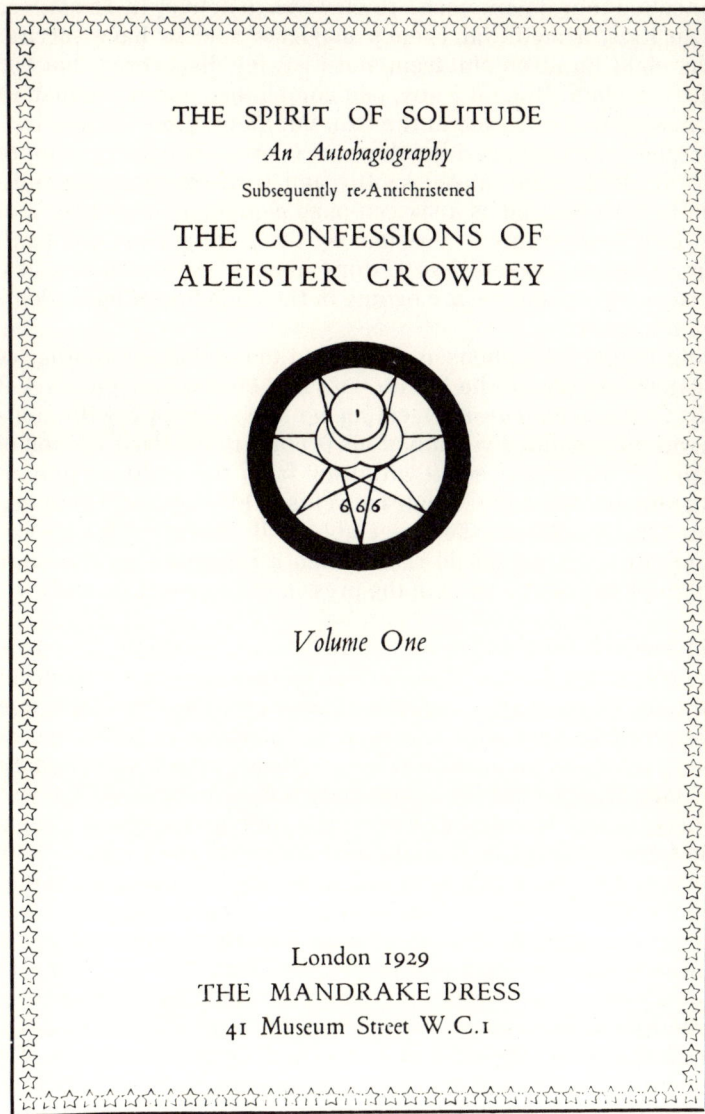

More phallic magic, this time on the title page design

for the Oxford University Poetry Society in January 1930. Threats of disciplinary action against the society were rumoured, and the lecture was cancelled four days before Crowley was to deliver it. The subject was Gilles de Rais, a medieval French magician said to have sacrificed as many as eight hundred children, and Crowley discovered that Oxford's Catholic Chaplain, Ronald Knox, had complained about the planned lecture. Crowley was outraged at the ban, but Stephensen knew what to do. Encouraged by his own residual bitterness over his political suppression at Oxford, Stephensen moved swiftly and with considerable relish. He had the lecture printed as a sixteen-page pamphlet 'at an hour's notice', as the back cover proudly boasted, by the Botolph, his old Fanfrolico printers. Then he travelled to Oxford himself with a thousand copies which were put on sale next morning in the High Street by students with sandwich boards.[42]

During January, Stephensen contracted to publish yet another censorship protest and one of the Mandrake's last books: Lawrence's *A Propos of Lady Chatterley's Lover*. Deciding he was unhappy with the essay, which was an expanded version of his preface to the Paris edition of *Lady Chatterley*, Lawrence tried to withdraw from the contract only a week after signing it. When the Mandrake refused his request, Lawrence commented: 'Oh, that Mandrake—vegetable of ill omen!'[43] This was a reference to Crowley's bad magic rather than a reflection on the Mandrake itself, though the deaths of both the press and Lawrence himself were not far off.

An investor or company promoter by the name of Major Thynne formed an alliance with Crowley's supporters to take over the Mandrake as a limited liability company, Mandrake Press Ltd. The Crowley supporters were induced to part with a couple of thousand pounds, and several hundred pounds were obtained from a Harley Street psychoanalyst, Dr Grace Pailthorpe, whose Freudian study *What We Put in Prison* was to be published by the Mandrake. Under the new arrangement Stephensen became for a few months the editorial manager, and in May 1930 Mandrake Press Ltd issued its first and only major catalogue, announcing twenty new titles including the Dujardin translation suggested by Joyce, and an edition of the *Revelation of Saint John the Divine* with a foreword written by D. H. Lawrence just before his death. These and most of the other new titles never appeared under the Mandrake imprint.[44]

Stephensen's business dealings had become a series of intrigues, claims and counter-claims, threatened and actual legal proceedings. Crowley was not only suing the old Mandrake partnership but also trying to divert £500 from the new company's capital to purchase yet another publisher, the Aquila Press.[45] These machinations exasperated Stephensen and he told Crowley to keep out of the Mandrake office and not 'extort' money before it was 'earned by good honest royalties':

> I want absolute *carte blanche* for Mandrake Press Ltd to go ahead publishing your work, as and how I think fit, in consultation with

Thynne and Yorke. I want you to regard Mandrake Press Ltd solely as your publishers, and not to prejudice the purely commercial side of that purely publishing concern with any of your fits and starts, Thelemite politics, earthquakes, and the other distracting phenomena of art and nature, such as pin pricks, dogmatism, human chess, brawls, faux pas, bravado and braggadocio, pure bluff, brainwaves, and dementia precox, which tend to accompany your too personal intrusion into the world of practical affairs.[46]

This was typical of their bantering, quarrelsome but essentially good-humoured relationship. Crowley had scribbled off to Inky at Easter: 'I wrote you at great length ... Entrusted letter to thief. Suppose it lost. Main points: (1) I love you dearly. (2) You impress people as unreliable. (3) You pub-loaf. Cut it out ...' In another letter Crowley was more specific: 'Pub loafing with Liam [O'Flaherty]—the very wombats would protest!' Stephensen and Crowley were at least honest about each other's shortcomings, if not about their own. Crowley warned him: 'You shouldn't wave the axe you want to grind'. Invariably, the wickedest man in the world ended his letters to his Australian friend with the affectionate 'Dear Winifred love to you'.[47]

This correspondence gives a fleeting image of the human Aleister Crowley beneath the bravado and braggadocio. It is interesting that Stephensen's close friend Robert Hall found a similar duality in Inky: 'We got on much better by ourselves than when he was carried away by company and wanted to impress or outdo them'.[48]

During the summer of 1930 Stephensen had a disagreement with Thynne and possibly with other Mandrake directors. Hall remembered the outcome: '[Stephensen] became convinced that the new men were not paying him enough, and could not get on without him. He therefore made the curious decision to stay away from the office until they protested and then give them his terms for a return'.[49] This 'silent' resignation was a gesture of frustration as much as wounded pride. The board, however, called Stephensen's bluff and crossed his name off the company letterhead, installing as manager W. L. Hanchant who was then editing a collection of Victorian ballads and broadsides for the press. The company limped along towards the autumn and failed to publish any more books, at least one title being remaindered before publication.

Having used Mandrake capital for his own purposes, Crowley had now exhausted his publishing opportunities in London. The third volume of his *Confessions* reached proof stage at the Mandrake Press but was not printed. Crowley returned to Germany where he dropped Marie and picked up a new scarlet woman, a nineteen-year-old artist, taking her to Portugal in September. On a wild piece of coastline, appropriately named *Boca do Inferno* ('Hell's Mouth'), Crowley finally staged the fake suicide he had been contemplating for some time. The new scarlet woman had abandoned him, so he addressed his 'suicide' note to her, and a very pretty example of his wit it was too. 'I cannot live without you', he wrote, in mock desperation. 'The other "Boca do Inferno" will get me—it will not be as hot as yours!' Crowley thoughtfully weighted the note with a cigarette lighter so it would not be blown away, and the news of his mysterious death was published in Portugal, France and England before he appeared at an exhibition of his paintings in Berlin, shamelessly resurrected and still up to his old tricks.[50]

Meanwhile, Stephensen had retreated further from the Mandrake and further from the metropolis to a quiet village in Kent. Early in the summer of 1930 he and Winifred had taken a lease on Ailsa Lodge, a three-storey house on an acre of land near the tiny village of Toys Hill. They were almost at the crest of the North Downs, and on a clear day had a splendid view right across the weald of Kent to the coast. The village had a store and a post office, and the inevitable local pub, The Tally Ho, in which Stephensen spent 'many happy hours'.[51] There were no other amenities, however, and it was necessary for someone in the household, usually Winifred's son Jack, to walk down and bring back drinking water from the gable-roofed village well. As there was no sanitary service either, Inky enlisted his regular visitors Robert Hall, Liam O'Flaherty and the artist Lionel Ellis to help dig a deep pit on the far boundary which adjoined the local Anglican hall. As they tossed up the earth, the crew sang lusty shanties with lines like:

> Oh my god it's bloody cold in the bloody rigging,
> Sister Susy's getting old, all along of frigging.

It was not long before an embarrassed parson called at the house and drew their attention to the hall's lack of sound-proofing.[52]

On another occasion O'Flaherty and Ellis arrived back from a drinking spree at a nearby village carrying a church noticeboard which they had souvenired on their noisy journey home. A constable called next day on his bicycle to say he had traced the procession of thieves as far as Ailsa Lodge. There was an awkward standoff until, at Winifred's whispered suggestion, Stephensen placed five shillings on the table. At an appropriate moment, the money disappeared. 'Ah, well, I don't suppose I'll be able to solve this after all', the constable observed, and pedalled away on his bicycle.[53]

O'Flaherty stayed at Toys Hill with the Stephensens while he began work on a book about his recent trip to Russia. He later recalled that his friend Inky had incited him to write a 'thoroughly propagandist book' for the Mandrake Press about the Soviet state, but that from the first page the book had become 'maliciously satirical'.[54] O'Flaherty not only mocked the Russian experiment but also revealed a definite anti-Semitism, characterizing Jews as 'clever little tricksters' with 'nefarious habits' and comparing them unfavourably with 'that glorious race', the Vikings.[55] In his later autobiography *Shame the Devil* (1934), however, O'Flaherty renounced the 'criminal mockery' of his flippant account of Russia, describing the country as 'that workshop, where the civilization of the future is being hammered out by the gigantic labour of heroic millions'. In the light of Nazi excesses, O'Flaherty was prepared to modify his

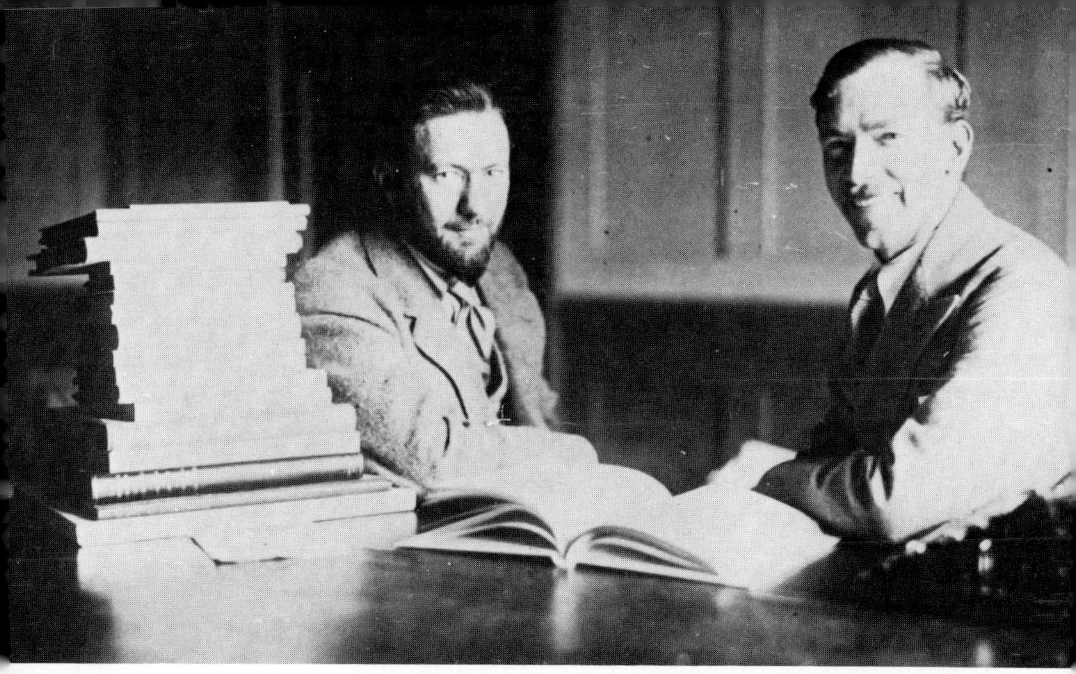

Jack Lindsay (left) and Stephensen beside a stack of their publications at the Fanfrolico office, Bloomsbury Square, London, May 1928

THE ANTICHRIST OF NIETZSCHE

A NEW VERSION IN ENGLISH BY P. R. STEPHENSEN

WITH ILLUSTRATIONS BY NORMAN LINDSAY

THE FANFROLICO PRESS LONDON

"POLLICE VERSO"

HERE ENDS THE ANTICHRIST OF FRIEDRICH NIETZSCHE TRANSLATED BY P. R. STEPHENSEN AND ILLUSTRATED WITH DRAWINGS BY NORMAN LINDSAY NOW PUBLISHED BY THE FANFROLICO PRESS IN LONDON FORTY YEARS AFTER NIETZSCHE COMPLETED THE WORK

The Book was Printed in Poliphilus Type upon Arnold's Handmade Paper at the Botolph Printing Works in Gate Street Kingsway London under the Supervision of William Dieper and the Plates were Engraved by Alexander & Sons the Book Bound by Kelly & Sons Typography and Production Arranged by Jack Lindsay and P. R. Stephensen

Dies Buch gehort den Wenigsten

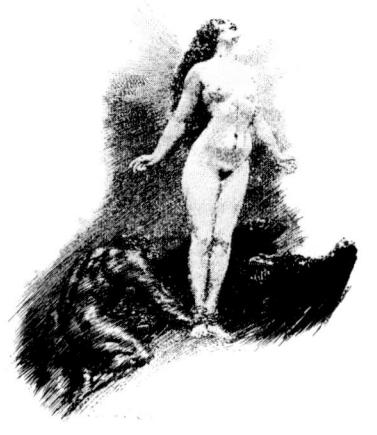

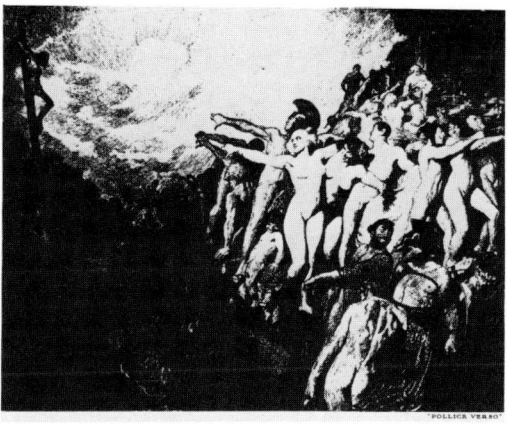

The title page and the last page of The Antichrist of Nietzsche, *translated by Stephensen*

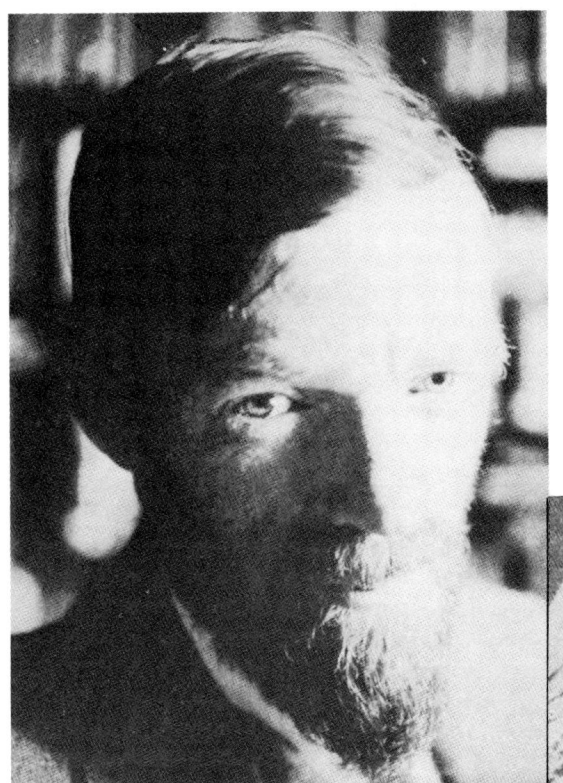

D. H. Lawrence in Florence in 1928 (from a photograph taken by Robert H. Davis, reproduced by courtesy of the Davart Company, New York)

This photograph, showing a clay bust of Lawrence sculptured early in 1930, was used by Stephensen as the frontispiece to his secret London edition of Lady Chatterley's Lover

Stephensen in 1929

Aleister Crowley about 1929 (from The Confessions of Aleister Crowley, Mandrake Press, 1929)

The row houses in Knockholt, Kent, where Stephensen lived in 1929 alongside Crowley and his entourage

Ailsa Lodge, Toys Hill, Kent, where Stephensen lived from 1930 to 1932

comments on Jews also, writing that 'a Germany governed by Jews might be a lesser danger to human happiness than a Germany governed by Prussians'.[56] He never renounced Irish nationalism and independence, however, and during World War II lived in America where he spoke in defence of Irish neutrality, a cause curiously parallel to that which Stephensen came to espouse.

During the summer and autumn of 1930, at Toys Hill, after abandoning the Mandrake Press, Stephensen concocted several outlandish and improbable publishing schemes. Perhaps following the example of Jack Lindsay's hand press, he pencilled a prospectus for a 'Toys Hill Bible', to be printed on a private press at the house, using 'moveable wooden type especially designed for the purpose by Lionel Ellis'. Working with just enough type to compose two pages at a time, Stephensen and his stepson planned to complete the 2000-page Bible in three years.[57] This extraordinary and absurd plan was probably dreamed up by Inky and Ellis over a few drinks but it was an indication of Stephensen's lack of direction at this time.

Equally unlikely was his idea for a 'hard-hitting weekly critical paper', to be called *The Voice* or *The Free Voice*. Since the *London Aphrodite*, in fact ever since his first taste of editorial power with the University of Queensland magazine, *Galmahra*, Stephensen had wanted a paper or magazine of his own. It was a desire which persisted right through the 1930s, with ultimately disastrous consequences. In July 1930 he asked an Australian journalist visiting London if he knew of any 'wealthy Australians' to finance *The Voice*: 'Something along the [*Bulletin*] lines, with plenty of punch to it, would go over big here'. All that was needed was a backer with 'plenty of money and a sense of fun'. It would be no trouble at all, Stephensen thought, to 'rake up a couple of dozen talented exiles' to supply the new London weekly with material.[58]

O'Flaherty, now roaming Brittany, sent him £20 to help start the paper, and other friends may have contributed small amounts, but no wealthy philanthropist appeared, except in Stephensen's imagination. It was, after all, the time of the Great Depression. A printer, however, quoted for fifty thousand copies of *The Voice*, and made up a couple of sample issues, dated 3 and 10 October 1930.[59] With features such as 'The Round of Society' by 'Peeping Tom', 'The Drama' by 'The Scene Shifter', and 'Our Gambling Page' by 'The Sucker', *The Voice* aimed at sharp and witty iconoclasm such as D. H. Lawrence had suggested in 1929 with his idea for a magazine called 'Squib'.[60]

Stephensen's contributions to the sample issues of *The Voice* included a satirical chess column and a serious if jaundiced critique of the book trade. He portrayed the struggling publisher as both a selfless visionary and a 'mug', while the parasitic bookseller was the epitome of 'Sloth, ignorance, insolence and avarice'. Such a splenetic outburst may have been aimed at his former partner, the bookseller Goldston, and Stephensen's publishing experiences in London accounted for the article's rather misanthropic and melancholy tone. *The Voice* needed more dispassion and wit than this if it was to criticize the contemporary scene 'without fear or phobia', as Stephensen intended it should. In the absence of capital as well as inspiration, *The Voice* was never heard of again.

The autumn of 1930 saw not only the abortive magazine plan but also the final demise of the Mandrake Press. Dissatisfied creditors were pressing for payment, and in October Stephensen was still arguing with Major Thynne, the Mandrake 'chairman of directors', about transfers of worthless shares and about money Thynne said Stephensen owed him. But Stephensen could pay neither his nor the Mandrake's debts. Finally, towards the end of November, a shareholders' meeting was held to voluntarily wind up the company's affairs. When Stephensen asked for a financial statement he was informed that more than £2000 was owed to printers and other creditors, with almost £4000 worth of stock still unsold. The next day Thynne dropped Stephensen a note wishing him luck: 'When one looks at this [Mandrake] catalogue and thinks of all it means then the present position is a tragedy'.[61]

According to the later accounts of both Crowley and Stephensen, Thynne was a share hustler who pocketed Mandrake capital.[62] In Crowley's case, this undoubtedly explained away his own pocketing of Mandrake funds, but in Stephensen's it was also a way of rationalizing the ultimate failure of the business. For him the causes included Goldston's cupidity and weakness as well as Thynne's machinations, complicated all along by Crowley's antics. Not that Goldston was blameless. He had drawn out of the company almost as much cash as he had put into it. Stephensen too had drawn out more than £700 which he had spent in a matter of months, in typically extravagant style.[63]

The depression had also intervened, but its significance seemed greater in retrospect than it was at the time. The fact was that the Mandrake only had one real publishing success, the Lawrence paintings, and Stephensen's gamble with Aleister Crowley to repeat that success failed. Instead of propelling the press forward once more on controversy, the magician sent it into oblivion. Well, not quite. Crowley, and the Mandrake Press, suffered one last if not lasting metamorphosis: into an American cartoon strip, 'Mandrake the Magician'.[64]

For Stephensen the approaching winter of 1930 brought deep depression. Each year at this time he grew more and more homesick for the Australian summer, and the withering away of his publishing enterprise made him more conscious than ever that his own roots, not just those of the Mandrake, had been pulled up. He telegraphed his family in Brisbane that he had lost his money in the 'general slump', and then in the depths of winter he suffered a kind of breakdown. Robert Hall made available his tiny house at Pond Place in London, and Inky retired to bed there, fog bound, hating the dreary weather. In effect he went into hibernation for a few weeks, refusing to go out, and not even permitting the blinds to be lifted.[65]

By a coincidence, Jack Lindsay was asked to attend a meeting of Fanfrolico creditors at about the same time as the Mandrake went into voluntary liquidation. The Mandrake Press had not survived two years, and the Fanfrolico had struggled on for almost four. A financial statement showed that the Fanfrolico Press owed creditors nearly £3000, and Lindsay handed over all his stock in a deed of arrangement to clear as much of the debt as possible.[66] Jack and Elza were left with nothing but some furniture and a few pounds.

Entering his own, more prolonged phase of despair and impoverishment, Lindsay attempted to re-establish contact with Inky, writing to him care of Oxford as he had done on arrival in England five years before. This time, however, Lindsay's letter lacked the spark of friendly anticipation, which was not surprising as they had earlier clashed about money owing on a reprint of the *London Aphrodite*. On Christmas Day Stephensen replied in very bitter terms, accusing his former friend of fanaticism and narcissism, but signing off 'with genuine affection'. The 'psychic rubble' and 'crisis of nerves', which Stephensen diagnosed, applied also to his own state of crisis. His admission that he held views 'sceptically and for convenience' was a significant clue to his often contradictory nature. 'I agree with you that men are all animals and scared to realise it', he wrote to Lindsay. 'Why realise it however? My own impression, held somewhat sceptically and for convenience, is that man the animal fluked a consciousness which quite transcends the abyss of animalism.'[67]

A week before Christmas their mutual friend, the composer Philip Heseltine, had committed suicide. Educated at Eton and Oxford, he had alternated between his own gentle and introverted spirit and that of his rollicking persona 'Peter Warlock', the drinker and womanizer who reeled off bawdy limericks. On Heseltine's death Stephensen scribbled a memorial ditty, noting at the bottom, 'Before turning on the gas Philip put out the cat':

> Here lies the body of Peter Warlock, Composer
> Who lived next door to Soames the Grocer.
> He died of drink and syncopation
> To the lasting disgrace of the British nation.[68]

The schizophrenic Heseltine/Warlock had much in common with Stephensen and Lindsay, being anti-Christian, an admirer of Nietzsche, and steeped in the lore of booze and ribaldry. A connoisseur of beer in particular, Heseltine's 'sole recreation ... was the tavern', and before his suicide he was often drunk and quarrelsome. Like his Australian friends, he had seen his hopes and income evaporate, and his schemes for making money were 'touchingly naive'.[69] Such whimsical plans as the 'Toys Hill Bible' were common enough among the cultural proletariat of Bloomsbury, but Stephensen's artistic ambitions were never so high, nor his depths of depression so low, that he ever considered suicide.

Like Crowley, Inky Stephensen forged ahead with picaresque panache, dismissing all past failures as the fault of others. At the age of twenty-nine, he was not struggling under a heavy burden of guilt, and he rarely faltered long enough to look behind, just as he never troubled to think too far ahead. He expended too much energy in the continuing moment of existence.

7
Cutting Adrift

After Christmas 1930 both Stephensen's faith and his finances were restored as if by magic. Winifred received a £600 legacy from a wealthy Australian woman, Nancy Weston,[1] and Stephensen was offered some moderately lucrative writing commissions. He ghosted Walford Hyden's memoir of the dancer Pavlova, who had died suddenly in January 1931, and then wrote a volume about Harry Buckland, a master of hounds and the model for 'Harry Buckman' in Sassoon's *Memoirs of a Fox-Hunting Man*. Stephensen spent much of 1931 on these and similar assignments. One project which fell through was a course on success through physical and mental health for the 'Saxon Success Institute'. This was not an organization so much as an enterprising idea by one Val Valentyne. When the scheme came to nothing, Stephensen wrote Valentyne an angry letter which began sarcastically, 'Sorry the "success" scheme is a failure...'[2]

Pavlova: The Genius of Dance and *A Master of Hounds: Being the Life Story of Harry Buckland*, however, were successful, the former appearing in an American edition and the latter being reprinted soon after publication. Stephensen's share of fees and royalties even enabled him to cable his sister in Brisbane the fare for a trip to England. He was expanding his staff, and took on as well Aleister Crowley's cast-off secretary, Israel Regardie, who brought his stenotype machine with him to Toys Hill.

Stephensen and Regardie spent weeks soaking up the atmosphere of the hunting set for *A Master of Hounds*, and Stephensen's separation from the Communist Party was unconsciously completed. He had been sliding away for five years, very gradually at first and defending the left against cynics like Norman Lindsay and D. H. Lawrence. Communism had become an old garment which, though it was not thrown away, hung unused now in his ideological wardrobe. His self-image clothed him more in the style of a professional man of letters, rather wild but also witty and even charming when it suited him, a raconteur with as many literary anecdotes as political. At just the time when conspicuous poverty and rising unemployment were sending many intellectuals and writers towards the Communist Party, Inky had left the party behind.

He had always opposed privilege while enjoying its advantages, most notably at the universities of Queensland and Oxford. Now he began to savour the pleasures of flirting openly with the Establishment. The woman who had commissioned *A Master of Hounds*, Helen Gibb, was unmarried and about Stephensen's age, and she was attracted to the vigorous Australian who rode with as much confidence as he talked. He adapted easily to the formal English style of riding, with its peculiar sartorial embellishments, and was horrified when his young amanuensis Regardie came back from London with ill-fitting khaki drill jodhpurs and leather gaiters more reminiscent of a Light Horse charge than of a hunt meet. Despite the embarrassment, they went off to Hastings where Helen Gibb maintained stables, and Inky even spent some time later at her small estate in Scotland, enjoying the trout fishing and highland rambles.[3]

A Master of Hounds not only marked the point at which the thirty-year-old Stephensen turned his back on his radical beliefs, it also showed that his vision of pre-war innocence was coming more and more to be associated with rural values and with a nostalgic memory of his own pre-1914 childhood. In *A Master of Hounds* he lamented that machinery, cars and jazz had now disturbed the peace of the countryside, and he talked of the prosperous days before the war, when people were 'well-fed and happy, scarcely taxed at all, high-spirited—shall we ever see those days again?'[4] As a young communist, Stephensen would have declared that no such time ever existed, yet now he was accepting and mythologizing the old order in a way which became increasingly significant during the 1930s. Harry Buckland himself symbolized for Stephensen the rural ideals of honesty and integrity. Buckland had been forced to relinquish his mastership of the Ashford Valley Foxhounds in favour of the fat, bespectacled son of a wealthy American businessman who had virtually bought the hunt. For Stephensen in the decade ahead, this signified the evil power of English and American imperialism which had to be resisted.

Winifred became pregnant again during the summer of 1931, and Inky warned his sister Rosaline, steaming towards England on the *Moreton Bay*, that she would arrive 'in the middle of a certain amount of drama'. He told his sister he might be getting married, but Winifred suffered another miscarriage. Stephensen also promised his sister the 'greatest holiday' of her life, though she too joined his staff, along with Regardie and Winifred's son, at the domestic and professional ménage in Kent. Rosaline helped check the galley proofs of *A Master of Hounds*, and was then transferred to Stephensen's new venture, a weekly greyhound racing form guide which he had just started in partnership with a printer he knew.[5]

Unfortunately, the wet summer kept both race crowds and sales of the form guide down, and it was necessary to hire boys to hawk it outside the gates. Selling to shops became unprofitable and onerous work, and Stephensen's partner gave up in disgust. An investor was persuaded to put in £100 and Stephensen floated a company called Greyhound Form Ltd. Although this was never more than a shoestring operation, it tied up much of Rosaline's time and that of Winifred's teenage son Jack, for little or no return.[6]

After the prosperity of 1931 another bleak winter set in, and Stephensen and his extended family fell on difficult times once more. Faber and Faber, the publishers of *A Master of Hounds*, were interested in similar books, including a life of Lord Lonsdale, another master of hounds and also the owner of almost a quarter of a million acres, but nothing eventuated.[7] On his leased acre in Kent, though, with home-grown fruit and vegetables and other farm produce close by, Stephensen was not as hardup as some of his Bloomsbury friends like Lionel Ellis, the artist. In between visits to Toys Hill, Ellis survived by painting an elaborate Biblical mural on the dingy walls of a London fish shop, in return for free fish and chips. To prolong the commission, Ellis kept scrubbing out scenes as he went, professing dissatisfaction with the work.[8] It made a good story anyway, and no more apocryphal than their wild scheme to print the Bible on a hand press at Toys Hill.

In the first weeks of 1932 Stephensen suffered his usual fit of winter depression, exacerbated this time by rheumatism and a bad ankle. A week with Helen Gibb and the horse set at Hastings improved his temper, however, and he coached his sister Rosaline to ride in the English manner. At ease in this aristocratic milieu, Stephensen was nonetheless virtually destitute. Robert Hall paid the rent owing at Toys Hill, and made his London house available once more so Stephensen could look for a job. Hall also gave Winifred an allowance of ten shillings a week to pay grocery bills.[9]

This rescue operation was well timed, for Stephensen's removal to London coincided with the arrival of Norman Lindsay from New York. Lindsay had left Australia the year before in disgust at its narrow puritanism, after the banning of his novel *Redheap*. He had threatened never to return, but a lengthy stay in America failed to diminish his love for his native Australia, however much he despised its inhabitants. For some time this had been Stephensen's ambivalent nationalism as well, and when he finally met Lindsay in person in January 1932 they agreed on the need to establish a strong publishing industry in Australia. This was Lindsay's new crusade and it took no time at all to become Stephensen's.

A friend had written to Lindsay in New York that the price of imported books in Australia had increased by more than a third, and Lindsay had assumed this to be a tariff increase. He had immediately tried to interest major New York houses like Farrar and Rinehart in setting up a publishing operation in Australia, only to discover that by traditional agreement the Australian book market was strictly the property of British cultural imperialism. Britain took the raw material of Australian writers, processed it, and sent it back along with other surplus production to saturate the Australian book market. On an impulse, Lindsay had decided to make the uncomfortable mid-winter crossing of the Atlantic, taking his proposal straight to the headquarters of this imperial racket.

In London, however, he was in for another surprise. The new Australian tariff was only 10 per cent, the rest of the increase in the price of imported books being caused by currency fluctuations during the depression. Books were in fact exempted from duty a year later. Knowing their colonial market was not under serious threat, the London publishers patronized Lindsay and refused to consider his scheme for an Australian subsidiary. The director of Faber and Faber, Lindsay's own English publisher, told him the idea was far too premature.[10]

Lindsay's young friend Brian Penton was at that moment working on *Landtakers* in London, and Lindsay was convinced that Australia had the literary talent to support local publishing. So he decided to raise capital independently, from wealthy Australians if possible, to create an Australian publishing company. He admitted that the negative response from London publishers had rather 'flattened' his hopes, but proceeded bravely despite his own lack of business experience.[11] What spurred him on most of all was Stephensen's enthusiastic support. Stephensen visited Norman and Rose regularly at the flat they had taken over from Brian Penton in Bloomsbury, and Norman was impressed with Stephensen's energy as well as with his wide range of contacts and his years of publishing experience.

By the end of February 1932 their plan had the support of Sir Frank Fox, Lindsay's friend from *Bulletin* days, and it was announced to the newspapers that Stephensen would come to Sydney to manage the new company.[12] Fox assured Lindsay and Stephensen that the backing 'could be raised easily', but little was forthcoming save a cautious £20 from Fox himself and a more generous £100 which Stephensen persuaded the chairman of Aspro Ltd to part with over lunch.[13] Lindsay sailed for Australia in April to try to find the necessary backing there, leaving Stephensen to do what he could before making his own way back to Australia.

Stephensen's financial situation, however, had become even more desperate than ever. The greyhound form guide was briefly resuscitated, to no avail, and only Rosaline was now employed, earning a couple of pounds a week in an office as well as helping with the form guide at night. What money remained after the sale of the Toys Hill lease went on rent for an expensive flat near the British Museum. Winifred complained about the expense and about Stephensen's inability to economize or settle debts. 'Bills, bills, bills', she wrote in her diary, 'I never in my life owed money and ignored it'. In another entry she observed: '... when we have money he is lovely but oh how he spends it and then he gets a headache when the cash goes'.[14]

In May, Lindsay arrived back in Australia to a fanfare of publicity about the publishing venture, including a speech over the newly introduced radio network.[15] From London, Stephensen wrote about the continuing lack of success with investment gathering, and warned Lindsay that he might have to cable for assistance to pay the fares home of his entourage, which consisted of four people and a dog. Many potential investors had claimed that, with Jack Lang as premier in New South Wales, it was too dangerous to risk any capital there. In exasperation Stephensen told Lindsay that 'Australians as a mob' took politics too seriously: 'I think one of the first lessons we shall have to inculcate is that Life Goes On irrespective of politics'. This was perhaps to reassure Lindsay that Stephensen had turned his back on his own political past. He had not lost his impulsive optimism, nor his sense of humour. 'Surely in that essentially rich and naturally vital country', he wrote to Lindsay, 'there is someone who has £1,000 to spare to make things easier for us to begin. If not, after I have swum to Sydney, I shall rob a bank...'[16]

Meanwhile, Stephensen worked hard to draft a prospectus, stating that the new company would have 'virtually a monopoly in its field of operation, as publishing in Australia at the present time is sporadic and elementary'. The wide-ranging prospectus was both a testament to Stephensen's enthusiasm, and an example of how Soviet ideas had permeated his thinking, for his plan could have been modelled on the state-run Russian publishing house. In Stephensen's totalitarian vision, the Australian company would not only publish and reprint books but also act as overseas agent for Australian writers, and produce a fiction magazine as well as a literary review.[17] He had always wanted a magazine, and now he was proposing two! To get them he was prepared to compromise, at least initially, and he let Lindsay know that his youthful phase of 'astonishing the citizens' was now over:

> Regarding the periodical, I have in mind a monthly magazine, mostly fiction, not high-brow or polemical, but good solid reading matter. To hell with 'literariness'. I think we don't want to astonish the citizens so much as to *please* them; at any rate for a start ... We can also start a rowdy periodical if we feel like it—a fortnightly or even weekly full of pep. But I think the first step is to win the confidence of the persons with good solid stuff...[18]

Ever since his first article in the Queensland University magazine, Stephensen had been conscious of the need to foster a national literature. Now, thirteen years later, he took up the cause of Australian letters with unmatched zeal. Realizing the significance of Australian women writers, he set out immediately to win them over to the new company.

In July 1932, just a few weeks before leaving England, Stephensen went to a London literary party specifically to meet 'Henry Handel Richardson', and she promised him a small book for the new press.[19] At the same party he met Miles Franklin and struck up an instant camaraderie which developed into a lifelong friendship. In the short time Stephensen had left in London, they met several times, corresponded at length, and went for rambles in Hyde Park with Winifred and Franklin's flat-mate who had a pet monkey. As Winifred recorded in her diary, with the monkey and her son's dog Jimmy, they made quite a circus in the park. Winifred had known the novelist in America during the war and this strengthened the relationship.[20]

Stephensen gave Franklin a copy of *Bushwhackers*, and she wrote to him enthusiastically about his stories, urging him to write a 'big book, which surely should be among the few indigenous GREATS'.[21] Realizing Franklin was also 'Brent of Bin Bin', Stephensen let her know that he would respect and keep the secret. Then, tongue in cheek, he wrote to 'Brent' care of the pseudonym's Edinburgh publisher, Blackwood: 'Please do not consider this an attempt to discover your identity ...'[22] 'Brent' continued the game, typing a long reply on the recognizable Franklin typewriter, and amplifying Franklin's praise for *Bushwhackers*:

> Indeed we are well-met already, for when I read your 'Bushwhackers' I began a letter to tell you that the book made a milestone day for me ... I suppressed this letter for your sake, lest you should think it senile decay for me to feel it any matter whether I approved you or not; but I shall confess now that when I read your stories—all of which are gems, and two or three of which are great—the mist came—and still comes—to my eyes, and I closed them and *felt*. To have that effect on a hardened sophisticated reader is to be able to *write* ... It will be a big day when I hold a full length saga by you in my hands. I shall tremble lest—no: all will be well—you have the touch. Australia has cradled you in her magic.[23]

'Brent'/Franklin ended by thanking Stephensen for his 'restful attitude' about the pseudonym, and asking him to be 'god-father of the secret and ... help maintain it'. By this shared subterfuge, Franklin was able to offer Stephensen various manuscripts for the new publishing house: a detective novel under her own name and, among other things, a collection of stories as 'Brent of Bin Bin'. Although Stephensen was scarcely able to keep it to himself, he advised 'Brent' to tell her secret to 'nobody'.[24]

Stephensen had already written a long and excited letter to Nettie Palmer about the new company, with the postscript: 'I have discovered the identity of Brent of Bin Bin—a terrific sensation is in store. Perhaps you know ...' He addressed Palmer as if she were the literary godmother of Australia, though his ebullient tone was rather miscalculated:

> Dear Nettie Palmer,
> Here's news! We are going to begin a 100% fair dinkum Australian publishing house immediately—the kind of institution you have dreamed of, I imagine, for years ...
> I think you may recall my name as author of a deplorably hasty booklet 'THE BUSHWHACKERS' or through mention by our mutual friend, Jack McLaren—or perhaps from your scallywag brother Esmonde who has been I hear more steadfast in the Bolshevik faith than I. We have other mutual friends too ...
> Anyway I have been a publisher in London since leaving Oxford in 1926 and now Norman Lindsay has enticed me (I didn't need much enticing) to become Factotum and Serang of a genuine Australian publishing effort. I am proceeding with the details and we begin operations (in Sydney) early next year ...
> I have admired for years your magnificent fight for Australian letters. Practically alone you have kept the faith going in Australia as a

> fountain of literature. I would esteem it a very great privilege to make your acquaintance and I implore you to join us and help us to establish our publishing venture on the correct lines. Will you live in Sydney and accept a directorship? ...
> ... My idea is to find 100 shareholders for £100 each—to make the company as widely representative as possible. I hope you will be able to put the hard word on patriotic plutocrats (if any) of your acquaintance to become shareholders—as of course we can't begin properly without the capital. Inspiration will follow when the bank balance is sufficiently large and my first job is to secure that.
> Norman Lindsay of course is doing all he can to raise what we need, but I want various groups represented, and not only Norman's ...
> I hope to be able to print 'REDHEAP' in Australia and to reprint 'JONAH' to begin with and I have already *signed a contract with Miles Franklin for a new book!* (four handsprings). I am negotiating with H.H.R. for a little book for our first list and with Havelock Ellis for 'KANGA CREEK'. Patience, patience, this is a new dawn for Australia ...

This unconvincing call for patience echoed D. H. Lawrence's advice to him. Now uttered aloud to himself like an incantation, it indicated not restraint but Stephensen's headlong rush of excitement:

> We can't rush things. I have got to be absolutely satisfied that every detail is organised before the first book is published. The ultimate aim is one new novel each month buttressed by reprints, biographies, educational books, etc. We are also going to publish a monthly fiction magazine (one shilling) and a literary quarterly and found a Book Guild and it will all take time ...
> ... Perhaps you and Vance Palmer will have books ready for our first list ...[25]

When Nettie Palmer received this letter six weeks later on Green Island, off north Queensland, her first reaction was caution, with just a trace of suspicion that this high-spirited newcomer was striding rather too eagerly into her territory. She noted in her diary: 'Mail ... included an amazing letter to me from P. R. Stephensen, proclaiming the Australian Publishing House and calling on me to collaborate. A little too fast, but his hopes and plans are very invigorating to behold and perhaps to share'.[26] She told Frank Dalby Davison that she had enjoyed 'every inch of [Stephensen's] enthusiasm and hope', but that her reply may have sounded 'very cold and disheartening' because she had warned him of the 'apathy and hostility' which awaited him in Australia.[27]

Even had he received Palmer's reply in London, it is unlikely it would have deflected Stephensen from his course. He was sick of English winters, and after eight years away was easily tempted to imagine Australia as the sunny promised land of his youth. He had in any case begun to associate Britain and the rest of Europe with decay and decline, and he knew only too well what advantages he would enjoy as a former Rhodes Scholar returning from the metropolitan heart of English culture. That he was broke and still owed a hundred pounds to the man who had invested in his greyhound form guide deterred him not a whit, nor did the fact that his chances of finding a hundred willing investors during a worldwide depression were negligible. In more ways than one, he felt he was abandoning a sinking future, and there was nothing for it but to jump. His spring still had something of the old agility from his pole vaulting days.

A few days before his ship left, Stephensen wrote to Katharine Susannah Prichard at the suggestion of Miles Franklin. He hoped to make contact with Prichard when the ship docked at Fremantle, and his letter was more restrained than that to Nettie Palmer. It was in fact a carefully worded publisher's introduction, solicitious and flattering. He told Prichard that her work had 'the power of D. H. Lawrence (whom I knew well personally) without his faroucheness', and he politely inquired if she might have a 'small book' for the first list. His optimism for the new venture was not altogether unqualified, and there was no mention of Norman Lindsay:

> I shall be a passenger on the *Otranto* which arrives at Fremantle on 4 October en route to Sydney where with others I am going to found a publishing house to do what is necessary (at long last) for Australian authors in the home market and abroad. Hopes are high; perhaps this is a real emergence of Australia into world status. This is the gesture which must be made from the depths of world depression—a literary affirmation of a new hoping life, defined in some new setting: in this case young Australia become adult. Can we do it?[28]

'Of course we can' was the implication. When he described the 'new hoping life, defined in some new setting', Stephensen was all too transparently thinking about his own future.

Leaving Robert Hall to settle his business debt, Stephensen boarded the *Otranto* at Tilbury on 3 September 1932 with Winifred and her son. His sister Rosaline followed on the *Mongolia* several days later with Jimmy the dog. Inspired by Stephensen's hopes, Miles Franklin also left England by ship early in September to return to Australia.[29]

Stephensen had cabled Norman Lindsay for some money 'to complete arrangements' for his departure, and it was ironical that Norman had paid for his son Jack's fare to England but helped Stephensen return to Australia. Struggling with poverty and the tormented Elza in the west of England, Jack Lindsay had not come to see his father in London. In a futile attempt to recover something of their once buoyant relationship, Inky had written Jack a note before sailing, to place some 'remarks on record':

1. I deplore estrangement from you ...
2. we have done something together.
3. I want to publish your collected poetry ... in Australia.
4. write a cable to me if in real need ...
5. when civilisation collapses in Europe I will help to move you to Australia ...

6. I consider you are easily the most authentic poet alive hence I don't care if you are a fool in action. You are wrong to quarrel with Norman...

The remarks, however, seemed addressed to some future historian rather than to a former friend. Stephensen left the note with Phil Lindsay who never forwarded it on to his brother because of what he saw as its 'offensive tone'.[30]

One person who took special note of Stephensen's departure from England was Colonel Sir Vernon Kell, the director of MI5. From Oliver House in South Kensington he wrote to the head of Australia's Investigation Branch that the Queensland Rhodes Scholar 'concerned in the formation of revolutionary groups... at Oxford' was heading back to Australia. 'You may just care to know that STEPHENSEN is returning... in the S.S. "Otranto"', Kell reported, implying that it was now up to the Australian secret service to keep an eye on him.[31] Most likely this letter travelled all the way to Australia on the same ship as the suspect himself. Stephensen had in many ways cut himself adrift, but not completely, from his stormy past.

Part Three
Sydney, 1932–1942

A publisher, to achieve success, needed charm, financial acumen, a knowledge of the future, a stony heart, and a very rich wife.
>R. McLean
>*Victorian Book Design*, 1963

I am the same Quixotic tilter, reckless of personal safety; and always going towards the same goal, the mirage (it may be) of Australian nationalism.
>P. R. Stephensen
>letter, 1941

Point: Then raise the Scarlet Standard high.
Counterpoint: But he abhors Communism.
Point: Then let him espouse Fascism.
>P. R. Stephensen
>*Point Counter Point* parody, 1928

The authoritarian character is never a 'revolutionary'; I should like to call him a 'rebel'. There are many individuals and political movements that are puzzling to the superficial observer because of what seems to be an inexplicable change from 'radicalism' to extreme authoritarianism.
>Erich Fromm
>*The Fear of Freedom*, 1942

8
A New Endeavour

Stephensen had left London on the first day of autumn 1932. Within hours of boarding the *Otranto* he had discovered a fellow chess enthusiast and was set for the voyage, a journey which in a few weeks would transport him from his chilly and depressing English future to a more promising Australian spring.

Back in Sydney Norman Lindsay had also embarked upon a new phase of his chequered career. His attempts to raise capital for the publishing venture had been disappointing and, with the income from his artwork having all but dried up, he had found it necessary to re-enter journalism. The chairman and managing director of the *Bulletin* company, S. H. Prior, welcomed Lindsay back as the magazine's chief cartoonist in August with the announcement that the 'world's greatest black-and-white artist' was rejoining the *Bulletin*. The subject of Lindsay's first cartoon was the economic depression, one of the reasons the new book publishing scheme had so far failed to attract financial backing.[1]

While Stephensen's ship was steaming homewards, however, Lindsay discussed their vagrant project with Sam Prior and managed to convince him that such a publishing company was not only culturally necessary but also potentially profitable. Although it had for some years sponsored a novel competition, the *Bulletin* had long since lost its reputation as the focus for new creative writing. Prior no doubt saw Lindsay's scheme as a chance to recover something of that early brilliance. He may also have been anxious not to lose Lindsay's services. After discussions with his son Ken and the other *Bulletin* directors, Sam Prior agreed to back the new book publishing house, and when Stephensen's ship berthed at Fremantle on 4 October a telegram was waiting for him, offering him the position of manager. Stephensen's aim of a widely representative shareholding was not to be realized. Despite his optimistic announcements to the Australian press on his arrival, the fact was that the new publishing firm would be a *Bulletin* subsidiary.

When his ship reached Melbourne, he gave more newspaper interviews, listing the books he planned to publish, including novels by 'Henry

Handel Richardson', 'Brent of Bin Bin', A. G. Stephens, Vance Palmer, Jack McLaren, Katharine Susannah Prichard, and Miles Franklin.[2] Norman Lindsay was at work on a 'boy's book' based on the stories of his own boyhood which he had published earlier in the *Lone Hand* and *Bulletin*. There was now no chance of publishing an Australian edition of Lindsay's banned novel *Redheap*, as Stephensen had first hoped, and Prior only reluctantly agreed to consider the 'boy's book'.[3] Compromise and safety had become the hallmarks of the once adventurous *Bulletin*.

Leaving Winifred and her son Jack in Melbourne, Stephensen came on to Sydney in the *Otranto*, arriving in mid-October 1932. He returned to a city which had changed significantly since his last visit in 1924. The harbour was now dominated by the steel arch of the Sydney Harbour Bridge which had been opened in controversial circumstances just a few months earlier. But despite this imposing symbol of industrial achievement, Australia's economy was at its lowest ebb, with a third of the workforce unemployed. As Stephensen's younger brother Eric later recalled, it was a grim period characterized by long queues at job sites and soup kitchens, and at police stations where money or ration tickets were doled out. Eric Stephensen missed out on the educational opportunities his much older brother had received, and travelled up and down the country with other 'bagmen' of the depression, riding bicycles or freight trains and looking for work.[4]

It was against this background of social unrest and even desperation that plans had been made for a quasi-military coup against Lang's New South Wales Labor government. Eight years before, Stephensen had sailed out of Sydney inspired by the possibility of social revolution. In the intervening years the political climate had changed and in Australia, as in Europe, the widespread discontent and dislocation were being exploited by ex-soldiers seeking a more disciplined order. Revolution was now threatened more seriously by pro-fascist forces than it ever had been by communists.

After his arrival in Sydney towards the end of 1932 Stephensen may have heard Eric Campbell give a series of radio broadcasts outlining the establishment of a future Australian fascist state. Earlier in the year the secret armies of Campbell's New Guard had been planning a coup when the state governor, Sir Philip Game, dismissed Lang from office. After this the New Guard became less active and less militant, though it had as many as fifty thousand members at the beginning of 1932. In March, Francis de Groot, a Sydney antiques dealer and leading guardsman, had brushed Lang aside and 'opened' the new Harbour Bridge himself on horseback, cutting the ribbon with a sabre. This was a symbolic act of defiance and a warning that the New Guard was prepared to overthrow an elected government by force of arms.[5]

The Australian fascist movement, however, differed from the European model. In effect Australia was still a colony, and the New Guard swore allegiance to the British throne and to the British Empire. Their bitter opponent, Jack Lang, was a nationalist and an isolationist, and it was this style of nationalism which Stephensen took up with such vigour and dedication. Although no longer politically committed, in such an atmosphere Stephensen was able to combine a distaste for fascism with an increasingly strident cultural nationalism.

Encouraged by reports from M15, however, the Australian secret services still regarded him as a potentially dangerous communist. On the day the *Otranto* docked in Melbourne, the director of the Commonwealth Investigation Branch in Canberra had circulated a memo about Stephensen's arrival to the various state forces. These had responded with innocuous press reports of the new publishing scheme, but one Sydney officer wrote that he had learned from a source 'which is usually very reliable' that Stephensen was regarded within the communist movement 'as a factor of some potential importance'.[6]

This was nothing but out-of-date gossip. Sailing through Sydney Heads, Stephensen had his mind on the business of culture rather than politics. More ambitious now, and with a family to provide for, he intended to press the *Bulletin* company for a good salary, and he was holding out for £1000 a year. Within a week negotiations with Sam Prior and the board were concluded and Stephensen was to receive a £750 salary and shares in the new book company.[7] He spent a weekend with Norman and Rose at Springwood to discuss publishing strategy, and the firm was tentatively named The Australian Book Publishing Company. A trading or imprint name was still to be decided. Manuscripts and authors were already turning up at the *Bulletin* offices, and Sam Prior himself approached Vance Palmer, urging him to submit work. Lindsay wrote to his friend Louis Stone to facilitate an agreement to reprint *Jonah*, Stone's novel which had been out of print since the war.[8]

Lindsay drew a cartoon for the *Bulletin* showing the Australian Book Publishing Co. office being rushed by an eager herd of Australian fauna all clasping manuscripts.[9] As Stephensen and Lindsay soon discovered, there was little work of quality in this stampede of manuscripts. Many had been rejected years before by the publishing houses of Britain and Australia, and their authors had about as much hope of success as the wombats, koalas and platypuses depicted with such gusto in Lindsay's cartoon.

Although not yet formally incorporated, the company had begun to develop a momentum of its own, and Stephensen pushed ahead with characteristic zeal. His London publishing experience had been almost completely in the fine press field so he requested quotes from machinery merchants for expensive sewing, case making, folding and other machines, and he became impatient at the time it was taking the *Bulletin*'s lawyers to draw up company documents. Newly arrived from London, he was frustrated also by the limited range of papers and inks available in Australia.[10]

He had not been back a month when he wrote a long piece for the *Bulletin*'s Red Page on Australian books. Brash and confident, it gave notice that Stephensen intended to educate as well as serve the local

THE WELCOME.
"An Australian Book Publishing Co. has been established in the shelter of 'The Bulletin.'"

Norman Lindsay's *Bulletin* cartoon, 2 November 1932

literary community. His first job was to banish colonial prejudice against Australian themes:

> The brief history of this continent is crowded with incidents and characters which will one day astonish the world, when the epic is adequately told. The sophisticated White Man's rape of this virgin land is a sustained feat of heroism and fortitude no less than of greed and macabre cruelty.[11]

Here again was the ambivalence of his attitude towards the European invasion of Australia, so evident in his *Bushwhackers* stories. There was a discrepancy also between his populist style nationalism and his adherence to European culture. In a talk to the Fellowship of Australian Writers (FAW) two weeks later on 'The Future of Australian Literature', Stephensen criticized the Australian tendency to be 'slap-dash' in printing work. 'Like the bungaloid growths which disfigure Australian landscapes', he told the FAW, 'many Australian books show the hand of the jerry-builder'. It all came back 'to the question of taste, of civilised convention, of cultural maturity'.[12] The awareness of sophisticated and 'civilised' European intellectual standards caused Stephensen, and the Palmers to a lesser extent, to become frustrated by Australian realities at the same time as it allowed them flights of idealism about the national future.[13]

Unfortunately, along with his concern for high quality printing and serious literature, Stephensen had a tendency to be unrealistic about book sales. In his Red Page article he mentioned average sales of six thousand copies per title. Then in his speech to the Fellowship of Australian Writers he doubled this already optimistic figure, asking if there were not 'twelve thousand good readers and true' to support Australian literature. He acknowledged that although Angus and Robertson had a name for publishing, they were primarily booksellers. Yet he did not stop to analyse the reason. In a country with so small and scattered a population, publishing was just too uncertain and unprofitable.

Their own finances boosted by the *Bulletin*'s generous gamble, Stephensen and his family moved from their city flat during November into a comfortable house at Mosman, overlooking the harbour. Ken Slessor, then on the staff of *Smith's Weekly* and himself a lover of Sydney Harbour, dropped Stephensen a friendly and encouraging note after seeing the Reg Page article. 'The road lies open', Slessor wrote enthusiastically, 'and I can't see you failing'.[14]

Another poet, 'William Baylebridge' (William Blocksidge), visited Stephensen's makeshift office in the *Bulletin* building in mid-November. He was, like Stephensen, a Queenslander but for private reasons maintained an air of reticence about himself.[15] His family were prominent in Brisbane real estate, and a private income enabled him to print his own works. Yet he made few copies of his books available, and only his wartime tales, *An Anzac Muster* (1922), were at all widely known. Baylebridge was a man of fifty when he approached Stephensen at the *Bulletin* office with 'a vast volume of philosophical poetry'.[16] Entitled *This Vital*

Flesh, it consisted of revised versions of earlier work and was not published until 1939, and then by Baylebridge's own private press.

A contradictory mixture of recluse and sociable littérateur, Baylebridge had the appearance of a prosperous sheep farmer. He was a perfectionist as well as a nationalist, with a highly romantic vision both of himself and of his country. He believed his imitative verse would eventually be compared with the poetry of those he admired and sought to emulate, including Shakespeare. Yet despite his delusions and his imitativeness, Baylebridge's talent was not inconsiderable. Judith Wright has suggested that Baylebridge could have been 'perhaps our foremost writer', but for the 'element of preaching and political fervour which has always haunted the Australian poetic tradition'.[17]

Stephensen knew next to nothing about this shadowy writer who happened to share his own enthusiasm for Nietzschean philosophy. At a 'first glance', Stephensen agreed with Norman Lindsay that the style of *An Anzac Muster* was 'over-precious', but the four-hundred-page typescript of *This Vital Flesh* Stephensen recommended a few weeks later as work of 'high literary quality'. Baylebridge, he said, was rumoured to be a Queensland station owner and to have been in the British secret service in Austria before the war. Wealthy Baylebridge certainly was, and he was prepared to guarantee any sum for an edition of *This Vital Flesh*, wanting only nominal royalties of five pounds.[18] Although the book was not published by Stephensen's new company, which was concentrating on fiction and popular non-fiction, Stephensen became friendly with Baylebridge and a lifelong champion of his work.

Norman Lindsay had been wading through many of the manuscripts initially submitted to the press and, not used to such a task, he became increasingly dispirited. He found numerous examples of 'conscious cultural inferiority' and lumps of 'pretentious drivel'. Even before their company had been formally incorporated, Lindsay told Stephensen he was beginning to 'entertain a serious alarm for the chance of anything good' coming from the younger generation of Australian writers.[19] Lindsay informed Sam Prior's son Ken that the few professional writers in Australia turned out 'workmanlike stuff' which was dull, while the unpractised were producing excellent material but badly constructed. Seeking to remedy this, Lindsay even suggested that a group of the most promising younger writers should receive coaching from Stephensen and from Lindsay himself at a series of informal evenings.[20]

Stephensen meanwhile was still trying to organize company details, and he considered several names for the new house including 'Waratah Press'. Despite Lindsay's later claim that he had suggested it, Stephensen in early December 1932 came up with 'The Endeavour Press', an imprint which reflected the aspirations of the cultural voyage on which they were embarking. Both Priors liked the name, and Stephensen asked Lindsay to do a 'careful and correct drawing' of Cook's ship *Endeavour* as the press's trade mark.[21]

The company itself was formally incorporated on 9 December as the

Australian Book Publishing Company Limited with £10 000 of share capital, three-quarters of which was held by the *Bulletin* Newspaper Company. The only other significant shareholders were Stephensen and Lindsay who had been granted just over a thousand shares each, fully paid up by the *Bulletin*.[22] The board of directors also reflected the dominance of the *Bulletin* management. The elder Prior was chairman and, with his son Ken and head printer G. L. Bombelli, he could outvote Lindsay and Stephensen. Installed now as managing director, however, the thirty-one-year-old Stephensen retained the temporary illusion that he could run the book company his way. Until the new letterhead was available he continued to use his own elegant stationery, announcing him as 'P. R. Stephensen, Publisher, Bulletin Buildings, 252 George St., Sydney'.

It was on this notepaper that Stephensen wrote to A. G. Stephens, asking him to lunch 'for a chat about the Australian publisher's problems, past, present and future'. It would be a 'great privilege', he said, to make Stephens's acquaintance, as he was belatedly following Stephens 'in this present attempt to publish books under the aegis of the "Bulletin"'.[23] Then a sick man of almost seventy, Stephens had mellowed from the 'fiery pagan' of the old *Bulletin* into a 'fulsome patriot', obsessed with eugenics and the evils of decadence.[24] Stephensen regarded him as Australia's greatest critic and editor, and his decline ominously foreshadowed Stephensen's own embittered later years. Although he never did meet Stephens, who died early in 1933, Stephensen was nevertheless delighted to receive a brief reply from the old man, written in purple ink on a postcard:

> The name of Stephens has long been the most prominent in Australian literature. I hope, with your Nordic patronymic, that you will raise it from prominence to eminence.
>
> A.G.S.[25]

With the Endeavour Press now organized and well capitalized, Stephernsen set out to do just that. His ambition was to realize his and Norman Lindsay's dream of an Australian publishing house which would set standards and encourage indigenous literary culture. Their chief obstacle would be the apathy and colonial-mindedness of the book-buying public, something Stephensen was aware of, but which in his optimism he did not realize would prove so intractable. The well established Australian publishing firm, Angus and Robertson, had in fact reduced their local output during the 1920s and had reprinted overseas bestsellers like *Anne of Green Gables*. Their only substantial local novelist at this time was Frank Dalby Davison, yet A & R had taken up Davison's *Man-Shy* only after it had won a major literary award, the author having paid for the original edition himself.

This canny old bookselling and publishing firm played safe not only financially but also in terms of subject matter. Descriptive and travel writing was safer and more lucrative than socially conscious fiction, and

A & R had rejected Leonard Mann's war novel *Flesh in Armour* (1932) and Prichard's Aboriginal story *Coonardoo* (1929), as well as M. Barnard Eldershaw's *A House Is Built* (1929) and Christina Stead's first book. Apart from other bookseller-publishers like Robertson and Mullens in Melbourne or the New South Wales Bookstall Company, there was only a scattering of small Australian publishers in the early 1930s. Typical among these was the Macquarie Head Press which issued some poetry and drama as well as light romance.[26] English publishers still enjoyed a virtual monopoly of Australian writing talent.

During December 1932 Stephensen was finalizing the first list of Endeavour titles and thinking about more long-term projects such as an Australian drama library, a series of popular fiction, and even a *Who's Who in Australia*.[27] No doubt in an attempt to keep his *Bulletin* financiers on side, Stephensen planned his list with an eye to saleable works. The first title, in fact, would not be a book at all, but rather a booklet on contract bridge, a game then much in vogue. Of the initial half-dozen titles planned, only two were novels and one of these was the reprint of Stone's *Jonah*. Norman Lindsay's novel based on his tales of boyhood, *'Saturdee'*, would be the first substantial volume to launch the Endeavour imprint, followed by books with obvious popular appeal such as A. B. Paterson's *The Animals Noah Forgot*, illustrated by Lindsay, and a book on the filming of *In the Wake of 'The Bounty'* by its director Charles Chauvel.

Encouraged by Norman Lindsay and by Miles Franklin's enthusiastic response to *Bushwhackers*, Stephensen had decided after his return to Australia to expand his hasty sketches into a novel, 'The Settlers'.[28] Following the example of Lindsay, who had converted his stories of boyhood into the novel manuscript of *'Saturdee'*, Stephensen drafted twenty to thirty thousand words during the Christmas holidays and into the new year. The novel was planned as a pioneering saga of Queensland and was divided into four sections: 'Settling', 'Settled', 'Unsettled', and 'Resettled'. Stephensen, however, only drafted the first part and a few pages of the second. The opening was derived from the title story of *Bushwhackers*, and the novel was focused on 'an old Australian town, one of the oldest in central Queensland'. This was the fictional town of 'Bindai', based on Stephensen's home town of Biggenden, with elements also of Maryborough where he had gone to grammar school.

D. H. Lawrence had advised him to go deeper into his 'scene', and Stephensen set out to explore not only the historical reality of European settlement in north-eastern Australia but also to develop his own ideas about Australian culture, about the significance of Aboriginal themes, and about the future direction of Australian society. It was a polemical as well as a fictional work, and some of his traditional bogeys, like banking, were singled out for special attention:

> The temple of finance was the Queensland National Bank ... managed by Mr. Randolph Lancaster, a man who looked like a kangaroo, with a sagging paunch, squat legs, narrow shoulders and long head ... Mr.

> Lancaster was assisted in the bank by Little Willy Welsh, a city bred rat, with watery eyes and pale hands, who snivelled.

The accent here was on rural values opposed by metropolitan evils, and even the names—Lancaster and Welsh—were strongly associated with Britain and the decline and decadence Stephensen perceived in financial/industrial society.

One character in Stephensen's partially completed novel deserves attention, the eccentric Dr Morpeth, a heavy drinker but also a knowledgeable man with great feeling for Australia. The outlines, at least, for this character were probably taken from the Maryborough doctor who had set Stephensen's broken wrist after his school initiation accident. Morpeth expressed Stephensen's respect for the Aborigines, angrily telling one of the early settlers:

> The Aborigines have more brain than any of you tree-chopping, murdering lot! You think you're superior to the black-fellows ... You drove the blacks out of this country with guns, not brains. If any of you were naked and alone in the bush, ye'd starve! ... The Australian natives are the most intelligent people on the earth.

Stephensen was familiar with anthropological theories of the diffusion of the human race, popular in the early decades of the century, but one theory in particular attracted him. It may have come to his notice that a German anthropologist, Professor Carl Täuber of Zurich, in a book published in 1932,[29] had put forward the idea that human life had originated in Australia. Such diffusion theories are now largely discredited but in 1932 Täuber's Australian thesis was a radical and startling idea. Not only did it support Stephensen's respect for the Aborigine but, with a metaphysical leap back in time, it also allowed him to justify the white European occupation of Australia. As his attitude to the violent and greedy settlers had shown, Stephensen carried a burden of racial guilt along with his racial pride. This new anthropological theory, supported by geomorphological speculation about the great age of the continent, allowed Stephensen a vision of Australia as both the oldest and newest frontier of human civilization, linking the original Aborigines and white Anglo-Saxon settlers across time.

Appropriately, in the novel Morpeth revealed this astonishing theory to the Rev. Brinsley Clough, the town's representative of Anglican Christianity, smug in his doubly reinforced sense of superiority as a man of God and a man of Oxford. After reading Clough a simple lesson in Darwinian evolution—'Life evolved naturally, not supernaturally'—Morpeth announced that 'Life began here', in Australia:

> This is the Oldest Continent. There used to be a land-bridge from here to Asia. Man evolved here from tree-marsupials which had evolved into monkeys and apes. *On the Australian plains Man learned to walk upright*! Then he crossed to India, the home of the Aryan race ... *The Aryan race began in Australia*. Australia is the original home of the white man. In coming to this land we are returning home. Australia is

home to the white man. Marvellous things will happen as a result of this homecoming.[30]

For Stephensen this 'homecoming' was an assertion of his own hopes about returning to Australia as well as a partial answer to his guilt over the Aborigines. There were echoes too of Lawrence's sense of the ancient spirit of Australia. Continuing his old dialogue with *Kangaroo*, and with himself, Stephensen suggested a complex and almost mystical relationship between European culture and its supposed roots in ancient Australia.

> *Australia is the original home of the white race* ... The European here returns to his source; a most disturbing experience. The white man here is afraid of the bush, because it stirs primitive memories in him. He destroys it, destroys it! He does not know why he loves and hates this country.[31]

Someone else with an ambivalent attitude to Australia finally returned home towards the end of 1932. Miles Franklin had lived away from Australia since 1905, in America and Europe, but after the death of her father in 1931 she made the decision to return and live with her mother at Carlton, a southern suburb of Sydney. She came back, not to the bush which had inspired her best fiction, but to the city and a suburban selection. The optimism of her young friend Inky Stephensen had made her homecoming seem more promising than it really was. On New Year's Day 1933 she and Stephensen went up to visit Norman Lindsay at Springwood, for an 'orgy of discussion' as Inky related it to Nettie Palmer. He described Franklin as the 'most gifted woman writer in the world', an indication of his own buoyant spirits on the occasion. 'Images fall from her like ripe fruit', he said, 'even when she is talking'.[32]

Word must have got to Nettie Palmer in Melbourne about Stephensen's speech to the FAW in which he had alluded to the passion of Australians, both black and white, for sunbathing. Stephensen assured Palmer that he at least was not 'lying aboriginally on beaches':

> I am working like a man demented, to get something done before the Great Australian Drought dries me up. During the holidays I wrote thirty thousand words of a novel, which seems a desperate thing for a publisher to do, surrounded by manuscripts. However, don't be alarmed. My novel won't be ready for a year, as I can only do it in spare time. The first wild dash at it was to get the rhythm right. Now it will be easy to add bits.[33]

It wasn't. Publishing absorbed all his spare time, and three of the planned four sections of his novel, 'The Settlers', never took shape except in his imagination.

On New Year's Day, as well as entertaining Stephensen and Franklin, Norman Lindsay also found time to write to an English friend that no work by an Australian would sell well in England unless it made an 'act of submission to the national English ego'. Not that such approval mattered; Australia must be 'its own liberator or its own hangman', Lindsay rather wearily decided:

> That is, if it does not first hang its own publishers. Stephensen is out here and now vigorously managing what appears to be a publishing house in embryo. At least, the affair is well backed, and the first books will be out this month, and I am sunk in an abyss of MSS.... The maddening thing is that some of the stuff I am getting here is so good that the mystery is how it can also be so bloody bad.[34]

Among the good stuff were some stories and poems sent in by the twenty-one-year-old Hal Porter. Lindsay wrote to Porter that his fluency was remarkable and encouraged the young writer to put together a 'definitely shaped book' for publication. However, it was ten years before Porter's first story collection appeared in print.[35] Among the exasperatingly uneven manuscripts submitted to the Endeavour Press was a romantic fictional treatment of Aboriginal legends by Theo Price of Townsville. No doubt because of his interest in Aboriginal culture, Stephensen later took over the handling of the novel from Lindsay, but Price did not altogether appreciate Stephensen's collaborative editorial approach.

Even Lindsay, an experienced author whose own novel 'Saturdee' was nearing publication in January 1933, proved very sensitive to such editorial intervention. Lindsay welcomed Stephensen's constructive criticism of his unpublished novel 'Isolates in Limbo', but reacted angrily when Stephensen queried a passage in 'Saturdee' referring to a 'loony'.[36] Lindsay was used to dealing with more deferential American publishers, one of whom had even cabled him for permission to alter some punctuation. So Lindsay objected to what he saw as Stephensen's interference, based as it was on the younger man's experience in London where the tradition of editorial power was greater.

'At present the author has no standing in Australia', Lindsay complained to his fellow director Stephensen, 'and therefore will submit, with whatever ill grace, to having his work cut about by a publisher'. Lindsay threatened never to use the Endeavour Press again as his publisher if 'our firm takes liberty with my MS'.[37] Lindsay denied that his position as a director of the firm affected this principle of authors' rights, but his irritability was evidence of other, deeper frustrations. Not only had Lindsay found it almost impossible to do anything new or significant with his pens and brushes since returning to Australia, but he had begun to quarrel with his wife Rose and their marriage was approaching a crisis. His relationship with Stephensen and the Endeavour Press therefore began to wane, even as the first titles were coming from the press.

At the end of January 1933 advance copies of 'Saturdee' arrived, and Stephensen's Australian company was at last 'in full sail'.[38] Early in February his staff moved up to their new offices and workroom on the third floor of the *Bulletin* building in George Street. But Stephensen's optimism was short lived. Down at street level was the big rotary press which spun out, to the wonder of passers by, the *Bulletin* and *Woman's*

Mirror magazines each week. This machine was the responsibility of the head printer, Bombelli, with whom the younger Stephensen soon clashed. Bombelli had to look after the flat bed press which printed the Endeavour books, and he regarded this additional work as a nuisance, busy as he already was with the *Bulletin*'s rotary press.[39]

The actual working area of the Endeavour Press was also subject to pressures from the *Bulletin* operation below. Up on the third floor Stephensen's editorial offices were at the front of the building, partitioned off from a work area where the folding, rounding, stitching, case blocking, and guillotining machines were operated by a staff of four or five. For a while things went smoothly, only the aroma of wool bales from the wool agent on the floors above invading the atmosphere. However, when shipments of newsprint for the *Bulletin* company's magazines came in, the rolls were stored on the Endeavour Press working area, cramping operations and leaving its employees in little doubt as to which publishing activity took precedence.

Despite Stephensen's ambitions and the company's substantial backing, the Endeavour Press was certainly the poor relation of the *Bulletin* dynasty. The Endeavour Press too became a family affair but it was more like a cottage industry. Stephensen's sister Rosaline was his secretary, and Winifred's son Jack helped bind the books as did Bombelli's son Ron. Before long, Stephensen's younger brother Eric came down from Brisbane to work as storeman and office boy. The whole binding operation was run by an experienced English tradesman who was a distant relative of Winifred's. Depression unemployment was partly responsible for such convenient nepotism, though both Stephensen's sister and his stepson had some previous experience of printing and publishing.

Stephensen's newly recovered nationalism did not mean that he embraced anything like indigenous habits. In fact he imported from London not only ideas and values but also some social polish as well. This came as rather a shock to his brother Eric who was used to a more casual Queensland lifestyle. Stephensen took him straight in to buy a suit and instructed him to wear it at all times in the city, when at work and when sitting down to dinner. Stephensen and Winifred were particular about their evening meal, not drinking tea or beer as was usual in Australian households, but sipping sherry and other wines, usually claret or burgundy. Along with his brother and sister while they were staying with him, Stephensen took the ferry across to Circular Quay each morning.[40] He never owned a motor car, and as he lived close by Sydney Harbour there was really no need for one.

It was typical of Inky's energy that within a few months of his return to Australia he had organized a publishing company, written part of a novel, and taken an active part in Sydney literary life. He had joined the FAW and was soon made one of the fellowship's ten vice-presidents, along with such luminaries as Mary Gilmore, Henry Handel Richardson, 'Steele Rudd', Vance Palmer, and Hugh McCrae.[41] He began amassing a library of Australian books and planned to reprint important works which had long been unavailable.

The *Contract Bridge* booklet was published in January 1933 and Lindsay's '*Saturdee*' in February, but trouble erupted as the third book, Paterson's *The Animals Noah Forgot*, was being proofed. Stephensen had already complained, both in private and in public, about the lack of quality in Australian printing, and *The Animals Noah Forgot* was potentially the Endeavour Press's best selling title. So Stephensen rejected the first printing as not up to standard because the type appeared heavy and blurred. During a heated exchange the head printer Bombelli accused Stephensen of knowing nothing about printing. Despite his relative youth, however, Stephensen probably did know more about book production than the older man. 'It is my job to know something about printing', he informed Bombelli, and insisted the book be done again.[42]

Still not satisfied with the reprint, Stephensen complained in a confidential memo to the two Priors that the half-tone frontispiece of Banjo Paterson was 'crude and amateurish' and the whole printing job was still out of register. 'In what capacity am I here, if not in an advisory and consultative capacity?', he demanded of the Priors. Although Bombelli's name was not mentioned in this confidential memo, the implied criticism of the head printer was obvious and intemperate.[43] As Stephensen had been only a short time in the company's employ, his complaint was a miscalculation. The Priors would obviously back their printer who had served them for years. Stephensen tried to get the Priors to agree to using outside printers for Endeavour Press books, but they continued to insist on all the production work being carried out under the *Bulletin* roof.[44] Miles Franklin's *Bring the Monkey*, published in May 1933, was the only Endeavour title not typeset and printed on the *Bulletin*'s machines.

Distribution and advertising became another difficult area for the Endeavour Press though this was not entirely the fault of the *Bulletin* hegemony. Australia's only major book and magazine distributor, Gordon and Gotch, had demanded a 50 per cent discount and sole distribution rights, so it was decided that Endeavour Press books would be handled by the *Bulletin*'s own state branch network.[45] Although hundreds of copies of each title were shipped to these branches, they were not equipped or staffed for book distribution. Stephensen felt that the *Bulletin* company's magazines, and in particular the *Bulletin* itself, were not publicizing and advertising the Endeavour list.

Stephensen's relations with Norman Lindsay, though still cordial, were becoming strained, and he began to blame Lindsay for saddling the new company with its *Bulletin* overlords. 'These are the fruits of collaboration!', he complained to Lindsay about the 'wretched' printing of *The Animals Noah Forgot*.[46] Their personal friendship had begun to cool just as earlier Inky's deteriorating relationship with Jack Lindsay had contributed to the collapse of the Fanfrolico Press partnership.

The fault did not lie with one side, and the situation was further complicated when the thirteen-year-old daughter of Norman and Rose began writing love letters to Stephensen. He had met her at Springwood and lent her books but there is no evidence that he encouraged what was probably nothing more than an adolescent crush. For obvious reasons, Stephensen was worried and told Rose about it. Winifred's diary for February 1933 gave a hint of the tension between Stephensen and Lindsay which the incident had exposed. 'Inky says Norman sooled the child on to annoy him and to get the kid away from him', Winifred wrote, 'as in the jargon of today "she has a fixation on her father". Inky has always insisted that Norman is malicious'.[47]

Winifred still patiently endured the attention other women paid Inky from time to time. He was a handsome young publishing executive of thirty-one while she was now in her mid-forties, and their age difference always caused her anxiety. When they were married in the late 1940s, after the death of her first husband, she was able to maintain the guilty secret by understating her age by about seven years. Their relationship, though, was always close, despite his moodiness and his flirtations. In early March 1933, while he was still in a 'filthy temper' over the clash with Bombelli, Winifred noted in her diary:

> Velia Ercole[48] who fell in love with Inky because he took an interest in her writing as a publisher, came in [to the Endeavour office] and feasted her eyes on him and he went to see her off, came home and told me all about it. Oh Ohh his attractive manner and smile, how many women have fallen for it, little knowing it is to him a stock in trade which he switches on and off at will. They ought to see him in the mornings...[49]

Stephensen's deafness began to worry him, and this increased his natural propensity for talking rather than listening. Rose Lindsay sympathized with Winifred, and wrote to Inky that Winifred was not looking well and he should not make her feel worse by talking too much. D. H. Lawrence was not the only one to be worn out by a conversational session with him. Rose told Stephensen that he talked 'so hard, so long and with such gusto' that she was totally absorbed but also exhausted.[50] She suggested Winifred should come to Springwood for a rest, but Rose's own marriage was faltering. By May 1933 she was thinking of selling Springwood and even taking her two daughters out of Australia. Not long after, Norman partially separated from his family and began living alone in Sydney.[51]

Lindsay's various frustrations meant that he was increasingly pessimistic about the future of the Endeavour Press, writing to a Melbourne friend in March that the 'cultural impulse is so weak in this country that it may not respond to our efforts'.[52] He thought the success of the press depended on the sales of the initial volumes, but Miles Franklin saw the main problem as one of literary standards. In a letter to the American journalist Hartley Grattan she summed up the *Bulletin* management with her characteristic sharp wit:

Stephensen has already published a number of books, and a light novel by me is already in the press, for which Norman Lindsay has done delightful illustrations. The scheme has suffered a sea change. It is not what I helped envision in London, and I have no part in it. It should be a very successful concern as it is the Bulletin plan and has heaps of capital for equipment etc. There are five directors—Lindsay and Stephensen the brains, and the others embalmed capital. Read the Bulletin and you will see that it is a petrified affair. The genius went out of it a generation ago and those carrying on merely crystallised but added nothing. I should judge their ideal of the right fiction to publish would be cautious mediocrity that will 'best sell'.[53]

Lindsay himself discovered the constraints of such a commercial régime, writing to Peter Hopegood that 'Stephensen and myself are having a hard job fighting for the author's right of free expression'. They were not winning the fight, Lindsay reported, because they had 'no power to force works on our publishing board, which as it supplies the coin, retains power to outvote opinion from us'.[54]

Yet in its first six months of operation the Endeavour Press published a lively and varied fiction list. The *Bulletin*'s Red Page reviewer, probably John Dalley, described Lindsay's '*Saturdee*' as a comic masterpiece by a humorist of genius: 'Mark Twain himself never recaptured the idioms of his childhood so completely, and no one has penetrated so far into certain murky recesses of the small boy's soul'.[55] Although it did not sell particularly well, the Endeavour Press's next new novel, Miles Franklin's *Bring the Monkey*, was a light and witty piece of satire, dispatching everything from the English aristrocracy to American film stars and producers, aviators and war heroes. In one memorable aside, the eccentric Lady Tattingwood summed up Australian tea parties as 'full of flutter and misplaced deference to a title, and free from any mental stimulation'.[56]

It was because of Miles Franklin that Stephensen published a novel by another woman writer, 'G. B. Lancaster' (Edith Lyttleton). This was the pioneering saga of Tasmania, *Pageant*, which had been published in London earlier in 1933 and had quickly become a bestseller and book society choice. It was very popular in the United States as well. On Franklin's recommendation Stephensen obtained the Australian rights, and Lancaster's novel became the best selling work of fiction for the Endeavour Press in 1933. More works of fiction followed, including a selection of Ernest O'Ferrall's farcical stories which had originally appeared in the *Bulletin* and *Lone Hand* under the pseudonym 'Kodak'.

In general, however, the press's better selling titles were non-fiction. At the end of June 1933 the Endeavour Press sales figures revealed that Paterson's *The Animals Noah Forgot* was the company's best seller, with more than 3000 copies sold, followed by the *Contract Bridge* booklet at 2000 copies, and Chauvel's *In the Wake of 'The Bounty*' (1600 copies). By comparison *Pageant* had sold 1260, '*Saturdee*' 1070, *Jonah* 810 and *Bring the Monkey* 560. This was not quite the six to twelve thousand copies Stephensen had hoped for a few months earlier, though *Pageant* was reprinted twice in 1934. As Stephensen admitted in his disappointing manager's report for the half-year, 'Sales at this rate will barely pay cost of printing and certainly will not enable the company to show any profit'.[57]

Just a few days before, Stephensen had told a meeting of the FAW that it was necessary to sell about two thousand copies of a book just to cover expenses. He had entitled this talk 'What a Publisher Wants' and, with the nagging worry of the Endeavour Press's poor sales, his conclusion was that publishers wanted just one thing—*best sellers*. In his frustration, Stephensen told the assembled writers that if they would buy books instead of 'merely writing them', then Australian literature would quickly become established.[58]

The Endeavour Press chairman of directors, Sam Prior, had died early in June and this left Stephensen with no defence against the growing commercial impatience of Bombelli and Ken Prior. The *Bulletin* company maintained control of the Endeavour board by nominating staff member Cecil Mann to replace Prior senior. As Stephensen wrote to Vance Palmer, 'The death of S. H. Prior has slightly altered the atmosphere, and we have not yet made re-adjustments'.[59]

Stephensen's solution to the Endeavour Press's problems, as outlined in his half-yearly manager's report in June, was to expand the business with an extra £5000 capital and more editorial, publicity and sales staff. He predicted that Christmas trading would lift sales, and suggested that the *Bulletin* and *Woman's Mirror* should each devote half a page per issue to promote Endeavour titles. The aim would be to produce a new book every week. As the company had lost about £700 in the first six months of trading, however, the prospects for further expansion, and possibly greater losses, did not impress the board.[60] Yet his grievances about publicity and distribution were genuine and it is difficult to see what more he could have done in the circumstances to improve the press's balance sheet. A solid backlist as well as a sprinkling of bestsellers are necessary before any publishing operation can become profitable, and inadequate distribution remained the Achilles' heel of the Endeavour Press and many another publisher. Stephensen was later criticized, especially by Norman Lindsay, for causing the failure of the press through excessive haste and extravagance, but Lindsay was also covering his own embarrassment and sense of failure over what had been just as much his scheme.[61]

Lindsay later claimed that he had found only one good novel by a new writer, *The Doughman* by Robert Tate. Yet early in July 1933 Stephensen was complaining that Lindsay had kept Tate's manuscript for several months without reading it. Stephensen got the novel back from Lindsay the next day, read it quickly, and wrote to his dilatory co-director:

Dear Norman,
    I took ROPE [later published as *The Doughman*] home last night and read it. There is no doubt that Tate shows signs of being a great writer,

but ROPE is actually not a great book. There is too much straining after effect, and the construction of it is too confused.'

Stephensen reported that the novel contained many memorable scenes, especially in the Sydney bakery where the story was set, but that the work contained 'the usual fault of the novice—too lavish use of material'. Tate apparently would not revise the novel any further, and Stephensen thought this was a pity since Tate's next book would probably be a good one. 'We should take him up somehow, as that's what we're here for', he told Lindsay, adding as a postscript, 'I could blue-pencil the book into publishable form in a few hours'.[62] Tate's novel was in fact published by the Endeavour Press later in the year under the title *The Doughman*, though it slipped into undeserved obscurity.

Another new writer approached Stephensen at the Endeavour Press about mid-1933, but unlike Tate his future was to be anything but obscure. Xavier Herbert left the long typescript of a novel, *Capricornia*, with Stephensen.[63] The novel had been written in London the previous year and had already been rejected by publishers there, but Stephensen at once recognized the power and vitality of Herbert's work. He also saw the need for further extensive revisions—for the same 'ruthless blue pencil' he had recommended in Tate's case. Stephensen's first letter to Herbert is the earliest available piece of criticism on the novel, and it shows Inky Stephensen at his best as a publisher: brisk, professional, and yet sympathetic.

Dear Mr. Herbert,   14 July 1933

I think it is absolutely necessary for you to revise, shorten, and retype CAPRICORNIA before we can give you our decision on it. In view of your very great gifts as a writer, I presume that you want my candid opinion as a publisher, willing and anxious to help you into print, but aware of the practical requirements of book publication.

In its present state the story is over-loaded with far too much detail, and with too many explorations of side-tracks. I would like to see you shorten it, with a ruthless blue pencil to 100,000 words.

Where you have a story to tell, as for example the journey with little Nawnim in the train, you tell it marvellously well. You handle action and dialogue like a master. Where the book goes wrong, I think, is in the elaboration of subsidiary action, and the intrusion of irrelevant characters. This, together with a certain amount of long-winded moralising, over-weights the book. Reading it has confirmed my surmise that you have been too lavish in use of material. If you keep the story strictly to Norman's life, deleting everything extraneous, the book, I believe, will make a powerful impression on readers. Without some such revision and drastic shortening, we could not make you any offer to publish it. This is a more honest reason than the one given you by the London publisher you mentioned.

Whatever the difficulties, I hope you will prune and retype the work and then let us have it for serious consideration. We are very anxious to issue books of the highest class, written on Australian themes by Australian authors. A first book, to be really up to world standard, needs a tremendous amount of planning, re-writing, again and again, and diabolical persistence. Will you come in for another talk about it? I hope I can be of some practical use to you.[64]

Although Herbert appreciated Stephensen's praise and encouragement, he offered the manuscript unrevised to Walter Cousins, the publishing director of Angus and Robertson, but it was once more rejected, as it had been in England, for excessive length.

Meanwhile the work of another hopeful author, Theo Price, was being ruthlessly blue pencilled by Stephensen. In a series of pleading letters, Price wrote that he and his daughter were penniless and almost starving in Townsville, and he desperately requested payment of an advance of £25 for his 'Australian Mystical Romance' entitled 'Moongooloonga'. Finally, in July 1933, he sent Stephensen an urgent telegram that he had been on his death bed for a week and unless Stephensen could send money 'negotiable today' then Price would 'suicide tonight'. Stephensen telegraphed a reply straightaway that Price should keep calm, and posted his abridged version of the novel for Price's approval. Obviously wary of Price, Stephensen was careful not to say who had actually made the extensive revision to the manuscript.[65]

The author realized, of course, and in a long missive he lamented that Stephensen had done away with nearly all his adjectives and reduced his 'poetical prose' to '*school-boy simplicity*'. Price said his threat of suicide had not been a bluff, but that Stephensen had so incensed him it had awakened his interest in life again. He thought it was also a mistake for Stephensen to change the 'Abo chapter headings' into English ones. 'I cannot help feeling that your somewhat lengthy residence in England has put you rather out of touch with things Australian', he chided Stephensen.[66] In order to ensure his £25 advance on royalties, however, Price signed the Endeavour Press contract without delay.

Despite the fact that three Endeavour Press titles—*Pageant, Jonah* and *Bring the Monkey*—were the only Australian novels recommended on the *All About Books* July bestseller list, Stephensen was now well and truly under siege from the new chairman of the Endeavour board, Ken Prior. In response to Stephensen's half-yearly report, Prior in July circulated a memo to the other directors that he resented Stephensen's comments, and especially the suggestion that the *Bulletin* was responsible for poor Endeavour sales. Advertising would not sell books which lacked quality, he observed icily. The message was now clear: Stephensen's position as Endeavour Press manager was now untenable and he would have to take sole responsibility for the company's early trading loss. Two days after receiving Prior's aggressive memo, Stephensen wrote to his new ally Baylebridge that he wanted to discuss with him the formation of an independent Australian publishing house. Stephensen also fired off a volley of complaints to Prior, about 'faulty publicity' and advertising, and about the defective printing of Endeavour books which would 'not bear scrutiny by experts'.[67] Some days later, formal agreements were drawn up, limiting Stephensen's term of office as manager to twelve months and clarifying the ownership of certain copyrights. This last precaution was necessary because Stephensen and Lindsay had signed contracts in London in 1932 with writers like Henry Handel Richardson and Miles Franklin, and so technically held the copyright licences.[68]

All this was clearing the way for Stephensen's imminent departure. In one last attempt to improve the Endeavour Press profit and loss account, Stephensen drafted a letter to George Robertson of A & R suggesting a 'publishers' agreement' to increase the retail price of Australian novels from six shillings to the same level as that for imported English novels, 7s 6d. Then, at Ken Prior's suggestion that books were already too dear, Stephensen turned around and sketched out a plan for direct mail-order selling which would cut out the bookshops altogether. But the scheme could only succeed, he told Prior, with 'sustained publicity' from the *Bulletin* and *Woman's Mirror*.[69] As this was the main point of contention between Prior and Stephensen, Prior would not play into his hands by agreeing to such a proposal.

Stephensen's newly drawn up service agreement expired in October 1933, so during August he approached other friends such as Miles Franklin for assistance to plan his new independent company. His ideas for a truly national publishing house were now centred on the nation's capital Canberra rather than on the vicissitudes of private entrepreneurial capital. He planned a headquarters and printing works in Canberra, with an output of fifty or more books a year as well as a monthly literary magazine of the *Mercury* type. His hope was that nationally minded federal politicians and their friends would ensure sufficient backing and contracts, and he proposed an advisory editorial committee of seven eminent Australian authors.[70]

In September Prior and his two fellow *Bulletin* nominees on the Endeavour board, Bombelli and Mann, met and decided not to renew Stephensen's contract as manager, conveying this decision to him on 15 September. The next day Stephensen offered his formal resignation as manager, though he wished, as a major shareholder, to retain his place on the board.[71] Norman Lindsay did not have the stomach to attend the board meeting on 18 September which accepted Stephensen's resignation, and stayed away pleading illness.[72]

On the day he resigned, Stephensen asked Baylebridge to lend him £25 to set up a new office quickly.[73] Apart from his books and papers, his only possessions were a desk, some chairs and a typewriter on which he tapped away two-finger style. The 1933–34 edition of *Who's Who in Australia* still listed him as the managing director of the Endeavour Press, and he described his recreations with playful mockery as 'chess, eating and sleeping'. In the lean and difficult years ahead he would be doing less eating and sleeping, but playing chess more compulsively to take his mind from his mounting anxieties. He was chain-smoking a couple of packets of cigarettes a day, and his fingers and teeth had become stained with nicotine. He had discovered the 'lot austere/That ever seems to wait upon/The man of letters here', and had also encountered the apathy and hostility of which Nettie Palmer had warned him.[74]

Yet despite its frustrations, life still seemed to entice him with amusement and challenge. In the eventful ten years since he had left Queensland as a Rhodes Scholar, Inky Stephensen had been a principal of three publishing companies as well as a student, writer, journalist and political agitator. At the Endeavour Press he had published a number of significant Australian novels in less than a year, and more were forthcoming from the press including Penton's *Landtakers* (1934). However, the London publishers who had poured cold water on Norman Lindsay's scheme had been right. The Endeavour Press was premature, and instead of becoming Australia's major book publisher it joined the ranks of the other presses which failed during the 1930s.

Norman Lindsay was quick to accept this disillusionment, but not so Stephensen. In Bruce Muirden's words, Inky 'never easily dropped an idea, a friend or an enmity'.[75] Now he wanted some more time to work out the ideas and hopes he had built up over the past eighteen months for a new Australian publishing house. With *Bulletin* company backing this had been possible, but he had been beaten by the impatient balance sheet and by the lingering financial depression as much as by the apathy and colonial-mindedness of readers and booksellers.

Yet he refused to admit defeat. With typically Quixotic flourish, he moved his publishing vision closer to Sydney Harbour, took with him authors as well as his office furniture, and attempted to carry on a losing battle without even the working capital to help him sustain his vision.

9
Xavier Herbert, P. R. Stephensen & Co.

With the loan from Baylebridge, Stephensen found an office within a couple of days of his resignation from the Endeavour Press. He had letterhead printed on heavy creamy paper with his new address—'P. R. Stephensen, Publisher, Waltham Buildings, 24 Bond Street, Sydney'—and wrote his first letter on it to Norman and Rose Lindsay, outlining his plans. 'I am just going ahead, and not losing a day', he told them, 'but at the same time not over-hurrying'.[1] It was his fatal contradiction.

Stephensen's assertion of independence from the *Bulletin* did not hinder his dealings with his former employer. He negotiated with Prior for the rights to a number of works already under contract to the Endeavour Press. About the only thing Stephensen did not immediately take with him from the Endeavour Press was his loyal staff of family members. His brother Eric, stepson Jack, and sister Rosaline all stayed on for a while at the *Bulletin* building. Towards the end of 1933 Rosaline joined him again at Bond Street. Jack Kirtley, his associate in the early days of the Fanfrolico Press in London, became his 'business manager', reading manuscripts and assisting with production details.[2]

To set up on his own, this time with no assured financial backing, was folly enough, yet by early October he had proofs of a long and detailed prospectus for his new company, to be named P. R. Stephensen & Co. Limited. He envisaged a vast enterprise, with the establishment of a complete printery in Canberra (cost: £8000) as well as branch offices in four states and New Zealand (running cost: £2800 per annum). Stephensen planned to pay himself £1000 a year, and his head office would include a staff of seven or eight, at an annual cost of almost £4000.[3] The scheme was advertised at length in the magazine *Book News*, and late in October 1933 he visited Canberra to try to organize his dream publishing house. But nothing like this plan was ever put into effect.

Meanwhile, Nettie Palmer and the literary community were looking on with some amazement but even more with concern and scepticism. Palmer asked Frank Dalby Davison about Stephensen's latest venture, and Davison replied that he had been the first visitor to Stephensen's new office. He characterized the publisher as a 'delightful chap', but detected a 'streak of irresponsibility' in his make-up: 'When he is talking I just let him rattle on and don't take him too seriously'.[4]

Early in November the Stephensens left their rented house in Mosman and moved right down the other end of Raglan Street to 'Hartley', a block of flats overlooking Balmoral Beach and Middle Harbour, with a view also of the Heads. Once more the Stephensen household became an extended family, with various lodgers including for a while Kirtley. Xavier Herbert had made contact with Stephensen again and brought along his much-travelled London typescript of *Capricornia* which had just been rejected by Angus and Robertson. Together with Sadie he sent the Stephensens a Christmas telegram, offering them 'perennial but hopeless affection'.[5]

Stephensen had become acquainted with most of the local writers during his year at the Endeavour Press and through Sydney literary gatherings such as the FAW. Now, however, he concentrated on those who could assist his business, signing several contracts with authors who paid him amounts of up to £100. In the case of Eleanor Dark's *Prelude to Christopher* this was in the form of a guarantee, to be repaid to her at two shillings for every copy sold. Another author, Ruby Lemont of Potts Point, was allocated shares in Stephensen's company in return for her £100 contribution.[6] This was in contrast to the practice at the Endeavour Press where many of the authors had actually received advances on royalties.

The first P. R. Stephensen & Co. title, Henry Handel Richardson's twelve-page 'Aquarelle', *The Bath*, was published in December 1933 along with Louise Mack's *Teens Triumphant*, a sequel to her bestselling volume *Teens*, which had been published thirty years earlier in London. Stephensen was at last free to indulge the passion for fine book production he had developed in London, and Kirtley was once again available to encourage and assist. One reviewer described Richardson's booklet *The Bath* as a work of art in miniature: 'The format, and the use of a fine modern type face, as well as the colour work, indicate that the publishers bring up-to-date London technique to the business of local book production'.[7]

Yet by Christmas Stephensen's infant company had already registered a trading loss of £141, and the capital provided by authors had almost dried up. During January Kirtley arranged introductions to stockbrokers, recommending Stephensen's 'integrity and his remarkable qualifications'. In a note to Rosaline Stephensen, Kirtley said he hoped her brother would concentrate on brokers and other serious investors, and 'drop the bohemian bums hard'.[8]

Taking Kirtley's advice, but not completely, Stephensen approached Ruby Lemont's husband who was an architect. Most likely Stephensen had met him at the FAW, and Ruby's novel *Makala Farm* was already under contract to the press. The much more modest plan Stephensen outlined to Lemont was for a 'small company' with only a couple of directors, each subscribing £250. This would finance another half-dozen titles or so. More realistic now about sales, Stephensen was thinking in terms of a thousand copies, rather than tens of thousands, though his estimated revenue calculations showed a sizeable profit which he claimed would be increased still further by subsequent editions. 'I bring expert knowledge and a considered enthusiasm to the task', he assured Lemont. 'The opportunity undoubtedly exists. At this stage I only need a little support of the right kind from the right people.'[9]

Even before the company was incorporated, however, the solicitor for one author who had paid Stephensen a £100 guarantee demanded the return of the money along with the manuscript of 'Hell's Airport', an illustrated story of central Australia.[10] P. R. Stephensen & Co. Limited was formally incorporated on 18 January 1934 with only two directors, Stephensen and Lemont. Other initial shareholders included Winifred Stephensen, Rosaline Stephensen, Ruby Lemont and George Berrie whose novel of outback life, *Threebrooks*, was then in preparation at the press. In return for the goodwill of the business, his stock and furniture, Stephensen received an allocation of 750 shares in the new limited liability company. Perhaps more importantly, the company took over all debts as well.[11]

P. R. Stephensen & Co. occupied first-floor offices in Bond Street. The main office was on the corner of the Waltham building, and another, smaller room down the corridor was used as a storeroom. The staff consisted of Stephensen, his sister Rosaline, Kirtley, and later a manuscript 'reader', Arthur Dibley, an arts graduate from the University of Sydney. Dibley was taken on as a copy editor and proof reader, but he was useful in another way. With the assistance of his father, who was the joint managing director of a large music firm, Dibley compiled a list of possible investors for Stephensen. All those named were 'in a good financial and social position', and Dibley was to receive a commission on any shares sold. The Dibleys' anonymity was to be guaranteed.[12]

The list included knights and Macquarie Street doctors as well as others with a smattering of the best Sydney addresses from Woollahra, Longueville and Potts Point to Double Bay and Point Piper. Patrick White's father, V. M. White of Darlinghurst, and one of his uncles, A. G. White of 'Belltrees', Scone, were also suggested as potential investors. White's parents each purchased £50 worth of shares in P. R. Stephensen & Co. and later increased their investment, making theirs possibly the biggest shareholding.

Most of the investors in the company, though, were authors or prospective authors, including J. J. Mulligan, Ambrose Pratt, and George Berrie, and their shareholdings were generally small. Former prime minister, W. M. Hughes, for example, whose book of reminiscences Stephensen was planning to publish, only contributed £10. Parents of prospective authors formed another category, and even Xavier Herbert's working-class father was prevailed upon to purchase ten shares in February 1934.[13] Stephensen's interest in the White clan was of course only financial, but his affinity with Xavier Herbert developed into a close and often stormy relationship.

Stephensen still insisted that the lengthy typescript of *Capricornia* needed to be entirely rewritten, with more careful story plotting and construction. Busy as he was with the establishment of P. R. Stephensen & Co., he agreed to advise Herbert on the revision, and the author brought *Capricornia* along regularly to the Stephensen flat overlooking Balmoral Beach. During the course of a number of evenings, weekends, and even all-night sessions in January 1934, Stephensen worked with Herbert at the flat. They pored over the typescript, Herbert reading passages out aloud to the publisher.[14] This close consultation enabled Herbert to clarify the novel's faults and plan the rewriting.

He was then living with Sadie Norden in a house they rented cheaply at Narrabeen which boasted a Roman bath, a billiard table and a fine view of the ocean. About February Herbert began to redraft *Capricornia* along the lines he and Stephensen had discussed. His publisher friend visited him a few times at Narrabeen, staying usually for the weekend and reading parts of the revised manuscript as they were completed.

Stephensen's monthly publicity *Circular*—with its usual editorial harangue on the apathy, doubting, provincialism and hostility of the Australian reader—announced at the end of March 'a Giant Novel Coming'. In an earlier *Circular* Stephensen had carefully set himself up by asking: 'Who will write, and who will publish, the Great Australian Novel for which the world is waiting?' The answer was thus dramatically, and prematurely, given in the March issue:

> Stephensen's have in the press a novel of epic proportions, over 200,000 words in length, entitled *Capricornia*, by Xavier Herbert. On a vast canvas the author, whose stories in English, American, and Australian magazines have made his name well known, depicts the whole sweep of life in Northern sub-tropical Australia ... Publication of this gigantic novel, which will appear subsequently in both England and in the United States, will be an achievement on a scale never before attempted in Australia. (*To be published in May.*)[15]

As Herbert was still revising the novel, May publication was an optimistic fiction. However, Stephensen needed ammunition like this. With only a few publications released, and probably most of his initial working capital gone, he wanted to convince investors, as well as authors and book-buyers, that he could bring off such a coup. The claim that Herbert was well known in England and America was simply not true, and his stories in the *Australian Journal* before 1933 had been published under the pseudonym 'Herbert Astor'. There is also no evidence that any overseas editions of *Capricornia* had been arranged.

Yet Stephensen's enthusiasm for the novel was genuine, and he recognized in Herbert a kindred nationalist. They were contemporaries, having been born in the year of Australian federation, and both had grown up in relatively isolated areas of Australia, Stephensen in Queensland and Herbert in north-west Western Australia. As children they had gained a first-hand knowledge and love of the bush which they drew upon in their short stories.

Where they differed, though, was in training and family background. Herbert's father had been a railway engineman and Stephensen's a wagon builder, but Stephensen's upbringing had been much less working class. He had been exposed to European high culture and to the intellectual sophistication of Oxford and London. Herbert's experiences, on the other hand, had been scientific and practical, and more physically adventurous. A pharmacist who had qualified under the apprenticeship system, he had given up a medical course at the University of Melbourne to wander through northern Australia gathering material for his fiction. When Stephensen was mixing in London literary society and enjoying long vacations in Paris, Herbert was navvying in the Northern Territory on the north-south railway line, mustering cattle, hunting crocodiles, or working as a diver on a pearling lugger.[16]

Both Stephensen and Herbert, however, shared a fascination for the Aborigines and a sense of outrage at their mistreatment and degradation. In his novel manuscript 'The Settlers' and elsewhere, Stephensen defended the unique culture of the Aborigines against those who 'habitually deride poor Binghi'.[17] More than once, his publicity *Circulars* suggested that Aboriginal culture should be treated with respect, and in an article on publishing for the *Australian Rhodes Review* Stephensen described the Aborigines as 'ancient and wise' people who had conserved Australia's resources and practised many arts including 'poetry, music, painting, drama, and religion'.[18]

Herbert's involvement with the Aboriginal cause was less theoretical than his publisher's. He had seen Aborigines treated as slaves, chained by the neck at night to stop them running away, and he was closely acquainted with the black communities of the north coast. While working as a railway navvy, he had inherited a harem of lubras from another white labourer who had, in Herbert's words, 'died of a surfeit', and this interracial theme formed the basis of his early attempt at a novel, 'Black Velvet'. It was also a significant component of *Capricornia* which had been written in a London garret in 1932.[19]

By a coincidence, both Herbert and Stephensen had returned to Sydney within a few weeks of one another. They had left a Europe increasingly dominated by the politics of racial purity, and had come back to a happy-go-lucky country which had already exterminated or 'concentrated' most of its racially 'inferior' inhabitants. For both men during the 1930s, therefore, important cultural and political struggles remained to be fought on Australian soil.

Temperamentally, Herbert and Stephensen were almost opposites, and this undoubtedly contributed to the instability of their relationship. For all his sentimental adherence to pre-war bush values, Stephensen was a thoroughly metropolitan type; a flamboyant talker, drinker and polemicist. Though Herbert could be as talkative as Stephensen, cities threw him off balance, and he preferred the life of a wandering bushman and recluse. It was the landscape and people of the north which sustained his creative spirit and powered his narrative genius.

Idealists in their own ways, the two men shared a strong sense of the *genius loci*, the special spirit of the land which a number of Australian writers sought to express in the 1930s.[20] Herbert later recalled that he used to go for 'smoke-o' with Stephensen to a coffee shop or pub in Sydney, and talk for hours about 'our True Commonwealth'. For Herbert, Stephensen was a man of 'wildly exuberant moods' alternating with periods of 'silent, even sulky, majesty'. Herbert remembered that his publisher would literally shake with excitement.[21] In a less indulgent assessment of the man who did so much for his early literary career, Herbert also claimed that Stephensen's ideas on Australian nationalism had been derived from him. Yet Stephensen's nationalist programme had been developed well before he had ever met Xavier Herbert. It is fair to say, though, that the two supported and developed each other's faith. Herbert's strong personal commitment to the Aborigines helped convert Stephensen's theoretical and rather sentimental sympathy for 'Binghi' into practical support for the Aboriginal protest movement later in the 1930s.[22]

From Narrabeen Herbert wrote to Stephensen of their 'joyous' friendship, and addressed him with great warmth and affection. Herbert also elaborated on a plan they had discussed for a popular magazine to rival the *Australian Journal* and the *Women's Weekly*. The name Herbert suggested for the magazine was, appropriately enough, 'The Spirit of the Land', and he intended it to publish not only Australian fiction but also gossipy columns, cookery, fashion and farming. He sketched a cover design depicting the sun and a blue flag with a silver Southern Cross, and insisted there would be no Union Jack on the flag, illustrating the anti-British sentiment he shared with Stephensen.[23]

Another suggestion Herbert made was that Sadie could be useful to the publishing business, and Stephensen did take her on as a general helper at Bond Street to replace his sister who had left for Melbourne. Sadie dispatched books and mail, acted as receptionist, and even lived in the Stephensen ménage at Balmoral for a while. The revised manuscript of *Capricornia* was completed about the end of April 1934 and on 1 May Stephensen paid Herbert a £10 advance on royalties.[24] By the time copy editing and typesetting of the 'gigantic' novel had commenced, however, the publishing firm was running seriously short of funds.

Stephensen had sent out his company prospectus and publicity *Circulars* to everyone he could think of in the literary community, but these only caused further ripples of concern. Nettie Palmer wrote to Davison that she was anxious Stephensen might collapse if his scheme failed, but could see no way of helping: 'He's such a splendid bubble when he's up, but bubbles have notorious powers of failing'.[25]

By March an aggressively disappointed Stephensen had begun scolding his potential supporters:

Dear Nettie,
   Not a word from you to acknowledge receipt of my first circular and the prospectus! What's wrong? I find it difficult to believe that you, too,

are one of the former shouters for Australian literature who are now flabbergasted at the arrival of a real Publisher. I have been vastly amused by the celerity with which Australian litterateurs vanish from my vicinity as soon as I suggest that the first practical step is to raise Capital to help me to do my job here. It seems that I will have to start with an entirely new set of writers, because the old ones are too dejected to make an effort to help themselves by supporting or encouraging me.[26]

After receiving this, Palmer wrote to Leslie Rees that she was 'very anxious' about Stephensen's financial situation, 'though I'm afraid he thinks I'm not anxious enough'. She strongly suspected that authors were subsidizing Stephensen's publications, and Vance Palmer predicted the company would not see out the year. Both the Palmers advised Rees to try his novel with English publishers because Stephensen's firm was so dubious, the Endeavour Press was now 'incalculable', and A & R were 'uninterested' in serious fiction, catering only to an 'unsophisticated public'.[27]

Even those interested in Australian writing were prepared to abandon the local publishers for more respectable English houses. Marjorie Barnard urged the Palmers not to let Stephensen have Vance's next novel, but to try Cape in London instead. Despite the fact that Stephensen was then considering an Australian edition of *A House is Built*, which had been published in London in 1929, Barnard wrote to Nettie Palmer in April 1934:

Yes Stephensen and A & R seem to be vying with one another as to who can publish the greatest rubbish with the most éclat. Each is very scathing about the 'literary' taste of the other. A somewhat acid joke ... Of course all publishers praise their rubbish as energetically as their good stuff, but while one can ignore overseas rubbish the home-grown article is very much with us.[28]

One such example of literary 'rubbish' was J. J. Mulligan's novel, *A Gentleman Never Tells*, then in the press at P. R. Stephensen & Co. The jacket blurb described it, with painful alliteration, as the 'surprising adventures of Lord Gerrard Fitzgerald, playwright, polo-player and popular personality in his peregrinations to Paris, the Riviera, Egypt, and elsewhere in the Beau Monde...' As Nettie Palmer had suspected, it was lightweight titles such as this which were subsidized by their authors. Mulligan had paid £50 towards the cost of production, and for that he received 150 free copies of his novel. In this case Stephensen was doubly bound, since Mulligan was also a company shareholder.[29]

In May, a couple of weeks after *A Gentleman Never Tells* was published, Miles Franklin wrote to Australia's literary godmother, Nettie Palmer, that she should 'immediately if not sooner' get hold of Mulligan's appalling novel. 'If this one had been a gentleman instead of a gent he would never have told on himself', Franklin told Palmer, fairly bursting with indignation. 'The implications of this book are such that it nearly gives me black rings around the eyes. I could write a major brochure on Australia, what it does to writers and what writers do to it, upon a specimen like this.'[30]

If his literary friends were privately disappointed with his list, Stephensen was himself not reticent about publicly lambasting booksellerpublishers like A & R, Robertson and Mullens, and the New South Wales Bookstall Co. Without actually naming these 'booksellers-who-dabble-in-publishing', he used his *Circular* to criticize their products as 'puerile in ideas and slovenly in literary and printing technique'.[31] Yet Stephensen was in danger of hurling his polemical stones from a publishing house composed largely of glass. The same issue of his *Circular* contained rather apologetic descriptions of the featherweight novels by Mulligan, Berrie and Lemont, all of whom had subsidized their books' publication.

There was, however, almost universal acclaim for the improvement in book production and design which Stephensen brought about. The jackets of Price's *God in the Sand* and Berrie's *Threebrooks* were praised by the Melbourne *Sun* as 'cover artwork at its best—arresting, imaginative, delicate'. Price's book, based on Aboriginal legends, had a particularly effective black jacket, and the *Labour Daily* thought the best part of the book was its 'well-designed cover', a sentiment shared even by Price's hometown paper, the *Townsville Bulletin*.[32]

Although Stephensen had in effect introduced two of the country's major novelists, Eleanor Dark and Xavier Herbert,[33] his only immediate achievement as a publisher was to show that a small and undercapitalized Australian company could produce books as stylishly as any London publisher, helping thereby to dispel the cultural inferiority which so angered and exasperated him. And if he published lightweight books in order to keep his exceedingly fragile enterprise going, it was because of his faith in important writers such as Herbert and Dark. Stephensen well knew that it took years, not months, to build a worthwhile fiction list. He promised Furphy's indefatigable champion, Kate Baker, that he would try to reprint *Such is Life*, which had been out of print for years, and he did in fact issue Australian editions of Franklin's *Old Blastus of Bandicoot* and Lancaster's *Sons of Men* in his 'Southern Classic Library' series.[34]

In April 1934, with his co-director Lemont, Stephensen went to Melbourne for a few days to establish an office there and, more importantly, to find some much-needed capital. They appointed a sales representative, and Stephensen had discussions with the local literati including Nettie Palmer, Kate Baker and E. J. Brady. However, by the end of May, with nine books already published, P. R. Stephensen & Co. was slipping further into financial trouble, most of the titles selling just a few hundred copies. The Melbourne salesman wrote in frustration that all his running about had been useless and he had had to argue with booksellers and others who harboured 'preconceived prejudices' against Stephensen or 'Australian publishers in general'. He had only managed to talk a friend into buying one copy of *The Bath* for 'patriotism's sake'.[35]

Stephensen was angry because his company had sold £400 worth of books in Sydney. But, after costs and discounts, the profit margin even on this turnover was negligible. At his first shareholders' meeting at the end of May, required under the Companies Act, he wisely made no extravagant predictions about the future. 'Though this company is a small one', he told the little band of shareholders, 'its future development may be great'. He thanked his co-director and the staff, including Kirtley and Dibley, for their 'unselfish assistance' and 'sustained enthusiasm', which were indeed praiseworthy since their salaries were paid in company shares. Just over £700 had been invested in the company by thirty-two shareholders, and the lack of capital had 'hampered' development. Although Stephensen tried to be cautiously optimistic, his company was now in urgent need of funds, with debts totalling almost a thousand pounds and the Bond Street storeroom full of unsold books.[36]

Disillusioned, the 'business manager' Kirtley left early in June, and a couple of weeks later Stephensen offered a Brisbane school teacher the position of 'Director of Educational Publications' if he would invest £1000 in the company. The teacher only had £350 available, and in any case was frightened off by the indecent haste with which Stephensen tried to absorb him and his cash. 'WOULD ACCEPT 350 DEPOSIT AND BALANCE LATER WILL YOU COME TO SYDNEY THIS WEEK', Stephensen had wired him.[37]

Some financial relief was provided by Ruth and Victor White, who were already prominent shareholders. Early in July 1934 they each purchased another hundred shares, bringing their total holding in Stephensen's company to £300. This further injection of funds was almost certainly part of a deal where P. R. Stephensen & Co. agreed to publish a volume of poetry, *The Ploughman*, by the Whites' son Patrick, then a Cambridge undergraduate. The additional two hundred shares were allotted to the Whites on Monday 2 July, and before the end of the week Stephensen had accepted a quote from W. T. Baker & Co. to print *The Ploughman*, requesting the printer to treat the job as urgent. No fewer than three sets of galley proofs had to be ready by the following Tuesday, possibly to enable the Whites to send off a set to their son in England by the next mail steamer.[38]

Ruth White in particular was closely involved in her son's early writing career, having arranged for the production of his *Thirteen Poems* when he was still a teenager. From her Stephensen not only received the handwritten copies of her son's *Ploughman* poems, but also a novel manuscript, 'Finding Heaven'.[39] Because of the delay in sea mails to England, and because White was away in Europe for the Cambridge summer vacation, he did not return the proofs of *The Ploughman* till October. Stephensen had apparently encouraged him to rewrite 'Finding Heaven', but he replied from King's College that he did not know if he could bring himself to revise the novel 'after all this time'. He said he had written it in a 'frame of mind' with which he did not now sympathize.[40]

White asked Stephensen to estimate the novel's 'greatest weaknesses', but there is no trace of Stephensen's reply, if any. His comments on this early work would have been particularly interesting, as he had no taste for White's later novels which he criticized as formless and un-Australian.[41] The contract for *The Ploughman*, in Ruth White's name, is available but undated.[42] Because of Stephensen's various unpaid accounts, W. T. Baker refused to complete the printing and White's mother arranged for the volume to be privately printed elsewhere in Sydney the following year.[43]

Nettie Palmer's network of informants had kept her up to date with the latest crises at P. R. Stephensen & Co., and she was already writing of Stephensen's 'downfall' to Miles Franklin early in July 1934.[44] Perhaps in an attempt to boost his spirits, Palmer wrote to Stephensen a couple of weeks later that she and Vance had been looking through copies of the old *London Aphrodite*. She had been reading Stephensen's Bakunin article in the train and 'nearly fell out of the door'. It was, she told him, 'Vigorous, significant!' She, too, appreciated the contribution he had made to publishing and to public debate:

> Dear Inky, I hope you're not feeling as down and defeated by circumstance as the mere factual logic of the case might suggest. I have a feeling that you are resilient somewhere. If the time for you to be a successful publisher is not yet, perhaps you are to be a writer first. From the outside, your work as a publisher has had two special virtues: you have raised the standard of book production here beyond measure, and your statements in the press have all been valid and important . . .[45]

Palmer had just been reading Penton's novel *Landtakers*, published by the Endeavour Press, and was impressed that such a 'lively mob' had come from Queensland in the early 1920s.

Her tone was sympathetic and consoling, but Stephensen had not given up yet. An investment firm had provided him with two commission agents, Cecil Sedgwick and Commander Chesleigh, and in a Hupmobile car hired by Sedgwick they all set off for Canberra to try to float the flagship which had been Stephensen's vision the year before: a national publishing house operating from the nation's capital. He issued a press release about the Canberra company which was to be called, rather grandly, Stephensen's National Book-Publishing House Limited.[46]

His plan was to invite parliamentarians and other prominent figures to join the board, though none did. The draft prospectus listed new projects including a mail-order bookselling scheme from Canberra, a 'Tourist Guide to Australia', a popular biography series, 'Lives of the Pioneers', and the launching of a 'National Magazine' to advocate 'Commonwealth ideals' by

1. Strengthening and Defence of Federation
2. Preservation of forests and Australian native fauna
3. Preservation and study of the Aborigines
4. The encouragement of literature, science, and art
5. Foundation of a University at Canberra[47]

This welter of proposals, designed to attract Canberra's statesmen, was the result of an energetic imagination stretched by financial tensions. Although the new company was incorporated late in July 1934, the relevant documents were never filed at the Canberra registry, so the investors were in effect lending money to the Sydney company.[48] Stephensen and Sedgwick stayed at the expensive Hotel Canberra, giving an impression of security and prosperity, but they experienced great difficulty in meeting the bill.

The letters Stephensen wrote to Winifred during his month or so in Canberra that winter showed that he and Sedgwick did secure more funds, including a cheque for £250. 'That is a great relief', he told her, 'as it means that the business can carry on very nicely now ... So cheer up. I'm feeling fine and optimistic'. Winifred, however, did not share his optimism, and her letters and diary notes expressed her mounting anxiety. In the midst of threats and accusations from creditors and investors, she wrote and phoned Stephensen, urging him to return to Sydney. Instead he sent her a few pounds, and gave vent to his own anxieties:

> What I must impress upon you is *first* it is *NO USE* my returning to Sydney unless I bring £300 or £400 with me. This money I intend to get here, and I won't leave Canberra until I get it. Second. I am perfectly aware that things are getting into a muddle at the Sydney office but nothing fatal will happen. I shall arrive with the answer to all criticism, viz. the hard cash.[49]

Somehow he did return from Canberra with sufficient funds to stave off creditors for a few weeks and to pay outstanding office expenses such as telephone and rent. However, most of the company's printing work had been suspended and Stephensen's supporters were becoming more critical if not mutinous. Kirtley had already left and Sadie had been stood down. Herbert, too, had become disillusioned with his publisher. He had been trying to hunt up desperately needed funds so that *Capricornia* could be published, but now decided that Stephensen was cynically making use of him. He refused to give Stephensen a substantial cheque from G. Inglis Hudson, a wealthy manufacturing chemist who had made a fortune out of 'Hudson's eumenthol jubes'. Herbert had visited Hudson at his waterfront mansion at Rose Bay and discussed a deal whereby the old man's memoirs would be published. As a chemist, Herbert seemed just the right person to assist him. Although *Capricornia* was almost completely typeset, Herbert decided to abandon Stephensen's sinking company. He gave Hudson back his cheque and headed for the hills, as it were, to stay with his brother at Peat's Ridge, north of Sydney.[50]

Addressing him as 'Alfred Xavier Herbert, Esqre', Stephensen wrote him a long and eloquently outraged letter, characterizing Herbert's protestations of love and devotion as nothing but 'gas'.[51] Stephensen was particularly angry about the returned cheque, but did manage himself to secure £200 from Hudson. Together with the few hundred pounds contributed by Canberra investors, this meant that another four P. R. Stephensen & Co. titles could be completed. But not *Capricornia*.

Stephensen concluded his letter to Herbert by saying he was fond of the author still, despite his disloyalty. Yet worse was being plotted. The plan, which Herbert melodramatically called the 'Black Betrayal', was to send, without Stephensen's knowledge, a carbon of the final typescript of *Capricornia* to Piers Gilchrist Thompson, the one London publisher who had shown some interest in the novel two years earlier. Thompson was now in partnership with Lovat Dickson, and for most of the remainder of 1934 Herbert was on tenterhooks awaiting the verdict of the English firm.[52]

In order to clear the way, however, he had to ensure that Stephensen did not succeed in publishing *Capricornia* first, even if it meant hastening the inevitable demise of the company by tipping off printers and binders that Stephensen could not meet his debts. Herbert's letters from Peat's Ridge revealed both his hopes and his anxieties about Stephensen, now characterized by Herbert as 'The Bum'. All his former affection for Stephensen he transferred to his new ally, Arthur Dibley, who was still working at Bond Street.[53]

Stephensen at this time was treading water frantically to stay afloat, and he warned Winifred to state that everything in the house was her property should the bailiff call. During September and October various newspapers sued the company for unpaid advertisements, and a number of typesetters and printers also took legal proceedings for recovery of debts. Even the company's 'best selling' author, J. J. Mulligan, sued for £20 in unpaid royalties.[54] Unluckily for Stephensen, Mulligan was a solicitor as well as a writer.

Desperate, but still not yet drowned, Stephensen tried in October to raise additional money through the 'Stephensen Book Agency Syndicate' which would market the company's books including *Capricornia* and others in preparation. Under the syndicate agreement, subscribers' funds would be frozen in a trust account until £1250 had been raised, but Herbert suspected that Stephensen might try to use some of these trust funds to pay for *Capricornia*.[55]

Even during the time that Herbert was dedicated to stopping Stephensen from publishing *Capricornia*, his feelings towards 'The Bum' were ambivalent. He wrote to Dibley that he sincerely hoped Stephensen would win through all the 'machinations'. Still anxiously awaiting word on his novel from the London publishers, Herbert was kept informed by Dibley of the latest developments at Bond Street—the 'Madhouse' as Herbert described it. The news that the bailiff had been in shook Herbert 'to the bones', but when he discovered that Stephensen had fended off even the bailiff he exclaimed to Dibley: 'Amazing situation! Astounding man!'[56]

Fearing that Stephensen might now stay afloat long enough to see the novel published, Herbert approached a lawyer who pointed out a loophole in the contract. This would become effective three months after Herbert gave Stephensen a demand in writing for money owed, which he did in October. The contract would be void in any case if the book did not appear before 14 January 1935.[57] To sweat out the time until January, and also to wait for news from London, Herbert secluded himself in the rugged Barrington Tops area north-west of Newcastle, and panned for gold with a half-caste Aboriginal friend.

Although work on *Capricornia* was held up, Stephensen did manage to publish several other books including *C. J. Brennan: An Essay in Values*, a critical memoir by Brennan's friend and former pupil Randolph Hughes. Criticizing the 'jigging jingles' of Lawson and Paterson, and the 'vulgar sentimentalities' of C. J. Dennis, Hughes turned to Brennan with eloquent praise and sophisticated analysis. At four universities in Europe, including Oxford and Paris, Hughes had never met anyone with scholarship 'as wide and profound, as massive and delicate' as Brennan's.[58] Stephensen also published Vivian Crockett's novel *Mezzomorto* wrapped in a magnificent scarlet and gold jacket. It sold about six hundred copies in a few weeks before receiving a scathing notice in the *Bulletin* under the headline 'Through Muddle to "Half-Death"'. The review was written under cover of a pseudonym by the malicious Brian Penton who had not forgotten his clash with Stephensen several years previously, and who looked upon Crockett as a rival novelist. Because of this rivalry, and because Stephensen's estranged employer, the *Bulletin*, published the review, both Crockett and Stephensen were later able to sue for damages.[59]

During October 1934, however, with the failure of various schemes to move stock, the net of company creditors was moving closer and Stephensen was in deeper trouble. The secretary of his now abandoned Canberra company, who had not heard anything from Stephensen for a month, wrote requesting some news. It was not good. At the end of November P. R. Stephensen & Co. Limited was more than £3000 in the red, with little in the way of useful assets: £5 in the bank, a few sticks of office furniture, and a large stock of unsold books. Stephensen's authors were owed a total of £200 or more, his own staff had not been paid, and he owed himself £53.[60]

In December Herbert finally received the London publisher's criticisms of *Capricornia*. The firm's reader had taken issue with the characterization and, once again, with the length. Like Stephensen, Herbert was entering a period of despair and he wrote bitterly to Dibley on New Year's eve that he was considering a trip into 'eternal obscurity' in the north, convinced that he would never succeed as a writer.[61]

A hopeless proposal to try to reconstruct Stephensen's publishing company, seeking an additional £3000, failed and all production work stopped. Three weeks before Christmas Stephensen too was almost prepared to admit defeat. 'Things are not going well with me', he wrote to Ken Prior, chairman of the *Bulletin*'s virtually defunct Endeavour Press. 'I may have to shut up shop soon and possibly return to England.'[62] W. M. Hughes requested the return of his anecdotes manuscript which had been listed for November publication under the title 'By the Way'.[63] Stephensen wrote to Hughes that he would never give up the idea of establishing a 'real publishing house in Australia'.[64]

A week before Christmas the bailiff threatened to sell by auction Stephensen's typewriter, furniture and books at his Bond Street office if certain debts were not met.[65] Yet Stephensen was still able to show unrestrained enthusiasm for *Love Redeemed*, the sonnet sequence William Baylebridge had just published under his own Tallabila Press imprint. 'This day is the most significant day in Australia's literary history', Stephensen wrote to Baylebridge on 21 December 1934. 'That a poem of such fineness and dignity should be produced in our land is a sufficient guarantee of our national future.'[66]

His relationship with Baylebridge had accentuated an anti-democratic trend in his thinking. Along with Bakunin, Stephensen had little faith in governments, whether elected or not, and his increasingly strident nationalism was driving him further towards the right. To Baylebridge Stephensen had written that political leadership in Australia could 'no longer rest on the "democratic" ideal' because leadership was something 'enforced by those sufficiently strong to lead'.[67] The depression, with its heightened ideological and class conflict, seemed to signal the destruction of liberal democracy. After a decade in power, Mussolini was now being taken more seriously, and Hitler had been chancellor in Germany for almost two years.

Rudyard Kipling had banned the use of swastikas—an Indian emblem—from his book jackets, but in Australia the fascist concept enjoyed a surprising degree of support, and not just from Eric Campbell and his New Guard. In the same issue of the *Sydney Morning Herald* as a review praising Baylebridge's Elizabethan-style love sonnets as an 'unusual tour de force', there was a long and eulogistic report of an interview with 'Herr Hitler' at his 'Mountain Home'. As twilight fell over the 'snow-sheeted alps', a jovial Herr Hitler, resplendent in grey golfing clothes, had been a 'PERFECT HOST' and a 'perfect gentleman', offering assurances of peace and good will. The article was accompanied by a photograph of the impressive Matterhorn, inset with a cameo portrait of the great dictator himself, and the *Herald*'s readers could have been forgiven for thinking this was Father Christmas in disguise, spreading so much good will.[68]

A year earlier Miles Franklin had written to Hartley Grattan that she had heard Australians talk about wanting a 'Hitler or Mussolini to straighten up Australia', but that Hitler had now gone too far; his exhibition was 'too much for the free and easy tyrants out here'.[69] Stephensen, however, was no longer directly involved in politics, absorbed as he was by his own *Kulturkampf*. In January 1935, as his company foundered, Nettie Palmer wrote to Franklin that she was 'still pretty sad and bewildered' about Inky. 'I like him very much', she told Franklin, 'but I feel he's impossible, the more I think of his contradictions and uncertainties'.[70]

Still trying to complete the printing and publication of his company's

Rosaline Stephensen on 'The Ship' and her brother on 'Plain Jane', two of Helen Gibb's horses, at Hastings, January 1932 (photograph by courtesy of Rosaline Stephensen)

Miles Franklin with her London flat-mate's pet monkey, in 1932; the monkey featured in Franklin's novel, Bring the Monkey, *which Stephensen published in Sydney in 1933 (photograph from the Miles Franklin collection, by courtesy of the Mitchell Library, Sydney)*

Stephensen just after his return to Australia, with Norman Lindsay at Springwood, October 1932

Xavier Herbert in London in 1932 after completing the manuscript of Capricornia

W. J. Miles in the 1930s (photograph courtesy of Julie Munro)

most important novel, *Capricornia*, Stephensen offered the entire edition to a marketing group in exchange for the £300 it would take to pay the printer.[71] Stephensen had commissioned several jacket designs for the novel, and one was particularly striking: a red, white and black design using Aboriginal art motifs and showing a black head in profile.[72] However, Herbert came back to Sydney and advised the printer that Stephensen's contract had lapsed. The share hustler Sedgwick tried to talk Herbert into agreeing to the marketing scheme, but the collapse of P. R. Stephensen & Co. was not only inevitable but long overdue, and Herbert wearily took back his novel. He offered it again to Angus & Robertson, this time in standing type, but once more Walter Cousins rejected it as too long and depressing.[73] So the two tons of printer's type for *Capricornia* were melted down, dissolving all the hopes of its author. Herbert left for the north on Australia Day 1935, returning to obscurity and to the country which had inspired his fiction.

P. R. Stephensen & Co. Limited went into voluntary liquidation early in February, just a few months before its progenitor, the Endeavour Press, was likewise wound up.[74] Stephensen's two Sydney companies had been a daring experiment at a time of financial depression and cultural indolence, but this did not reduce the bitterness he always felt over their failure. Had he been a decade later, he might have survived to lay the foundations for a really worthwhile and enduring publishing house. Instead, only debts remained.

10

Mercurial Nationalism

For writers as well as publishers in the 1930s the material rewards were negligible and the frustrations immense. Only those with independent means, such as Baylebridge and Dark, were cushioned against financial pressures. The downfall of P. R. Stephensen & Co. was also, coincidentally, a time of personal crisis for the Palmers and for members of their literary circle.

Early in 1935, just as Stephensen's firm was going into liquidation, Marjorie Barnard had a nervous breakdown and Frank Dalby Davison was also suffering from 'nerves'. In February Miles Franklin wrote to Nettie Palmer that she was 'jaded into stagnation' and 'dry as dust spiritually and mentally'. She was concerned about Stephensen's failure and about his 'poor little wife'. In this bitter and depressed frame of mind, Franklin denigrated Penton's novel *Landtakers* as 'spurious spirituality' and described it as harsh, flat and 'as arid as a police report'. Passing on the news and gossip that Palmer liked to have, Franklin told her Penton was known as the 'Sydney cad' because of his destructive review of Crockett's novel *Mezzomorto*.[1] The Palmers themselves left Australia in March 1935, Nettie worn out by her literary journalism, and Vance feeling bitter and angry at the critical reception of his novels in Australia.

The Palmers were both turning fifty that year and Miles Franklin was approaching sixty. But if the older generation was dispirited, there was at the same time a new sense of militancy within the literary groups, and especially in the Fellowship of Australian Writers. The FAW had been formed in 1928 but by 1934 it was scarcely more than a conservative debating club. Late in 1934, however, the controversial visit of Czech-born journalist and writer Egon Kisch caused a furore in the FAW and indeed right across Australia. A respected literary figure, and one of the first writers arrested by the Nazis, Kisch had been invited to represent the international committee of the Movement Against War and Fascism at a peace congress in Melbourne, only to be denied entry on arrival in Australia. He literally 'jumped ship' in Melbourne and broke his leg, but eventually beat the government ban on him by a High Court action.[2]

Kisch's visit quickly became a cause célèbre, embarrassing the federal government and focusing attention on the threat of war caused by fascism. It also disturbed the club-like atmosphere of the Fellowship of Australian Writers and helped propel Stephensen back into the political arena.

Kisch was not the only writer then visiting Australia. The English Poet Laureate, John Masefield, had come out for the celebrations to mark Victoria's centenary, and he was invited to be guest of honour at an FAW luncheon in Sydney on 22 November 1934. The president of the Fellowship, George Mackaness, and others who thought they could keep politics out of literature, were appalled when the honorary secretary of the FAW, Frank Clune, invited Kisch along to the luncheon. A Vaucluse accountant and author of the rollicking autobiography *Try Anything Once* (1933), Clune was not especially radical. In fact he had once been a member of the New Guard. But he and many others including Stephensen were disgusted at the blatant infringement of free speech which the Kisch ban had revealed.

After a series of stormy meetings Mackaness resigned as FAW president, an event which caused Marjorie Barnard 'savage glee'. She wrote to Nettie Palmer that Mackaness illustrated the paradox that it was possible to be both a climber and a bounder.[3] Stephensen's former room mate at Oxford, Tom Inglis Moore, was elected to replace Mackaness, and Stephensen chaired a reception for both Kisch and Katharine Susannah Prichard held at the Cafe Shalimar in January 1935. This was in some ways a victory celebration for those who wanted the FAW to take a more active role in promoting not only culture but also social and political awareness. Stephensen had obtained a European encyclopaedia from a Sydney consulate, and he read out to the assembled writers at the reception a long list of Kisch's publications to counter the suggestion that the Czech was nothing but a communist agent. Apologizing to Kisch for the attitude of the government, Stephensen assured him that there were some Australians who resented the attempt to ban authors along with books.[4]

A series of articles on 'The Future of Australian Literature' in the Melbourne *Age* during February 1935, however, had a more profound effect on Stephensen than all the excitement over Kisch. The first article, by Vance Palmer, affirmed that 'scattered literary work of great value' had been done in Australia. What the country lacked most of all, though, was a 'lively and intelligent criticism', something which had 'lagged badly behind creative work'. Having written for London journals such as the *New Statesman* and the influential *New Age*, Palmer was by no means a parochial literary nationalist. However, his article was followed a week later by one of lofty scorn written by an Englishman resident in Australia, Professor G. H. Cowling. Stating at the outset that he regarded an Australian as a 'Briton resident in Australia', Cowling judged the country to be '"thin" and lacking in tradition' because of its lack of 'ancient churches, castles, ruins'.[5]

One correspondent facetiously retorted that perhaps Australian authors should be 'banished to Europe, where their flagging invention and prosaic imagination might be stimulated by the constant contemplation of castles, ruins and ancient churches'.[6] With her usual forthrightness, Miles Franklin wrote to Hartley Grattan that Cowling's arguments were 'weak piffle' and typical of the 'small-grade Britons' imported to man Australian universities.[7] In a long letter to the *Age*, Frederick Macartney wrote that other countries would take Australian literature seriously only 'when we take it seriously ourselves'. Even the recently deposed FAW president Mackaness suggested a number of measures, including a series of cheap reprints of 'great Australian books' like *Such is Life*, the establishment of a 'Commonwealth university press', and the imposition of a prohibitive duty on the millions of garish thrillers and Westerns flooding into Australia from overseas.[8]

Trying to revive his collapsed publishing business early in 1935, Stephensen too was appalled by Cowling's imperial arrogance. While Prichard and other left-wing writers formed the Writers' League, Stephensen and Clune worked within the FAW for the cause of Australian literature rather than international peace. Galvanized into more direct political action by the Kisch incident and the Cowling debate, they discussed issues such as censorship and the importation of cheap overseas 'rubbish'. By May the FAW had a Cultural Defence Committee of which Stephensen was chairman and Clune honorary treasurer. The committee held more than a dozen meetings and issued the pamphlet, *Mental Rubbish from Overseas: A Public Protest*.[9]

Spurred on by frustrations both cultural and financial, Stephensen spent the first half of 1935 trying to establish various literary ventures. Within a week of the shareholders' meeting early in February which put P. R. Stephensen & Co. Limited into voluntary liquidation, he had arranged some funding for a new enterprise, the Literary Guild of Australia. Guild members would receive each month a book and a copy of 'The Literary Times' with its 'comprehensive review of modern world literature'. This would dispose of surplus P. R. Stephensen & Co. stock and provide him with a magazine in which to harangue the apathetic and scold his enemies.[10] All but disgraced financially, he was still restless for a public platform.

The headquarters for this operation would be his old office at 24 Bond Street, and Stephensen sent his mother in Brisbane a draft prospectus for the Literary Guild, with the note: 'If it succeeds, we shall be all right'.[11] It did not succeed, and his new partners quickly deserted him. Stephensen was still being assisted by the investment agent Sedgwick who may have introduced him to A. S. R. Boynton, a salesman with money to invest, and another man, Captain L. A. Connolly, a journalist formerly of the British army. Both Boynton and Connolly took shares in a company Stephensen floated in March, Australian Book Services Limited, to handle the Literary Guild and produce the 'Literary Times'. Connolly was Stephensen's co-director and Boynton the sales manager.

Stephensen asked his friends in the FAW to keep their eyes open for other potential investors, and he even wrote to Frank Packer at the *Women's Weekly* in a hopeless attempt to link up once more with the real world of big business in Sydney.[12] As Vivian Crockett was bringing a libel action against the *Bulletin* and Brian Penton over the *Mezzomorto* review, Stephensen could not expect much sympathy from his old employer, and in fact he became convinced the *Bulletin* company was trying to destroy him. The truth was of course that Stephensen had self-destructive capacities far beyond anything even his enemies could muster against him.

About the middle of May 1935 Stephensen was amazed to discover that his co-director Connolly had published the first number of a new magazine, *The Opinion*, to rival the planned 'Literary Times'.[13] Angered but not silenced by the appearance of the *Opinion*, Stephensen immediately prepared a draft announcement of 'Cooee', the 'Australian National Literary Magazine' which would be the 'organ of Australia's ignored intellectual minority'.[14] Gone were the aspirations which would have made the 'Literary Times' a journal of 'world' literature. Instead 'Cooee' was to cry out for Australian writing, including that of Baylebridge, Miles Franklin, Christina Stead and Vance Palmer. As well, Stephensen planned a 'Retort Courteous to Professor Cowling', that imperious and imperial detractor of Australian literary endeavour.

Stephensen had now abandoned any thought of reaching a wide audience; he was anxious just to make contact with some like-minded enthusiasts. 'Are we all boobs, interested solely in race-going, cricket, borrowing money, daylight political robbery, suburban gossip, weather reports, wool growing and such like?', he asked. '*Is there no intellectual minority in Australia to foster indigenous culture?*' He admitted that 'Cooee' was a 'yell uttered in the vast open spaces of the Australian Mind', and quite possibly a 'despairing call' as well.

But there was a new edge to his injured pride. His isolationism not only stemmed from his fears about Australia being swamped by British and American popular culture, but also revived the spectre of involvement in another bloody overseas conflict. 'Europe has gone war mad, and is headed for Chaos', he wrote in the draft announcement of 'Cooee'. 'When the inevitable smash comes, followed by revolution and turmoil in Europe, Australia won't be there: *Australia will be here*. And what then? We shall have to develop the European inheritance on our own soil with our own resources and in our own way.' The first number of 'Cooee', to be published in June, would appear 'for sure', Stephensen wrote rather uncertainly, adding that further numbers would 'most probably appear'. He crossed out 'most probably' with a blue pencil, and changed the name of the magazine from 'Cooee' to *The Australian Mercury*.

In his 'confidential' memo seeking subscribers to the establishment fund for the *Australian Mercury* Stephensen was wildly over-optimistic as always. He mentioned a possible capital of £50 000 and concluded his investment pitch with the ingenuous comment that 'You can do many things with your money less satisfying than to help P. R. Stephensen launch the *Australian Mercury*'. Unfortunately, less satisfying investments must also have been safer, for he received only a couple of hundred pounds, including £10 from E. Morris Miller.[15] Yet he felt the magazine could win a payable circulation amongst 'the intelligent and sophisticated minority' in Australia provided that it was modern (but not 'modernistic'), local (but not parochial), national (but not 'colonial'), and vigorous (but not 'larrikin-crude').

'I have in mind the standards set by the *London Mercury*, the *American Mercury*, and the *Mercure de France* . . .', Stephensen wrote to Dr F. W. Robinson at the University of Queensland, enclosing his memo. Despite his nationalist zeal he was not afraid to use overseas examples to impress the local lads. His letter ended with a note of urgency, indicating that the initial response had not been all he had hoped for: 'Will you please do whatever you can, and immediately?' He signed off with the salutation 'YOURS FOR AUSTRALIA', reminding Robinson: '. . . as they used to say 40 years ago when our literature was beginning to flourish'.[16] Printed on the reverse of the fund application form was the heading DO IT NOW with two quotations showing how firm and deliberate an identification Stephensen felt with his adopted mentor, the late A. G. Stephens:

'The great names of Australia and of literature must not be taken lightly.' (A. G. Stephens in *The Bookfellow*)
'A nation without a literature is incomplete'. (P. R. Stephensen in *The Australian Mercury*)

Addressing him as 'Inky, dear old soul', Robinson replied that he was unmoved by the news that Australian literature was being reborn or revived, and refused to send a subscription to Stephensen's 'new mercurial venture'. If the magazine proved a success, Robinson said he would be pleased for Stephensen's sake, but added 'I don't want it, and I don't want to want it . . .'[17]

Although Stephensen had been frustrated in the months since his publishing company had collapsed, his very frustrations had been shaping themselves into a spirited manifesto on Australian culture which was to have great significance for him personally as well as for literary nationalism. He not only scrambled to produce the first, July issue of the *Australian Mercury*, as well as an August issue which never got beyond proof stage, but he also began writing *The Foundations of Culture in Australia: An Essay Towards National Self Respect*. Two major instalments of this appeared as editorials in the July and still-born August numbers of the *Mercury*, and, along with a third section written the following summer, the complete essay was published in book form in 1936.

Stephensen's achievement was not so much the originality of his ideas but rather the singular force and wit with which his polemical essay was armed, and its stimulating effect on other Australian writers and thinkers. As Margriet Bonnin has shown in her study of descriptive and travel writers in the 1930s, there was a preoccupation amounting almost to an obsession with the 'spirit' of Australia. Writers were concerned with national character, with the Aborigines, soil erosion, and the 'vast open spaces' of the interior. The failure of soldier settlement schemes, the declining birth-rate, the widespread droughts of the late 1920s and early 1930s, and the dislocation caused by the depression had all contributed to a state of deep insecurity and a corresponding yearning for stable national values.[18]

Within the literary community, issues such as censorship, the inability of local publishing companies to compete with overseas houses, and the implications of the extraordinary Kisch case had turned the FAW into an active lobby group. Yet this was also part of a broader cultural impulse and insecurity, something Stephensen felt keenly because of his own thwarted ambitions. There were other parallel crusades as well at this time. The composer Percy Grainger conducted an Australian tour in 1934–35 during which he staged concerts and made radio broadcasts designed to encourage self-respect in musical culture. Like Stephensen, Grainger urged Australians to look beyond the traditional European viewpoint, and to consider the cultural possibilities of other regions so that an individual Australian music could develop.[19]

The first two instalments of *The Foundations of Culture in Australia*, which Stephensen wrote in mid-1935 for his *Australian Mercury*, developed from the 'Retort Courteous' to Professor Cowling he had promised for the *Mercury* prototype, 'Cooee'. His answer to the effortless Anglocentricity of the professor of English at the University of Melbourne was indeed courteous, as well as balanced, intelligent and rather mockingly respectful. 'I would deplore the bad-mannered "Australianism" of anyone needlessly decrying English culture', Stephensen wrote in his essay, 'as much as I deplore Professor Cowling's denigration of the local culture'.[20] Stephensen described Cowling as 'well-meaning', and even thanked him for 'putting the Unteachable Englishman's point of view so succinctly on record'.[21] This was the skilled polemicist at work. Elsewhere in the essay, Stephensen reminded his readers that, in its brief white history, Australia had been a British colony, just as Britain had once been a colony of Rome.[22] Finding further support in the wide sweep of English history, Stephensen showed just how blind Cowling was:

> His attitude is precisely that of the Latinists who, perceiving Wycliffe and Chaucer writing books in the English vernacular, sniffed (no doubt) at the very idea of literature in English. Here we are on the threshold of Australian self-consciousness, at the point of developing Australian nationality, and with it Australian culture, we are in our Chaucerian phase, and this Professor cannot begin to perceive the excitement of it, overlooks his grand opportunity of studying and recording for posterity this birth-phase of a new literature in formation under his very nose . . .[23]

Stephensen rejected Australia's continuing status as a colony because it had 'an acknowledged right to become one of the nations of the world'. Within or without the British Empire, Australia had to find its own culture and define it, for 'we cannot suck pap forever from the teats of London'. Independence was now a necessity because English culture was showing signs of 'decline and "decadence"'. As examples, Stephensen cited Huxley's *Brave New World* and Lawrence's *Lady Chatterley's Lover*, though he hastened to define the term 'decadence' as 'ultra-sophistication', not in any 'simple "moral" sense'.[24]

The Foundations of Culture in Australia was based on Stephensen's lively summary of the history of Australian literary achievement. He began with a detailed exposition of W. C. Wentworth's poem *Australasia* which had won second prize in the 1823 Cambridge Chancellor's Medal competition. Wentworth was a native-born Australian—one of the earliest—yet the writer whose poem actually won the competition (on the prescribed theme 'Australasia') was 'an Englishman who had never left England', W. Mackworth Praed.[25] This set the tone for Stephensen's whole Australian/English dichotomy:

> Both poems were written in stilted couplets, in the high-falutin style of the period, the verses decked with classical allusions. Praed's winning poem runs smoothly and sweetly, and tells us precisely nothing about Australasia. Wentworth's poem is in parts impassioned and fiery, full of exact knowledge about Australasia. Praed is genteel and refined, Wentworth is shouting and vigorous. Praed's poem is purely 'literary' and bookish; Wentworth's poem is from life direct.[26]

Stephensen went on to look at each poem closely in order to elaborate and amplify this distinction, but his inspiration was to see Wentworth's final, patriotic vision as having direct relevance for the 1930s when England was looking more and more like a 'tamed lion':

> And, oh, Britannia! shouldst thou cease to ride
> Despotic Empress of old Ocean's tide—
> Should thy tamed lion—spent his former might—
> No longer roar, the terror of the fight;
> Should e'er arrive that dark, disastrous hour,
> When, bowed by luxury, thou yield'st to power...
> May this, thy last-born infant then arise,
> To glad thy heart, and greet thy parent eyes;
> *And Australasia float, with flag unfurled,*
> *A new Britannia in another world!*[27]

Stephensen went so far as to suggest that by the year 2000 Australia might rival England as a world power, a suggestion which looks less far-fetched now than it would have in the 1930s (not to mention the 1820s).

The essay developed this competitive dichotomy between England and Australia by tracing a line of 'melancholics' and exiles (including Clarke, Boldrewood, Gordon and Kendall) who had deferred to English conventions and to the 'idea of Australia as a permanent colony', and then comparing this with another, more vigorous and indigenous 'line of succession' composed of writers who were 'optimistic and humorous about Australia'. Among these were Paterson, Lawson, Furphy, the 'young'

Miles Franklin, Steele Rudd, and others of the *Bulletin* school. Stephensen criticized both the convict and bushranger themes as 'mainly the prerogative of English-minded writers'. As the convict writers Clarke and 'Price Warung' had conveniently been succeeded by Stephensen's personal enemy, Brian Penton, he was therefore able to describe *Landtakers* as a novel 'which wallows in the sensationalism of convictism and flogging'.[28]

Stephensen acknowledged the historical role of the old Sydney *Bulletin*, but criticized the 'Irishman', J. F. Archibald, for making his magazine a '*lark played by a literary larrikin*'. Stephensen apologized for his alliteration, but scolded the '*Bullet-een* (as it used to be called)' for thumbing its nose 'at England and at respectability'. Having thus settled a few scores with Penton and the *Bulletin*, he then took the opportunity to pay his respects to A. G. Stephens, 'Celtic-Australian literary critic of genius' who had shown 'what literary criticism really could be in Australia'. Now, Stephensen lamented, the once 'radical ragamuffin' *Bulletin* had become 'violently and hysterically anti-radical and anti-labour in politics, with a tendency to a Fascist outlook'.[29]

In the two instalments of his essay which he penned as editorials for the *Australian Mercury*, Stephensen expressed respect for England and concern about the development of 'Hitlerism and Fascism' in Australia. The danger he saw was not from the left, but from groups like the New Guard and from the political censorship imposed by state and federal governments. He repeatedly described Hitler as a schoolboy bully, lacking in culture, and commented that the '*Heil Hitler* buncombe' of fascism would be treated in Australia with the 'contempt such preposterous saluting and goose-stepping deserves'.[30]

His attitude to Australia's own military history was a combination of anti-imperialism and anti-militarism, but with a respect for individual soldiers such as his former Queensland University friends, Dennis Fryer and Fred Paterson. The men who had volunteered for the AIF were 'splendid fellows' who detested rather than glorified militarism. In Stephensen's view they had '*Made history*—not jingo death-and-glory history, flag-flapping history, chauvinistic history—but a new kind of history'. This was a history 'founded on individual initiative which became an astounding collective *morale*'. Although Stephensen had had no personal experience of World War I, it remained of vital significance to him and he urged the careful study of 'that turning-point in our national life, 1914 to 1918, in its moral, its psychological, its national aspects'.[31]

Vehemently opposed to the militarism of the New Guard, Stephensen attacked them in his essay as 'would-be Fascists' and 'Fascist tykes' who boasted about the AIF as though it belonged to them, and who wanted to 'impose a military, or semi-military, regimentation upon Australian civil life'.[32] This was the real threat which the 'timid intellectuals' needed to be on guard against. Stephensen's warning about right-wing extremists in Australia was a clear indication of his continuing sympathy with the anti-fascist commitment of writers such as Prichard and Jean Devanny.

It was also an ominous and ironical comment on his own unthinking slide 'down a steep place to Fascism' just a few years hence:

> When the Hitler-minded in Australia develop a little more self-confidence, enough, it may be, to seize power, the press which now tacitly encourages them, and the cowardly intellectuals who merely stand by and lift their eyebrows, *will feel the weight of the rubber-truncheon*, as the press and the intellectuals have felt it in Germany.
> Fascism is a greater menace to us than Bolshevism could ever be; for Fascism is a schoolboy bully, armed. It has no intellectual pretensions, aims at imposing discipline 'from above,' is a Junker-idea, a Hun-idea which Australians have fought to abolish from the earth. Bolshevism at least has a humanitarian goal, a cogent philosophy, and a professed respect for ideas and the raising of cultural standards in the community-in-general. Probably we shall not have either of these cults, in their European forms, in our Australia of the future; we shall work out our own destiny. But not without thought. Unthinking, we could go down a steep place to Fascism. Let our intellectuals awake from their reveries of faraway Europe, and deal, if they can, with *this* danger.[33]

Perhaps one of the keys to Stephensen's later dalliance with fascist ideology was suggested by a section of his essay where he attempted to distinguish between the 'sabre-rattling' of 'Huns like Hitler' and the more respectable love of country which Stephensen himself expressed with such emotional force and conviction:

> A nation is nothing but an extension of the individuals comprising it, generation after generation of them. When I am proud of my nationality, I am proud of myself...
> The nation as an extension of the ego, as a permanent idea which lives when the individual dies, is essential to an individual's well being.[34]

Stephensen's theories of individualism were inspired by Bakunin and Nietzsche, and there was always the danger that, under stress or excitement, even the most benign and theoretical identification of self with nation might approach the dangerous territory of megalomania, especially in someone with Stephensen's sense of destiny as a cultural prophet. The weapons of cultural assertion which Stephensen wielded with such force in *The Foundations of Culture in Australia* could, with the wrong encouragement, be put in the service of those who admired rather than deplored the examples of Hitler and Mussolini.

In terms of the rich texture of the essay itself, however, Stephensen's ideas on politics, on fascism and anti-fascism, were in fact peripheral to the cultural foundations he was at pains to unearth and display. And his essay was read as it was intended to be read: as an intelligent, lively, and entertaining case for Australian culture generally, and Australian literature in particular. What excited his many readers was that his forceful arguments, and the stimulating examples he adduced from his wide reading and experience of other cultures, all proved beyond doubt that the foundations for an independent Australian culture were already firmly in place. It is difficult in retrospect to appreciate just how dominated Australia was at that time by debilitating Anglophilia. Stephensen's essay was aimed at the 'intellectual minority', and many in this group did find the work refreshing and inspiring.

The response to his first editorial in the *Australian Mercury* was immediate and mostly gratifying. Xavier Herbert, who had received a copy of the magazine in Darwin, wrote that his feelings about Stephensen's essay were 'too deep for expression', and a range of other people from former prime minister W. M. Hughes to the scholar Randolph Hughes praised the aggressive editorial.[35] There were also more critical assessments. Frank Wilmot, one of the magazine's financial supporters, thought there was too much 'boost', too much talk about Australian culture, and 'not enough evidence of performance'.[36] This was a justifiable criticism since the first *Mercury* also published some banal epigrams by Bartlett Adamson and a slab of stilted verse by Ambrose Pratt. Ken Slessor praised the *Mercury* as a 'wonderfully good production', but made a similar point to Wilmot's, that the poetry in the magazine was an 'unfortunate anti-climax' after the 'debunking' of the editorial.[37] The first issue did, however, also include a powerful Eleanor Dark story about the suicide of an actor, as well as the texts of radio talks given by Miles Franklin and Frank Dalby Davison during Writers' Week in April.

Most of the 2000 copies of the *Mercury* were distributed to booksellers and newsagents throughout Australia, only a few hundred going directly to readers and subscribers. Fewer than a hundred people took out annual subscriptions, so the magazine was soon in trouble financially.[38] Stephensen's own financial foundations were collapsing, and his former partner Boynton had instituted legal action against him, claiming £1000 damages.[39]

It was a busy period for literary litigation. In June, Crockett had been awarded £1000 against Penton and the *Bulletin* after a Supreme Court hearing lasting several days. It was a remarkable case, and one in which an author successfully sued a reviewer. Crockett was represented by no fewer than two King's Counsels, including A. B. Piddington who had been victorious in defence of Kisch six months previously. In the Crockett case, the KC who defended the *Bulletin* described *Mezzomorto* as a novel which 'just reeks of blood, immoral women, sadism and disgusting things'. Turning to the all-male jury, the defence counsel put the time-honoured Victorian question to them: 'Ask yourselves, gentlemen, in your own hearts, is this a book you would like your own wives and daughters to read?'[40]

The gentlemen of the jury, however, remained unimpressed, and found for Crockett, to Stephensen's delight as well. He dined out that night in celebration, and with good reason, for his publishing company had gone bust not long after Penton's damaging review had appeared in the *Bulletin*. After Crockett's successful action, Stephensen took out his own writ, claiming £20 000 for the loss of his business, though it was another year before the case finally came to court, and by then his finances were in diabolical disarray.[41]

In mid-1935, however, the *Mercury* operation was already beset with difficulties. Stephensen had been rushed to hospital with appendicitis just as the July number was coming out, and the August issue was never printed. It was typeset and proofed, but the printers would proceed no further unless Stephensen paid the £100 still outstanding for the first number. The stalled August *Mercury* continued Stephensen's editorial essay and included a Dal Stivens sketch, a Davison story, poems by young Adelaide writer Ian Mudie, and an essay and review by Miles Franklin. It was a stronger issue than the first, but Waite and Bull, the printers, stopped waiting and the *Mercury* sank along with Stephensen's earlier publishing ventures.[42]

Virtually destitute, the Stephensens were forced to sell a valuable copy of the Mandrake Press *Paintings of D. H. Lawrence* for £20 to meet living expenses. During September various investors and contractors began pressing for payment, and the electricity department threatened to cut off power, at the Balmoral flat as well as at the Bond Street office.[43] Boynton, who had invested in Australian Book Services Limited, finally obtained a judgment for more than £500, and bankruptcy proceedings were instituted against Stephensen. He therefore resigned from the 'Board of Directors' of Australian Book Services Limited, leaving the commission agent, Sedgwick, as 'managing director'. The company headquarters were moved to a small, cheap room on the roof of the Manchester Unity building.[44]

Even Stephensen's friends and supporters began to turn against him. Miles Franklin wrote to Nettie Palmer, now in London, about the 'awful mess' the *Mercury* operation was in. Franklin claimed it had not been lack of financial support which had defeated Stephensen since his return to Australia, but rather his methods—a view shared by Norman Lindsay and other disgruntled former allies. Franklin wrote to Palmer that, with the money Stephensen had collected, they could have begun a successful magazine themselves. 'Stephensen must have had thousands', she told Palmer sorrowfully, and it was 'all gone for nothing'. Yet despite his faults, Stephensen possessed 'many qualities that would have been useful in leading the wandering Australian writers to their rightful harvest'.[45]

Franklin was right to a large degree. Stephensen had used thousands of pounds of *Bulletin* money as well as the funds of many smaller investors to stagger from one publishing failure to the next. But he had also introduced and sponsored a number of important new writers, improved book production standards and, perhaps more significantly, had helped to raise the level of debate on literary issues. In June, for example, with the *Mercury* still in preparation, he had convened a meeting at the Shalimar Cafe to form a New South Wales branch of the Book Censorship Abolition League. Among the members of the provisional council were Dulcie Deamer, Jean Devanny, Bartlett Adamson and Clive Evatt, brother of the High Court judge. The League had originated in Melbourne in response to increased political censorship.[46]

Stephensen's greatest need now was money, not causes, and he signed a contract with Australian Trans-Continental Airways Limited to compile and publish various material including the life story of Captain Ernest Mustar,[47] a brochure on Junkers aircraft, and a pamphlet on barter trade with Germany. This pamphlet was published by Stephensen's company under the title *Trade Without Money!* and the author was given as 'An Economist'. Stephensen wrote it just as the Nuremberg decrees were being used to segregate Germany's population and persecute Jews and other 'non-Aryans'. Yet the pamphlet was very sympathetic towards Germany, describing the huge war reparations as a 'tragedy'. Possibly working from material he had been supplied with, Stephensen described the German people as 'exceptionally tough' in spirit. They had made a 'gigantic effort at national reconstruction' since the war and, in their desperate economic situation, had fallen back on a system of '"Autarchy" (or national self-sufficiency)'. Only months after describing Hitler as a bully, Stephensen was now prepared to sell his services so that the Nazi dictatorship could be clothed in euphemisms. The business justification, though, was quite simple: Stephensen had to have income, and Trans-Continental Airways wanted Germany's Junkers aircraft which they hoped to purchase in a barter exchange for shipments of Australian wool.[48]

The airline company agreed to pay an advance of £50 and then £50 a week while the various publications were in preparation. Stephensen travelled to Melbourne, engaged a secretary, and took a suite of rooms at Scott's Hotel costing 25 shillings a day to work on Captain Mustar's memoirs. Winifred was annoyed that he could not make do with an ordinary 8s 6d room, but Stephensen replied that he had to have favourable conditions for 'such a high speed job'. In the aftermath of Crockett's action against the *Bulletin*, and with bankruptcy proceedings hanging over him, Stephensen had almost convinced himself that the *Bulletin* company really was trying to crush him. 'I have had such worries and many more every day for more than a year', he wrote to Winifred. 'It is all due to trying to run a business without enough capital, while there is a real group worth millions of pounds trying to crush me. Now I just won't be crushed...'[49]

On his return from Melbourne he received a 'nasty letter' from one of his former partners, and would not let Winifred read it. She wrote in her diary:

> We are desperately hard up and Inky still lives in a dream of 'tomorrow' and chess. Meanwhile I'm driven nearly silly with bills, demands, anxiety, and damned little food. A day of terrible woe. I felt very ill and utterly depressed. Inky came home at eight and played chess for hours. He will not discuss the bills and what's best to do.[50]

After a couple of weeks the airline company money suddenly stopped coming in, and Stephensen returned once more to hopes of resuscitating the *Mercury*. He wrote to supporters in October 1935 that the magazine was 'having the fight of its life' but would pull through 'for certain'. His xenophobia as well as his paranoia showed signs of increasing. The

Mercury must survive, he wrote, in order to replace 'so much Yankee and other foreign rubbish' entering Australia.[51]

Nettie Palmer wrote to Baylebridge from London that she was 'very anxious about Inky' and quoted Baylebridge's own assessment of the paradoxical publisher: 'All the defects of the very finest qualities'.[52] This had now become the pattern. Stephensen's literary acquaintances could no longer reconcile his idealism with his increasingly dubious business dealings. One old friend, the cynical and misanthropic Jack Kirtley, wrote to Winifred that her husband's talent was as a 'controversialist', and a magazine was a better proposition than book publishing in 'this tight-fisted country'. In any case, Inky was too 'good-natured' to be a publisher, and also 'a little ahead of his time'. Kirtley thought a newspaper editorship would be 'an easy stage towards a political career'.[53] Eventually Stephensen got both an editorship and a brief political career, but it was more than he or Kirtley had ever bargained for.

His *Mercury* editorial had in fact greatly impressed one Sydney magazine 'proprietor', William John Miles, a wealthy accountant and company director. Miles had been a longtime rationalist and, by coincidence, the same month Stephensen's *Mercury* appeared, Miles launched the first number of his *Independent Sydney Secularist*. His pseudonymous editorial noted that the 'chief cause of Australians' lack of patriotic feeling' was the 'diversion of their thought from Australia's future to the future of Britain's Empire'.[54] To Miles's surprise and pleasure, he stumbled on Stephensen's editorial in the *Mercury* which professed similar sentiments but at greater and more eloquent length.

By nature a cautious and meticulous man, Miles was not given to sudden enthusiasms, yet the appearance of P. R. Stephensen seemed, even to his rational imagination, almost miraculous. In July 1935 he sought Stephensen out and had a talk with him. At first Stephensen treated Miles as a potential investor who might be inveigled into funding further issues of the *Mercury*, but Miles had no special interest in literary culture. His hobby-horses were nationalism, rationalism, and the evils of British imperialism. In August Miles wrote to Stephensen that he could not recommend any investors for the *Mercury*, and cautioned Stephensen against being 'too optimistic'—something which only led to 'fits of depression'.[55]

The sixty-four-year-old Miles was, like Stephensen, a competent chess player, and he shared the younger man's anti-Christianity as well as his love of polemical games. Stephensen later described him as being armed with 'mordant wit and ruthless logic'.[56] Miles's nationalist spirit had been fostered when, as a boy, he had been taken to England by his parents and had witnessed the famous 1882 Ashes cricket test, narrowly won by the colonials. Miles had joined his father's accountancy firm and eventually took control of the exclusive menswear store, Peapes, which his father had owned.[57]

During World War I Miles had founded a New South Wales branch of the Rationalist Press Association and published his pamphlet, *The Myth of the Resurrection of Jesus, the Christ* (1914). He had also become caught up in the anti-conscription movement, speaking at rallies in the Domain and elsewhere alongside his class enemies, the socialists and 'Wobblies', and contributing to the left-wing *Ross's Magazine*. About 1917 he organized an Advance Australia League in Sydney with the letterhead slogan, 'Australia First!'. The objects of the League included the maintenance of 'White Australia' and the fostering of 'Australian national sentiment'. Miles was still using his League letterhead in 1920 when the first number of the magazine *Australian Post* appeared with a map of Australia on the cover and the same slogan as Miles's: 'Australia First'.[58]

After many years devoted to his business activities and to his other interests such as rationalism, Miles by 1935 had decided to take up once more the political cause of Australia First. Late in that year he left his office in Challis House, Martin Place, which he had occupied for more than twenty years, and moved to a smaller one at Wingello House, Angel Place, a suitably witty address for a dedicated atheist. (This building had also housed the headquarters of the New Guard.) Although Miles had a knowledge of literary classics and had been an enthusiast for *Such is Life*, his interest was not in the literary aspects of Stephensen's *Mercury* essay but rather in its 'Australia First' propaganda potential.

As the summer of 1935 approached, with no other possibilities for salvaging the submerged *Mercury*, Stephensen tried once more to attract Miles's patronage. The canny old businessman was probably his last chance of finding someone wealthy and altruistic enough to support a cause without thought of profit. In November Stephensen submitted to him a far-reaching plan for an 'Australia First Party', elements of which Miles considered too far 'ahead of the times'.[59] The platform was Swiss-style nationalism, based on the principle that Australians should never participate 'in wars of conquest or aggression', but would defend their own territory 'to their last drop of blood'.

Stephensen's political programme included aspects of republican, fascist, and even communist policy. The six states of Australia were to be replaced by thirty 'provinces', each capable of maintaining a million 'small holders' by the 1980s, and the commonwealth government would control all national legislation. There would be a government monopoly of banking, and all overseas borrowing would cease. Population would be encouraged by various bonuses and land grants, and immigration would bring in 100 000 people a year on a 'racial quota' made up of 70 per cent 'Teutonic and Celtic races', with the other 30 per cent provided by 'Latin', 'Slav' and 'Asiatic' races. All such immigrants, however, would be required to conform to 'Australian standards' of education and social customs. Appeal to the Privy Council would be abolished, all imperial honours and titles would be replaced by an Australian Order of Merit, and the governor-general and members of parliament would have to be Australian born.

There were more bizarre and ominous plans as well. The Commonwealth Bank would purchase all overseas-owned property, and national culture would be fostered by ensuring that key positions in education, libraries, bookshops and the media were held by Australians. This echo of Nazism was contradicted, however, by the plan to abolish all forms of censorship and to arm the citizenry as a safeguard against invasion or 'any attempt at Fascist military dictatorship within the Commonwealth'. Stephensen's Australia First Party platform was thus a revolutionary and yet conservative confusion of aims and ideologies, representing the rag-bag of political ideas he had picked up in the decade and a half since his Queensland university days. The remnants of his Swiss grandfather's democratic ideals were still discernible as well.

To give the party plan special appeal for Miles, it was specified as strictly 'non-sectarian and non-religious'. While it would rely on 'peaceful persuasion', the party would, if opposed by force or declared illegal, 'retaliate by force and illegality'. Seditious ideas still excited Stephensen, and it was little wonder that the cautious Miles regarded this political programme as daringly and even dangerously 'ahead of the times'.

Although he rejected the party plan as too premature, Miles kept Stephensen on a string about the possibility of a new Australia First paper. Around Christmas 1935 he paid Stephensen £10 to help him complete the final instalment of *The Foundations of Culture in Australia*. The Stephensens had moved from their Balmoral flat to a cheaper one in Kings Cross where they at times actually went hungry while Stephensen was finishing his book. One day Miles visited them and, unknowingly, ate the last of their bread and butter. Winifred's diary entry for 14 January 1936 gives the exact flavour of their impoverishment:

> What a day. I produced my last shilling for cigs and we have only had a few oddments of food left, a tiny drop of milk which I had to part with to give————a cup of tea ... I had one egg, a cold leftover sausage and tomatoes. I fried them all up and decided to read whilst eating so it would seem more. But just as I was feeling it was not too bad and trying to forget the fruit I'd longed for and the chops I'd smelt and the prawns I'd admired, the wireless started to talk about strawberries and armfuls of food and in my book my eyes fell on a paragraph about food—ham which I do enjoy—the word ham caught my eye and held it.[60]

Relief was in sight, for two days later Miles wrote that his enthusiasm for a larger 'monthly paper' was increasing, and by the end of January 1936 he had paid the Communist Party printery a deposit for the publication in book form of *The Foundations of Culture in Australia*.[61] The book was to be styled exactly like *On the Pacific Front*, an account of Egon Kisch's visit which the same printer had just produced for Stephensen's company, Australian Book Services Limited. The author was left-wing journalist Tom Fitzgerald who had written the Kisch book under the pseudonym 'Julian Smith'.[62]

The significance of the third and final section of *The Foundations of Culture in Australia*, written during January 1936, was its greater political commitment. This had come about largely because of Stephensen's contact with Miles, the man who was now sponsoring the publication of the complete essay. 'The question of Australian nationality, as I now think', Stephensen wrote, introducing the final section, 'is not merely a cultural question: it is financial, political, economic'. Although he denied any personal interest in *'party politics'*—in 'sectional bickerings' or 'the dog-fights of the market-place'—the whole thrust of his argument had become political. Australia's 'literary dependence' was probably a result of economic subordination to Britain, he concluded, and therefore emancipation could only be achieved by 'some form of political action to free Australia from English (or other international) control'.[63]

Stephensen went on to discuss the Statute of Westminster and 'Equal Status', the need for increased population and industry, and the necessity for Australia to trade with major Asian countries, principally Japan. He thought national morale had been undermined by the protectionist mentality of relying on the British navy, and prophesied, with accuracy as it turned out, that British military forces would be preoccupied defending 'England first' when the 'dictator-ruled countries' went 'berserk in Europe'. Likening Australia's role to that of a young man leaving his parents' house, Stephensen forecast that Australians would then be *'in the exhilarating position of having to defend their own country, unaided'*.[64]

Contact with Miles, the old anti-conscription campaigner, had sharpened Stephensen's bitterness at the wartime sacrifice of Australian lives, and he asserted that 'every man, every shilling'[65] would be needed now for the defence of the country. Australia could not rely on British protection in any case, since a Japanese attack would only be launched 'during another self-decimating war of the white races in Europe'. Europe itself was 'war-crazed and power-crazed', a 'den of cutthroats, thieves, and barbarians', and the 'world's cockpit and bearpit'. Stephensen made it clear he was not advocating the aggressive, 'sub-civilised' nationalisms of 'Hitler, Mussolini, and Winston Churchill', and reiterated his distinction between 'chauvinistic' and 'cultural' nationalism.[66]

He concluded *The Foundation of Culture in Australia* by returning to the refrain, 'A New Britannia in Another World!', and a vision of Australia as the new home of the British race, maintaining 'our Ideal of White Australia'. He was right to use the word 'our', for the obsession with White Australia was at this stage Miles's, rather than his. Conveniently forgetting Aborigines for the moment, Stephensen tried to reassure white Australians, including himself, that 'Visions of race-grandeur become dangerous only when they imply the extermination or subjugation of other races'.[67]

With this slab of political rhetoric, prophecy and prejudice added to his earlier, more balanced cultural analysis, Stephensen delivered the manuscript of *The Foundations of Culture in Australia* to Hector Ross, who was on the central committee of the Communist Party and also managed the Forward Press, the party's printery. Two thousand copies of the book were printed with yellow paper covers in February 1936, and Stephensen presented a signed copy to his former Ipswich friend, the radical Albert Welsby, inscribing it to the man 'who first taught me the meaning of Dialectical Materialism'.[68] Miles agreed to pay royalties at the rate of tenpence a copy, which was indeed generous, representing about 40 per cent of the retail price of two shillings, and in March and April Stephensen received payments totalling more than £60.[69]

At a small dinner at the Carlton Hotel to celebrate the publication of the book, Miles announced his plans for a new magazine, *The Publicist*, which would begin in July. Also present at the dinner were three of Miles's friends who formed the core of his Australia First political group: S. B. Hooper, a bank manager and fellow anti-conscriptionist; C. W. Salier, another rationalist and a senior executive of the AMP Society; and the thirty-year-old Edward Masey, who was a foundation member of the Australian Institute of Political Science.[70] Stephensen was the newest and most enthusiastic recruit, and it was the provocative *Foundations of Culture in Australia* which provided Miles's re-activated wartime movement with its first and perhaps only propaganda success.

The response to the book from Stephensen's wide circle of acquaintances was little short of ecstatic. Benjamin Fryer, the editor of a printing trade journal, congratulated him on his 'straight speaking', and joked that the book would no doubt be censored by the following Monday. E. J. Brady wrote from Melbourne that by 'the thunder of Caboolture—which is the loudest thunder I have heard in this country—you have done a good job'. Writing as a 'social and financial outcast' and an 'amused spectator', Jack Kirtley said he had read the book with great interest, but did not share Stephensen's optimism. Within the next ten years, Kirtley gloomily but accurately forecast, Australians would once again participate in the 'gory arena of Europe'.[71]

Others from Xavier Herbert to Mary Gilmore wrote in glowing terms, although E. Morris Miller told Stephensen not to expect much thanks for his efforts:

> Your iconoclastic 'Foundations' reached me yesterday. By the time I hurriedly finished it I wondered whether any foundations were really left. Nothing seemed to be upstanding. You intended to create a shambles and left us all in as though shovelled out of a barrow when asleep. It is good to awaken people out of smugness . . . Although you will get it in the neck for your disrespectful handling of authority, calm minded supporters will eventually follow up what is substantial in your work and forget the racketing they have received . . .[72]

Writing from Barcelona just before the outbreak of the Spanish Civil War, Nettie Palmer told friends that *The Foundations of Culture in Australia* had begun as a valuable and even brilliant commentary, but that Stephensen had fallen 'headlong into many of the crudities and boostings he has had to condemn'.[73]

The book, however, created as much excitement amongst reviewers as it had amongst friends. Not surprisingly, the most detailed and thoughtful assessment, in the March *Australian Quarterly*, was by Edward Masey,

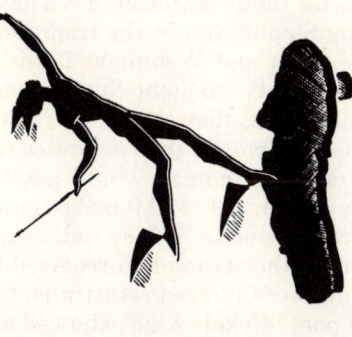

A copy of *The Foundations of Culture in Australia*, inscribed to Stephensen's WEA friend, Albert Welsby

one of Miles's inner circle. Masey was especially impressed by the 'wealth of matter', by the elegance of Stephensen's diction, and by the 'vigour and clarity' of his argument. But the scholarly Masey questioned some of Stephensen's views on 'nationalism and economic dependence' as 'insular and protectionist'.[74]

The Melbourne *Herald* thought the book a 'brilliant piece of pamphleteering', and a Melbourne radio reviewer described it as 'vitally and cleverly written', placing Stephensen in the tradition of social critics of the calibre of H. L. Mencken and Wyndham Lewis.[75] While Frederick Macartney, in *All About Books*, thought Stephensen's ideas were 'not always as closely co-ordinated as they should be', he excused these blemishes and also the touches of 'spleen', and concluded that despite its faults the book was so important no summary could possibly do it justice. 'It must be read', Macartney remarked, 'and it makes entertaining reading'.[76]

In May Stephensen was invited to Sydney radio station 2KY to discuss on air the numerous letters the station had received following an earlier session on *The Foundations of Culture in Australia*. Stephensen said that one correspondent, the poet 'Rickety Kate', showed a 'delightful sense of humour' in thinking that Stephensen wanted to burn all imported books in a huge bonfire. 'Well, maybe it would be no great loss', Stephensen commented facetiously, adding that 'Rickety Kate' would not find a publisher for her humour 'as long as Australians prefer P. G. Wodehouse's jokes'.[77]

During April, after the first printing of 2000 copies had quickly sold out, Stephensen amd Miles disagreed over plans for a reprint. In the space of a couple of days they fired letters backwards and forwards, trying to score points and no doubt getting each other's measure. In clarifying his own 'personal prejudices, shortcomings or idiosyncracies', Stephensen proudly informed Miles that he came of a 'stiff-backed generation' and would 'beg for favours of no man'. Yet straightaway he appealed to Miles, and not without some charm, that 'With you in particular I like to discuss ideas rather than coin and I hope you will get the coin part of the discussion over quickly'.[78]

Miles not only paid him a generous royalty on *The Foundations of Culture in Australia* but also agreed to pay for a reprint of the book about the middle of the year, and put Stephensen on a retainer of £5 a week as his 'literary adviser' for the forthcoming *Publicist* magazine.[79] Stephensen was still facing bankruptcy proceedings, and the allowance he and Winifred received every Friday from Miles was barely enough to cover their rent as well as food and other bills. Winifred, who turned fifty that year, had been ill with pleurisy, and her medical expenses and need of special attention added to their financial burden. Her health continued to deteriorate during the 1930s, and they moved restlessly from flat to flat, never having the money to buy a house of their own, something Winifred had wanted since they first began living together in England.

Not yet thirty-five, Stephensen had produced what many considered to be a brilliant Australian polemic and one 'more assiduously consulted than acknowledged', in the words of Miles Franklin.[80] Although *The Foundations of Culture in Australia* managed to disturb a few Anglican archbishops, the most hostile reaction came, rather surprisingly, from the scholar Randolph Hughes who had praised the first *Mercury* instalment. In the English journal, *Nineteenth Century*, Hughes described Stephensen's book as a 'fumy elucubration ... clumsily conceived and barbarously written', and the product of a mind 'muddled and ill-furnished'. Revealing his own pro-fascist tendencies, Hughes objected to Stephensen's abusive descriptions of 'Herr Hitler', and was also angered by what he saw as the 'malignant distortion of English history'.[81] In Australian literary and intellectual terms, however, *The Foundations of Culture* remained one of the most influential books of the decade.

Immediately he had finished reading it at the Aboriginal Compound in Darwin, where he now had a job as temporary superintendent, Xavier Herbert scribbled an excited letter to Stephensen about the book's 'inspired message'. He wrote that he was 'filled with longing to be by your side, fighting'.[82] Stephensen regarded his own book as a 'Rubicon-crossing manifesto',[83] but it was also one of his last public utterances as an anti-fascist and a liberal.

As Europe lurched towards the certainty of another violent conflict, Stephensen offered thoughtful Australians a hectoring but also highly stimulating polemic, with a vision of past and future which incorporated elements as diverse as Aboriginal and English pre-history, communism, and the dangers of fascism. It was the most significant achievement of his tempestuous career, and it coincided with the most impoverished period of his life. His vision was unquestionably a prophetic one. The irony was that it would lead him ultimately to personal disaster.

11
War of Words

With his own business in ruin, Stephensen sought at least temporary shelter under the patronage of the wealthy Miles. 'The present campaign in the "Publicist"', he wrote to Xavier Herbert, 'as far as I am concerned is by way of a preliminary to the establishment of a True Australian National Publishing House'.[1]

However, as Miles stated in his first editorial, 'A publicist is a writer on current political topics'. Right from the start, Stephensen's own regular 'Bunyip Critic' column, subtitled 'Experiments in Australianity', was oriented towards politics rather than literature. The proofs of the first *Publicist* were completed, as Stephensen noted with some relish, on American Independence Day, and Australian independence was now his consuming ambition. Without the application of the two 'magic' words, 'Australia First', he wrote, 'we live continuously in a mirage, in a Fata Morgana of Europe, reflected upside down in the sky'.[2]

The *Publicist* was launched in July 1936, the month the Spanish Civil War broke out, and the magazine developed against this background of heightened ideological conflict and violence. In Australia as elsewhere there was considerable support for Franco among Catholics who saw the civil war as a ruthless assault on the church. The *Publicist*, however, was anti-communist as well as anti-Christian, and wanted no part of this far-away struggle. Stephensen and Miles were convinced there would be another major European war, but they were both determined to fight to keep Australian troops for home defence. Stephensen's first Bunyip Critic column included three satirical recruitment posters seeking half a million young Australians 'for use in Europe as soil-fertiliser' and to act as 'lethal-gas inhalers'. In literature, too, Europe seemed to offer only a dead end, and Stephensen instanced Spengler's *Decline of the West* as the fountain of 'intellectual decadence and literary defeatism'. The 'simpering war neurosis' of Europe had produced work with titles like *The Waste Land, Decline and Fall* and *Those Barren Leaves*.[3]

Stephensen made it clear in this first *Publicist* that he and the magazine's editor, 'John Benauster', were not responsible for each other's opinions. Miles was never named in the magazine other than by pseudonyms, but Stephensen made no attempt to cloak his identity except on occasions when he playfully adopted names such as 'Rex Williams' (that is, King Billy—a typical *Publicist* joke). Stephensen conceded that his 'propaganda for an Australian national culture' would be waged under a great disadvantage since the *Publicist* was 'a paper of big ideas and small circulation'.[4]

Comprising usually sixteen large pages of double-column type between yellow paper covers, the *Publicist* was sold by subscription and through news agencies for almost six years. The average print run was 3000 copies, though never more than two-thirds of these were sold and Miles did not seek advertising revenue. He did not need to. His losses on the *Publicist* enabled him to write about £2000 a year off his heavily taxed income. As Edward Masey, one of the contributors, later wryly remarked, the magazine was in fact jointly subsidized by Miles and the government.[5]

Miles was never afraid to acknowledge that the *Publicist* was an 'extremely unpopular' journal,[6] and he and his hired pen Stephensen even seemed to take a perverse delight in being oracular outsiders. In Stephensen's case, this confirmed his self-image as a national visionary, and Miles was both by fortune and temperament an élitist. Not a charitable man, he indulged himself by spending considerable amounts of money on another whim, gambling. Every Saturday he attended the races to bet on a special losing system. As with his *Publicist* hobby, this may also have been an amusing way of outwitting the Taxation Department.

The *Publicist* operation was run from a ground-floor office in the T & G building in Elizabeth Street, facing Hyde Park. The office had a plate-glass window and also served as a bookshop which was something of a misnomer since much of the stock consisted of old books Miles had brought from home. The 'shop', though, did at various times handle books by Miles Franklin, Frank Clune, William Baylebridge and Ian Mudie, and there were always copies of *The Foundations of Culture in Australia* available.[7]

For most of its half decade, the *Publicist* headquarters was run by Miles himself. He arrived punctually each morning by taxi from his house in Gordon to write letters and articles at a big oak table, and was assisted by a secretary and by Stephensen's stepson Jack who acted as office boy. Stephensen mostly wrote his contributions at home, which from about 1936 to 1940 meant flats at Darling Point, York Street and Potts Point. He did regularly visit the *Publicist* office to edit and prepare copy, and to help his stepson check proofs. His time was also taken up by discussions and arguments with Miles.

As Edward Masey recalled, Miles was a stimulating but difficult man to deal with, having a ferocious temper and insisting on thoroughly 'rational', or logical, conversation.[8] He was not tall, with a grey moustache and thinning hair, but in his dress and bearing he conveyed an air of authority. He was distinguished most of all, however, by his tearaway daughter, Beatrice, the notorious 'Bee' Miles with whom he had some spectacular confrontations. By the 1930s she had become a familiar figure in Sydney, wearing a green eye-shade, riding a bicycle, or commandeering taxis and private cars by jumping on to their running boards.

It has been said that Bee Miles suffered 'more from sanity than madness',[9] and Stephensen wrote a foreword to her unpublished memoirs, describing her as an extraordinarily intelligent person with great vitality and candour. Mencken, Swift, Nietzsche and Schopenhauer were among her favourite writers, and her memory for Shakespeare was so good that she gave impromptu recitals around the city, often from the steps of public buildings. Suspending his own sexism, Stephensen wrote that in her non-conformism Bee anticipated a 'woman of the future, a type not yet fully evolved'. He applauded her anarchism as well as her intelligence, and indeed he might have felt another affinity with her as they both drew a weekly allowance from the coffers of her father.[10]

Not that Stephensen relied entirely on this pocket money. During the winter of 1936 he spent time away from Sydney on trips with Frank Clune, down the south coast and then west to Bourke and back. They had become friendly through the Fellowship of Australian Writers and especially through their leadership of the FAW's Cultural Defence Committee. Several years older than Stephensen, and a veteran of Gallipoli, the adventurous Clune had wandered the world. *Try Anything Once* (1933) was the first of his many popular books, quickly followed by *Rolling Down the Lachlan* (1935) and *Roaming Round the Darling* (1936). These three early Clune books had been written with the assistance of a more experienced writer, most probably his friend Bartlett Adamson.[11]

During 1936 Stephensen began what was to be a lifelong collaboration with Clune, first as his 'editor' and then later as his ghost writer. Clune prided himself on coming from the school of hard knocks but he also suffered from a sense of educational and cultural inferiority, especially among his writer friends, so he took on the Oxford-educated Stephensen to make up the deficiency. When their partnership was well under way, Clune provided the principal research material and anecdotes from his travels, and Stephensen put together and polished the narratives, imitating Clune's jocular style. They first collaborated on *Dig* (1937), the story of the Burke and Wills expedition, and Stephensen received £35 for his assistance.[12]

Their winter trips out west became an annual event during the late 1930s. As an accountant, Clune went on tax pilgrimages in August each year, doing the books for country storekeepers and graziers. Stephensen tagged along for the ride, learning more at first hand about the country whose spirit held such significance for him. At the same time Clune was picking up stories and information about various regions and particularly about bushranging, his favourite historical theme and one which yielded numerous books.

During their first trip together in 1936 Stephensen made notes for an extensive Bunyip Critic column on one of the central obsessions of the 1930s: the 'Vast Open Spaces', a cliché Stephensen reduced to the acronym VOS. He said he had hoped to discover whether there were any trees left west of the Blue Mountains, whether the emus, kangaroos and Aborigines had all been exterminated, and whether jazz and 'body-odour advertising' had yet reached the outback. His report in the *Publicist*, however, was not entirely facetious. He described the treatment of Aborigines as the 'most disgraceful chapter of our national story'. They were being 'steadily exterminated by christianity' or living on the 'slum fringe' of towns, yet their cultural level was intrinsically higher than that of the sheepmen who had displaced them. Nothing had been done, Stephensen reported, 'to fill the Vast Open Spaces of the Average Australian Mind', and his picture of outback civilization was sharp and evocative:

> Small-town gossip, small-visioned politics, stagnation of mind generally, and outbursts of boozing provide the cultural amenities of the west. The Schools of Arts contain serviceable billiard-rooms, and some Zane Grey romances: not much more.[13]

In the first year of the *Publicist*, Miles and Stephensen began a regular discussion group at the Shalimar Cafe, in the basement of the T & G building. The cafe was just a few doors along Elizabeth Street from the *Publicist* office and it had already been the venue for various literary groups and functions, including the FAW reception for Kisch and Prichard. Every Thursday afternoon Miles and Stephensen left the *Publicist* office and dropped in at the Shalimar for an informal editorial conference which often included Edward Masey, S. B. Hooper and C. W. Salier as well.

During the 1920s and 1930s there were a number of similar literary, artistic and political groups meeting in teashops and hotel back rooms, and the gatherings at the Shalimar soon came to be known as the 'Yabber Club'. The name was chosen by Stephensen who also later had cards printed inviting friends and associates to the 'Discussions of Australianity' every Thursday from 4.30 to 6 p.m. (coffee sixpence). There was a predominance of literary and artistic people on the list of those 'permanently invited' to the Yabber Club, including William Baylebridge, Vivian Crockett, Eleanor Dark, Frank Dalby Davison, Dulcie Deamer, the cartoonist George Finey, Miles Franklin, Xavier Herbert, Lionel Lindsay and Tom Inglis Moore.[14]

Although Miles and Stephensen did support and develop each other's nationalism, their approaches were fundamentally different. As a successful capitalist, Miles was attracted to the idea of corporate structure, the basis of fascist-style organization as well as big business, yet Stephensen preserved the suspicion of financial institutions he had had since his days as a communist student. His cultural concerns were reflected in the many book reviews he wrote for the *Publicist* in the fields of Australian fiction, poetry and non-fiction. The magazine also published a certain amount of poetry, including the full text of Wentworth's 1823 work *Australasia*. There were some of Stephensen's own satirical ditties, too, but the *Publicist*'s main poets were Ian Mudie, the Adelaide writer, and John Manifold, then studying at Cambridge along with David Campbell.

THE PUBLICIST PUBLISHING COMPANY.
THE PUBLICIST. MONTHLY. 5/- PER ANNUM (INCLUDING POSTAGE).

TELEPHONE: MA 7683
G.P.O. BOX: 1783 K.
"AUSTRALIA FIRST."

THE PUBLICIST BOOKSHOP.
209A ELIZABETH STREET, SYDNEY.
(T. & G. BUILDING, HYDE PARK.)

22nd March 1937

Dear Ian Mudie,

Delighted to hear from you again. I am not dead, nor sleeping. The Mercury will rise again, at the proper time. For nine months past I have been actively helping "The Publicist" — of which I am not the editor, however. I send you the whole nine issues to date, also a copy of my book, "The Foundations of Culture in Australia." Please write quick & let me know your responses to all this. Are you a cultural nationalist? If so, perhaps you will send some Australian-tinted verse to "The Publicist". (No pay.)

Best of regards to you
always
yours
P.R. Stephensen

Stephensen's letter to Ian Mudie, 22 March 1937 (from the Mudie Papers, State Library of South Australia)

More than thirty of Mudie's poems appeared in the *Publicist* and this in effect launched his writing career.

Stephensen also used the *Publicist* to fight any necessary literary battles which had to be fought in the interests of national liberation. When Cape, the London publisher who had handled Radclyffe Hall's *The Well of Loneliness* a decade before, commissioned Vance Palmer to abridge Furphy's classic, *Such is Life*, Australian writers and critics were appalled. Miles Franklin wrote to the *Bulletin* that if cutting 50 000 words from the novel was the only way of attracting English attention, 'then our very feeble status as colonial writers is painfully exposed'. Kate Baker, Furphy's champion for many years, complained that no vestige of the novel's 'offensively Australian' irony remained in Palmer's 'edited' version.[15]

Stephensen's reaction was more violent, and another lifelong enmity was sealed. In the *Publicist* he said he regarded the 'mutilated edition' of *Such is Life* as the 'parting of the ways between Vance Palmer and me'. The edition was 'an outrage', and Palmer had 'committed the unforgivable literary sin of altering and vulgarising a classic, one of our very few, very rare, Australian classics'. In the next issue of the *Publicist*, Stephensen returned with even more vitriol to the 'murder' of the novel. 'Nothing has so much depressed me in five years', he wrote, and went on to attack Palmer's own novels as 'written with ink-and-water' and 'too thinly-spread to be considered as art'.[16]

Despite all his continuing literary activities, Stephensen still found time to float his own ideas for money-making ventures. In September 1936 he helped plan a scheme for the air transport of fish from the coast to inland centres. A prospectus for Direct Air Transport Limited was issued and the company formally incorporated with three directors including Patrick White's uncle, Arthur White, of the 'Hotel Australia, Sydney' and of 'Belltrees, Scone'. Still facing bankruptcy proceedings, Stephensen was not officially involved in the venture but assisted with the preparation of brochures and other publicity. He also prepared a prospectus for Commonwealth Pictures Limited which planned to produce Australian and 'South Seas' feature films for release throughout the world.[17]

Stephensen's best chance for money making, however, was litigation, and in October 1936 he brought his case against the *Bulletin*, its printer Bombelli, and Brian Penton, claiming £5000 damages for libel and conspiracy to libel. This was a more realistic figure than the £20 000 he had earlier suggested. The case was heard in the Supreme Court, Stephensen basing his claim on the *Mezzomorto* review Penton had written in 1934 under the pseudonym 'Conn Bennett'. As P. R. Stephensen & Co. Limited had been liquidated a few months after the damaging review of Crockett's novel, it appeared that Penton's review had contributed to the downfall of Stephensen's company. The fact that Crockett, as the offended author, had already won £1000 damages in a similar action meant that Stephensen's case was a strong one, and he secured the services of Crockett's counsel, A. B. Piddington, KC, just to make sure. The remarkable Piddington was supported by two other barristers while a battery of four barristers defended Penton and the *Bulletin*. Among those taking a special interest in this unusual case were Stephensen's numerous creditors, and Stephensen himself hoped that an award of damages would not only save him from bankruptcy but also allow him a new start in publishing.

During the week-long court hearing Stephensen's past activities in publishing were exposed in detail, including his involvement with D. H. Lawrence and the erotic productions of the Fanfrolico Press. His deafness was not yet acute enough to put him at a disadvantage, and he parried the aggressive cross-examination with ease. When pressed about whether he had read *Lady Chatterley's Lover*, Stephensen threw his interrogator off guard with the different editions, expurgated and unexpurgated, and the barrister was unable to pin him down as to whether he had read both editions or only parts of them. The judge finally intervened, bringing the cross-examination back to the novel in question, *Mezzomorto*, but not before the defence counsel had read aloud from *Lady Chatterley's Lover* and passed one particularly unspeakable passage directly to the shorthand writer to avoid embarrassment in court. Parts of Stephensen's *London Aphrodite* essay on philosophy, 'The Whirled Around', were also read out. 'There are too many long words in that article', he nonchalantly replied; 'I do not write in that style nowadays'.[18]

Stephensen was in the witness box for five consecutive days, and the official transcript of the hearing ran to several hundred pages. He published long excerpts from it in the *Publicist*, though he was very careful to edit out the details of his various company failures in Sydney, details which the *Bulletin* reproduced with relish in its equally biased report of the hearing. This was potentially the most damaging evidence for it demonstrated that Stephensen's company was in fact floundering, well before Penton's review had appeared.

Summing up for Stephensen, Piddington took two and a half hours to convince both judge and jury that, as a result of personal animosity, Penton had written a deliberately damaging review which the *Bulletin* had then published for equally sinister reasons. Describing Stephensen as a 'brilliant young Australian', Piddington asked the four-man jury to 'put P. R. Stephensen back where he was, in the publishing world of Sydney'. Miles Franklin, who was present during several days of the hearing, wrote to Nettie Palmer that the case had amounted to a trial of Stephensen and that his 'business misses' had been exposed. It was all a 'pitiable mess', but she thought Penton was the 'evil genius in the affair' and a 'most repellant personality'.[19]

The jury took only an hour to award Stephensen £750, a small fortune but not nearly enough to cover his heavy legal costs and the claims of his creditors. The moral victory restored some of his fire, if not his finances. 'What a shame I did not get £2,000 damages', he wrote to Xavier Herbert, 'enough to compensate me and set me up in business again. As things are,

I still have to battle for a bare existence'.[20] It meant Stephensen was still tied to the cantankerous Miles.

The creditors quickly moved in like birds of prey, and his lawyers alone claimed more than half of the £750. As he wrote to Herbert a few weeks later: 'The ravens, mollyhawks and vultures are getting all the proceeds of my verdict against The Bulletin. Never mind, I am full of go. Steel must be forged by fire . . .'[21] A meeting of his creditors was held a month after the libel case, and he avoided being declared bankrupt by agreeing to a deed of arrangement under which he made available any assets including the £750. Eventually the trustee paid off creditors at the rate of 6s 3d in the pound.[22]

His debts now behind him, Stephensen continued to nurse a romantic hope of returning to book publishing, and one last victory in fact remained, the greatest of his publishing career. He had retrieved from Herbert a mouldering set of *Capricornia* galley proofs, and about Christmas 1936 Miles read the novel and agreed to publish it 'without thought of profit'.[23] Stephensen assured Herbert that although Miles would finance the edition, Stephensen himself would be 'identified wholeheartedly with its production in all technical aspects'. He had indeed burned his boats, as he told Herbert, and was now committed to a political rather than literary future:

> Probably I shall not become an 'independent' book publisher again for some years. I have undergone a metamorphosis and am now become a propagandist of 'Australia-First' on political rather than literary lines. (By political I do not mean 'parliamentary'). I am a political publicist rather than a book publisher at present, and I have burned all my boats and crossed every possible Rubicon. As far as I am concerned unless 'Australia-First' wins in Australia, I have no business or professional or commercial future here.[24]

Almost as a symbol of this irrevocable political commitment, in January 1937 Stephensen began his weekly *Publicist* radio talks on Sydney station 2SM, the Catholic-owned station. This was appropriate, too, since the more extreme elements of the Catholic church at times supported *Publicist* policies, and Mannix had helped publicize the slogan Australia First a generation earlier. Introduced every Monday evening at 7.30 by the first bars of Bizet's *Carmen* overture, Stephensen's ten-minute talks supplemented *Publicist* propaganda with Australia First material over the air. These broadcasts continued for two and a half years, until just before the outbreak of war, and Miles paid the not inconsiderable sum of £10 each week for them, reaching a far greater audience than with the *Publicist*.[25]

In his first broadcast Stephensen explained that the 'Australia First Group' was not a sectional organization like the capitalists and socialists, or the communists, fascists and pacifists. The *Publicist*'s one political objective, he said, was *'to encourage in Australians a distinctive national culture by the specific propaganda of Australia-First'*. Showing that much of his own frustration was literary in origin, Stephensen mentioned his work for the Cultural Defence Committee of the FAW, and the 'clever' sneers of those who maintained that there was in fact no culture for Australians to defend. 'No matter how weak Australian literature may be', Stephensen told his radio audience, 'it could not possibly be as feeble culturally as these crime, sex, horror, and wild west magazines that are dumped into Australia in millions'.[26]

Stephensen and Miles may have seen Australia First as a clearly defined cultural and political struggle, but others were not so sure. Tracing the history of the *Publicist*'s propaganda right back to the 'radical movements of the Victorian era', George Waite of the Sane Democracy League commented that 'Australia First' was 'a catchcry used by conflicting groups lacking cohesion, with ideals as far apart as the poles, by local Sinn Feiners, Soviet Nationalists, chaotic-minded labourites and highbrow eccentric intellectuals'.[27]

As well as the *Publicist*'s magazine and radio propaganda, a plan was laid in 1937 for Stephensen to write a book-length history of Australia. He would receive from Miles £20 a month for this, over and above his weekly stipend as *Publicist* assistant. The aim was to capitalize on the sesquicentenary celebrations in January 1938, Australia's 150th colonial birthday. Conscious always of such significant national events, Stephensen dated his letter to Miles confirming this plan 26 January 1937.[28] Although his 25 000-word history of Australia was in many ways as stimulating and polemical as *The Foundations of Culture*, it was not published in book form, appearing instead in a special issue of the *Publicist* for January 1938 under the title 'A Brief Survey of Australian History: Our Story in Fifteen Decades'.

While he was writing this history, and also preparing *Capricornia* for publication, Stephensen became actively involved with Aboriginal protest. He was encouraged of course by Herbert and also by Miles whose own nationalist iconography delighted in anything native, from kookaburras and kangaroos to blacks. It would be too cynical, however, as well as too simple to write off the involvement of Stephensen and Miles in Aboriginal protest as nothing more than an interest in Australian fauna. Such zoological principles had already been partly responsible for the herding of Aborigines into reserves—a system, Stephensen was fond of pointing out, which had more than a passing similarity with Nazi concentration camps.

During 1936 Stephensen had seen a 'dear old friend', an Aboriginal woman he had first met at Wilcannia on his trip with Clune. While visiting her at a Sydney hospital, Stephensen also saw a three-year-old Aboriginal girl with syphilis, and promised to get her a doll. He told Xavier Herbert it would 'not be the right thing' to buy the girl a white doll but as the only black ones available were golliwogs he 'compromised' and bought her a 'chinky doll, price 7½d., which absolutely appeared to delight her' when he placed it in her hands.[29]

There was nothing sentimental, however, in Stephensen's survey of Australian history for the January 1938 *Publicist*. Decade by decade, he chronicled the 'terrible atrocities against the blacks' as they were 'outnumbered and dispossessed' and 'callously driven towards extinction'. He described as cruel slavery Queensland's blackbirding system, and characterized the 'Yellow Peril' as a 'creature of British militaristic and navalistic propaganda' and Australia's 'most permanently-recurring nightmare'. By the 1920s, he observed sarcastically, Australia had gained a reputation as an 'exterminating civiliser of backward peoples', and the new opportunity to become 'Pukka Sahibs' in Papua New Guinea had appealed 'instantaneously to Australian democrats'. Stephensen's conclusion was that few would join him, on Australia's 150th anniversary as a 'Pommy' colony, in mourning 'with the Aborigines'.[30]

Britain's claims of racial superiority, Stephensen asserted in the *Publicist*, amounted to nothing less than fanaticism, and Australians too had adopted this racialist approach:

> ... the White Australia policy, with its deportations of Asiatics and Kanakas, with its extermination of the Aboriginal blacks, has been a more ferocious and inhumane demonstration of racial prejudice than anything that Hitler's anti-semitic policy can show.[31]

Bearing in mind Stephensen's scepticism of World War I anti-German propaganda, this was probably fair comment, even in 1938, for although pogroms had already taken place in Nazi Germany it was another five years before the 'final solution' made Stephensen's analogy more questionable. In 1939 Stephensen wrote that official laws against Aborigines, supported by 'social ostracism' and 'cruel jokes against blackfellows' in the press, had put 'Herr Julius Streicher's crusade of anti-Semitism a long way behind our Australian policy of anti-Aboriginalism'.[32]

Stephensen was not himself able to resist an occasional joke at the Aboriginal's expense. One of his first Bunyip Critic columns included what purported to be a transcription of an Aboriginal protest song—perhaps the first ever published—which he had heard on the streets of Wollongong. Stephensen's account was a typical blend of sentimental idealizing and sardonic humour. 'The singer smelled of methylated spirit, as well as of the Spirit of the Land', he wrote, 'but his eyes were as gentle as those of any marsupial, and his voice had the clear tenor lyricism of the tall-timber native people'. Unfortunately there was no indication whether the version which appeared in the *Publicist* had been edited or otherwise 'improved' upon. The last two verses, in particular, strongly suggest the work of Stephensen's own sense of humour.

JACKY'S SONG.

Jacky was a smart young fellow,
Full of fun and energy.
He was thinking of getting married,
But a whitef'l'a took the girl, you see.

> *Kookity Booboola Woldy Mah*
> *Billingai! Djai! Kingeri Wah.*
>
> . . . .
>
> Hunting food was Jacky's business
> Till the whitef'l'a came along,
> And put their fences across the country—
> Now the hunting days are gone.
> *Kookity Booboola*
>
> Whitef'l'a now he's got to pay taxes
> To keep Jacky Jacky in clothes and food.
> Jacky don't care what becomes of the country—
> Whitef'l'a tuckers him very good.
> *Kookity Booboola*
>
> Now Australia is short of money,
> But Jacky sits and laughs all day.
> Whitef'l'a wants to give Australia back to Jacky,
> No fear! Jacky won't have it that way.
> *Kookity Booboola Woldy Mah*
> *Billingai! Djai! Kingera Wah.*

Stephensen regretted that a translation of the chorus could not be provided since it represented 'Jacky's private, personal, and quite uncensored opinion of us whitefellows'.[33]

During 1937 the Stephensens bought about an acre of land at Heathcote in the bush just south of Sydney. This was intended as a weekend retreat for the Stephensen family, and over the Christmas holidays they all pitched in with some friends to erect a shack. Among the helpers were Stephensen's Aboriginal friends, Monty and Mary Tickle, 'full-blood Abos' as Winifred noted in her diary. By that stage Stephensen and Miles had become involved with the Aborigines Progressive Association (APA), recently formed in Dubbo by a shearer and unionist, William Ferguson, and a former boxer, Jack Patten. Both were Aborigines, Ferguson in his late fifties, while Patten was younger than Stephensen.[34]

The APA demanded Aboriginal citizenship rights with equal opportunities for education, employment and social services. 'They do not ask for charity, or for anthropological unction', the *Publicist* explained in its November 1937 issue, and when APA members appeared in person at the *Publicist* office, Stephensen agreed to become 'Hon. Sec. Pro. Tem.' of an APA support group, the Aboriginal Citizenship Committee. Membership of the APA itself was open only to blacks.

Stephensen's immediate aims were to assist Ferguson and Patten in preparing evidence for the New South Wales select committee into Aboriginal affairs, and to call a protest conference to coincide with the sesquicentenary celebrations in January 1938. He also helped write and produce various material for the APA, including posters, manifestos and press releases, and he shadow-edited the APA journal, *Abo Call*, which was published from the *Publicist* office with Miles's financial and personal assistance.[35]

Stephensen at Gundagai, July 1939, on one of his outback trips with Frank Clune

Sadie and Xavier Herbert with children at the Kahlin Aboriginal Compound, Darwin, where Herbert was acting superintendent, 1935–36

Experiments in Australianity . . .

THE BUNYIP CRITIC

A MONTHLY CAUSERIE BY P. R. STEPHENSEN

The Ninety Seven Per Cent Joke: Are Australians "British"?: Race and Place: The Novels of Eleanor Dark: Top-Conscious and Below: Sydney University's Million Pound Cadge: A Morgue of Culture: Needs in Australian Criticism: Australian versus English Literature.

One of these two is P. R. Stephensen

"AMERICAN" OR "BRITISH"?—We no longer consider it funny when British visitors come to Sydney and voice their opinion that Australians are becoming "Americanised". This is not news; we merely yawn when we hear it: but, on the other hand, it really is funny, and it really is news, when an American visitor comes hither and states his opinion that Australians are becoming "Britishised". *Fact is the seed of truth*, says Baylebridge: *sow hideous facts and hideous truths you'll harvest.* A visiting American (whom I need not name, as he would prefer to speak for himself) surprised me recently in conversation by remarking on the "monotonous British faces" to be seen in the streets of Sydney. Looking at them, he felt bored; his standard of comparison was with the streets of American cities, where a variety of physiognomy adds interest to a stroll out-of-doors. I had to laugh at Australia's proud boast of being "ninety-seven per cent British" thus turned Yankeely against us. My American friend may have been speaking aesthetically in condemning the "monotonously British" Australian phizoscape; but, for my part, I think he was speaking merely "from the book" — i.e. from the leader-writers' "ninety-seven per cent" cliché. In my view, Australian hard dials are merely Australian. British visitors do not think that Australian faces look British. For example, D. H. Lawrence came here, "a Pommy with a beard" (his own phrase), and was affrighted by the "naked Australian faces". Another Pommy, of quite a different kind, Sir Phillip Gibbs (a clumsy observer), remarked during the Great War that the Australian soldiers were "hatchet-faced" — whatever that might mean. Usually, Englishmen merely notice that Australians are non-English in appearance; and, for want of a better adjective, they describe us as Americanised. The Americans, however, repudiating such a slur, and noticing that we are non-American, describe us as Britishised. Both analyses are superficially true, but fundamentally wrong. We are Americanised in some superficial particulars, and we are Britishised in some other particulars; but *fundamentally* we are Australians — it must be so. The "English-speaking World" has more than two major types. Australians are already a third distinct kind of "Saxon" cross-bred, locally modified. All that remains to do now is to bring the Australian traits, the Australian differentness, into recognition. This is the work for Australian critics, writers, artists, thinkers, dreamers, and schemers. Self-consciousness, self-awareness, is every nation's national need.

*

THE NINETY-SEVEN PER CENT JOKE: The "ninety-seven Per Cent British" joke is one of the best British jokes ever put over in Australia. It had its origin after the census of 3rd April, 1911, but was not thoroughly disseminated until the second or third year of the Great War, when it proved to be a good recruiting slogan, in a period when sloganisation was rampant. Having served its primary purpose of inducing Australians to enlist for British slaughter, the Joke has been perpetuated ever since the War, in order to induce Australians to keep on paying interest to their "kinsmen beyond the seas". Sloganism has its uses, but THE PUBLICIST is a serious paper, with only one slogan, namely Australia First; so I set down the actual figures of the fateful Census of 1911, which was the first time that information as to birthplace was demanded. These are quoted from the Commonwealth Year Book of 1922, No. 15, and will be found there on page 1057:

BIRTH-PLACES OF AUSTRALIA'S POPULATION
(At Census of 3rd April, 1911)

Place of Birth	Commonwealth Total	Per Cent
AUSTRALIA	3,667,670	82.90
New Zealand	31,868	0.72
United Kingdom	590,722	13.35
Other European Countries	73,949	1.67
Asia	36,442	0.82
Africa	4,958	0.11
America	11,278	0.25
Polynesia	3,410	0.08
At Sea	4,238	0.10
Not specified	30,470	
	4,455,005	100.00

Those of unspecified birthplace are not included in the percentage.

On the letterhead of his Aboriginal Citizenship Committee, Stephensen wrote in December 1937 to a similar group of sympathetic whites in Victoria, the Aboriginal Fellowship Group (AFG). He felt that neither the labour movement nor the churches had the interests of the Aborigines at heart, and told Helen Baillie of the AFG that Ferguson and Patten had addressed the New South Wales Labour Council 'with negative result'. Stephensen reminded her that the trade unions had been largely responsible for the White Australia Policy which had 'injured the Aborigines so terribly', and he was not impressed with the AFG's aim of uniting Christians 'to work and pray for the welfare of Aborigines'. Christians had 'prayed the Aborigines almost into extinction', Stephensen told her bluntly.[36]

To some extent, of course, both Stephensen and Miles were supporting the APA for similarly suspect motives, as *Capricornia* was now nearing completion at the Stafford Printery in Chippendale which also produced the monthly *Publicist*. They both had good reasons for wanting *Capricornia* to be a success, and Aboriginal protest would provide useful publicity. So anxious were they to enter Herbert's novel for the sesquicentenary literary competition that Stephensen came down from Heathcote between Christmas and New Year and helped to bind one copy of the novel himself so it could be entered before the competition deadline. Miles Franklin wrote to Herbert that Stephensen was in a 'state of jubilation' over *Capricornia*'s entry for the prize, and she told Herbert that Stephensen had 'raised such a ballyhoo about Capricornia that the judges won't dare to turn it down'. In her letter Franklin discussed Herbert's main competitors, including Helen Simpson's *Under Capricorn* and Eleanor Dark's *Sun Across the Sky*, but assured him that all these were 'tiny rush lights compared with Capricornia'.[37]

Stephensen, Herbert and Franklin were not the only ones relieved to see the appearance of *Capricornia* after so many years of struggle and frustration. W. J. Miles, the businessman who was actually financing the first edition of the epic novel after it had been turned down repeatedly by publishers in Europe and Australia, sent Winifred Stephensen a Christmas card with the following ditty:

> The Publicist's my porridge,
> Capricornia my cake:
> For more I needn't forage,
> For more I couldn't take.[38]

Miles had never been so succinct. He too had clashed with Herbert.

The year 1938 proved to be the turning point, not only in international power politics, but also for Miles, Stephensen and their garrulous *Publicist*. The January issue featured Stephensen's long and stimulating 'Survey of Australian History', in which he idealized the bush ethos, but the issue also included Miles's overtly anti-Semitic and pro-fascist '40 Symptoms of Decadence'. Among the bizarre symptoms he deplored were the increase of insanity and bad teeth, the spreading of Jewish and 'feminine'

CAPRICORNIA

A NOVEL

by

XAVIER HERBERT

Of this book a first edition of 2,000 copies has been printed, including 50 numbered copies on pure rag paper.

This is Number Out of Bones

To W.R.E. from W.J.M.
with more memories than of X.
9/6/41.

"THE PUBLICIST"
209a Elizabeth Street,
Sydney

A copy of the special rag paper edition of *Capricornia*, inscribed from W. J. Miles to Stephensen, at the time of Herbert's clash with them (copy formerly in the possession of Jack Lockyer) influences, and the corresponding decline of 'home-life; with decrease of parental control and influence'.[39] It is tempting to see in Miles's 'symptoms' his own anger and frustration with his independently-minded daughter Bee. But he was also preoccupied with more common conspiracy theories.

Increasingly over the next three years Miles and Stephensen became Jew-baiters and anti-Semites, through their *Publicist* articles and also by distributing copies of *The Protocols of the Elders of Zion*. They may have adopted the popular image of the Shylock as no more than a metaphor for financial imperialism, anti-nationalism, and religious exclusiveness, but their timing could not have been more unfortunate, and their justification was frequently illogical. Stephensen, for example, argued that Jews brought persecution on themselves by their exclusiveness.[40] A fervent supporter at the same time of Aborigines, Stephensen apparently did not consider that they had likewise invited persecution by being black.

In the January 1938 *Publicist* was a statement on 'Citizen Rights for Aborigines', signed by Patten and Ferguson, as president and secretary respectively of the APA, but bearing the unmistakable marks of Stephensen's aggressive style.[41] He also arranged for the Stafford Printery to run off a couple of thousand copies of the APA manifesto in pamphlet form, and this was circulated to newspapers and other groups. In the weeks before the sesquicentenary celebrations Stephensen interviewed both Patten and Ferguson on his weekly *Publicist* radio session, and organized posters and handbills announcing the 'Australian Aborigines Conference' which would celebrate the sesquicentenary with a 'Day of Mourning and Protest' at the Australian Hall, Sydney. 'Aborigines and persons of Aboriginal blood only' were invited to attend.[42]

In preparation for the APA conference, Patten, Ferguson and other Aboriginal activists including Pearl Gibbs met frequently at the *Publicist* office. On the day when all the pamphlets and posters arrived from the printer, however, there was a misunderstanding and Ferguson became angry at what he saw as Miles's arrogance and paternalism. Gibbs had innocently queried the number of pamphlets in a parcel, and Miles had taken this as a slur on his honesty and integrity. His sharp retort upset Ferguson, and only Stephensen's intervention secured a rare apology from Miles.[43] It was the younger Patten, however, who continued to enjoy the patronage and friendship of Miles and Stephensen when a split developed in the APA later in the year.

Despite the almost universal frivolity of the sesquicentenary celebrations, the press showed considerable interest in the APA 'Day of Mourning', and *Capricornia* was also published as part of this protest on Australia Day 1938. Further attention was focused on the organization and on *Capricornia* by the notorious 'Packsaddle' case in Darwin. Early in March 1938 two 'widely known and highly respected white women' were 'brutally' attacked in Darwin by an Aboriginal. The *Sydney Morning Herald* report went on to describe in lurid detail how he had sunk his teeth 'deep' into the neck of one woman who was 'prostrated with shock'.

The women's husbands were 'almost demented with rage', and even before Packsaddle was picked up and charged with the assault, the mild-mannered whites of Darwin were organizing vigilante groups composed of flogging and lynching enthusiasts, all blaming the attack on missionaries and anthropologists who had 'pampered' the blacks.

Missing the opportunity to call it the Darwin vampire case, the *Sydney Morning Herald* instead termed it a 'Fiendish Assault', though in fact both women had been discharged from hospital and were 'progressing favourably'. On the same page was a smaller item reporting one of the protest meetings of the Aborigines Progressive Association at the Adyar Hall, Sydney, at which Patten and Ferguson had been joined on the platform by Mary Gilmore. She had told the meeting that as a child she had seen 'aborigines massacred in hundreds'. They had been poisoned or run down by organized hunting parties, she said, and savage dogs had been imported from Europe for such hunts. Gilmore remembered seeing 'little children dead in the grass, and scalps of blacks paid for as if they were dingoes'.[44]

Describing Darwin Aborigines as 'town boys', the *Sydney Morning Herald* reported that, in the wake of the assault on the white women, no black would henceforth be allowed on the streets of Darwin and none would be permitted outside an employer's residence except when travelling to or from work. An Aboriginal would be liable to arrest 'even if sent on a message by his employer'. Between 'sunset and sunrise' there would be a total black curfew. Faithful as always to journalistic objectivity, the *Sydney Morning Herald* also reported the view of APA president Patten that 'Assaults by white men upon black women' were 'much more common than the reverse'.[45] Stephensen developed this line in one of his radio sessions, observing that newspapers 'seldom or never' reported attacks on Aboriginal women.[46]

Although at his trial Packsaddle said he had been 'intimidated' by police into making a false confession, the presiding judge ignored this and sentenced him to four years jail. The judge even publicly lamented the fact that he was not permitted by law to order a flogging, the 'only punishment an aboriginal would appreciate'. At a subsequent meeting of the APA, this time at the Radiant Health Club in Sydney, Pearl Gibbs rhetorically asked the meeting if the learned judge would advocate flogging for white men who assaulted Aboriginal women.[47]

In the midst of this excitement it was announced that *Capricornia* had won the £250 sesquicentenary novel competition, judged by Frank Dalby Davison, Flora Eldershaw and Marjorie Barnard. When he heard the news in Darwin, Herbert went out and bought a case of beer and assembled all the 'bums and bagmen and Greeks and Chows and yella-fellas' he could find, most of whom had no idea what they were celebrating. As Herbert told Miles Franklin, he got 'quietly drunk' and stayed that way for three days.[48] Eleanor Dark, whose own novel *Sun Across the Sky* had been a contender, wrote to Stephensen congratulating him as publisher after the 'years of delay and disappointment'. Admitting that she had wanted to win the competition herself, Dark said that after reading *Capricornia* she would have 'resented' any other novel but Herbert's taking the prize.[49] Ian Mudie wrote quickly from Adelaide that the win 'might wake a lot of people up to the fact that P. R. Stephensen is Australia's finest literary critic'.[50] This would have been high praise indeed, except that Stephensen was also an enthusiast for Mudie's poetry.

Congratulating himself no doubt on his good business sense, Miles approached the winner of the sesquicentenary poetry competition, R. D. FitzGerald, with a 'view to publication'. FitzGerald responded that a couple of years before he had chased Stephensen 'for months and never caught him', but he nevertheless submitted a poetry manuscript to the *Publicist*. For Miles, however, business ethics and the financial balance sheet took the place of a religious or moral code, and FitzGerald had to retrieve his manuscript again after the astute businessman realized it was not possible to publish a poetry volume 'without actual loss of money'.[51] Miles had no doubt taken any taxation savings carefully into account.

While the 'Publicist Publishing Coy.' edition of *Capricornia* was widely reviewed and had sold out before the end of 1938, the Aborigines Progressive Association, which Stephensen and Miles had also sponsored, began to break down. A split developed between Patten and Ferguson, and there were accusations of conflicting white influences. Led by Ferguson, some APA members felt the association was becoming the plaything of political extremists. Patten's earlier mentor, the socialist Michael Sawtell, accused Stephensen and the *Publicist* of exploiting the APA. At a noisy general meeting of the association at La Perouse Aboriginal settlement on Easter Sunday 1938, Patten and Ferguson each claimed leadership, Ferguson complaining bitterly about 'lies, corruption and dictatorship'.[52] Although this was as much a personal quarrel between the young and fiery Jack Patten and the more experienced unionist Ferguson, the *Publicist*'s involvement with the APA had become a contentious issue between the two men. Ironically, by trying to support and foment Aboriginal protest, Stephensen and Miles unwittingly helped to divide and weaken it, as did the APA's communist supporters.[53]

The APA dissidents were not the only ones disquieted by the *Publicist*'s fascist complexion which became apparent during 1938. The magazine's monthly Anglophobia and pro-fascism began to disappoint and worry even old friends of Stephensen's like Herbert Burton and Robert Hall. In his study of British enthusiasts for Nazi Germany, *Fellow Travellers of the Right* (1980), Richard Griffiths observed that it was during 1938 that the distinction became clear between fearful 'appeasers' and open 'enthusiasts', though both groups were working towards the same end, avoidance of war.[54]

Miles's pro-fascism is rather easier to account for than Stephensen's. The corporate state held no fears for Miles, and his position for many years at the top of a corporate pile had convinced him what a good and efficient system it was. But Stephensen's transition from the left-liberalism of *The Foundations of Culture* (1936) to his *Publicist* pro-fascism in 1938 has puzzled most observers from his close friends to historians of the 1930s.[55]

The short answer is that when Miles recruited him in 1936 Stephensen was not only impoverished but also desperately frustrated as a publisher, writer and public figure. Having observed the headquarters of Empire at close range, he was infuriated by the colonial subservience of Australians. The pro-Empire sentiments of the ABC radio commentator 'The Watchman' (E. A. Mann) in the late 1930s are a good example of what roused Stephensen's volatile political temper.[56] As E. M. Andrews summed it up in *Isolationism and Appeasement in Australia* (1970), apathy was the traditional Australian response to international affairs, and this apathy 'provoked and frustrated the small group of intellectuals'.[57]

In *The Appeal of Fascism* (1971) Alastair Hamilton noted that for most of the European writers and intellectuals who were attracted by fascism it was 'an amusing means of provocation, a feather with which to tickle the throats of the English liberals'.[58] Stephensen's provocative polemics, however, caused anger rather than irritation. His article on 'The Decline and Fall of the British Empire', describing the empire as 'an historical patchwork' with a glorious past and a dubious future, appeared in the *Australian Rhodes Review* early in 1938, resulting in the censure of the editor and the withdrawal of the magazine's grant.[59]

Hamilton also observed that few pro-fascist writers were themselves English. Belloc was part-French, Yeats and Shaw Irish, Roy Campbell South African, Ezra Pound American, and T. S. Eliot and Wyndham Lewis American born. All to some extent provide useful comparisons with Stephensen and his Danish-French-Swiss background, though perhaps Lewis, Campbell and Pound are the most illuminating examples. Wyndham Lewis was an anarchistic 'provocateur' who was 'prepared to go a long way for the sake of giving offence'. The South African poet Roy Campbell was an 'extroverted and obstreperous' man who loathed the 'perversion and effeminacy' of London literary decadence, while Pound was an anti-Semite obsessed with monetary reform.[60]

Stephensen's make-up combined similar elements of personality and persuasion, though his peculiar complexion was exaggerated by the colourlessness of much Australian intellectual life in the 1930s. In David Walker's terms, Stephensen was a 'primitive' nationalist, harking back along with Miles Franklin to a bush ethos, but he was also a sophisticated Nietzschean Bakuninite for whom anarchism was an unrealizable ideal in the midst of a nightmare of historical decay.[61] In the April 1938 *Publicist* he admitted to being a 'philosophical anarchist'. All governments, whether 'Democratic' or 'Fascistic', were to him totalitarian and 'repressive of individual liberty'.[62]

Hamilton observed a similar strain in European intellectuals:

> Fascism combined the idea of discipline with another prospect which was found equally exciting intellectually, although we now have some difficulty in dissociating it from the genocide which, however indir-

ectly, descended from it. This was the prospect of the 'new man', the elite of heroic supermen, '*artist*-tyrants', of whom Nietzsche had dreamt.

This myth, Hamilton wrote, was connected with the 'desire for renewal' and the age-old idea that 'civilisation had reached a point of crisis', an idea which pervaded intellectual circles and seemed to be confirmed by World War I and the depression:

> More and more writers began to find the apocalypse not only inevitable but desirable. Partly in order to forestall it, partly in order to survive it, they chose to commit themselves to totalitarian ideologies and to support régimes that would hasten the destruction of the civilisation which they believed in a state of putrefaction.[63]

In the *Publicist* Stephensen wrote that 'Without national pride, soaked in British and other European "ideology", the pathetic lost generation of post-Great-War Australians stares into the future, listless and afraid'.[64]

This now became Stephensen's political scenario: that the coming war would devastate and disillusion Australians but also provide real opportunities for national renewal and independence. With modifications, of course, this was exactly what did happen. Stephensen also had very definite but more dangerous and deluded ideas on political economy. He had retained both a fear and a hatred of imperial exploitation which he now labelled, provocatively, as the 'unholy trinity': composed of British imperialists, communists and Jews.[65] In the *Publicist* world-view these 'internationalists' had conspired to enslave Australia to foreign interests.

Disillusionment with 'democracy' and with Stalin's Moscow trials of 1936–38 had pushed Stephensen towards the extreme right.[66] With the depression and approaching war, political activists of many shades had become convinced of the need for an alternative to liberalism and the conventional party system. Those on the left could see the conflict in more clearly defined class terms, but for those on the right like W. J. Miles, with unquestioned ruling-class allegiance, the 'real' enemy had to be more elusive and cunning, hence the attraction of a 'sinister internationalism' in which Jews could be seen as controlling not just the communist movement but also insidious imperialism.

It must be stressed once more that, because of his cynicism about World War I, Stephensen regarded anti-German press reports as wildly exaggerated propaganda. Ever since his Oxford days he had sympathized with Germany's crippling burden of war reparations.[67] Impatient for the 'British Garrison' to get out of Australia, Stephensen probably looked upon Hitler's reoccupation of the Rhineland as a worthwhile example of national liberation.

Stephensen's isolationism and even his anti-Semitism were not unusual. He was just more outspoken about his prejudices, and he never could resist a provocative metaphor. Anti-Semitism in Australia was, and still is, a pervasive but largely invisible phenomenon. For Miles it was part of his crusading rationalism, but he was also in the 'rag trade', and commercial competition may have had something to do with his subscription to Jewish conspiracy theories. For Stephensen the emphasis was racial and eugenic as well as cultural, rather like Norman Lindsay's anti-Semitism, and the whole modernist/anti-modernist debate in art and literature was involved, Jews being regarded as purveyors of disintegrative modernism. This can be seen most vividly in Lionel Lindsay's anti-Semitic references in *Addled Art* (1942).

The attraction of conspiracy theories for someone of Stephensen's flamboyant temperament was also a factor. His earlier communist activism revealed this capacity, and even then it was the cunning hand of international Jewry which gave these fantasies bodily shape, and not only in Stephensen's imagination. The notorious *Protocols* had given the delusion a quasi-documentary shape as well. Though Stephensen may in fact have realized that it was a fantasy, it nevertheless continued to titillate his sense of tribal injustice, first as a bohemian communist in the 1920s and then as a nationalist in the 1930s.

Having objects to scorn and deride was an essential feature of his polemical armoury, and he was more apt than most to be carried away in the heat of the battle. During a discussion in the *Publicist* columns early in 1939 one reader questioned the Australia First policy of 'absorbing' racial minorities, including Aborigines. The reader favoured reserves for 'non-detribalised natives' because 'absorption' was a 'gentle word for "extinction"'. Stephensen interpolated: *'Then why not segregate the Jews also?'*[68] This was a debating point, the sort of logical technicality Stephensen knew would amuse his editor, Miles. Yet a far more vicious if similarly tongue-in-cheek remark was made just a few weeks later in Berlin by the 'Reich Cultural Leader', Dr Alfred Rosenberg. Rejecting the idea of Palestine as a home for the world's fifteen million Jews, Rosenberg told diplomats and the foreign press that Jews should be settled, not in a Jewish state, but on a '"reservation", supervised by a police-trained administration'. The good doctor suggested Guiana or Madagascar as eminently suitable sites.[69] What made such fantasies and gestures truly malevolent was not the whimsical imagination, nor even the prejudice, but the inclination and means to turn them into reality.

When Hitler absorbed Austria in March 1938 Stephensen used his regular *Publicist* radio session to extol the virtues of Nazi Germany which he described as 'a model of order, discipline and national enthusiasm'. Germany, Italy and Japan, Stephensen warned, would no longer permit Britain to act as 'world policeman'.[70] In the April and May issues of the *Publicist* Stephensen engaged in a full-dress debate with Hartley Grattan during which the American described him as a 'tub-thumping' nationalist, an 'incorrigible debater', and a 'staggeringly florid rhetorician' with a 'brawling manner'. Stephensen's 'striking verbal coruscations' were frequently borrowed from 'past crusaders', Grattan pointed out. He had already taken the Australian to task in the *New York Times Book Review*, commenting that Stephensen had 'stuffed his cannon not only with tried and true ball and powder but also with old nails, bolts, screws and odd bits of rusty iron he has found roundabout and fired the thing off with a childlike delight in the bang it made'.[71]

What most upset Grattan, of course, was not Stephensen's style so much as his politics. Grattan said he found Stephensen's 'recurring invocations of the kind of nationalism current in Germany, Italy and Japan deeply offensive'.[72] That Stephensen and Miles actually published Grattan's stinging attack was perhaps an indication of the intellectual health and confidence of the *Publicist*, however suspect many of the germs of ideas lodging between its yellow covers may have been. Miles and Stephensen welcomed criticism because it afforded them the luxury of a lengthy reply.

With one whimsical eye on the future as always, Stephensen began his retort to Grattan in the May 1938 *Publicist* with a 'Note for Research Students': 'Will Carnegie, Rhodes, or other scholars of the year 2038, A.D., fingering this crumbling page, please take my greetings—*Heil* and What Ho?' Describing Grattan's more splenetic outbursts as 'Broadway bounce', Stephensen went on to elaborate his own isolationist position under the sub-heading 'The Second World War':

> For every one word uttered by *The Publicist* for Australian peace, there are a million words uttered in Australia, in the press, radio, and on pulpits and platforms, for Australian war.... When the Second World War warms up (for it has *already* begun, in Spain and China), just where will Australians be expected to go overseas to fight "in defence of democracy"?.... Australian champions of democracy will be able to take their choice of dying on any one of several dozen non-Australian battlefields, next time.

In the modern world, he wrote, democracy was the 'war-cry of the world's worst gang of imperialist permeators—the moneylenders of London, Paris, and New York', while fascism, 'scientifically considered', was at least 'a revolt of people oppressed by the Shylocks of the Paris-London-New York financial axis'. Feeling 'nothing but friendship' for the people of Britain, France and the United States, Stephensen nevertheless 'loathed' their rulers for fastening the chains of debt, exploitation, and military servitude upon Australia. Stephensen also reiterated his distinction between the colonial nationalists he supported—including Gandhi, de Valera, George Washington, Robert Bruce and Boadicea—and the 'imperial nationalists' whose expansionist aims he did not endorse. This list not only included Hitler and Mussolini, but also Julius Caesar, 'Jenghis Khan', Napoleon, Bismarck, and 'D'Israeli'—thereby associating British imperialism with Jewish influence.[73]

On balance, Stephensen's was the more persuasive and also the more witty and engaging broadside in the *Publicist* war of words with Grattan. Stephensen defended his flamboyant style by advising Grattan that 'banter and persiflage may be the garb of a serious intent'. But it was just this serious intent which most troubled Grattan and other critics. In the June 1938 *Publicist* Stephensen again attacked democracy as 'a lie and a

THE PUBLICIST.

1st June, 1938. 13

Hail, Hitler!

A SPEECH TO THE REICHSTAG: FIRST INSTALMENT

Not being German, we write "Hail"! — and mean it. Not being German, we do not pretend to be. Hitler has our high regard, so we write, Hail, Hitler! We have one King, 10,000 miles away, one Governor General of the Commonwealth of Australia (our King's vice-regality because our King himself maintains domicile far away), and six State Governors (six vice-regalities, also because our King himself maintains domicile far away), one Prime Minister of the Commonwealth, and six State Premiers. Hail, also, to them all! We have no dearth of leaders (*fuhrers*), nor has Germany. Advance Australia! THE PUBLICIST stands for Australia First, as it logically should; but it advocates goodwill towards all peoples with whom we are not at war.

Hitler's great non-rhetorical speech of January 30, 1937, elated THE PUBLICIST because it gave peace to Europe, depressed the League of Nations, and startled Anthony Eden on his decline. Two-fifths — the international part — of that famous speech were printed verbatim in THE PUBLICIST of May, 1937, and was deliberately contrasted with the rhetorical nonsense of the last (then) public speech of our widest-known Old South Welshman.

My reasons for calling the meeting of the Reichstag for today were twofold: in the first place I wished to make a number of changes in important posts and it seemed to me fitting to make them after, rather than before, January 30; while in the second place I deemed it advisable to effect a further and very necessary understanding in a certain department of foreign affairs before addressing you.

You all expect, and justifiably, that on such a day there should be not merely a report on the past, but also some suggestion as to what may be expected in the future. My speech today shall, then, contain both.

When five years ago at noon, on January 30, Field-Marshal von Hindenburg, the President of the Reich, entrusted me with the Chancellorship and thus with the leadership of the Reich, we National Socialists felt that this act marked a turning point in the history of the nation.

This may perhaps have seemed to our opponents comparable to many other similar occasions when a man was appointed Chancellor of the Reich, only to have to yield place a few weeks or months later to a successor who was already treading on his heels. *What was to us National Socialists a moment of unique importance, thus seemed to the others merely but one of a course of events.*

Now we have Hitler's great non-rhetorical speech of February 20, this year, and we shall give it to our readers in full. But it is of about 20,000 words, so we have divided it into four as equal parts as its matter makes reasonably convenient for serial reading. We shall make no comments till afterwards: the German Fuhrer (Leader) speaks for himself and the Germans: some Australians may be able to learn something to their own advantage — those Australians whose heads are not too bony; or whose minds are not too narrow, or too muddled with prejudices or fuddled with anti-German propaganda. We shall put some of the German Leader's words and sentences into italics when they appear to us to contain matter of particular value to Australia-Firsters. A word or note in square brackets would be ours.

We have entitled the four "quarters" of the speech —

1. — Retrospect.
2. — Development.
3. — National Socialism.
4. — Germany, 1938.

(Editor.)

Speech Delivered in the Reichstag,

February 20th, 1938.

by

Adolf Hitler, Fuhrer and Chancellor.

[Part 1. — Retrospect.]

MEMBERS OF THE GERMAN REICHSTAG, I am well aware that you, and with you the German Nation, were expecting to be called together on the occasion of the fifth anniversary of the day on which we entered into power, to the end that you, the elected representatives of the Reich, might celebrate with me the beginning of a new period in the development of our nation, a date that is fraught with so many memories for us National Socialists.

But who, gentlemen, assessed *the meaning of that moment aright.*

Five years have passed since that day. Do the events of this period entitle us to deliver our judgment as to the epoch-making importance of that moment, or have they merely proved a confirmation of the opinion of our opponents, who on that occasion held that all that was taking place was the addition of but one more Cabinet to the vast number which had held office?

Even if unanimity on this one point only prevailed among the nation, there would today be but one opinion as to the importance of at least one event in history. Even our opponents of that time can scarcely dispute that any longer.

The day on which I entered the building in Wilhelm Platz as leader of the biggest party in the opposition and left it as Fuhrer and Chancellor of the nation, was a turning point in the history of our people, *then, now and for ever.*

There is nobody who fails to realize that January 30, 1933, formed the end of one epoch and the beginning of another. *So uncontested, indeed so obvious is this fact that men now divide the history of our country into two periods, before and after the coming into power of National Socialism.*

It is not my intention, gentlemen, to sketch for you today a picture of the chaotic condition of affairs existing before we came into power. Our adult contemporaries are far from having forgotten it, while the rising generation could scarcely conceive it, even if one were to paint them a picture of the Germany of that time. I therefore propose to deal only very briefly and in general terms with that tragic period in the history of our nation, which now lies behind us.

After the collapse of the old German Reich and especially of Prussia at the beginning of the past century, Palm, a bookseller in Nuremburg, published a remarkable and impressive pamphlet entitled *Deutschland in seiner tiefsten Erniedrigung (Germany in the Depths of Humiliation).*

The June 1938 *Publicist* which featured one of Hitler's speeches humbug' which reduced everything to the 'dead level of mediocrity'. It was in fact already a doomed concept, he said, as the world headed towards another catastrophe. A new élite was needed, a 'group of Australian Samurai' to control the civil service.[74]

Turning his back on his past campaigns against censorship, Stephensen forecast correctly that censorship would be stepped up in the future, but now he approved of this, provided 'British propaganda' was censored along with 'pornographic and crime-inciting American and British publications and cinema films (mostly of Jewish origin and inspiration), which would be instantly banned in Germany, and ... in Russia'. In the same issue of the *Publicist* Miles ran the first instalment of Hitler's February speech to the Reichstag, under the heading 'Hail, Hitler!', and flanked by swastika ornaments. Miles himself introduced Hitler's speech by acclaiming it as a 'great non-rhetorical speech' from a man who 'has our high regard'.[75]

By the middle of 1938, therefore, both Miles and Stephensen had stated their position quite unequivocally: they were anti-British, anti-Semitic, and anti-democratic, as well as sympathetic towards many fascist ideals. In Stephensen's case, however, the sympathy was somewhat qualified. Comparing Hitler's concept of 'blood' with the 'vital flesh' idea propounded by the 'elusive and reticent William Baylebridge', Stephensen denied that Australia could make use of Hitler's 'inspirational concept' of race, because of the Asian and Aboriginal component of Australian society. Stephensen felt that inspiration must be found instead in the spirit of place, the *genius loci*.[76]

It was at this time that Stephensen and his Adelaide correspondent, Ian Mudie, began to discuss one such attempt to formulate a cultural philosophy embodying not only place spirit but also Aboriginal pre-history and myth. This was Rex Ingamells's recently published *Conditional Culture* (1938) which had been inspired as much by Stephensen's *Foundations of Culture in Australia* as by Ingamells's earlier reading of Spencer and Gillen's *The Arunta* (1927) and Devaney's *The Vanished Tribes* (1929). The result of Ingamells's deliberations was the formation of the Jindyworobak poetry movement, based in Adelaide but including amongst its fellow travellers at one time or another major poets such as Judith Wright and David Campbell. As Brian Elliott has shown in his authoritative Jindyworobak anthology, Stephensen's *Mercury* essay was the 'first really powerful stimulus' to Ingamells, and it had encouraged him to study Lawrence's *Kangaroo* from which he 'gained a strong sense of the *primaeval* in Australian nature'.[77]

Stephensen, however, shared Mudie's doubts about the successful integration of Aboriginal words and mythology into what was essentially a European poetic tradition. Writing to his Adelaide friend, Stephensen said he was not convinced Ingamells was a 'real scholar of Aboriginal languages'. The possible confusion of different languages 'mixed ridiculously with English words' in the one poem was 'pretentious' and a 'spurious Australianisation of poetry'. Mudie's own work, on the other hand, Stephensen praised as 'place-local' and authentic. Yet Stephensen asked Mudie to be 'tolerant and long suffering' of Ingamells's attempts since 'ALL the Austral fanatics possible' were needed. Although Mudie was himself of German ancestry, and perhaps the *Publicist*'s most dedicated supporter, Stephensen still felt it necessary to excuse the publication of Hitler's speeches in the magazine. 'When we print Hitler's speeches', Stephensen told Mudie, 'it is merely because we have to do something to break the British spell . . .'[78]

For Mudie as well as Ingamells, *The Foundations of Culture in Australia* had provided a powerful stimulus, and Mudie wrote that Stephensen's Bunyip Critic columns in the *Publicist* had made him 'more fiercely happy than ever before'.[79] Ten years younger than his mentor, Mudie was to remain Stephensen's dedicated and lifelong friend. In common with Inky's other close friends such as Liam O'Flaherty and Frank Clune, Mudie was an extrovert. Brian Elliott has described him as 'a man of robust and energetic personality', sociable, easy-going, and a 'natural enthusiast, eager to proclaim what he believed in'. Mudie was 'a talker first and a poet after that', and Elliott recalled that the 'sound of his voice, his resonant accent, penetrated all his writing'.[80] His writing was also permeated by the spirit of the land which he hoped would drive out the 'alien' European spirits:

> Once, alien gods, Odin, Osiris, Pan,
> came crowding in upon our entering heels.
> Kill them, oh Land, free us and let us be
> of you, and of your totem-gods of stone and tree.[81]

This was from Mudie's poem 'As Are the Gums', published in the *Publicist* in 1938, and it was through such poems and through their correspondence that Stephensen came to know him.

During 1938 Stephensen once more became active in intellectual and public affairs in Sydney. In May he debated Australian independence with the barrister R. Le Gay Brereton at Sydney University, and in June he gave an ABC broadcast on Australian culture, describing the country as a 'culture-dump' for Britain and America, while Australia's own creative writers and artists were 'neglected, starved, or forced into exile'.[82] Towards the end of the year Xavier Herbert arrived from Darwin in a blaze of publicity as a prize-winning novelist, and was feted by the Yabber Club at a 'press luncheon' held at the Shalimar Cafe, followed by a radio interview with Miles.[83]

Between the Munich settlement and the widespread Nazi pogroms in November, Stephensen became determined to enter active politics again, as an agitator rather than as a propagandist or theorist. It may also have been an assertion of independence from Miles, to whom he wrote on 3 October 1938, setting out his ideas and hopes in a private memo. Stephensen stated that he had a 'passion for experiment' and liked to test a theory in practice, though it involved extra work and 'elements of danger'. This was a vital memo, because although Stephensen explicitly disclaimed any 'big responsibility', he was obviously becoming more ambitious as well as impatient.[84] He no doubt saw himself as the inspirational head of a Gandhi-style national liberation movement, but his enemies saw him as a future fascist dictator of Australia.

There were elements of both in Stephensen's thinking, as well as naivety and confusion, but the reality of his situation, as he well appreciated, was somewhat less grandiose. He informed Miles, as subtly as possible, that the *Publicist* had 'idiosyncracies' which prevented it from becoming popular. 'It is analytical, logical, ironic and philosphical', he told his editor, but it was also 'perverse in style and in method'.[85] Whether these criticisms referred to the content or the presentation of the *Publicist*'s Australia First propaganda was not clear, though as Bruce Muirden commented, Miles's own lengthy and pseudonymous contributions to the magazine were 'invariably unoriginal and wearisome'.[86] Stephensen no doubt began to feel that his talents were being exploited and wasted in polemical isolation, preaching only to a small band of the converted.

His suggestion was to organize 'Australia First discussion groups' supported by yet another monthly paper, 'Australian Action'. *Action* had been the name of Oswald Mosley's New Party magazine in England in 1931 when Mosley was becoming increasingly fascist, but there is no indication that Stephensen was aware of any connection with Mosley's British Fascists.[87] Thinking perhaps of the communist cell system, Stephensen planned the formation of a 'hundred agents (group convenors)' to begin the experiment.[88] With his eye now on a more political future, Stephensen had become increasingly sensitive about his past, and he threatened the *Australian National Review* with a libel action over a comment that advocates of Australian culture had 'failed to make money out of English culture'. Although Stephensen was not named, he took it as referring to himself, a disturbing indication of guilt if not paranoia.[89]

As he was already financing both the *Publicist* and his rationalist paper, *The Independent Sydney Secularist*, Miles did not accede to the request for yet another political journal. So instead, Stephensen ran a series of 'Australian Action' features in his Bunyip Critic column in the *Publicist* between November 1938 and April 1939. These were sub-titled 'Towards the formation of an "Australia-First" Party', and Stephensen suggested a 'Twelve-Point Policy' as the basis for discussion. These points were essentially anti-democratic, aiming to destabilize parliament by a campaign of informal voting which would eventually weaken the existing party system and lead to the 'ultimate formation of an "Australia-first" party' for the organization of 'self-dependence' and 'self-defence'.

His policy also advocated 'compulsory labour-training' and, for youths, training in the use of weapons, physical culture, and 'political training in ideals of civics'. This concept was probably no more subversive than the Boy Scouts but at the time it looked like an attempt to set up Hitler-youth-style organizations. Instead of immigration to reverse population decline, Stephensen suggested better child endowment, the 'encouragement of early marriage', and the 'statutory elimination of females of child-bearing age from industrial employment at wages lower than are paid to males'. The elimination of wage differentials between men and women sounded progressive, but of course it was designed to drive women back to housewifely and motherly duties, the cult of motherhood being another Nazi obsession.[90]

Stephensen's friends responded to this platform with a mixture of dismay and sadness. Herbert Burton wrote from Melbourne that he was 'very dubious and suspicious' of the fascist elements of the party proposal. 'If your real objective is dictatorship', he candidly asked Stephensen, 'what is going to happen to the rebels (like yourself) in the future?' Eleanor Dark's husband was also 'dubious' about the fascist complexion of the party, while Robert Hall wrote to Burton from England that he found it hard to understand how Stephensen had 'put all his ideas of humanity and brotherhood so thoroughly behind him'. Some of Stephensen's plans were good, Hall wrote, but a lot were 'rotten', some 'just wrong', and others 'terrifying'.[91]

The response from *Publicist* readers generally was more mixed, several describing the youth training plan as 'pure Hitler' and savouring of Nazism, but one woman asking in all seriousness, 'Why not labour camps for girls, too?' One reader far-sightedly suggested placing the Australian coinage on a decimal basis, while another thought free rail travel throughout the country would help prevent the congregation of minority groups.[92]

The Australia First party discussion faded away as 1939 progressed and war in Europe became inevitable. During the same period both Stephensen and Miles became more stridently anti-Semitic, pro-German and pro-Japanese in their attempt to keep Australia out of another war. In the March *Publicist* Stephensen celebrated 'Japan's 2,599th Anniversary' with a glowing tribute to the antiquity, respectability and 'clean-living' habits of Australia's 'Neighbours of the Near North'. Japan was a perfect example, he claimed, of a defensive island strategy, and he regarded the Japanese not as a potential enemy but as a 'potential friend'. This was of course prophetic as well as pragmatic Menzies policy, and the historian Geoffrey Blainey has suggested that Japan was driven to expansion and aggression during the 1930s by the policies of her rivals, Britain and the United States.[93]

Stephensen's increasing admiration for Japan was based on an image of the Japanese as a 'clean-living' and positive alternative to decadent and power-crazed Europe. The problem with such rhetoric is to decide whether Stephensen was in fact an outright fascist or just a polemical *'agent provocateur'*, trying to provoke Australians into an awareness of the urgent need for an independent and self-defensive outlook. His support for Japan was certainly another way of thumbing his nose at Britain and the rest of Europe, and he recalled with some pride that as a boy he had had a pony named Togo after the Japanese admiral who had routed the Russians in 1905.[94] Yet for all his cultural and intellectual breadth,

Stephensen was prepared to support fascist rule in the interest of national 'regeneration', as he wrote in the *Publicist* under the headline 'A War of Emotions':

> Australia needs a harder philosophy than University professors or an ancient singer of pretty clever Odes can supply. We need here a Mahomet, a Hideyoshi, a Cromwell—or a Hitler—a man of harsh vitality and vigour, a born leader, a man of action, not one sicklied o'er with the pale cast of thought. Fanatics are needed, crude, harsh men, not sweet and decorous men, to arouse us from the lethargy of decadence, softness, and lies which threatens doom to White Australia unless the regenerating force emerges here before the year 1950. Wanted, a Leader![95]

In April 1939 the Sydney *Workers Weekly* ran an article attacking Stephensen and the *Publicist* under the headline 'PROPAGANDISTS FOR NAZIS AND JAP. WAR LORDS'. Stephensen took court action claiming £5000 damages, the same amount he had claimed against the *Bulletin* three years earlier. It was three years, too, since he had commented in *The Foundations of Culture* that the '*Heil Hitler*' buncombe' would be treated in Australia with the contempt it deserved. A jury once again found in his favour but this time, instead of awarding him a small fortune, the court showed its contempt for his views by awarding him just two farthings.[96]

It was not the only insult in store for the *Publicist*. Just before war broke out in Europe, the Rabbi who officiated at the synagogue near the *Publicist* office in Elizabeth Street began calling out to Miles that he was a 'dirty Nazi spy' and asking him 'How's Hitler?' Then on Sunday 3 September 1939, the day war was declared, someone painted in large brown letters across the front window of the *Publicist* office: 'NAZI HQ'. Miles complained to the police that it was as likely to have been a communist as a Jew,[97] but the war of words had now given way to another and more dangerous phase.

12
Fascism and Australia First

Even before the outbreak of war in Europe, Australia's security services began to show renewed interest in P R. Stephensen. The accuracy of their reports, though, had not improved much since the early 1930s when he had been regarded as a potentially dangerous communist. During 1939 the Commonwealth Investigation Branch (IB) wrongly attributed the authorship of a book on Japan to Stephensen and claimed he was receiving a £500 annual retainer from the Japanese consul for propaganda work.[1] These allegations were unfounded. The only retainer Stephensen received was £10 a week from his *Publicist* editor Miles, income which he augmented by editorial work on Frank Clune's books. Since 1938 rumours had been circulating in Sydney that the *Publicist* was supported by German propaganda funds, when in fact the magazine continued to be subsidized by the Australian government through Miles's tax deductions.[2]

The war not only deepened national insecurity; it also caused a proliferation of civilian and military security agencies. Despite its misinformation, the most professional of these was the IB, attached to the Commonwealth Attorney-General's Department, but there were two other major groups operating in Sydney and not always in a spirit of co-operation with the IB. One was Military Police Intelligence (MPI), a division of the New South Wales police, and the other was Military Intelligence (MI), attached to the army's Eastern Command. All three groups sent agents along to the Yabber Club at various times to observe the proceedings, and at least one of them decided the club was as 'harmless as a curate's tea party and loyal as a Primrose League'.[3] Both Miles and Stephensen were aware of this surveillance, and Stephensen later claimed he and Miles had approved of it since the authorities would realize there was nothing 'seditious or disloyal' about their activities. As the genuine Yabber members conversed energetically and at length on a wide range of issues, Stephensen said it had been easy to identify the 'intelligence' officers at the Shalimar Cafe because of their almost complete lack of political knowledge and their inability to take an intelligent part in the debate.[4]

With the war against Germany, the *Publicist*'s pro-fascist tone became more subtle, though it was still unequivocal and was accompanied by a more sporadic but also more strident anti-Semitism. Jewish refugees were now reaching England and Australia in increasing numbers, and a Jewish settlement was suggested for the remote Kimberley region of Western Australia. Stephensen's Bunyip Critic comment was that 'Germany's rise to strength' had followed the 'elimination of Jewish influence in that country', and he could not believe that Australia would benefit from the influx of Jewish refugees. He could even foresee the day when it would be 'correct policy' for Australia to expel, exclude or restrict Jews.[5]

Miles's rabid anti-Semitism reached a peak in his editorial for the February 1940 *Publicist*, commenting on a pamphlet published in Melbourne about the plight of Jewish refugees. Miles summoned up all his cruel irony to observe that the disabilities suffered by these refugees were their 'just deserts as sinners'. He considered the notorious *Protocols of the Elders of Zion* a 'brilliant exposition of Jewish aims and ways', and yes, he regarded the Nazi race theory as fundamentally scientific. In answer to the question, 'What is the Solution of the Jewish Problem?', Miles replied simply, 'There can be none while a Jew lives'.[6] His timing, as usual, was impeccably grotesque. Auschwitz's gas chambers began to put this rhetorical solution into practical effect within a matter of months.

In 'A Reasoned Case Against Semitism' for the March 1940 *Australian Quarterly*, Stephensen likened Semitism and anti-Semitism to 'toxin and antitoxin', and noted that many liberal thinkers were horrified at the thought of 'organised anti-Semitism' because they felt this 'must lead to massacres of Jews'. Stephensen argued that there were solutions other than force, and that 'the Jewish Race should abolish itself, by becoming absorbed in the common stream of mankind'.[7]

Along with many others, including groups of Jews themselves, Stephensen seriously and tragically underestimated the Nazi capacity for transforming a political metaphor into mass murder on an almost unthinkable scale.[8] With his deeply ingrained suspicion of war propaganda, Stephensen later continued to deny the truth or extent of the Nazi extermination programme. To have accepted the holocaust would have been to acknowledge his own and Miles's support for a régime and an ideology which, far from arresting the decay of western civilization, instead provided history with its most unforgettable example of callous and obscene brutality. As I. N. Steinberg wrote in *Australia: The Unpromised Land* (1948): 'Our experience in many countries has taught us that these gentle, theorizing words can overnight become the blood-curdling yells of pogrommongers. The *Publicist* certainly does not represent Australian public opinion, but we must not disregard the underhand work of men like Stephensen'.[9]

Although Stephensen and Miles had little influence on public opinion, one regular reader of the *Publicist*, Miles Franklin, seems to have been swayed by the magazine's anti-Semitism. Early in 1939 she had written to W. J. Miles that she knew nothing of communists and less of the Jews, but a year later she informed Nettie Palmer that although she supported religious liberty, the Jews went 'beyond religion' and reduced racial intermingling to 'miscegenation'.[10] Franklin was never pro-fascist, although she was becoming more cynical and racist. As Drusilla Modjeska has shown, Franklin's attraction to strong leadership was accompanied by a scorn for the 'common minds'.[11] Although she sympathized with the cause of Australian independence, her opposition to the *Publicist*'s anti-feminism remained implacable and she refused to write for the magazine. She had received an indication of Miles's view of women when he had shouted her down at one Yabber Club session.

Despite the offensive nature of much *Publicist* propaganda, Australian independence remained its focus, and the war gave Miles and Stephensen a new resolve as well as a plan of action. Less than a week after the declaration of hostilities, Miles wrote that the *Publicist* would press for the formation of an Australia First party 'after the War'.[12] Miles viewed war as biologically inevitable, and both he and Stephensen were fond of comparing human with political organisms after the fashion of Morley Roberts's *Bio-Politics* (1938), a work they championed. The decay Miles thought he detected in western civilization happened to coincide with his own increasing ill health. Approaching seventy, and with such poor circulation in his legs that he was almost lame, he began referring pessimistically to the *Publicist* as his 'swan-song'.[13]

Stephensen on the other hand continued to plan and agitate for a new political party. When the following advertisement appeared on the back page of the *Publicist* between October 1939 and April 1940, the note of urgency was Stephensen's:

MEN WANTED!
Australian men, with public spirit and Parliamentary ambition, between 28 and 49 years of age, are invited to communicate personally with 'The Publicist', with a view to the formation of an Australia-First Political Party after the War.

The response was disappointing. In a later issue, and employing a pseudonym, Stephensen reported that those who had replied had been 'almost unanimously stupid', criticizing the wording of the advertisement or asking if it was to be a fascist party. 'The truth is that Australians generally do not desire to put "Australia First" in their thoughts', Stephensen commented in disgust. 'They enjoy and they prefer an inferior status.'[14]

For Miles, politics was an extension of his business interests, but for Stephensen the obsession with national liberation had now engulfed his concern for literature and publishing. Reviewing his friend Baylebridge's compendious volume, *This Vital Flesh*, in the February 1940 *Publicist*, Stephensen described the author as a 'poet-philosopher' though he was much more concerned with Baylebridge's ideas on 'Vitalism and Nationalism' than with any literary values.[15] The national hall of fame, however, was severely short of literary icons, Stephensen decided, so he and a couple of Yabber Club compatriots set up an 'A. G. Stephens Memorial

Committee' to organize fund raising for a bust of Stephensen's local hero. It was hoped to display this eventually in the Mitchell Library. Stephensen persuaded Miles Franklin to join the committee which in the course of a few months raised about seventy pounds from a wide cross-section of literary, academic and artistic people including Baylebridge, Eleanor Dark, C. E. W. Bean, and H. M. Green.[16] Not everyone, though, shared Stephensen's enthusiasm for Culture. One of W. J. Miles's grazier friends replied that he was not interested in literature or 'literary people', but would willingly subscribe to 'a sheepish memorial to Macarthur'.[17]

As a further contribution, Stephensen delivered a lecture on *The Life and Works of A. G. Stephens* to the Fellowship of Australian Writers in March 1940, and then had the lecture printed as a sixpenny pamphlet. It was a useful introduction to A.G.S. and just as revealing about Stephensen. The sympathetic treatment of Stephens's financial and literary frustrations was also a defence of Stephensen's past publishing failures and a gesture of defiance towards the future:

> Very seldom is the Man of Letters a 'good business man'. Almost necessarily he is not so. It is amazing what A.G.S. achieved through the long years when he had to battle so hard for a bare living. His pertinacity is the amazing thing, his refusal, his stiff-backed refusal, to acknowledge defeat: his unwavering faith in Australia—and in himself. If he had found a patron, in this land of so much wealth, Australia today would be a richer country, culturally, than it is.[18]

Stephensen was not faring much better. His patron Miles was in failing health and in any case remained a political rather than literary enthusiast. Miles regretfully told the *Publicist*'s captive poet, Ian Mudie, that it would not be possible to publish and distribute a volume of his verse 'except at a loss'.[19]

In April 1940 the *Publicist* was instructed under authority of the Commonwealth National Security regulations to submit all manuscript copy for censorship. Miles and Stephensen were anxious to comply and regarded this as an inevitable wartime restriction, but the *Publicist* was being paid very special attention. Along with only four other papers throughout Australia, including two which were communist, the *Publicist* was to be censored before publication. The rest of the press was just monitored. Miles hastened to assure the censor that he was not the well-known communist, J. B. Miles, but there was no mistake. The government was exercising the strictest control possible over any type of radical opinion.[20]

This careful scrutiny of *Publicist* material began to inhibit the magazine's anti-Semitism. The censor deleted a number of anti-Semitic articles and references, and Miles straightaway closed down his other journal, the *Secularist*, because he did not expect the censor to pass its 'anti-Semitic propaganda'.[21] Stephensen informed Mudie that the *Publicist* was 'prohibited' from publishing articles 'against Semitism', but the magazine in fact continued to snipe at individual Jews and at Jewish influence generally.[22] Because of the self-perpetuating logic of prejudice, these government restrictions only reinforced the *Publicist*'s belief in the widespread Jewish control of the media.

Yet if the *Publicist* had to tread more cautiously now, this did not affect plans for an Australia First party 'after the War'. Miles had agreed to this in principle, and about April 1940 he visited Stephensen's Potts Point flat to discuss the party platform. Together they came up with a typically provocative list, the *Publicist*'s Fifty Point Policy of what they were for, and against. This was amplified in the May *Publicist* and issued the following year in booklet form.[23] Many of the points were innocuously imprecise, and it was not surprising to find that Australia First was *for* Australian culture and self-dependence, and *against* imitativeness and colonial status. But Miles and Stephensen could not resist airing their prejudices in detail, so they were 'For "White" Australia' and 'For Aryanism; against Semitism', as well as for babies, a higher birth-rate, and women in the home. Leaving no doubt that their world view was regressive and authoritarian, they declared their support for discipline, loyalty, the police, private ownership, 'less taxation', and 'monarchism'. This display of allegiance to the Crown was a clever ploy. It both outraged the *Publicist*'s communist opponents and appeased those who might otherwise suspect disloyalty, especially during wartime. No lover of British imperialism, Stephensen was usually careful to define the monarch as the king of Australia.

There were other key points in the Australia First policy, however, which suggested by their very ambiguity that Nazi Germany remained the 'nationalist socialist' model for the party Stephensen and Miles were proposing:

6. For national socialism; against international communism.
32. For legitimate speech; against 'free' speech.
33. For responsible journalism; against 'freedom of the press'.
34. For political education; against political apathy.[24]

The reaction to such a policy was predictable. Communist speakers in the Sydney Domain called for the suppression of the 'fascist' and 'Nazi' *Publicist*, while even those who showed enthusiasm for Australia First were scornful of the repetitious and long-winded fifty points. 'Ye Gods' was the response of one of Stephensen's literary acquaintances who commented that the policy needed 'some realism' instead of 'hammering away at leftists and Jews'.[25]

The most damning indictment of the *Publicist* and its Australia First platform, however, was an article in the left-wing *Daily News* in May 1940. Listing the obviously fascist elements of the Fifty Point Policy, the *Daily News* also published the text of an interview with Miles and Stephensen. As no denial or rejoinder was ever issued by the *Publicist*, the *Daily News* report must have been substantially accurate. One exchange in particular conveyed the authentic flavour of the relationship between Stephensen and Miles, as well as the old man's peppery wit:

'The Daily News': Why are women to be excluded from your party?

Mr. Miles: We can't be bothered with women. They are no good to us. Their votes are useful to those who want votes. We don't seek votes.

Mr. Stephensen: That's a straight answer. We are for women in the home and against women in industry. We are for babies and against birth restriction.

'The Daily News': Why are you recruiting now for a party that is not to begin till after the war?

Mr. Miles: We are certain that the Allies will not win the war. Australians then will be bitterly disillusioned. Australia then will be a new and bad land.

Mr. Stephensen: A new and good land!

Mr. Miles: Stephensen is an incorrigible optimist.

Other parts of the interview seem less credible, though both Miles and Stephensen enjoyed baiting leftists as much as they did Jews:

'The Daily News': How are you going to finance your new party?

Mr. Miles: How was Hitler's party financed?

'The Daily News': By the big German industrialists.

Mr. Miles: We will do the same.

Mr. Stephensen: That's a straight answer for you.

Mr. Miles: In fact, we will accept money from anybody. Even from the Jews, though they cannot join our party; even from Hitler—after the war. If he gives us a million I'll think he has gone completely mad, but I will still take his money.[26]

A few weeks later France fell and Italy joined Germany to share the spoils of victory. For Britain, the war was now entering its darkest phase and on 15 June 1940 the Australian government declared the Communist Party an illegal organization under the National Security (Subversive Associations) regulations. A number of communist papers had already been banned by the conservative federal government, and Stephensen gloated over the suppression of his old party. He also attacked the Fellowship of Australian Writers as the 'dupes and stooges of Moscow'. In 1939 the FAW had amalgamated with the Writers' Association, a Communist Party front organization, and the new FAW was led by party member Bartlett Adamson. Stephensen continued to rail against the 'Muscovite Communists and Jews' of the FAW who he claimed were using the fellowship for the 'advancement of bizarre political causes'.[27]

Yet nothing was quite so bizarre as the pro-fascism of the *Publicist*, and had a Labor government been in power in June 1940, instead of Menzies's United Australia Party, then Miles's magazine would very likely have been suppressed at that time. On the day France signed an armistice with Germany, Friday 21 June, as the hail of German bombs began falling on Britain, both Stephensen and Miles felt an allied defeat was imminent. Inky was at Wagga Wagga on his annual winter trip with Frank Clune, and Miles wrote that he expected 'a thorough collapse in Britain'. It was very important now to form a nucleus for an Australia First party, Miles wrote, as thousands of Australians were already thinking Britain was sure to lose. He was even prepared to consider a *'short* preliminary series of lecture meetings'.[28]

Stephensen wrote to Winifred that there was 'big work' for him to do in Australia in the near future.[29] He envisaged that, after Britain's collapse, the real battle for 'Australia First' would begin. 'I'll make the most of my present holiday to rest my nerve and brain in the expectation or hope of getting an opportunity to serve Australia on the Home Front when crisis mounts', Stephensen told Miles. 'I have a strong premonition that I'll be in a maelstrom of politics during the coming three years!' He was more right than he knew. 'My future—like Australia's—is insecure', he concluded.[30]

In his July Bunyip Critic column, Stephensen supported calls for a one-party government to beat the Germans 'at their own game'. The whole thrust of his article was that fascism was both workable and necessary, and he applauded the 'virtually dictatorial powers' assumed by Australia and other allies to meet the war crisis. Even if the doctrines of Hitler and Mussolini were 'spurious', the fascist dictators had won the confidence of 'millions', and their 'glamour' resided in their claims to be 'progressive, venturesome, audacious in experiment'—in short the very things Stephensen himself admired in a man of action.[31]

This was dangerous as well as deluded Dionysianism, and Stephensen was intoxicated by the thought of what such a new order could offer Australia. In a sense, too, he was punch-drunk after years of wrestling with the dark phantoms of frustration and failure. He had tried to write a novel which would eclipse *Kangaroo* and reveal the true spirit of Australia; he had wanted to found a national publishing house and develop it into an enduring cultural monument; and he and Winifred had wanted to produce children. Yet he had not realized any of these creative ambitions, and the aggressive power of fascism became irresistibly attractive to him. He was unable to distinguish any more between instinctive rebelliousness and constructive revolution, or between his own besieged identity and that of his country.

In a letter to his friend and supporter, Ian Mudie, on the letterhead of the Publicist Publishing Company, Stephensen gave a glimpse of the role he might play in the coming social turmoil. Under the strain of both anxiety and excitement, this was the closest Stephensen ever came to the fascist megalomania of which his enemies accused him.

> Now, as to politics. Please understand that I have no personal ambitions of a parliamentary kind. I refuse to kow-tow to softness in the community by smoodging for 'votes'. I will not be the first man, but the last man, called upon to save Australia from British chaos because the medicine I will prescribe will be a drastic purge with a bitter taste to softies and weaklings. Like Petain, I will be called in at the death-bed, after the collapse of the British Garrison, not before. My medicine will either kill or cure the patient.
>
> I don't want POWER, for Power's Sake, but for Australia's sake. At present, I am best as a critic and propagandist. I don't want to lead a lot of sheep! Wait until they become Kangaroos![32]

Despite the bantering tone and typically metaphorical style, this was the expression of a serious ambition. Mudie would have also picked up the reference to the political aspects of Lawrence's novel *Kangaroo*. If intelligence surveillance had been more rigorous such a letter might well have hastened Stephensen's demise. His comparison with Pétain was particularly unfortunate, for it was only a matter of weeks since Marshal Pétain had become premier of France and arranged an armistice with the invading Germans. The implication was that Stephensen would likewise make an accommodation with an invading enemy.

Whether this indicated a potential fascist collaborator, or whether the key was extreme Anglophobia and the 'collapse of the British Garrison' in Australia, one thing remains clear. Stephensen stood almost alone at a time of do-or-die loyalty to Britain; when AIF recruitment increased six-fold and when the ABC's popular radio commentator, 'The Watchman' (E. A. Mann) described the Union Jack as 'our own flag' and 'an object of deep affection'. It was 'The Flag on which the sun never sets', Mann intoned proudly.[33] That Stephensen saw the lie in such propaganda, and that the world would soon witness the destruction of the myth after the Japanese had swept away European control of southeast Asia, still failed to vindicate his political opportunism. Applying the words of T. S. Eliot, Stephensen's greatest treason was to be right—about British imperialism —but for the wrong reason.[34] He idolized the rise of fascism and remained as deluded as those who clung to Britain's declining glory. Fascism was no more a new hope for national reconstruction than Britain was the perfect model of democracy and freedom.

In his flight from 'democracy' and parliamentary government, Stephensen was expressing his Bakuninite disillusionment with all systems of government. He had witnessed the degradation of the working class in Britain in the 1920s and knew the Empire had been built on violence and exploitation. Had circumstances not conspired to blind him to the truth of Nazi repression and persecution, he might have been spared his bitter twilight.

Yet if he never actually tasted the reality of political power, Stephensen did come in close contact with those who did. In August 1940, when H. V. Evatt was deciding to abandon the High Court and enter federal politics, Stephensen was one of those invited to his chambers to discuss his resignation and the general state of Australian politics. It was not so unusual that Evatt should approach Stephensen as they were both widely published intellectuals and had met previously at one of Hartley Grattan's 'talk-fests' in 1937. Stephensen admired Evatt and had praised his books in the *Publicist*.[35] However, it does seem mildly astonishing that with Britain on the point of defeat, a leftist should seek the views of a somewhat notorious pro-fascist. Possibly Evatt did not follow the eccentric progress of the *Publicist*, and remembered only Stephensen's stimulating conversation and his provocative, anti-fascist *Foundations of Culture in Australia*. Alternatively, Evatt may have wanted to find out what the enemies of the left were planning at this time of international crisis just as he was about to embark on his own stormy political career.

Whatever the reason, Stephensen gave all his sympathies as well as antipathies away. After their meeting, he wrote to Evatt about the failure of democracy and the dangers of American and Jewish influence in Australia. 'I look to reform along "authoritarian" lines', he told Evatt, 'namely rule by a politically conscious minority, organized and trained for the express purpose of rule'. There is no record of Evatt's response, if any, but Stephensen followed up his letter with a Bunyip Critic column praising Evatt's 'outstanding... intellectual ability, scholarship, and public spirit'.[36]

Stephensen too was prepared to accept a more public role, but the initiative for forming an Australia First party was to some extent taken away from him and from the Sydney *Publicist* group. During 1940 the Melbourne soapbox orator and former communist, L. K. Cahill, started his own 'Australia-First Movement' in Melbourne, telling Miles that it would be too late after the war was over. Although there was no formal connection between the Melbourne and Sydney Australia First groups, Cahill's reports began appearing regularly in the *Publicist*. For the January 1941 issue, Stephensen wrote that Australia needed not a new political party but a *'New Political Order'* and a 'Leadership based on strength'. The organization of that leadership was the task of the 'Australia-First Movement', Stephensen concluded, adopting Cahill's name for the movement. Fanaticism had now thoroughly invaded Stephensen's rhetoric, which seemed to resound with the echoes of Hitler's oratory:

> 'Australia-First' will build a nation here, not for an age, but for all time ... Are there one thousand young Australians who would dedicate themselves unswervingly to the task of re-vivifying our community? A thousand fanatics, prepared to live and die, for Australia, in Australia, prepared to build a Nation that will endure?[37]

During May 1941 Miles was predicting riots and even civil war in Australia, and Stephensen thought that Australian nationalism would 'soon reach the phase of action'.[38] It was at this time of excitement and anxious anticipation in the Australia First camp that Xavier Herbert conclusively parted company with Stephensen and Miles, the two men who had done so much to launch his literary career. Since the Publicist Publishing Company had first issued *Capricornia* on Australia Day 1938 the novel had been reprinted three times by Angus & Robertson and also published in England. Herbert had tried several times to complete a second novel, only to give up in despair because he felt the material was too much like *Capricornia*.[39]

Now living in Sydney, Herbert had become friendly with a number of left-wing writers including Dymphna Cusack. He attended the Yabber Club occasionally, but the *Publicist*'s increasingly offensive anti-Semitism disgusted him, particularly since Sadie was Jewish. So in May 1941

Herbert wrote a number of strongly worded letters to Miles and Stephensen, eliciting the usual elaborate and unnecessary response. Stephensen denied possessing 'irrational racial resentments' and urged Herbert not to abandon 'a really poor and oppressed people, the Aborigines' for the 'political machinations of Zionist Jews' who formed a 'rich, powerful, and cunning minority'. Signing himself as a 'former friend and comrade', Stephensen exchanged 'benedictions' for Herbert's 'curses'.[40]

Herbert had begun a friendly correspondence with his 'blood brother', Ian Mudie, whom he affectionately addressed as 'Kaijek', songman. Herbert tried to disillusion the Adelaide poet about Stephensen, revealing just how deep and violent his hatred for his former publisher had become. Without actually naming him, Herbert described Stephensen as a 'poison snake', a 'Thing' with a shrivelled soul and little Nordic eyes. Herbert promised Mudie that if this Nordic snake outlived the magic Herbert had made against him, then there would be nothing for it but to shoot a hole through the place where 'other men' had hearts.[41] Thirty years later this bitterness was distilled in *Poor Fellow My Country* (1975) in a contemptuous caricature of Stephensen as the 'Bloke': opportunistic and paranoid, a 'renegade Communist' and an 'erudite wrangler' who aped Hitler.[42]

Although Mudie remained Stephensen's staunchest supporter, other poets attracted by the Jindyworobak philosophy became dubious of the aims and origins of Australia First ideology. Flexmore Hudson was surprised at Mudie's support for the 'cheap alien fascism' of the *Publicist*, and Victor Kennedy criticized Australia First as a lot of 'superman stuff' imported from a 'Hitler beer-garten'.[43] Stephensen had constantly defended his nationalism as purely Australian, untainted by European isms and obsessions, yet the Jew-baiting and other elements of fascist and Nazi ideology espoused by the *Publicist* were nothing if not European.

In an essay on modernist poetry he wrote for a collection being put together by Victor Kennedy, Stephensen showed that his message now had less to do with nationalism than with indiscriminate explosions of polemic and prejudice. Entitled 'The Modernistics in Retrospect',[44] his essay began with some useful observations about poetic form, but quickly degenerated into a paranoid diatribe on the evils of Jewish-inspired modernism and decadence. He viewed the 'bazaar theories of Marx, Freud, and Einstein' not as innovations but as 'Jewish medievalism'. Stephensen's intellectual distortions were mixed up with the iconoclasm of past crusades. His attack on America—'rotten to the core with commercialism and Tin Pan Alley jimjam jitters'—strongly echoed the antimodernism he and Jack Lindsay had espoused in the *London Aphrodite* in their youthful 1920s. Now, confused with nationalism and antiSemitism, it was nothing but a compleat Nazified conspiracy theory:

> Released from the ghetto, Marx, Freud and Einstein have become the false messiahs of modernistic aesthetics. Instead of learning, what the Aryans have long ago learnt, that life is something to be *lived*, these Jews are still trying to alter life, to make it conform with an abstract

pattern of thought. They are still knocking their heads against the Wailing Wall, complaining, petulant, discontented, dogmatic, metaphysical . . .

Eliot, Epstein and Gertrude Stein—they were for Stephensen lamentable symbols of the two decades of his adulthood, the 1920s and 1930s, that 'interim period of uneasy peace'. Like many others, Stephensen had never been able to cope with the scale of horror represented by World War I. His anarchic acceptance of a new totalitarian blood bath indicated the depth of his anger and impatience—with the direction of his own thwarted career as much as with that of Australian culture. The remedy he proposed was therefore correspondingly desperate. 'The Eliotic world ended', he wrote in his essay, 'not with a modernistic whimper, but with a totalitarian bang'. The long expected revolution would come, he said, 'not from the whimpering left, but from the banging Right, banging on the doors of time'. The fascist revolution would 'clear away a lot of debris, to build anew and better, on the ascending scale of Aryan consciousness'.

Although he did not fight in either world war, Stephensen suffered from the cynicism of the first and the false prophecy of fascism which led to the second. A Danish-French-Swiss Australian, he had rejected Britain's imperialist propaganda only to fall uncritically under the spell of an ideal of racial and political purity which was as meaningless and regressive as it was inhuman. This not only perverted his sympathy for the Aborigines and other oppressed groups but so twisted his nationalist faith that he became a traitor to his conscience and, to many Australians, a hollow patriot.

Now entering a final and prolonged illness, Miles was confined to bed but continued working from his home at Gordon where Stephensen visited him regularly on *Publicist* business. With Germany's attack on Russia there had been a new allied accommodation with the left. Despite Churchill's previous vehement opposition to communism, his photograph now began appearing beside that of a smiling Stalin. In Australia the banned Communist Party was revitalized in its fight against fascism, and the *Publicist* fringe became further isolated.

During June 1941 Stephensen was impelled once again towards active politics. The Melbourne Australia-First organizer, Cahill, visited Sydney that month and made a favourable impression on Miles and Stephensen. Cahill's past had been at least as rebellious as Stephensen's. Expelled from the Communist Party in 1932, Cahill had attempted to set up a rival 'Fourth International' and was skilled as a Yarra Bank speaker. He was also quick with his fists and had been fined by a Melbourne court in 1940 for assaulting a communist interjector. Needless to say, his local 'Australia-First Movement' had attracted more communist disruption than popular support.[45]

Melbourne had long been a focus for Irish Catholic political dissent, and Daniel Mannix had helped originate the cry of 'Australia First' during World War I. Some of the younger right-wing Catholic radicals began to show interest in the *Publicist* and one, S. J. Ingwersen, contributed articles and corresponded with Miles and Stephensen. Ingwersen, however, was wary of Cahill and let Miles know that although the Yarra Bank speaker was an 'excellent organiser', he was 'very ignorant'. Mudie also warned that Cahill would need curbing. Hastening to the defence of Cahill and his 'native Australianism', Stephensen criticized Ingwersen for being too 'university' and 'snobbish'. Australia needed men of 'rough fibre', Stephensen said, to carry the nationalist message to the 'masses'.[46]

He also valued the role of nationalist poets like Mudie and Baylebridge, so when Jindyworobak chief, Rex Ingamells, declared his allegiance to Australia First, Stephensen took this as an important sign of solidarity. Mudie was not so sure, regarding Ingamells as 'horribly sincere' but also frequently 'self-deluded'. Stephensen, though, wanted to believe that Ingamells's influence, along with that of Mudie, would stimulate a 'New Australian poetic synthesis'. That Stephensen derived such satisfaction from Ingamells's support showed how desperate he really was for disciples, and how easy it still was to provoke his irrational optimism. 'After five years lonely battling for Australian Nationalism', he explained to Mudie, 'I now feel that our infant New Australia idea is launched and that it will swim'.[47] But not for long, with the tide of events running so strongly against them.

During July 1941 the first blackout tests were conducted in Australian cities because of the likely threat from Japan. With Miles's deteriorating condition, plans were made to close down the *Publicist* office in Elizabeth Street, and Stephensen's workload as well as his worries increased. His ardent supporters were now expecting big things from him, yet his position was in fact becoming weaker and more isolated. On the same day he received a warm letter from Ingamells and another from Mudie hailing him as the 'National Leader'.[48] He wrote to Ingamells disclaiming any dictatorial ambitions, giving instead a romantic and Nietzschean vision of his role as prophet and 'forerunner'. Yet the influence of Hitler's dream of a thousand-year *Reich* was as unmistakable as the persistent remnants of Stephensen's idealistic communism:

> Viewing the life of the nation as of a thousand years or more yet to come, the individual ceases to be of paramount importance; and only the Idea endures. I am therefore completely devoid of personal ambitiousness, and I detest being projected into anything resembling a messianic role ... At most my role is that of John the Baptist, a forerunner ...
>
> Our spiritual (perhaps our physical) ancestors (for the Aboriginals are the oldest Aryans on earth) had no kings or personal leaders. They deliberated around the camp fires ... This is the True Communism ...
>
> Here there is no room for ambitiousness, jealousies, personal glamorising, strutting, posturing, megalomaniacal exhibitionism on the European tribal model. Let's be Australian, different ...[49]

In a letter to Mudie, Stephensen reiterated his illusory synthesis of fascism and 'true' communism. 'We don't want a leader', he told his friend, 'we want a thousand leaders thinking in unison'.[50] After an absence of more than fifteen years from active politics, Stephensen's return to the arena of his youth was accompanied not by a coherent political philosophy (as in his communist days), but by a haphazard assortment of elements, many of which were harmless, some faintly ridiculous, and others explosive.[51] Unfortunately he could no longer distinguish which was which, nor could he see where they were leading him.

Stephensen was overwhelmed with *Publicist* business as tension mounted in Australia during August 1941. The remaining members of the Japanese community prepared to leave Sydney[52]—an indication of imminent hostilities—and at the end of the month Menzies resigned as prime minister, handing over to the Country Party leader, Arthur Fadden. Federal politics had become so unstable, however, that Fadden lasted only a few weeks as prime minister. In the August *Publicist* Stephensen dusted off the old Fifty Point Policy and arranged for its publication as a separate pamphlet with the title *Fifty Points for Australia: A Forecast of the New Order*. The 'new order' he envisaged was the dissolution of 'sectional' parties into some form of totalitarian régime under which journalists would be 'compelled to act with a sense of public responsibility'. Stephensen had hitherto been against military-style fascism such as that advocated by the New Guard, but now he wrote that 'Military rule, the imposition of authority "from above", may yet, under harsh necessity, prove the only practicable method of eliminating Australian slackness and casualness of mind and manners'.[53]

The *Fifty Points* pamphlets went to *Publicist* subscribers or to newspapers for review, and Mudie and Ingamells were among those who helped distribute another several hundred copies. To Ingamells, Stephensen wrote that, not having children of his own, he had to imagine himself as 'a kind of uncle or alcheringa godfather to younger Australians'.[54] One of his surrogate sons, Ian Mudie, who had just dedicated *This is Australia* to Stephensen, was coming to Sydney early in September, and Inky planned a reception for him at the Yabber Club.

Miles passed his 70th birthday in a coma but recovered sufficiently to announce that he would sell the *Publicist* to three of his supporters, including Stephensen. Although Stephensen formulated plans to try to make the *Publicist* self-supporting, he must have realized that Miles's fall would bring down the magazine and jeopardize the whole Australia First effort. Winifred suddenly became ill with tuberculosis, and Stephensen began to buckle. 'I am just about distracted', he wrote to Ingamells, 'my personal world appearing to be on the verge of collapse'. Despising fate, however, he refused to be 'smashed right down'.[55]

On 7 October 1941 two independents in federal parliament switched their support to the ALP and Curtin's Labor government took office, with Evatt as attorney-general and minister for external affairs. In an exercise book Stephensen drafted a letter which he sent to Evatt,[56] offering the new cabinet minister advice as he had done the previous year when Evatt was stepping down from the High Court. Stephensen still believed Britain could not win the war, and he warned Evatt that Britain's defeat would have a 'catastrophic effect' on Australia, resulting in 'psychological and economic collapse'. Facing possible psychological and financial collapse himself, Stephensen urged Evatt to consider an 'emergency plan' for 'National preservation', to stop Australia 'falling into the avaricious clutches of the U.S.A. plutocracy'. Stephensen expected that the United States would remain neutral until Britain was 'thoroughly smashed', and then pick up the pieces of her empire. 'If (or rather *when*) Britain is defeated', he wrote to Evatt, 'an entirely new constitution and also a new way of thought will be necessary in Australia—a new *leadership*'.

In the same exercise book as he drafted this remarkable letter, Stephensen whimsically scribbled some notes under the heading 'A School for Statesmen'. He wrote that if he were invited to act as dictator of Australia[57]—'(as seems very unlikely)'—he would ensure that no one could become a member or parliament without having first carefully studied certain texts, including Plato's *Republic*, Machiavelli's *The Prince*, Hobbes's *Leviathan*, Rousseau's *Social Contract*, and Morley Roberts's *Bio-Politics* (for which Stephensen had compiled a glossary).[58]

Then, out of the blue, Stephensen accepted overtures from Adela Pankhurst Walsh to form an Australia-First Movement (AFM) in Sydney, and the final act of this strange drama began. A member of the English suffragette family, Adela Pankhurst had come to Australia and married militant unionist Tom Walsh during World War I. Although they were foundation members of the Communist Party of Australia, the Walshes, like Stephensen and Cahill, broke with the left and became vehemently anti-communist. During the 1930s Tom Walsh joined the New Guard and Adela's Women's Guild of Empire acted as a pressure group against strikes and against women in the workforce. About 1940, after a visit to Japan apparently paid for by the Japanese government, the Walshes became public enthusiasts for that country.[59]

Despite the fact that Adela Walsh's Guild of Empire group had clashed with the *Publicist* a few years previously,[60] and despite Miles's low opinion of her,[61] Stephensen suddenly agreed to join with Walsh and some of her friends in a weird hybrid Australia-First Movement. At first he had been reluctant to be associated with Walsh, but she had threatened to start her own AFM if he did not co-operate.[62] Others had already taken the initiative away from Stephensen and he was anxious not to be left behind. Cahill had been running his 'Australia-First Movement' in Melbourne for more than a year, and Cecil Salier, one of the *Publicist* group, had begun an 'Australians Progress Movement' in Sydney in September 1941 with a planned series of lectures.[63] In any event, Stephensen no doubt felt a special affinity with other renegades from communism, so he wrote to Cahill and invited him to Sydney to join the Australia First group and Walsh's 'women's auxiliary' friends:

> [Miles] is very weak indeed in health and thinks he will not recover. Events, however are moving so fast that we can no longer wait. We must

now start doing something to get mass support. The time of talking is past, the hour of action has struck.⁶⁴

A preliminary meeting was held at the flat of one of Adela Walsh's associates on 15 October 1941, just a week after the Labor government took office, and Stephensen circulated a draft ten-point manifesto along with a constitution and rules. These were all adopted five days later at the first general meeting of the Australia-First Movement which was held at the Yabber venue, the Shalimar Cafe. Stephensen was voted AFM president and chairman of a motley executive committee which included the two paid 'organisers' Walsh and Cahill, three of Walsh's Guild of Empire women, Ian Mudie, a shoe shop proprietor, and a truck driver and his wife.⁶⁵ A series of public meetings was planned to begin in November at the Australian Hall in Elizabeth Street, not far from the *Publicist* office and the scene of the 1938 Aboriginal Day of Mourning and Protest.

Miles took no part in the AFM, and Stephensen's new ten-point manifesto looked more progressive and less prejudiced than the earlier Fifty Points he had concocted with Miles's assistance. There was no specific mention now of National Socialism or anti-Semitism, though the AFM wanted to control the 'numbers or quality' of immigrants and to oppose any restrictive overseas 'monopolies, combines and political powers'. The key to the manifesto was '*Australian Independence*', yet the old contradictory affirmation of 'loyalty to the King' was added, just in case.⁶⁶

Although the AFM was strictly a political pressure group, Stephensen became involved in further cultural debate and controversy. The November 'Nationality Number' of *Meanjin Papers*, then only a few issues old, contained a piece by Ingamells and also one by Stephensen on Queensland culture, stressing the importance of the *genius loci*. In the interests of balance, perhaps, these were opposed by Brian Vrepont's critical poem 'Nationalism' which deplored the 'black Aryan nightmare' of fascism. Under the cloak of the pseudonym 'Mopoke', Vrepont also slated Mudie's *This is Australia* as fanatical, monotonous and futile propaganda. 'As an Australian, on poetry's behalf', Vrepont wrote, 'I apologise to Australia for Mr. Mudie's seriously purposed intellectual and emotional sterility'.⁶⁷

Stephensen replied in the *Publicist* with a stinging attack,⁶⁸ but such literary skirmishing was now far from the centre of his thoughts. As he wrote in a memo to his prospective *Publicist* partners, S. B. Hooper and Valentine Crowley, the propaganda of Australia First was his 'life work and all absorbing interest' and he would 'stand or fall on that ground'.⁶⁹ In November 1941, the month Stephensen turned forty, his dying patron Miles agreed to sell for the princely sum of five pounds the whole *Publicist* operation, including office equipment, stock, copyright, and 'goodwill (if any)'.⁷⁰ This was another of Miles's wry jokes, since he had always taken a perverse pride in the *Publicist*'s unpopularity. With only a matter of weeks to live now, Miles had little interest in the political movement he had spawned, and instead revealed his macabre sense of humour by running a sweep on the exact time he would die. Punctuality had always been one of his obsessions.

With Stephensen as president, and Cahill and Walsh as organizers, the AFM held public meetings at the Australian Hall in Sydney each Wednesday evening throughout November and December 1941. Stephensen, Cahill and Walsh were usually the speakers, assisted by Edward Masey, and the meetings attracted an average of about a hundred people, including journalists, hecklers, and officers and shorthand reporters of both Military Police Intelligence (MPI) and the Commonwealth Investigation Branch (IB). Right from the start Stephensen was aware of their presence. No doubt mindful of future historians, he was pleased to see them taking such a detailed record. He even invited the spies up to the press table, to 'make themselves comfortable', but they declined his offer, and instead 'sat at the back, among the interjectors'. From the tone of the MPI reports in particular, they would have felt more comfortable down with the hecklers.[71]

At the first meeting on 5 November Adela Walsh could barely be heard over the noise of a dance band playing in the adjoining building. One of the communists in the audience, however, knew enough about her Japanese sympathies to shout 'Get out you Japanese rat', and Cahill offered to fight another interjector who called him a goat. Cahill said it was up to Australia and Japan to decide the 'future of the Pacific', and both he and Walsh objected strongly to United States military bases in Australia.[72] Addressing the audience as 'Fellow Australians', Stephensen explained that the AFM claimed the same degree of independence for Australia 'as the people of Britain claim for Britain'.[73]

At the second meeting Adela Walsh again had to contend with the dance band next door, this time playing 'Rock Me to Sleep with Your Dreams', and towards the end of the evening a small group of half-drunk air force men joined about a dozen left-wingers in noisy interjections. Stephensen brought the meeting to a close by ordering the pianist to give a hasty rendition of 'God Save the King', and one of the MPI constables prevented a 'free fight' between two members of the audience as the meeting threatened to become a brawl.[74] It was after this meeting that the New South Wales premier wrote to Prime Minister Curtin about restricting AFM activities.[75]

Yet after three meetings membership of the AFM was still far short of a hundred, and it is difficult to see the justification for an MPI report which concluded that Australia First was the 'genesis of a Fifth Column of a most virulent kind'. In the past the movement had certainly been 'Anti-British, Anti-American, violently Anti-Jewish and Anti-Communistic, and pro-Japanese', as MPI officers reported,[76] but these were political opinions, widely disseminated through the *Publicist* and subject to the strictest censorship. There was, after all, a clear distinction between public statements, however eccentric, and subversive plotting.

Despite the strong wording of the intelligence report, when it was considered by the Commonwealth solicitor-general in the light of Stephensen's affirmations of loyalty, no action to suppress the AFM was considered necessary.[77] During this time, however, numerous groups including Labor Party branches, unions and the 'British Empire Union in Australia' approached Curtin seeking the suppression of the AFM and the internment of its members. The State Labor Party executive carried a resolution demanding a ban on the movement and the 'public trial' of its leaders.[78] In federal parliament S. M. Falstein, a Labor MP, asked the attorney-general, Evatt, for a report on the 'anti-war, anti-democratic, and pro-fascist' organization 'masquerading' under the name of Australia First.[79]

Evatt knew enough about Stephensen to be suspicious of him and the AFM, but there were more important preoccupations for the man who was also external affairs minister. At the end of November 1941 Curtin and Evatt received a 'Most Secret' cipher cable from London advising the Australian government that negotiations with Japan had broken down and that an aggressive move was expected 'possibly within the next few days'.[80] Just a week later, on Sunday 7 December, came the devastating raid on Pearl Harbour, and then on 10 December Japanese aircraft sank the British battleships *Prince of Wales* and *Repulse*. The Japanese forces advanced quickly down through southeast Asia, and Australia faced a real danger of invasion, after decades of 'yellow peril' nightmares. On 11 December Ingamells wrote to Mudie that there would be 'bloody hell to pay' and that many of the things Stephensen had advocated would now 'automatically take effect'.[81] Ingamells was right, but events were suddenly moving more swiftly than Stephensen had ever imagined.

At the first AFM meeting after Pearl Harbour Stephensen took the platform to speak against conscription for service abroad, mindful of the strong tradition of 'Australia First' protest which had originated in the World War I anti-conscription movement. Stephensen also took heart from the fact that Australia's declaration of war against Japan had not been automatic but 'separately declared', implying that Australia could sue for peace separately if necessary. Yet he declared himself unequivocally behind the war effort and the defence of Australia.[82]

In the wake of Japanese aggression, however, there was little room for the AFM to manoeuvre, especially with its pro-Japanese record, and the movement began to fall apart. Cahill and Walsh were at loggerheads, and Cahill resigned from the committee to enlist for military service. Walsh 'tendered her resignation' from the AFM, or more likely was pushed out because her public sympathy with Japan had now made her a serious liability.[83]

Even without Walsh and the provocative Cahill, the next public meeting became very rowdy as Masey tried to explain that trade rivalry had caused the war with Japan, and that a military defeat of Japan would 'not solve the problem'. Such sober analysis failed to satisfy an excited and

The Publicist

THE PAPER LOYAL TO AUSTRALIA FIRST

No. 67. SYDNEY 1st JANUARY, 1942. MONTHLY, 6d.

PRINCIPAL CONTENTS

Nineteen-Forty-Two	*(Editorial)*
Conscription-for-Service-Abroad	*P. R. Stephensen*
Charity Begins at Home	*M. F. Watts*
Art and Australia	*Anna Brabant*
Community Disunity	*Val Crowley*
Two Poems	*Ian Mudie*

1942

The year 1942 dawns, promising to be the most portentous year in all Australia's 154 years of British-colonial history. Now, the long-expected, long-deferred, War in the Pacific has started. It is a war which should naturally be fought mainly north of the Equator, between two principal protagonists, Japan and the U.S.A., whose home coasts are in the Northern Hemisphere.

To Americans, Japan is a Far West. To Japanese, the U.S.A. is a Far East. The main naval and aerial warfare between the two countries is raging, and will rage, across a vast extent of ocean. The distance between Yokohama and San Franscico is 4,750 miles. It is difficult to see how either of the parties could *decisively* damage the other at the extremity of such a long reach.

Almost equally great is the distance between Japan and Australia. On the north-south axis, from Yokohama to Sydney is a distance of 4,200 miles by the shortest sea-route; and between Yokohama and Port Darwin there are nearly 3,000 miles of sea. As it is an old military axiom that "distance is the best cover", the main protagonists in the Pacific Ocean war would all appear relatively safe in their respective homelands from danger of large-scale attack or invasion. (The distance from Yokohama to London, by sea via Cape Horn, is so great as to be not worthwhile calculating, for practical war-purposes.)

It follows, then, that this War in the Pacific will be mainly a matter of skirmishes between outposts of all the combatants, in positions considerably advanced from Home bases. There have been, and will be, naval battles in open ocean, between fleets fairly equally balanced in strength; there have been, and will be, assaults by land, sea, and air, on isolated outposts of the contending powers — assaults rather in the nature of raids than of territorial offensives. Such skirmishes and raids have done, and will do, much damage; but, unless followed by consolidation, they do not amount to much more than "hit and run".

In the Eastern Asiatic Zone, Japan enjoys the undoubted strategic advantage of "interior lines" of communication by sea, land, and air: just as Germany and Italy do in the European Zone. A similar advantage is enjoyed by the U.S.A. in the North American Zone; and by Australia in the Australian Zone. Compactness is a great advantage for defence: the lack of it is a strategic disadvantage for Britain's Empire, which is widely scattered in the seven-and-seventy seas. This disadvantage is well-known to Britain's strategists, who have built up an Empire of strong-posts: each virtually an isolated outpost, capable of standing siege.

From the British-Imperial point of view, Australia is one of the strongest, and most self-sufficient, of the isolated outposts in an Imperial Strategic Line which extends from Portsmouth via Gibraltar, Malta, Suez, Bombay, Colombo, Singapore, Darwin, and Sydney to Auckland, thence via Canada back to Britain. This is veritably a girdle around the earth; with alternative routes via the Cape of Good Hope and Cape Horn, if Suez or Canada were blockaded or impeded. From the purely British-Imperial strategic point of view, the fall of one or more outposts, though serious, would not be fatal. One of the most important links in this chain is Singapore, which defends the eastern gateway to India, richest jewel in the Imperial Crown. The fall of Singapore would be a very serious matter for the British Empire.

From the purely Australian insular point of view, however, the fall of Australia would be more than serious: it would be fatal. For us, Australia is not an outpost: it is Home. When we are at war with Japan, Singapore is on our Left Flank, as New Zealand is on our Right Flank. Our northern outposts are at Darwin, Thursday Island and Port Moresby, screened by the Dutch Islands, the Philippines, and Mandated New Guinea.

A casual glance at a map does not convey the immense distances implied in these strategical conceptions; distances which present formidable difficulties for the transport of troops and supplies. These difficulties are as great for Japan as they are for Britain, the U.S.A., or Australia. If the war is to be a mere matter of outpost raids and skirmishes, a decisive result would be unlikely for years. There is certainly no need for panic or despair in Australia, even if the enemy were to gain some initial successes in the skirmishing and raids. Distance, no less than time, operates in our favour. All that is needed in Australia is a workmanlike attitude of confidence and resolute self-defence, based, in the ultimate, on our compact strategical position and the cover of distance.

For 5½ years, this PUBLICIST, in its small field of influence, has consistently urged that everything possible should be done to preserve peace in the Pacific: a peace based on mutual toleration and understanding among the nations in this zone. Similar sentiments have been expressed by many Australian statesmen — among them Sir John Latham, Messrs Menzies, Curtin, Fadden, Spender, and Dr Evatt. The entire commercial newspress has been consistently hostile to such a view.

Now war has come between Australia and Japan. Like all wars, it is the result of a failure of diplomacy; and there is nothing now for honorable Australians to do except to stand loyally by their Government, to help their Government, to obey their Government in all things relating to the conduct of the war. The duty of the Government is also plain; and there is no reason to suppose that that duty is not understood. It is the duty of the Australian Government to defend Australia first, to safeguard Australia first, to uphold the interests of Australia first, in all circumstances of war and peace; but particularly in the present and immediately future times of unprecedented large-scale armed conflict in the vast Pacific Ocean Zone.

P. R. STEPHENSEN.

Stephensen's first *Publicist* editorial, in 1942, just before W. J. Miles's death and Stephensen's internment antagonistic audience. During the verbal slanging match which followed, Stephensen shouted that at least Australia First had not been declared illegal like the Communist Party. He did not help his cause by silencing one Jewish questioner with the comment, 'You have the press in which to make your propaganda'.[84]

Stephensen's mail was now being intercepted by the IB whose Canberra director recommended to Evatt just before Christmas 1941 that it was time for the 'freedom of the activities' of the AFM to be 'considerably curtailed'. A couple of weeks later a certain Captain Blood of Military Intelligence (MI) put in a submission for Stephensen's 'restriction'. Although this too was refused, all the various intelligence services, civilian and military, had now recommended action against the AFM. The IB director, however, did point out that the movement was seriously short of finance and, from reports coming in, it was apparent that Stephensen was 'rapidly losing heart in the movement'.[85]

Stephensen's first *Publicist* editorial, in the January 1942 issue, welcomed the new year as the 'most portentous' in Australia's 'British-colonial history', and anticipated that the fall of Singapore (then just a few weeks away) would be a serious matter for the British Empire but that the fall of Australia would be 'fatal'.[86] In a letter to Ingamells on 3 January, Stephensen said he regarded the 'Brit-Usa-Com-Jew' as the 'real invaders and opponents of Australia':

> I suppose I have less Japanic panic than any other man in Australia at the present time. Japos are frugal people and bombs cost money so they don't want to waste any on a place so far from the zone of East Asia as this. (It may be that Darwin will be air-bombed just as a gesture but I don't anticipate a Japanese Expeditionary Force ever to visit Australia).
>
> The future of Australian life depends wholly on the courage and clear headedness of a few of us . . .

As it turned out, Stephensen was right, and Darwin was bombed the following month, but to deny the imminent danger of military invasion in favour of some Jewish conspiracy was delusion rather than courage. Stephensen sent Ingamells a copy of the *Protocols of the Elders of Zion* which he said correctly set out 'the mad Jewish dream of dominating the world by guile'.[87]

Perhaps because of the threat of violence and property damage, AFM meetings could no longer be held at the Australian Hall, and moved instead to the Adyar Hall in Bligh Street where Aborigines Progressive Association meetings had taken place in 1938. Deserted now by his organizers and facing dissension within the AFM as well as negligible public support, Stephensen became even more isolated and defiant. He was the only speaker at the 7 January meeting, the chair being taken by the truck driver whose wife was AFM secretary.

Realizing he was in danger of suppression by the Labor government, Stephensen denied that his movement was subversive and defended the AFM's right to hold public meetings, a right he said had been lost years ago in Russia, Germany and Italy. He warned that Australia might be sacrificed by Britain and the United States in a strategy of 'reconquest'. 'If the Americans and Britain decide to let us go and recapture us later', he told the meeting, 'we will have to stand up for our principles, stand up for Australian nationalism'.[88] Again the implication was that Australia should have the right to make a separate peace with Japan.

A couple of days after this meeting, Miles finally died at his home, and Stephensen gave the funeral oration, noting that 'never again can we expect . . . to be angered or provoked by him'. Miles had warned Stephensen not to make his speech too long or 'eulogistic', but then had added, with 'typical ironic wit', that Stephensen should not be 'too hilarious either'.[89]

Now freed from the spectre of Miles's dying presence, Stephensen refined the Australia First policy down from an innocuous ten points to a more urgent and volatile three, including peace with Japan, as he wrote to Miles's Melbourne friend, W. D. Cookes:

> If there is any sign of the United States and Britain abandoning Australia while they concentrate on Hitler, then Australia would have no option except to conclude a separate peace with Japan . . . I expect to see opinions growing in favour of (1) Recall of the A.I.F., (2) Independence from Britain, (3) Separate peace with Japan. It would be premature to advocate this third point at present, but I believe the nettle will have to be grasped sooner or later by responsible leaders of the Australian community.[90]

At a 'members' conference' the next evening Stephensen put forward all three policies but, after discussion with the more cautious Masey, agreed to drop the demand for a separate peace with Japan.[91] An AFM leaflet was printed at the end of January 1942 with just two points for 'Australian National Defence':

1—Recall to Australia of all Australian Armed Forces
2—National Independence for Australia[92]

The IB agent's report of the conference, however, included the third point about peace with Japan, and the IB director passed this on as Australia First policy in a memo to the Attorney-General's Department. There, either Evatt or one of his officers marked Stephensen's controversial peace plan with a firm cross in the margin.[93]

At the next AFM public meeting, on 5 February, Stephensen praised the independent outlook of Evatt in external affairs, and went on to comment that the Labor government had 'established Australia's separate right to negotiate with other countries . . . in matters of war and peace'. However, he criticized the rest of the Labor cabinet as former pacifists who had failed to act with 'courage and resolution'. The Curtin government, he said, had exploited the Japanese threat to stay in office, and he held both the British and Australian governments responsible for the inadequate defence of Singapore and Rabaul. These comments were interpreted by MPI agents as prejudicial to the war effort.[94]

A few days later a rabid anti-Semite and AFM member, Thomas Graham, was arrested for possessing 'subversive literature', to whit a document warning Australians against the 'American imperialists' and 'Jewish financiers' who were invading Australia to prepare for an 'American-Jewish Dictatorship'.[95] The anxiety of the trigger-happy intelligence services was no doubt increased when they intercepted a letter on its way to Stephensen from the anti-Semitic architect, Hardy Wilson. There was no fear of the Japanese settling in Australia, Wilson had written, but he had prepared for this with proposals 'which the Japanese, probably, would respect'.[96]

In view of the weakening of the AFM, the IB in Canberra decided to reduce surveillance of the movement. The MPI in Sydney on the other hand requested permission from the police commissioner to conduct a search of premises occupied by key AFM members, and also wanted the movement declared unlawful.[97] Police Commissioner MacKay not only refused both requests, but pointed out that it was the role of the federal attorney-general to declare organizations illegal.[98] This was indicative of the confusion amongst the various intelligence networks which had proliferated since the outbreak of war. With the distinct possibility of a Japanese invasion, the military in particular had become extremely nervous.

While military intelligence was trying desperately to ferret out subversive groups, the AFM made a final bid to increase its size and influence. Under the heading 'NOW OR NEVER!', an AFM circular was issued on 14 February 1942 stating that a thousand new members were needed to make the movement an 'effective and solid body of public opinion'.[99] The next day Singapore finally fell to the Japanese, shattering any confidence Australians still retained in the Royal Navy and ending the centuries-old European domination of southeast Asia. What Stephensen and the *Publicist* had been predicting for almost six years had finally come to pass, and there was in the Australian community a widespread feeling of isolation and extreme vulnerability. Darwin was bombed a few days later, destroying ships and aircraft, and sending the panic-stricken population fleeing for their lives into the bush.[1]

Just after the fall of Singapore the MPI headquarters in Sydney intercepted a letter from a Perth man informing Stephensen that an Australia First 'party' would be established in Western Australia at a 'private meeting of supporters' the following Saturday night. The letter never reached Stephensen who had no idea that a few hapless and misguided readers of the *Publicist* in Western Australia were receiving the attentions of an undercover agent in the employ of Detective-Sergeant G. R. Richards of the Perth Special (political) Bureau.[2] Richards was later the deputy director-general of ASIO and the officer in charge of the controversial Petrov defection, so he was to enjoy a long record of involvement in politically sensitive intelligence operations.[3]

The agent he employed in Perth had already acted in a similar capacity against communists and knew enough about the AFM to manufacture highly and even ludicrously incriminating evidence.[4] Even if the agent did this only in the interests of his career as a police informer, the fact remains that Perth was an ideal place for such an operation against the AFM. Stephensen knew virtually nothing about the Perth movement, and Western Australia was at that time considered a likely target for Japanese invasion.

Powerful and determined groups were now moving against the AFM from a number of directions. On the day Darwin was bombed, the regular meeting of the movement in Sydney at the Adyar Hall was disrupted by waterside workers and communists. In the battle which followed an attempt to eject one of the wharfies, Stephensen was hit over the head with a water carafe, punched and kicked. Among the weapons found in the hall after the police belatedly arrived were an iron bolt, some eggs and bottles of 'evil smelling fluid'. The police advised Stephensen to close the meeting, but instead he took over the platform from Masey and proceeded to address the meeting at length, despite his battered condition. He said the capture of thirteen thousand Australians at the fall of Singapore was 'virtually the greatest disaster in Australia's history'. Physically bruised and bloodied, isolated and frustrated by the minority status of his beleaguered movement, Stephensen cried that the AFM, 'small though it may be', was the 'beginning of the Australian nation'.[5] Instead it was to be the end of P. R. Stephensen.

The actual mechanism of his destruction was in itself a conspiracy,[6] but Stephensen had invited trouble, and even seemed to relish it. As his suppression as a communist at Oxford ought to have taught him, opposing the government during a period of social unrest was highly dangerous. Further demands were made for the suppression of the AFM by members of parliament as well as by groups of servicemen who petitioned the army minister.[7]

Undaunted, Stephensen tried to rent the Sydney Town Hall for the next meeting, but when this was refused he managed to secure the Arcadia Theatre in Manly for 5 March. The handbill advertising the meeting proclaimed that the 'vigorous and courageous speaker', P. R. Stephensen, would address the meeting which would call for a national all-party government and the resignation of the 'minister or ministers' responsible for the inadequate defence of Rabaul.[8] Some newspapers were suggesting the formation of a 'People's Army' to defend Australia,[9] and it was in this atmosphere of desperate national crisis that the Manly meeting was planned.

A few hours before the meeting was due to start, however, police arrived at Stephensen's Rose Bay flat and took him for an interview with Police Commissioner MacKay who requested the cancellation of the meeting because of the threat of further violence. Stephensen countered by claiming police protection, but MacKay insisted that the meeting not proceed. He was armed with an order conveyed to him that day by dispatch rider from the attorney-general, Evatt, formally prohibiting the Manly meeting, but did not need to use it. Sensing at last what he was up against, Stephensen went down to Manly and announced the cancellation of the protest meeting.[10]

MacKay reported to the commonwealth solicitor-general: 'While it was possible on this occasion to ban the meeting and prevent it quietly it may not be possible on future occasions ... as Stephensen is a well educated man and knows his business'.[11] So apparently did MacKay who, just a few days after his interview with Stephensen, was appointed the first director-general of a new intelligence bureau, the Commonwealth Security Service.[12]

Stephensen had almost had enough. He issued a protest circular to parliamentarians and then on the morning of 9 March told the AFM's former treasurer that he was 'putting the movement in abeyance'.[13] Late that night an enciphered military intelligence cable from Perth reached the army's Eastern Command headquarters in Sydney. It read in part:

> Four principals [of the AFM] here ... detained this morning under section 13 National Security Act. Had in their possession most incriminating document. Shows intention to make contact with Japanese Army at moment of invasion. Plans for sabotaging vulnerable points this command. Plans for death of head of Army, Police, democratic politicians. Proclamation with heading 'Australia First Government' ... contains the following: 'This expression of belief of Australian nation tribute to valiant effort of Japanese who have so successfully fought for liberation of our people from Jewish domination and danger of communism ...' The proclamation contains 20 points of policy and instructs the [Australian Military Forces] to lay down arms on penalty of death. P. R. Stephensen your command named ... as leader of movement. Suggest urgent action ... [14]

Part Four

Liverpool, Loveday and Tatura Internment Camps, 1942–1945

I have a feeling that my Quixotic spirit will one day lead to my forcible repression...
P. R. Stephensen
letter, 1924

Unfortunately as soon as I departed for the Middle East, he had too much idle time and got into trouble.
Frank Clune
letter, 1943

Men like Stephensen lurk to seize power out of social upheaval.
Xavier Herbert
letter, 1961

This was a Grade B Hollywood movie ... Graham Greene could not have improved upon the ludicrous, espionage-like antics of the security forces.
Sondra Silverman
article, 1963

they could not fence you round with fear,
nor yet with rusted barbs of lies.
Ian Mudie
poem, 1943

13

Behind Barbed Wire: High Treason or Low Comedy

At 4 a.m. on Tuesday 10 March 1942 four police acting for Military Intelligence raided Stephensen's flat in New South Head Road, Rose Bay. Two officers approached the door while the others covered possible escape routes, thinking they were dealing with a dangerous spy rather than a deaf former publisher. The door bell roused Winifred but not Stephensen who was 'sleeping on his good ear' and had to be shaken awake. The leader of the police party, a detective sergeant, read Stephensen a warrant signed by the army minister, F. M. Forde, ordering Stephensen's detention and a search of his flat. Stephensen later claimed he was not told about the detention, but the early hour of the surprise visit and his poor hearing no doubt contributed to the misunderstanding.[1]

For more than two hours the police combed through his papers, accumulated over the ten years he had been in Sydney, and took away a large amount of material for closer scrutiny. Shown some Japanese literature from his writing room, Stephensen readily admitted that he had been friendly with the Japanese prior to the war. He was also asked if his wireless was a 'transmitter', and one of the police commented on the clear view of shipping in the harbour from Stephensen's window.[2]

He was then taken to the small Australia-First Movement office in Hunter Street. Co-operative as usual with the police, he opened the door for them with his key, and another two-hour search yielded more cartons, mainly of *Publicist* files and records. About 9 a.m. Stephensen was taken to Central Police Station, searched and locked in a cell with drunks. He had 'on his person' a pound note and a few coins, some keys, a pen and a pencil: indicating only that he was an impoverished man of letters. When he asked if he was under arrest, he was told it was a matter for the military not the police, and a request to contact his solicitor was refused.[3]

Although the decision to round up the Australia First leadership in Sydney had been made by Military Intelligence, acting on the cable from Perth, only police attached to the MPI had the authority to enter premises and detain suspects. So after about an hour in the police cell, Stephensen was taken out to join other AFM people who had been detained, including his *Publicist* partners, Val Crowley and S. B. Hooper. Along with Stephensen's younger brother Eric and some others picked up along the way, they were all taken by bus under armed guard to the Liverpool internment camp west of Sydney. Two of the AFM people on the bus, who were returned soldiers, made jokes about their predicament, and although Stephensen was 'jovial' he resented the presence of the armed guard. They all thought a 'big mistake' had been made.[4]

Later that day Stephensen's long-time publishing friend, Jack Kirtley, was arrested although he was not even an AFM member. In all, sixteen men were rounded up and interned at Liverpool on the order of the army minister. Half the original AFM executive had been women, but Military Intelligence officers believed it was government policy not to intern women. Ten days later the former AFM organizer, Adela Pankhurst Walsh, was in fact interned, because of her intense pro-Japanese sympathies rather than for her past connection with the AFM.[5]

Others with AFM connections were raided and searched. Ian Mudie was visited by Adelaide police on 10 March, as was Rex Ingamells, and in Brisbane another Jindyworobak poet, Paul Grano, received similar treatment. Nothing incriminating was found, although police took away from Mudie various books and papers including a copy of Hitler's *Mein Kampf* in English translation. They kept this along with the manuscript of a new nationalist poem Mudie had been working on entitled 'Australian Dream'.[6] As an AFM executive member, Mudie was lucky not to be interned, and his return to Adelaide a few weeks before the round-up apparently saved him.

Stephensen and his fellow Australia Firsters quickly settled down to the routine of their imprisonment at the Anzac Rifle Range which had been converted into a wartime internment or concentration camp. Before the war, rifle clubs had conveniently built huts for their members at Liverpool, so the army just threw a cordon of barbed wire around the perimeter and transformed the rifle range into a staging camp, mainly for 'enemy aliens'—Italian and German civilians. The hut Stephensen and the others occupied had belonged to the Mosman Rifle Club, and consisted of two rooms and a veranda, with straw mattresses to sleep on. The AFM group immediately dubbed their hut 'Australia House', and Stephensen's brother Eric, who had been studying art at the Julian Ashton school, painted this name on the front.[7]

Initially, a military officer informed the Australia First men that they could be detained for ten days on Forde's warrants, issued under section 13A of the National Security regulations. There had been so many calls for the internment of the AFM that their sudden capture must have come as a shock rather than a surprise. They knew nothing whatsoever of the Western Australian treason 'plot', and so were curious about this unexpected taste of military hospitality. The camp conditions were austere to say the least. Their first meal was bully beef and biscuits, and they were subject to military routine and discipline, being paraded and counted twice a day. Eventually their civilian clothes were replaced by POW issue—army uniforms dyed red. For ablutions there was a cold shower outside in a lean-to, and the toilets were earth-floored and roofless.[8] The internment was a strain, especially for the seventy-year-old Hooper and for the two World War I veterans, Harley Matthews and Martin Watts. A victim of gassing, Watts was on a military pension and in fact died not long after release from internment.

For the fifty-six-year-old Winifred Stephensen, the raid and subsequent events became a devastating nightmare. She had been ill for several months, and had no other support as her son was now in the army. Not realizing he was to be interned, Stephensen had taken nothing with him other than the clothes he stood up in, and it was three days before Winifred could even discover where he was held. Almost bed-ridden and with little money, she was in a state of great anxiety and helplessness. The terror of the pre-dawn police raid stayed with her, and for more than a year she could not sleep properly, waking every morning at 4 a.m. to relive the experience.

At first Stephensen was confident that whatever the misunderstanding or charge they would soon be released, and he wrote Winifred a note on one of the special camp letter-cards a week after his arrest:

> We are not 'interned'. We are only 'detained' for ten days under the National Security Regulations, pending investigation. This period elapses on Friday 20 March, when we will either be released or 'interned'. If 'interned', we have a right of appeal to a Tribunal . . . It is a great annoyance to be held like this, but I view the whole matter philosophically. A mistake has been made by the authorities, but these are not the times to grumble about small inconveniences, so I have settled down mentally to await developments.[9]

A heavy smoker, Stephensen assured Winifred that there was a camp canteen where he could buy cigarettes. After 20 March Stephensen assumed he was now 'interned' and wrote to Winifred to 'accept the position calmly'. Stephensen himself was 'quite reconciled to an indefinite period of internment', and asked her to send him his 'pyjamas, toothbrush, towel, woollen shirt, old *flannel* trousers, belt, Shakespeare's plays, old dancing shoes, safety razor and shaving brush'.[10]

The internees were permitted visitors only at the weekend, for half an hour. An armed guard was in attendance, and the men were separated from their visitors by thick wire mesh. Knowing how ill and depressed Winifred would be, Stephensen specifically requested her not to visit him. Correspondence was restricted to two letters a week and all mail was carefully censored. Some of the standard 22-line letter-cards issued by the camp included the instruction: DO NOT WRITE BETWEEN THE LINES. Because of the official scrutiny, inmates and their families invariably tried to read between the lines of these brief and cautious letters.

Through one of the visitors Stephensen got a message to Miles Franklin about his internment and about the need to protest. In response Franklin did little more than correspond with Ian Mudie about 'that unfortunate little Winnie in her desperate state of health'.[11] Although not in accord with some of the *Publicist* policies and prejudices, Franklin had attended a number of the AFM public meetings including the violent one on the day Darwin was bombed. Mudie, on the other hand, was both 'angry and exultant' about the Australia First martyrs who had been 'chucked into concentration camp like aliens'.[12]

On 25 March, five days after the detention orders under section 13A had expired, two MPI officers visited the Liverpool camp and informed the sixteen internees that, by an order dated 20 March and signed by the army minister, Forde, they were now interned under section 26 of the National Security regulations. This Draconian provision empowered the minister to detain indefinitely and without trial anyone who might act 'in any manner prejudicial to the public safety or the defence of the Commonwealth'. Appeal to a tribunal was provided for, but this was a secret tribunal where rules of evidence did not apply. Those few AFM members who did later submit to the tribunal found it was more like an inquisition and one which presumed their guilt.[13]

On the night of 25 March, during the adjournment debate in the Canberra House of Representatives, the Labor backbencher Maurice Blackburn revealed that a number of AFM members, 'all Australian born', were interned at Liverpool. Blackburn did not think any were sympathetic to the Japanese, and he protested about Australians being imprisoned like this without trial. 'The agent of a foreign enemy, or a spy, in Australia is not likely to be a person engaged in addressing public meetings and openly opposing government policy', Blackburn told parliament. When another MP asked if one of the suspects was a 'Rhodes Scholar', Blackburn said he did not think Stephensen was amongst those detained.

Having this inadvertently mentioned Stephensen's name, Blackburn went on to defend his character if not his opinions. 'I strongly disagree with certain views held by Mr. Stephensen', Blackburn said, 'but he is a man of great ability, energy and courage, for whom I have considerable admiration'. Blackburn did not believe that Stephensen was 'the kind of man who would be an enemy agent'. At the close of the adjournment debate that night, J. A. Beasley, acting attorney-general in the absence of Evatt who had left for America on 9 March, denied any knowledge of the Australia First internments.[14] It was more than two weeks since the Sydney AFM group had been imprisoned on allegations of treason, yet the commonwealth attorney-general was as unaware of these allegations as the suspects themselves. A bungle had obviously been made, but worse was to come before the cover-up began in earnest.

The following afternoon F. M. Forde, the army minister who had signed the orders for detention on the advice of Military Intelligence, made a carefully prepared statement to parliament, ostensibly in answer to a question. Forde's sweeping allegations of treason, made under parliamentary privilege, directly implicated Stephensen and his group, even though Military Intelligence in Western Australia had by then admitted that there was no connection between the Perth 'conspiracy' and the Sydney AFM:

> Mr. Forde.—(by leave)—I wish to state that twenty persons—nineteen men and one woman[15]—who were believed to have been associated with the so-called Australia First Movement have been arrested and interned. Documents and papers which have been seized purport to show that certain people in Australia intended to make contact with the Japanese army at the moment of an invasion of Australia. The documents set out elaborate plans for sabotage ... Plans for the assassination of prominent people are set out ... These documents indicate a fifth column activity of the worst kind by a very small band of people. The military authorities have been investigating the activities of the so-called Australia First Movement for a considerable time, and the arrests took place as a result of these inquiries. In view of the foregoing, I wish to warn people that, before associating themselves with any movement, they should assure themselves that it is bona fide and not an organization which, under the cloak of a pleasing name, is engaged in subversive activities. We shall stand no Quislings, whether they come from the highest or the lowest.[16]

Forde's statement was one of the most sensational of the war, and it was worded in such a way as to warn others about engaging in any activities which might be prejudicial to the war effort. At the same time, of course, it prejudiced any chance of a fair hearing for AFM members, tarring them forever with the suspicion of being traitors. It was perhaps no coincidence that Forde made his staggering allegations on the same day General Blamey was appointed commander-in-chief of the Australian Army, and on the day General Macarthur attended a meeting of the Advisory War Council in Canberra. Forde greatly admired Macarthur, and may well have tried to impress the American general with the efficiency of Australia's military intelligence network. It was a further irony that Macarthur had told the War Council he doubted the Japanese would invade Australia, a view shared by Stephensen.[17]

Forde's revelations made instant newspaper headlines across Australia, and led to a lengthy and emotional debate in parliament next morning. The Country Party opposition leader Fadden commented that the disclosures had come as 'a severe shock' and were 'without parallel in Australian history and in British history, at any rate since the Guy Fawkes plot'. He said the arrests 'must be followed by trial for treason', and in his excitement called for the internment of 'all enemy aliens' just for good measure. Fadden was followed by one member who seemed to have retained his sense of proportion as well as justice, and who was not afraid to criticize his own Labor ministers. 'Neither newspapers nor legislators should be allowed to prejudice [a] fair trial', Maurice Blackburn warned, but the damage was already done.[18]

Stephensen's former acquaintance, W. M. Hughes, and other MPs accepted Stephensen's guilt on the basis of Forde's misleading statement. A member of the Advisory War Council, Hughes was the most intemperate speaker that morning in parliament. He claimed to agree with Blackburn about not trying the accused in advance, but then held forth with his own violent allegations and threats:

> Mr. Hughes.— ... The real purpose of the Australia First Movement is to prepare the way for the coming of the Japanese. Its members emphasize Australia's right to make a separate peace. What is that but defeatism? What is that but the policy that overwhelmed France! We must never think of surrender. The man who first mentions surrender in this country is a traitor to Australia. So these people stand convicted. Their general purpose is revealed. They sent their spies and shock troops into Western Australia; and they were arrested. They are disclosing the real purpose of this movement. What is the government doing with the men who started the movement in New South Wales? They still walk the streets.
> Mr. Forde.—No.
> Mr. Hughes.—They do. Has Stephensen been interned?
> Mr. Forde.—I am not mentioning names. The bulk of the internments have been in New South Wales.
> Mr. Hughes.—If the Minister for the Army assures me that none of these men is still free I shall be perfectly satisfied; but while one of them roams at large I shall not be satisfied. We cannot make war in this fashion—blithering about the Bill of Rights and habeas corpus and things of that kind. This is war; and the man who says he will betray us deserves death ... If my name is on [the assassination list] I shall know what to do. I shall see to it that any of these gentlemen who are not interned will not need interning.[19]

The most intelligent criticism of Forde's statement came from the backbencher, E. J. Harrison, who commented that the army minister 'should have either withheld some of the information which he gave to the House yesterday afternoon or indicted the persons concerned before a criminal court'. This was the central point, and a number of others including Archie Cameron seized upon it. 'Interning a person is an entirely different thing from charging him with sabotage, conspiracy, attempted assassination, or treason', Cameron noted in the adjournment debate that night. Even the acting attorney-general, Beasley, revealed his irritation with Forde's handling of the case. 'I am unable to advance any reason why the Minister made the statement', Beasley admitted to parliament, though several weeks later he too began trying to prop up his colleague Forde.[20] The army minister had clearly miscalculated. If he had kept quiet instead of attempting to make crude propaganda out of the AFM cases, then the course of events might have been different.

The person to pay most heavily was Stephensen. Not only was he named in parliament—innocently by Blackburn and then more maliciously by Hughes—but the *Sydney Morning Herald*'s report included a summary of the AFM in which Stephensen's name and history were given prominence.[21] Unable to believe it, Winifred telegrammed Stephensen that the 'amazing concoction' was 'laughable as well as libellous', but the desperate seriousness of the situation quickly became apparent. A few days later she wrote to Stephensen that the whole thing was a 'nightmare'.[22]

Not surprisingly, Stephensen's enemies accepted the allegations with grim and even gleeful satisfaction. Brian Penton, then editor of the *Daily Telegraph* in Sydney, wrote an uncomplimentary profile of Stephensen for the *Sunday Telegraph*, which happened to be edited by another of Stephensen's enemies, Cyril Pearl. Penton described Stephensen as 'querulous, deaf, moustached', and the cartoonist George Finey drew a large and rather good caricature to accompany Penton's article.[23] Although the drawing featured Stephensen's toothbrush moustache, Finey at least resisted the temptation to give Stephensen any further resemblance to Hitler. The cartoonist had been at one time a welcome member of Stephensen's Yabber Club. The banned communist paper, *Tribune*, was not so restrained. Describing Stephensen as the 'fuehrer' of the AFM and a 'Nazi Japanese spy', *Tribune* called for the early trial of Stephensen and his fellow 'traitors'. The Sydney *Bulletin* had been critical of the government's handling of the internments, and was accused by *Tribune* of also being Nazi subsidized.[24]

Even Miles Franklin was prepared at first to entertain the possibility that some of the AFM people might have been willing to act as traitors, supplying a 'gauleiter' should the 'deadly enemy Japan' invade. Franklin was in two minds about the 'fantastic charge',[25] but Stephensen's other friends and acquaintances could not believe it. Paul Grano agreed with the *Bulletin* that the evidence most likely had been fabricated and planted on the AFM, while Mudie was convinced the whole thing was a plot against the movement.[26] In his bitterness and outrage at the allegations, Mudie penned the poem, 'If This Be Treason', which concluded:

> If love of land a dastard treason be,
> then black glows the sun and solid is the sea.[27]

At Liverpool the internees with literary interests composed their own expressions of bewilderment and protest. Harley Matthews, a poet, journalist and war veteran, wrote the following lines at 'Australia House' on April Fool's Day. Surely it was all a bad joke, or a bad dream:

> Why am I in this narrow yard?
> You ask. Well, I will tell you why.
> Outside some say that I should die.
> So here they brought me, stood the guard.
> There, shut the gate, made the barbed wire high,
> And all because so far as I can see,
> I loved my country and they hated me.[28]

Those with a more sardonic outlook on life—Stephensen, his brother Eric, Jack Kirtley, and the truck driver Gordon Rice—composed a satirical ballad 'Along to Internment' on the 'Waltzing Matilda' theme, and it was performed at a camp concert in April:

George Finey's caricature of Stephensen in the *Sunday Telegraph*, 29 March 1942

> Once a jolly publicist sat inside a wire fence
> pondering upon de-mock-ra-cy,
> and he sang as he sat and waited for the Tribunal,
> 'You'll come along to internment with me!'

'Down came the barristers grabbing at the money bags' began another verse of this mock ballad, while the ineptness of military and police intelligence was also satirized ('Demon' being Sydney slang for detective):

> Down came the MPI mounted in their motor car,
> Down came the Demons, one, two, three!
> 'Where's that bloody tommy-gun you've got in your
>   wireless set
> You'll come along to internment with me!'²⁹

Such a light-hearted response by men whose reputations had been ruined overnight was an indication of the devastating and at the same time ludicrous nature of the allegations against them. The internees also tried to keep up their morale by giving a series of evening talks at the long table of 'Australia House'. Eric Stephensen recited bush ballads like 'The Man from Snowy River' and received loudest applause for his rendition of Mudie's poem 'Corroboree to the Sun'. Stephensen gave a variety of talks including one on his home town of Biggenden, and he also conducted a study class in logic.³⁰

Meanwhile the War Cabinet was trying to extricate itself from the awkward situation arising from Forde's precipitate statement to parliament and the subsequent flurry of criticism. Cautious moderates and democrats sensitive to personal liberty and justice, such as Blackburn, had joined the cynics in doubting the facts on which Forde had made his sweeping allegations, while conservatives like Fadden and Hughes as well as communists demanded the speedy trial and punishment of the 'traitors'.

Within days of the stormy debate in federal parliament late in March 1942, the War Cabinet had decided to prosecute the four Western Australians involved in the bogus Australia First proclamation, but the solicitor-general, Sir George Knowles, indicated that there was as yet no evidence to implicate the sixteen Sydney internees.³¹ The crown solicitor, H. F. E. Whitlam, confirmed this opinion a couple of weeks later after perusing Stephensen's file. In a memo to the attorney-general, Whitlam reported that there was 'nothing in any of that matter which appears to indicate any contravention by Stephensen of any regulations made under the National Security Act or of any other Commonwealth law'. Whitlam gave this opinion after reading the intelligence reports of AFM meetings and a host of other material including intercepted correspondence.³² No charge therefore could, or ever would, be laid against Stephensen.

The handling of the Australia First affair by Forde and by Evatt's stand-in, Beasley, smacked of inexperience as well as ineptitude, but the Labor government moved to suppress further criticism, using press censorship and other legal powers.³³ Their task was made more difficult by an inaccurate report in the *Sydney Morning Herald* of 11 April which quoted Curtin as saying that legal proceedings would be taken against certain AFM members 'in Sydney who had been interned'. Winifred was relieved by this, and Stephensen began to prepare himself for a public trial to clear his name. He wrote to Winifred for a new pair of glasses and a 'deaf aid', as he would need both in a court action. More confident now, he told her that the whole episode was obviously just a stupid mistake.[34]

Because of her precarious state of health, Winifred did not visit Stephensen at Liverpool camp until May, and after another visit in June she wrote in her diary that the conditions for seeing internees were 'cruel—sadistic—cowardly and stupid'.[35] Despite her ill health and the considerable psychological and financial strain she had to endure, Winifred was adamant that Stephensen should not accept any compromise short of total exoneration. 'Don't allow yourself to forget for one minute that your enemies have tried to destroy you', she wrote to him, 'and don't forget that it is necessary that your good name should be given back to you'. Even after she became ill again with tuberculosis, Winifred remained convinced that 'Whatever happens to me, you are not to be goaded into coming out without a proper public trial'. Late in May 1942 she burnt two letters to Stephensen because they were so bitter about his imprisonment without trial.[36]

Protest at the AFM internments was being maintained with the support of Stephensen's old adversary, the *Bulletin*, and other papers. The *Publicist* had of course ceased publication but was not entirely dead. A 'Notice to the Public', dated 27 May 1942, was smuggled out of Liverpool camp and run off by the *Publicist*'s printer, explaining why the Australia First magazine had 'temporarily suspended publication'. The notice called on *Publicist* subscribers and others to demand a full inquiry and the release and exoneration of internees. It also criticized the censorship bans which prevented their side of the case being put in the press.[37]

Stephensen's friend, Dulcie Deamer, wanted to enlist the support of the Fellowship of Australian Writers in the protest, but there was little hope of that. As this case clearly showed, questions of civil liberties and freedom of expression depended very much on political sympathy, and most of the traditional protest groups had nothing but contempt for Stephensen's views. One socialist, however, Flexmore Hudson, who declared himself 'no friend of the *Publicist*', did make some attempts at protest and even planned a petition.[38] Others to register protests included the moderator of the Presbyterian Church in New South Wales, the secretary of the Christian Socialist Movement, and even Bishop Burgmann of Goulburn who had been criticized on a number of occasions by the *Publicist*.[39]

Although Labor Party ministers were now on the defensive they were not the only ones to be sensitive about the AFM. Having seen a report in the London *Daily Telegraph* on Stephensen's apparent involvement in the 'fifth column plot', the warden of Rhodes House, Oxford, wrote to the Australian secretary that it would be 'intensely humiliating' if the Rhodes Scholarships received any adverse publicity over the episode. Reporting back, the Australian Rhodes secretary explained that Stephensen's Sydney group was not really implicated, but he nevertheless proffered the opinion that a concentration camp was 'not at all a bad place' for Stephensen. The warden agreed that 'this incorrigible trouble-maker' was better interned, and informed his trustees about the black sheep of their scholarship scheme who had 'always been an extremist'.[40]

By coincidence, perhaps, the trial of the four Western Australian conspirators took place at a time of renewed panic about Japanese invasion as the war once more approached Australian soil. Late in May 1942 Japanese midget submarines entered Sydney Harbour and sank a ferry, and a week later coastal suburbs were shelled. Paranoia about intelligence surveillance increased too. Before his internment Stephensen had joked about phone lines being tapped, but in the wake of the AFM arrests, both Miles Franklin and Paul Grano censored their own letters for fear of possible repercussions. Grano cut half a page from one of his letters to Mudie with the note, 'excision by me', and Franklin changed course abruptly in a letter to the American, Hartley Grattan, remarking that 'one must not speak the truth these days'.[41] Grattan had himself been subjected to a political witch-hunt in America. Attacked 'almost simultaneously for being a Communist and a Nazi sympathizer', he had been forced to resign from his public service post.[42]

Stephensen's friend and literary 'employer', Frank Clune, returned in June from a six-month tour in the Middle East with the Australian Comforts Fund only to discover to his surprise that Stephensen was interned. Clune had taken little interest in his editor's politics, and no part in the ill-fated AFM, but he too fell victim to wartime paranoia. Clune gave broadcasts and lectures about his trip and found himself in trouble with the military authorities after making some pessimistic, though accurate, predictions about the Middle East campaign. When these were reported in the press, Clune was called to Victoria Barracks in Sydney and carpeted for his indiscretion. Although his remarks had been passed by the civilian censor, he had not realized there was an army censor operating as well.[43]

It was indeed a period when the country seemed to be crawling with spooks and snoops, and the Western Australian 'conspiracy' trial hinted at what sort of games they could get up to. The case was heard in the state supreme court in June 1942 and from the press reports Stephensen and the other Sydney internees finally realized the extent of the bizarre frame-up. Anxious now to get a hearing in any properly constituted court, Stephensen offered to give evidence at the trial in Perth, but this was refused.[44] Stephensen's offer may also have been a ploy to prove conclusively that he had nothing whatsoever to do with the alleged conspiracy in Western Australia which had in fact been the reason for his internment.

The defence barrister in Perth, T. J. Hughes, who had a history of exposing political scandal, opened his address to the jury by stating that the Australia First 'plot' was a straight-out 'police frame-up'. Without the police agent there would simply have been no case to answer, Hughes maintained, and the jury did acquit two of the four defendants, while the 'ringleader' received only three years gaol.[45]

On the evidence available, the suppression of the Sydney AFM was most likely organized by Military Intelligence who had viewed the movement all along as a security threat.[46] There had been a similar case in Britain, and also at a time of dire national emergency. During May 1940, facing the prospect of a German invasion, Churchill and Chamberlain had exploited a 'treason' case which MI5 agents had helped develop involving a United States embassy official and a fascist sympathizer. The object of the exercise was to justify amending and strengthening Defence Regulation 18B in order to arrest the British Union of Fascists leader, Oswald Mosley, and hundreds of his supporters. Mosley was interned without trial for almost two years at Brixton Prison and his wife was also imprisoned.[47]

The bizarre episode that destroyed Stephensen's career and virtually erased him from public life also had strong political implications, in that Stephensen had been criticizing the conduct of the war by Labor ministers in the weeks before he was silenced. Of more importance, perhaps, was the fact that the two Sydney Military Intelligence officers involved in the surveillance of the AFM had been convinced that the movement's leaders should be put behind barbed wire, and had tried unsuccessfully to secure Stephensen's detention in January 1942. It was after the refusal of this application that the Military Intelligence commander in Western Australia, Colonel Moseley, and his police intelligence chief, Detective-Sergeant Richards, suddenly decided to investigate the local AFM. The striking thing about their decision was that no AFM then existed in that state.

This did not deter Richards nor his police agent, F. J. Thomas, who had been working on a retainer of £5 a week, mostly infiltrating communist groups in Perth and procuring evidence, sometimes by questionable means. Calling himself 'Hardt', which was also the name of a Sydney Nazi, and claiming he had come from Sydney with the authority of Adela Pankhurst Walsh and the AFM, Thomas had approached *Publicist* subscribers in Western Australia, including L. F. Bullock. Thomas encouraged Bullock and a couple of others to establish an Australia First party or movement. Within a few weeks they had drawn up, no doubt under Thomas's guidance, a draft proclamation of the 'National Socialist Government of Australia'.[48] At the end of January 1942 Stephensen had advocated, but only in private, Australia's future right to make a separate peace with Japan, and this became the key to the next move. With the help of the agent Thomas, the gullible Bullock and his tiny band of disaffected eccentrics and dupes embroidered this principle of Australian independence into a crazy plan for sabotage, assassination and collaboration.

That the intelligence officers in Western Australia never took this plot seriously was shown by the fact that Thomas admitted to being in daily contact with his boss, Richards, while the whole thing was developing.

For more than a week after they had seen and photocopied the draft 'proclamation' of 27 February 1942, neither Richards nor Colonel Moseley made any attempt to alert the government about this supposed plot. It was not until the 'Western Australian section of the Australia First Movement' was formally set up by Bullock and his band on 7 March, and a more usefully incriminating document, now headed 'Proclamation of the Australia First Government', was concocted on 8 March that Richards and Moseley decided to send off their 'urgent' and dramatic cipher cable.[49]

The proclamation began by stating that the new 'Australia First' system of government was 'based upon a negotiated peace with JAPAN'. There was thus just sufficient resemblance between Stephensen's genuine AFM and the Western Australian group to provide Military Intelligence officers in Sydney with the ammunition they wanted to put away Stephensen and his colleagues. The important distinction between a 'negotiated peace' and a 'separate peace' did not bother the military.[50] No doubt thinking it would compromise the former suffragette, Adela Pankhurst Walsh, the Perth police agent also ensured that among the bogus Australia First policies were the 'Absolute equality of the sexes' and 'easier divorce'. What the agent did not know was that Walsh had already left the AFM, and in any case had renounced feminism along with communism years before. Stephensen's *Publicist* group could not have been more anti-feminist.[51]

The Commonwealth Investigation Branch played no part at all in this curious action and lodged a protest just a day after the internments had been carried out by the military. It has been suggested that one of the Australia Firsters rounded up by Military Intelligence was in fact an IB agent, giving the whole episode an even more farcical and embarrassing dimension.[52]

In July 1942, after it had become obvious he was not going to be charged with any offence, Stephensen applied for a writ of habeas corpus in the supreme court of New South Wales. He protested that he had been 'illegally and improperly imprisoned' and that the army minister had been 'maliciously misinformed'. Refusing Stephensen's application, the chief justice confirmed the minister's power to detain without trial and ruled that the courts had no jurisdiction in the matter. Stephensen was advised by the solicitor-general that the only course open to him was to be heard before the internment tribunal, but he consistently refused to appear before this secret inquisition.[53]

When Evatt returned from overseas in August and assumed responsibility for the internments, he arranged for ten of the sixteen Australia Firsters to be released, and by October 1942 only Stephensen, Cahill and Kirtley remained imprisoned. Evatt thereby hoped to satisfy critics and at the same time defend Forde's action by keeping some men interned, despite the fact that Evatt himself had admitted there was no 'guilty' association between the Western Australian and Sydney groups.[54] On 10 September the attorney-general compounded Forde's earlier prejudicial statement by reading to parliament some carefully selected extracts from correspondence to justify the continued detention of Stephensen, Cahill and Kirtley.

'These extracts strongly suggest the conclusion that the persons concerned were not friends of Australia but enemies of Australia', Evatt darkly warned, 'and were ready and willing to take advantage of enemy successes to support any movement for seizing power from the constituted authorities'. Defending his government's conduct of the Australia First cases, Evatt concluded that at a time of national crisis 'the safety of the people as a whole must override ordinary court procedure'.[55] Yet during the reign of the previous, conservative government which had actually introduced the National Security regulations, Evatt had protested strongly at the internment of two communists: 'Labor will not tolerate any attempt to imperil the security of this country. But we think that where Australian citizens are alleged to be guilty they should be prosecuted in the ordinary course and charged with some specific offence . . .'[56] Evatt's political principles had proved as flexible as anyone else's.

Until his internment, Stephensen had been an admirer of Evatt, but he never forgave the former judge for prolonging his detention without trial and for impeding his chances of legal redress. Stephensen became more and more suspicious of the attorney-general's role in the affair, and his prejudice against Evatt was confirmed a decade later during the anti-communist hysteria of the Petrov 'conspiracy'. The irony of course was that Detective-Sergeant Richards, formerly of Perth and later the ASIO agent in the Petrov case, attended upon the decline of both Stephensen and Evatt.

In mid-September 1942, a few days after Evatt's prejudicial comments to parliament, his three scapegoats were transferred from Liverpool to the Loveday internment camp in South Australia. Garbed in their humiliating red coats and trousers, Stephensen, Cahill and Kirtley made the journey on ordinary passenger trains, escorted by armed soldiers. Stephensen spent five months at the Loveday camp which he described as 'flat, dusty, treeless semi-desert country'. He was in the 'mixed' compound of camp number 14 with about a thousand others comprising nearly thirty nationalities. Most were Italian and German civilians but there were also European refugees, including Jews. Within a few weeks of his arrival, Stephensen complained to the official camp visitor that he was being victimized by 'communist and Jewish internees' who regarded him as a fascist.[57]

The bitter ideological conflicts of the 1930s were replayed, sometimes with accompanying violence, on the desert flats of isolated Loveday. When Italian anti-fascists and Jews in Stephensen's compound collected money to aid Russia, there was a brawl in the adjoining fascist compound, resulting in the death of an Italian anarchist.[58] Stephensen himself became involved in a protest meeting about unsatisfactory kitchen arrangements and was reported to the camp commandant for making pro-fascist threats, something Stephensen denied.[59] He was never com-

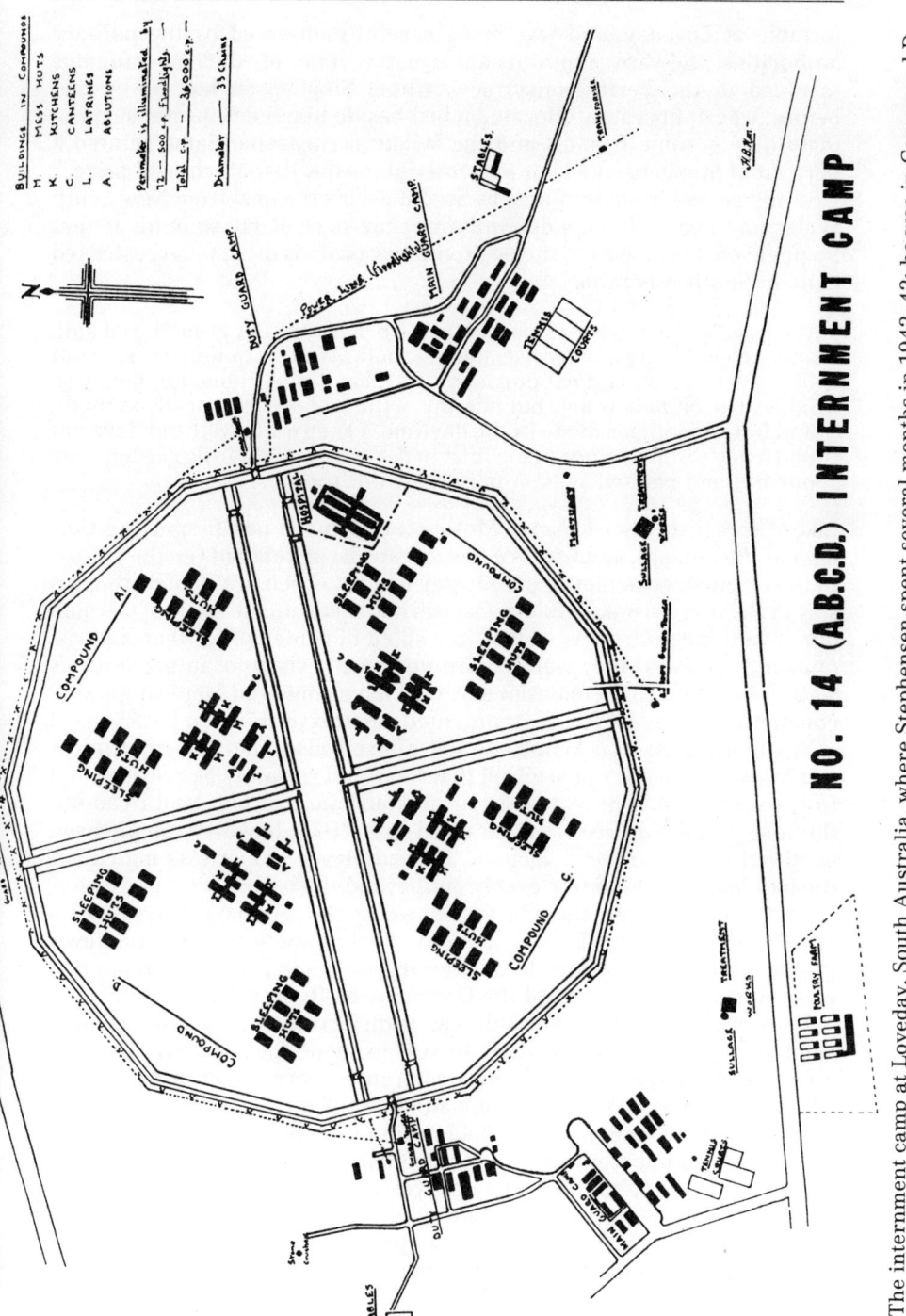

The internment camp at Loveday, South Australia, where Stephensen spent several months in 1942–43; he was in Compound D, a mixed camp mainly of Italian and German civilians (from *Internment in South Australia*, 1946)

fortable at Loveday, and was being carefully observed by the military authorities. Edward Cunningham Quicke, one of the unfortunates involved in the Perth 'conspiracy', whom Stephensen had never met before, was deliberately allocated a bed beside him. Perhaps not surprisingly they became friends, and the Western Australian later painted a portrait of Stephensen which was entered for the 1945 Archibald prize.[60]

Winifred had been desolated by Stephensen's removal from New South Wales and had suffered a debilitating recurrence of TB, so in his letters Stephensen tried to stress the positive aspects of his dreary and restricted exile in South Australia:

> We have a spacious enclosure, about 16 acres, of flat ground, red soil, and we get plenty of exercise and leg room. We live in long huts, about 50 men to a hut, and eat our meals in a big dining room, ten men to a table. The climate is dry, but healthy, with cool breezes mostly at night, and hot, sometimes dusty in the daytime. I keep quite well and have not had a day's illness since being interned. I have made a little garden near our hut and planted West Australian wildflowers . . .[61]

Like the British fascist leader Mosley, Stephensen began studying German in internment, and within a few months he could read Goethe's *Faust* in the original, an achievement Mosley had also been proud of during his stay at Brixton Prison. Both pro-fascists had taken up the study of German out of genuine interest as well as in a spirit of contempt for their imprisonment.[62] In *Faust* they were confronted with a vision of future hope as well as evil, though Stephensen may well have pondered Mephistopheles' comment that 'his fervent/Discontented soul drives him too far'.[63]

Stephensen assured Winifred, and himself also, that the internment was 'only a temporary phase' and that he would certainly be released and fully exonerated. 'I have a sense of humour', he told her, 'and I can see the joke in all this!' As 1942 dragged into 1943, however, Stephensen admitted he was in the 'doldrums'. He had played in a cricket match but the ball had been hit irretrievably out beyond the barbed wire perimeter. He watched Italians enjoying soccer while the Germans listened to a record of Beethoven's Fifth Symphony. Feeling more isolated than ever now at Loveday, he applied to do 'literary work' for Frank Clune but this was refused on the orders of the Commonwealth Security Service.[64]

In February 1943 Stephensen was transferred to Tatura internment camp in northern Victoria where he was to spend the remaining two and a half years of the war. Here he was granted permission to do Clune's editorial work and the camp commandant took a friendly interest in his 'literary staff'. Clune, however, had again crossed swords with the military, and been unceremoniously ejected from New Guinea where he had been trying to gather material for yet another travel book. General Blamey had not forgiven the ebullient travel writer for his indiscreet comments about the Middle East campaign, and this time Clune complained that a Military Intelligence officer in New Guinea had treated him with the brutal contempt of a 'Gestapo overlord'.[65]

Clune was the only friend to visit Inky Stephensen in Victoria, and during his long sojourn at Tatura camp, Stephensen worked on eight Clune titles including the bushranging saga, *Wild Colonial Boys*. Although this lengthy work was not published until 1948 because of the wartime paper shortage, Clune and Stephensen were able to carve a number of shorter books out of it in the meantime. One of the sad ironies of Stephensen's wartime incarceration was that, with severe restrictions on book imports, there was a minor boom in Australian publishing. Local books were readily sold now, even if they were printed on odd-sized or coloured paper. Stephensen's removal from the scene had coincided with a new assertion of cultural as well as political independence. Not until the post-Vietnam Whitlam era was such a spirit apparent again.

Stephensen had asked to be sent to Tatura and he appreciated the 'change of climate, scenery, food, company and conditions' at the camp which was pleasantly situated amongst trees. The military administration was more lenient, too, and a former chef from London's Savoy Hotel was among those preparing meals for the internees. Stephensen now bided his time quietly and philosophically, avoiding any political friction. He was even becoming accustomed to the company of 'foreigners' which he had found strange at first.[66]

Melbourne newspapers were available in the camp, and Stephensen worked hard arranging Clune's notes and other raw material into coherent narratives suitable for publication. Prison life had become more predictable as well as more civilized for him. There were hot showers, and a copper of boiling water close by for cups of tea or coffee. He listened to the news as well as to concerts on the radio, and played chess when he was not occupied with Clune's work. There were even route marches into the surrounding bush and later fishing expeditions to a canal near the camp. His flower and vegetable garden began to thrive.

If Stephensen became resigned to his crowded solitude, Winifred grew more tired and resentful during their long separation. 'The person who has had the real work and anxiety and struggle in this absurd, nonsensical affair is me', she wrote, exhausted after cleaning up the old *Publicist* office in Sydney and settling business matters connected with the ownership of the defunct magazine. As the wife of a man whom many considered should have been shot as a traitor, she had suffered public contempt and scorn. Winifred was also depressed by the violence and futility of the war which she described as a 'dance of death'.[67]

Her friend, Miles Franklin, expressed a similar sense of overwhelming despair about the 'raging madness' of the war, which made her wake at times in a cold sweat of 'sheer panic'.[68] For both women, age and loneliness made it harder to bear. Only in dream could Winifred escape anxiety and relive her youth as a ballet dancer. 'Last night I had a most lovely dream', she wrote to Stephensen in the winter of 1943. 'In my dream I was dancing again ... not bothered any more by my aching body. I was dancing on my toes with all the exquisite joy one feels when, rising in a spring, one feels for a moment suspended in air.' At that instant she was 'above all pain, fear, hate, and hopelessness', and it was her sadness which seemed a 'far distant dream'.[69] Financially, Winifred was only able to sustain herself with assistance from her son Jack, who was in the army. As well, Frank Clune occasionally advanced money to her for Stephensen's editing.

While Winifred was impoverished and ill, Stephensen remained suspended in limbo during his second year of internment. 'I feel like a chrysalis cocoon', he wrote to Winifred, 'and am waiting to spread my wings later'.[70] He was having his portrait painted by a German internee, and he sat for the artist each day for several weeks. Even though special transparent oil paints were used, so the camp authorities could see the portrait concealed no secret messages, permission to send it to Winifred was refused for several months.

Stephensen still hoped for a government inquiry into the AFM internments, and in the second half of 1943, with the aid of a Melbourne solicitor, W. H. Downing, Stephensen instituted a High Court action claiming damages for wrongful imprisonment. At considerable expense, no doubt, Downing retained the services of former Prime Minister Menzies, even though Menzies was sceptical of beating the Labor government in court. As he had introduced and administered the wartime internment Regulation 26 during his period as prime minister, Menzies gave the not altogether unexpected opinion that it was a valid and unchallengeable regulation.[71] Neither Stephensen nor his dedicated solicitor would give up, however, and Stephensen suggested some former literary acquaintances, *Publicist* supporters and other friends who might contribute towards the cost of his legal action.

One avenue of financial assistance remained firmly closed: the family of W. J. Miles. Earlier Winifred had unsuccessfully sought their help to purchase a hearing aid for Stephensen. They must have been deeply embarrassed by the internments and perhaps even relieved that Miles had died several weeks before the suppression of Australia First. During 1943 the Taxation Department began investigating Miles's tax losses on the *Publicist* after an eagle-eyed official found a statement that the magazine was 'run not for profit'. Stephensen provided the Miles estate with ammunition to fight the Taxation Department and used this opportunity to plead once again for assistance. Reminding them that he had 'sacrificed' other prospects, incurred hostility, and given 'six of the best years of my life' to help Miles, Stephensen said his internment was 'certainly in part the result of antagonism or misunderstanding aroused by the *Publicist*—not only my own writings but at least equally those of W. J. Miles'. Through their solicitors, the Miles family informed Stephensen that they felt no obligation to assist him.[72] Despite his bitterness, Stephensen never again laid any of the blame for his internment on Miles.

With that peculiar logic of prejudice, Stephensen was convinced that 'communists and Jews', and their 'crazy innuendo', had caused his downfall.[73] There can be no doubt that the *Publicist*—rather than the AFM

—had aroused the strong hostility of some groups, but this was the consequence of the magazine's strident anti-communism and anti-Semitism. There was a compelling irony in the fact that Stephensen, who disbelieved many of the stories about Nazi concentration camps, should spend most of the war in an Australian concentration camp. For those who respected his integrity, courage and intelligence, what happened to him was cruel and even tragic. But for those appalled by his persistent anti-Semitism, the crushing of P. R. Stephensen must have seemed like an act of rough justice.

During December 1943 a security service officer interviewed Stephensen at Tatura and informed him that the government was considering his release, subject to certain conditions. Weary of his internment, Stephensen readily agreed to live in a country town somewhere and to refrain from political activities, but Winifred was against such release unless it was accompanied by exoneration. In February 1944, just as the only other remaining Australia First internees, Cahill and Kirtley, were released unconditionally, Stephensen was informed that his own release had been refused.[74] Whether Evatt and his security officers had any real intention of freeing the last AFM scapegoat, this seemed almost a gratuitous act of cruelty on the eve of Stephensen's second anniversary behind barbed wire.

He had hoped for a change of government at the 1943 federal elections and had even tried to vote. Labor retained office, however, and Evatt remained as attorney-general with the sole power to continue Stephensen's detention without trial *ad infinitum*. Inky's spirits were at their lowest ebb. 'I am left like a whale on the beach when the tide has gone out', he wrote to Winifred on 9 March 1944, the anniversary of the cipher cable which had sealed his fate.[75] Winifred was ill again, and Stephensen had lost the desire to return to Sydney or any other city. Sydney in particular had become too 'Americanized' and, since Baylebridge had died of a heart attack fighting a bushfire in 1942, Stephensen felt he had no friends there any more. A naturally gregarious man, he had become withdrawn, suspicious and even misanthropic during internment. The old mercurial spirit had all but evaporated, and the only future he envisaged for himself was one of rural seclusion:

Dearest Win,
 ... *If* I am released, exonerated, and fairly compensated, I shall probably buy a farm, west of the Blue Mountains, and live quietly for a few years. I never have liked city life, anyway. Sydney is far too jazzy for my temperament. I am far more interested in horses and cattle than in human beings. As for politics, I have no real interest in it beyond obtaining exoneration for myself ... I shall probably lose all interest in political affairs for a considerable time to come, as it is a dirty game ...[76]

He wanted to be far away, not so much from the bustle of the metropolis, as from the glare of innuendo and accusation.

> Camp 2/A, Tatura, Victoria. Friday 10th March, 1944.
>
> Dear Ian: I have received your letters of 1st Jan. and 26th Feb., the former enclosing a holograph letter from four-year-old Bill which I value highly. Have also received a recent letter from Tom, full of optimism, but I can't answer all the letters I get, as I am allowed only two "personal" letters a week, so please tell him, if you see him, that his letter duly reached me. Today, praise the pigs! is exactly the second anniversary of my incarceration. Having now dwelled for two years in a barbwire cage, I have had ample time to reflect upon the rewards and punishments which my compatriots have bestowed upon me since I returned from England in 1932 and founded the Endeavour Press. Before being interned, I had ten years of hard work and worry, attempting to foster a national spirit in Australian literature. When I began to publish Australian books, the "typical" author was Ion Idriess. Practically no novels, and scarcely any poetry were being printed. I sincerely believe that my work from 1932 to 1942 gave a big impetus to Australian book-publishing, and that some day this will be recognised. Anyway, I did my best; but, as for the future, unless my name is cleared of the allegations which have been made against me, I could never hold up my head again. However, I am still hopeful. Love to Renée and Bill!
>
> Yours patiently,
> P. R. Stephensen

Stephensen's letter to Ian Mudie, 10 March 1944 (from the Mudie Papers, State Library of South Australia)

It was to literature and writers that Stephensen looked to salvage something of his reputation and spirit. On 10 March 1944 he wrote to one of his few remaining friends, Ian Mudie:

> Today, praise the pigs!, is exactly the second anniversary of my incarceration. Having now dwelled for two years in a barbwire cage, I have had ample time to reflect upon the rewards and punishments which my compatriots have bestowed upon me since I returned from England in 1932 and founded the Endeavour Press. Before being interned, I had ten years of hard work and worry, attempting to foster a national spirit in Australian literature. When I began to publish Australian books, the 'typical' author was Ion Idriess. Practically no novels, and scarcely any poetry were being printed. I sincerely believe that my work from 1932 to 1942 gave a big impetus to Australian book-publishing and that some day this will be recognised. Anyway, I did my best; but, as for the future, unless my name is cleared of the allegations which have been made against me, I could never lift up my head again ...[77]

The following year Mudie tried to have Stephensen's short story volume, *Bushwhackers*, reissued, and Miles Franklin agreed that some attempt should be made to rehabilitate him as a literary figure. 'Do you think you could [get] Inky out of politics and into literature?', she asked Mudie. 'I have never ceased to grieve about his loss in politics. But what experiences, searing and uproarious, he has had to enrich his literary possibilities.'[78] Stephensen, however, had become an observer rather than a participant now, and he was destined to remain a literary as well as political ghost.

At the end of March 1944 there was increased pressure in parliament on Evatt over the Australia First episode, and Stephensen's solicitor, Downing, discontinued the High Court action against the commonwealth, clearing the way for an inquiry into the internments. Just three days after Downing informed the crown solicitor that Stephensen's legal action would be called off, Evatt announced to parliament that he would be reviewing the Australia First cases.[79] There was also a renewed press campaign, with *Truth* describing the whole episode as a 'macabre mockery' of the democratic principle of fair trial. Commenting that 'Gestapo tendencies' were not limited to fascist countries, the paper thought Evatt was 'still fighting a sullen, shuffling rearguard action'.[80]

Fighting a defensive action he may have been, but Evatt quickly showed that he intended to vindicate his government's record rather than exonerate Stephensen and the AFM. In May 1944 Evatt announced that he had appointed a federal bankruptcy judge, T. S. Clyne, to inquire into the Australia First internments, and then he immediately prejudiced the inquiry by stating that the AFM 'was undoubtedly a quisling, a subversive, an anti-Australian and an anti-British group'. Evatt went on to warn anyone 'rushing in to make party political capital out of these cases' that they would find themselves supporting a group whose leaders 'were prepared to stab Australia in the back during the period of our greatest peril'. Evatt's director-general of security, who was also a personal friend, made a similarly prejudicial statement about the AFM.[81]

Stephensen was elated when he heard the announcement of the Clyne Inquiry on the wireless at Tatura camp. But when he read the newspaper reports of what Evatt and the security director had said, he immediately wrote to his solicitor that the inquiry had been prejudiced 'most violently' and to an extent 'almost inconceivable by traditional codes of law'.[82] Perhaps it was not so surprising that Stephensen maintained an undying hatred for Evatt. As Evatt's private secretary later commented, the attorney-general was 'never happy with the whole business of the Australia First Movement'.[83]

Shocked by Evatt's further accusations, and dubious about having his grievances aired before a judge rather than a jury, Stephensen nevertheless considered that a public inquiry must exonerate him. He even managed to convince himself that Judge Clyne would be less susceptible than a jury to the tricks government counsel might pull. Stephensen let Winifred know that he had full confidence in Clyne who had a reputation as a just and fair man. When the hearings of the inquiry began in Sydney, Winifred attended all the sittings and she too became assured of Clyne's impartiality.[84]

Stephensen finally obtained a hearing aid, paid for by Frank Clune out of the fees for Stephensen's editorial assistance, and he was taken to Melbourne under military escort to confer with his solicitor, Downing, in preparation for the inquiry. Only a few years older than Stephensen, W. H. Downing was a World War I veteran who had won the Military Medal in 1918. He was also an 'old-fashioned' professional, who would fight an action for no fee because he was convinced of the justice of the case. Although Winifred managed to advance him about £25 initially, this was possibly the only money Downing ever received for more than a year's work on Stephensen's behalf.[85]

Clyne came to the Australia First inquiry with some experience on a Victorian tribunal hearing applications for release by interned aliens. His terms of reference now were to decide if the original detention of the AFM people had been justified, whether the continuance of the internments had been justified, and whether further legal action should be taken or any compensation allowed. A close friend of Evatt's, W. R. Dovey KC, 'appeared to assist the Commission', as Clyne's report rather ambiguously put it, and another aggressive KC, J. W. Shand, represented military intelligence.[86] These two barristers were responsible for giving the inquiry the atmosphere of a political heresy trial.

In all more than a dozen lawyers were involved, and legal arguments alone consumed the first fourteen of the inquiry's sixty-nine sitting days. Delays meant that the hearings were not concluded for a year, and there were allegations that this was a government plot to slow down the inquiry. Among the 'exhibits' before the inquiry were more than a hundred extracts from the *Publicist* as well as intelligence reports, intercepted correspondence and other material. Although the hearings began in June

Stephensen (right) at Heathcote in 1937, with his brother Eric and friend Monty Tickle

Stephensen in 1939

Stephensen (right) with Xavier Herbert and W. J. Miles (centre), on the veranda of Miles's Sydney house, in 1937 or 1938

J. T. Patten in 1938 or 1939

Stephensen and Winifred, Sydney, June 1941

Ian Mudie in 1941; the photograph is inscribed 'Yours for Australia First'

A portrait of Stephensen painted by Robert Grothey at Tatura internment camp in 1943 using special transparent oil paints; the painting itself has not been traced

1944, the first witnesses did not give evidence until September. As well as the internees and others associated with the *Publicist* and the AFM, witnesses included the relevant Military Intelligence officers in Sydney and Perth, Detective-Sergeant Richards and even his police agent Thomas. Commonwealth Investigation Branch officers were not called, despite the fact that they had made detailed reports on the Yabber Club, the *Publicist* and the AFM. Their absence from the Clyne Inquiry was almost certainly Evatt's doing, as he apparently considered his IB agents had been 'too soft' on the AFM.[87]

As Bruce Muirden has shown, in his assessment of the 2500-page transcript of the Clyne Commission, the 'prosecuting' team, Dovey and Shand, could not establish any connection between the Sydney AFM group and the Western Australian 'plot', nor was there any evidence of contact between Australia First and the Japanese. Therefore the internments were defended 'by painting in the blackest terms possible the characters of those interned'. On the other hand, what also emerged were the suspiciously confused accounts and poor memories of the key Military Intelligence officers responsible for the internments. Whatever this concealed, it certainly revealed their 'blundering ineptitude'. Offered a quotation in praise of Hitler and asked if it warranted internment, one MI officer confidently replied: 'It is hardly what I'd call a Churchill speech'. To his lasting embarrassment, the quotation proved to be just that—an extract from one of Churchill's works.[88]

During Stephensen's more than five days in the witness stand, there was very little for him to smile about. After being sworn, he bravely admitted to being a 'Man of Letters', and was led through his evidence by Downing in an attempt to counter some of the accusations which had earlier been made. Stephensen described the Western Australian 'proclamation' as an 'outrageous travesty of the aims of the Australia First Movement'. He also emphatically denied that he was or had ever been anti-English, anti-American, pro-Nazi or pro-Fascist, but he protested too much when he referred to England as 'a kind of second home'. His assertive nationalism gave itself away several times during the inquiry. 'I am quite satisfied to see the Union Jack quartered on the Australian flag', he announced, 'so long as it is only a quarter and does not become the whole'.[89] But loyalty to Australia was not enough in the 1940s, and the cross-examination was at pains to expose his Anglophobia and anything else which might compromise him.

Shand, for the military, was the most aggressive inquisitor, repeatedly asking Stepehensen if he were not 'ashamed' of some of his writings. When Shand persisted about an extract from one letter which mentioned a 'separate peace with Japan', Stephensen said he was surprised rather than ashamed by the quotation.

Shand: What surprised you?
Stephensen: That you should read it out of its context.

Trying another tack, Shand asked him if he found the quotation 'startling'.

'Not greatly', Stephensen replied, 'I am used to surprises now.'[90] Reading out a letter from the Sydney artist and architect. Hardy Wilson, Shand suggested a resemblance to the Western Australian plot. Although Stephensen admitted that Hardy Wilson was obsessed with Jews, and in particular with the pernicious influence of Jewish art dealers, he ridiculed any suggestion of the artist's being involved in sabotage or collaboration:

> *Stephensen*: The Western Australian affair, as I have heard it read in this court, such as blowing up a viaduct, and so on, is such arrant nonsense that it is not at all similar to Hardy Wilson's statement. Hardy Wilson would not blow up a viaduct; he would make a drawing of it.
> *Shand*: And give it to the Japanese?
> *Stephensen*: No, he would give it to the National Gallery, with his other drawings. There is a whole room full of them in Sydney.[91]

Stephensen was more than a match for the experienced barrister in repartee, but Shand used other tricks to suggest disloyalty. He quoted from pre-war *Publicist* articles as if they were comments on the war. Once, however, Stephensen turned this to his own advantage:

> *Shand*: You had written on the occasion of the 2,599th anniversary of Japan in the most laudatory terms of the Japanese people.
> *Stephensen*: That was in 1937.[92] I was supporting the policy of the Australian Government at that time.[93]

More reprehensible methods were used to justify Evatt's claim that Stephensen and his band had been ready to 'stab Australia in the back'. Shand, for example, accused Stephensen of having had prior knowledge of the attack on Pearl Harbour. Stephensen denied this 'most emphatically' and the barrister failed to produce any evidence to support the wild allegation. Pressed by Shand about disloyalty—usually in terms of Britain rather than Australia—Stephensen finally burst out angrily: 'I don't care about being considered disloyal, as long as I am not locked up for it without a trial!'[94]

Shand continued, however, to chip away at some of Stephensen's *Publicist* rhetoric word by word and phrase by phrase. Defending himself as if it were a debating contest, Stephensen also damned himself with occasional outbursts of sardonic frankness. Shand could not believe his ears when Stephensen commented that 'in a general sense' Britain had deserved to lose the war because of giving Poland guarantees without the means to carry them out. 'What is that?' Shand asked, astounded that his intelligent victim had fallen into such an obvious trap. Equally surprised, Commissioner Clyne entered the questioning, and Stephensen admitted he had expected Britain to lose the war in 1940 and that the United States and Russia 'were trying to hold out of it and let Britain go down'.[95] Following up this line of attack, Shand asked Stephensen if, in the event of Britain's fall or decline, there would have been a 'new order' in Australia:

Stephensen: Yes, so there will be.
Shand: A New Order?
Stephensen: Yes, so there will be.

His use of tenses showed that he was still thinking ahead into the political future:

Shand: Well, Great Britain has not been defeated?
Stephensen: In any case, after the depression which will come after the war, there will be a New Order. I have no doubt about that.[96]

However innocuous these forecasts were, such an unrepentant and even defiant attitude undoubtedly helped prejudice Clyne against Stephensen. Ian Mudie congratulated Stephensen on his 'magnificent stand in the witness box' and compared it to a Bradman innings, while Winifred continued to have 'absolute faith' in Judge Clyne.[97] But Stephensen was exhausted by the strain of the trip to Melbourne and the long hours of remorseless cross-examination. The months dragged by and when Germany finally surrendered in May 1945 Winifred expected Stephensen's release. By June, with the Clyne hearings concluded and no sign yet of the judge's report, Stephensen became very impatient. He wrote to Winifred from Tatura camp that 'the joke has gone rather too far now'.[98]

Hearing that the grave of his younger brother Ted, an airman, had been found in France, Stephensen wrote that his brother's death had been 'heroic' and should not be mourned: 'He lived and died clean, and had no chance to become "disillusioned". He is the third of my near kindred to be buried in France. I wept over the other two, nearly thirty years ago, but I am too old for weeping now'.[99] Stephensen had become so bitter and disillusioned that he almost seemed to envy his brother's 'clean' death.

On the day an atomic bomb destroyed Hiroshima Stephensen peacefully listened to Bach's St Matthew Passion at a gramophone concert in the Tatura internment camp. Then on 15 August, the day after Japan's unconditional surrender, his detention order was finally revoked by Evatt. Angered by this further indignity, which suggested he had been just a wartime nuisance, Stephensen demanded that his release be deferred until he had been publicly exonerated. On 17 August, however, after three and a half years behind barbed wire, he reluctantly accepted his freedom.[1] He was never exonerated or compensated in any way, and remained a victim of the war and of his political ideals and delusions.

Part Five
Victoria; Sydney, 1945–1965

I have never cared what people might think of my
ideas or actions. To that extent I am unsociable
and I hope to remain so until death.
                           P. R. Stephensen
                           fragment of autobiography, 1952

I enclose a camera caricature of myself. It indicates
I am a somewhat dolichocephalic Nordic blond beast,
perceptibly aging, but with some sparkle remaining. I
am of athletic build, 5′10½″ high, wearing a Hitler
moustache since I was twenty years of age.
                           P. R. Stephensen
                           letter, 1960

Inky'll be a case for biographers for a thousand years
to try and sort him out, and they never will.
                           Walter Stone
                           interview, 1977

He was a poet in action—the most dangerous kind of poet,
and more dangerous to himself than to others . . .
                           P. R. Stephensen
                           The Viking of Van Diemen's Land, 1954

14
Ghost in Exile

Less than a month after Stephensen's release from internment, the report of the Clyne inquiry was published. Although the judge exonerated some of the Australia Firsters including Hooper, Masey, and the war veteran Harley Matthews, and recommended compensation for them, he found that there were 'substantial reasons' for Stephensen's detention. Along with Kirtley, Cahill and a few others, Stephensen was in effect 'blackwashed' by the government inquiry.[1]

After the years in a concentration camp, he had threatened to 'go berserk' if the Clyne finding went against him, and he wrote to one parliamentarian that he was now 'stigmatized for life, and utterly ruined'.[2] For years he remained in a state of bitter anxiety and lonely defiance. Yet he was later able to salvage and piece together out of the ruins enough of a literary life to sustain his wounded spirit, if not to restore his old swagger.

Patriotic antagonism was still strong after the war with Japan, and Clyne seemed to have had few qualms about justifying Stephensen's internment on a suspicion of disloyalty which was supported by evidence dating mainly from before the war. Clyne found that, in his *Publicist* articles, Stephensen had shown admiration for the Nazis and 'extreme admiration for Japan'. The question of a 'separate peace with Japan' during wartime compromised him also, and Clyne refused to accept Stephensen's protestations of loyalty to Britain. The commissioner thought Stephensen a 'clever and astute witness' who had been 'embarrassed' at times by the evidence of his own writings. Clyne's report also offered the gratuitously insulting comment that Stephensen had 'done little to realize the aspirations of Cecil Rhodes since leaving Oxford'.[3]

Stephensen was not the only one to be disappointed and angered by the Clyne report. His solicitor, Downing, had hoped for an award of costs to cover his many months of work. Now both Stephensen's reputation and finances were ruined, and when Downing presented him with a bill for more than £2000 he had no hope of paying it. Though for a time Stephensen and his solicitor directed at each other some of their mutual frustration and disappointment, Downing remained convinced that an injustice had been done. He described the Australia First cases as a 'brutal political kidnapping', and compiled his own detailed analysis of the evidence. Eventually he decided not to press Stephensen for further payment of costs.[4]

Without much enthusiasm, Stephensen continued to lobby parliamentarians and others for compensation, but was never successful. Evatt became permanently fixed in his mind as the villain of the drama, and to this plot he added various unlikely sub-plots about communists and Jews, including the sinister role played by certain Melbourne shoe manufacturers. He even began referring to Clyne as 'Klein', and speculated on the judge's probable Jewish origins.[5] This was indicative of Stephensen's disintegration and confusion, and also revealed his feeling of impotence in the face of an enemy he reasoned must be all-powerful as well as invisible.

In spite of the defensive mechanism of his conspiracy theories, the shock of internment so deeply affected him that he began to blame Australia itself as much as his own ignorance. 'My bitter experience of the past 3½ years has inured me to anything more that Australia could do to me in the way of rotten treatment', he wrote to Downing after the release of the Clyne report. 'I'm out of touch with prevailing trends, and never did understand the Australian business code.' Stephensen felt a kind of 'game' was being played in which he had no idea of the rules. 'I am forced to recognize', he said, 'that I am no longer a part of the Australian community'.[6]

During the last months of his internment, Winifred had been with her sister in Melbourne, so it was there he was taken on release from Tatura camp. After staying in Melbourne for a few weeks, he moved out of the city to become a rural recluse. With a loan from her sister for the deposit, Winifred had purchased a comfortable house on more than fifty acres at East Warburton, just beyond the terminus of the Upper Yarra railway line. The property was part of a defunct dairy farm, and extended from the Yarra up into the hills behind the house. Neglected during the war, much of this land had become overgrown with bracken, and there was very little farming potential in the property, though the house was almost incongruously luxurious, with a tiled roof, wall-to-wall carpets and wide verandas.[7]

'I'm a hermit', Stephensen wrote to Ian Mudie from Warburton in 1946. 'My present ambition is to become an old man of the mountains. Perhaps a silent yogi.' His only friends, he said, comprised a horse, cow, fowls, a dog and two black tom cats. If anything, though, he became more defiant than peaceful in his isolation. He was 'extinguished, suppressed, silenced and quite put out of business as a public critic', he told Mudie, because he had been 'too harsh for a weak people to endure'.[8] Although Stephensen sometimes dreamed of reviving the *Publicist*, it was left to a couple of other ex-internees in Sydney to arrange a reprint of the magazine's last three issues as a protest in 1946.

Stephensen changed the name of the Warburton property to 'Mountainside Farm' and planned to assist Jack Kirtley to produce limited editions there under the imprint of the Mountainside Press. Kirtley did obtain a press and took it up to Warburton where he stayed for a few months in 1947, but this nostalgic attempt to recover something from the lost days of the Fanfrolico Press was a failure. Kirtley too had become embittered and psychologically disturbed by internment, and he fell out with Stephensen. Assisted and encouraged by the Melbourne book collector and littérateur, J. K. Moir, Kirtley did however later establish his small Mountainside Press at Ferntree Gully.[9]

To help maintain the Warburton property, Stephensen employed a German he had met during internment, and he also paid a local girl to act as his secretary. She later claimed that security officers had asked her to report on Stephensen's behaviour, and Stephensen himself became suspicious of certain visitors to the farm.[10] As it was tedious and expensive even travelling the sixty miles to Melbourne, he and Winifred were more or less isolated at Warburton and spent their spare time listening to radio broadcasts of classical music. Winifred's husband had died, so she and Stephensen were finally married at the Melbourne registry office in November 1947 in the company of only two witnesses, a friend of Winifred's and Herbert Burton whom Stephensen had known since undergraduate days in Queensland. On the marriage certificate Winifred declared herself to be fifty-four, when she was in fact sixty-one.[11]

Still only in his mid-forties, Stephensen should have been entering his most productive period. Yet he was all but burnt out, a ghost of his former self—suspicious, bitter and often bad-tempered. It was only as a literary ghost that he was able to survive his ten years of self-exile in Victoria, avoiding cities and the terrible accusations which had haunted him since March 1942. His old friend, Frank Clune, had provided him with a gift of £50 on his release from internment, and continued to keep him occupied with work.

The two had similar temperaments and equally racist views, but Clune remained rather in awe of his Rhodes Scholar mate. Thick-set, with close-cropped hair, Clune looked more like a roughneck Texan than a Vaucluse accountant. He had worked his passage round the world at everything from selling mousetraps to lumberjacking in Canada, and had fought at Gallipoli. Boisterous and extroverted, he remained aggressively Australian, though not everyone appreciated his colloquial style. In the mid-1930s Marjorie Barnard had described him as a comic figure whose 'literary' ambition was a series of travel books which would roll all over New South Wales. Barnard said she had gazed 'spellbound' into his 'boiled looking eyes' while he spoke, automatically gathering up his dropped hs.[12]

Clune's anecdotal adventures and works of popular fiction in fact proved very successful. Like Stephensen's other patron, W. J. Miles, Clune was financially astute, and his tax business had more than six hundred clients in Sydney and country districts. He worked just six months each year on this, leaving him time for the travel and research which provided Stephensen with enough raw material for an endless succession of books. The travel sagas rolled not only over Australia, but also across Asia and the Pacific, Europe and the Middle East, with titles such as *Sky High to Shanghai* (1939) and *All Aboard for Singapore* (1942). The works of Australian history included biographies and accounts of bushrangers, explorers, murderers and other wild characters such as 'Chinese' Morrison.

Clune was second only to Ion Idriess as Australia's best-selling writer.[13] In 1945 he complained that the dozen books he had published with Angus & Robertson had sold 100 000 copies and netted him royalties of 'only' £2750.[14] Although most of this had gone in fees to his ghost writer, Clune enjoyed a wide public following and received free travel and other concessions. The jaunty Clune narratives, complete with awful puns and continual quips, were eagerly purchased by those for whom long-distance travel was neither practicable nor affordable. Clune loved to fly, though the main mode of overseas travel was still by ship. As Winifred remarked, Clune would 'quite calmly book a trip to the moon' if such excursions became possible.[15]

For transforming Clune's travel diaries and historical material into professional narratives, Stephensen was paid quite generously. In the years following his internment he was on a weekly salary of £20, and in the 1950s he received about six or seven hundred pounds per book. But he had to work hard for this, writing in addition feature articles for magazines like *Man* and *Smith's Weekly* as well as the radio serial 'Roaming around Australia'.[16] Apart from the wartime titles, whose length had been restricted by the paper shortage, Clune books were often 100 000 words, with some going as high as a quarter of a million words. 'For two pins I'd chuck up this distasteful literary hackwork altogether', Stephensen complained to Downing in a depressed mood. 'It ruins my nerves and eyesight, and wastes my talent.'[17] Yet it also supplied him with a regular income, and the thoroughly researched studies of bushranging and exploration contributed to a broader appreciation of Australian history.

For almost thirty years Clune and Stephensen remained a formidable and highly efficient team, producing an average of two or three books a year along with radio talks and magazine features. Clune whimsically referred to their joint enterprise as the 'literature factory',[18] and if their output was hardly literature it was certainly manufactured at assembly-line pace. In the year 1945–46, for example, Clune researched and Stephensen wrote almost 200 000 words, including *Ben Hall the Bushranger* (1947), five long stories for *Man* magazine, and fifty radio broadcasts.[19]

Their relationship was one of mutual need as well as friendship, though Stephensen had to bear the indignity of his status as a hack or ghost writer. Despite the ease with which he could imitate Clune's style, there were frustrations and regular arguments, usually conducted by letter. The two of them were, as Stephensen's stepson recalls, a real Gilbert and Sullivan pair.[20] For his part, Clune resented the fact that Stephensen received most of the financial return from the books. At times Clune borrowed heavily from Angus & Robertson in order to pay his scribe to complete more books in the hope of repaying the advances. Even for bestsellers the Australian book market was no gold mine, and publishing as well as personal pressures strained their relationship.

Towards the end of 1947, when Angus & Robertson wanted *High Ho to London* in time for the Christmas trade, Clune threatened to cut off Stephensen's salary. 'You are not doing your best', he told Stephensen. 'The go-slow waterside workers and miners have nothing on you for pure bloody downright unadulterated laziness.'[21] Stephensen's reply was typically defensive, revealing in turn his own resentments:

> Drop the idea that I'm lazy, or digging potatoes. That's all bunk, and I go flat out until one a.m. practically every night in the week on your job...
> You got £3,000 worth of free travel and accommodation during the first six months of this year... There are many other intangible benefits of your literary reputation, which stands higher than that of any other writer in Australia today. I have helped you, and gladly helped you, and I've been well-paid by you for helping you to achieve that status and those benefits of successful authorship. I have enjoyed doing it, but it's a soul-killer when you abuse me, as you do so frequently...[22]

Though Clune had been a member of the Darlinghurst section of the New Guard in the early 1930s, he expressed distaste for Stephensen's pro-fascism. 'Your communist Gods failed you', Clune wrote to him accusingly. 'Then you got a new God, a greater one than Christ, Buddha and Mohamet. His name was Fascism... Wrongly you were "concentrated" for your idyllic and childlike faith in these fantastic creations of mad dictators.'[23] When *Wild Colonial Boys* was finally published in 1948, it carried a dedication by Clune which was both a subtle protest at Stephensen's internment and also a criticism of his adherence to totalitarian principles:

Dedicated to
THE FREEDOM OF SPEECH
and the
DOWNFALL OF DICTATORS
WHO SUPPRESS IT

Stephensen had written the book in 1943 during the time of his own political suppression.

Although he did not in turn criticize his employer's politics, Stephensen sniped away at Clune for years about the 'hotch-potch' of 'clichés and Clunisms' which constituted the accountant's style.[24] Reviewers also took Clune to task for his cliché-ridden narratives.[25] For this and for other more complex as well as practical reasons, Stephensen resisted open co-authorship with Clune, though the ghost was sometimes acknowledged for his 'editorial' assistance. After Stephensen's release from internment, Clune told him quite bluntly his name was 'mud',[26] and both of them realized that the lingering suspicion of treason might spoil the Clune market if Stephensen's name were given any prominence. It would not have been possible anyway with the first-person travel narratives.

Yet Stephensen continued to hunger for some form of public recognition. When Rex Ingamells was writing a profile of Clune for *Walkabout* magazine in the early 1950s, Clune deleted a paragraph which Stephensen had himself inserted about their 'collaboration'.[27] Immensely proud of 'his' prolific output, Clune listed every one of his titles on his letterhead stationery. As the years passed, this list became a long column descending almost to the bottom of the paper. Such pride was partly commercial self-advertisement, for which Clune had a natural flair, but it also boosted the ego of a self-educated larrikin.

For Stephensen, involvement in the 'Clune Industry' was equally therapeutic, if less stimulating to his ego. It may have saved his sanity in the bleak years of exile, and it began to restore some of his old sense of humour as well. When Clune was setting out on yet another overseas tour in the late 1940s, Stephensen sent him some travel instructions. 'When in Italy *never drink water!*' Stephensen warned. 'You will get typhoid if you drink it as the Eyties piss anywhere.' It is possible to sense Inky's amusement and satisfaction as he pitched this sardonic advice at Clune —the archetypal ocker abroad. 'Italians like a man to laugh and joke, so don't scowl and snarl at them, or they'll knife you', he merrily informed Clune. 'You're only a foreigner to them, same as a Dago here so don't start chucking your weight about. Buy a phrase book and learn a few useful words. Viva vino.'[28]

This was all part of the symbiotic relationship they enjoyed. Where Stephensen patronized the roving accountant for his lack of culture and education, Clune in turn scorned his ghost's misguided politics and literary ambitions. Nevertheless, Clune respected the cultural accomplishments of his captive Oxford man just as Stephensen hailed Clune as a larrikin with the 'instincts of a scholar'.[29] They were both, in their own ways, wild colonial boys.

Early in 1949 the Stephensens moved to northern Victoria and to the less isolated but more provincial township of Bethanga near the Hume Reservoir. Stephensen had a theory that if they lived half-way between Sydney and Melbourne he would be able to communicate more easily with Clune in Sydney while Winifred could stay in touch with her sister in Melbourne. This idea proved to be about as visionary as the later Albury-Wodonga scheme, and they lived there for only three years before restlessly moving south again. At Bethanga Stephensen entered into the life of the small community yet was never fully accepted, as he explained to Ian Mudie:

> Much to my annoyance I am the only man in the district addressed as Mr. I go about in the oldest clothes, I haven't a motorcar, I yarn with everybody, and sometimes drink at the pub, go to all the dances, call everybody by their names or nicknames, but so great is the common

man's awe of learning ... they can't bring themselves to call me 'Steve' ...³⁰

It was at Bethanga in 1951 that Stephensen wrote the first of only two books on which his name appeared with Clune's.³¹ *The Viking of Van Diemen's Land* (1954) was also the most ambitious of all their books and certainly the one in which Stephensen invested the full measure of his creative energy. The reasons are not far to seek, for the book was a biography of Jorgen Jorgensen (1780–1841), the Danish adventurer, writer and political activist who was imprisoned by the British for his rebelliousness, and ended his days in Australia. Although Clune organized most of the research for the biography in Europe, England, Iceland and Tasmania, Stephensen clearly indentified with more than Jorgensen's Danish patronymic. One of the most bizarre episodes of Jorgensen's career was his proclamation of the independent state of Iceland in 1809, styling himself 'Protector', or 'Democratic Dictator' in Stephensen's oxymoronic description.³² No blood was shed, and Jorgensen's Cromwellian revolution lasted just two months, but the gesture strongly appealed to a radical nationalist like Stephensen.

In fact he lavished so much time and energy on the Jorgensen biography that it grew to a massive 400 000 words before being cut down to a more manageable 250 000. The irony was that Stephensen, who had blue-pencilled many a hapless author's script, was allowed no part in the 'butchery' of the biography. Clune himself carried this out at the instigation of Angus & Robertson who would not publish it otherwise.³³ This reversal of roles deeply offended Stephensen who was not even shown the revised version until proof stage. His detailed account of Jorgensen's early life, charting the Dane's psychological and intellectual development, was erased by the impatient Clune who considered such exposition secondary to the tale of Jorgensen's picaresque adventures. Stephensen's scholarly chapter references were dropped as well, though the extensive bibliography of Jorgensen material was retained in the published version.

Far from being apologetic about his hatchet work, Clune criticized Stephensen with characteristic bluntness, accusing him of being too ambitious and too fond of long or hyphenated words. 'That's what that bloody Fritz language did to you in camp', Clune declared, referring to Stephensen's study of German during internment. 'If you have a choice of a big word and a small one, you go for size. I don't know how many times I've blue pencilled "throughout", "particularly", "magnanimous" and God knows how many portmanteau jaw-breakers from your script.' The biography had already been rejected by London publishers as 'too pompous', Clune threw at his ghost spitefully.³⁴

'I am permanently disheartened by what has happened to this book', Stephensen wrote to Clune about *The Viking of Van Diemen's Land*, 'and will never again allow my name to be used and my work to be butchered'.³⁵ To E. Morris Miller, Stephensen poured out more of his frustration: 'When I saw the galley proofs, I was extremely dejected at the mutilation of a work which was conceived as the most ambitious attempt at biography ever made in Australia'. He said the philosophical material—including 'the influence of Swedenborg and the mystics, and of the French Rationalists'—had all been 'double dutch' to Clune, as had the Freudian analysis of Jorgensen's childhood.[36] This attempt to apply psychoanalytical theory was in itself surprising in view of his earlier dismissal of Freud as a medieval obscurantist. It was a rather belated indication of the discrepancy between Stephensen's polemical vocabulary and the real breadth of his intellectual interests.

Stephensen was paid £1000 by his partner and patron Clune to write the Jorgensen biography, and the published version was, like *Wild Colonial Boys*, a vivid mixture of fictionalized dialogue and authentic historical scenery, rich with detail and incident. E. Morris Miller thought Stephensen had made the figure of Jorgensen 'romantically real' as well as presenting him as 'a man of character and resource'.[37] In short Stephensen had taken Jorgensen and his ideas seriously, rather than accepting the traditional view of him as a ne'er-do-well adventurer.

Stephensen's full and sympathetic treatment is not surprising since the 500-page *Viking of Van Diemen's Land* is not only 'The Stormy Life of Jorgen Jorgensen', as the sub-title proclaims, but also an autobiographical account of Stephensen himself. Although it was gambling rather than politics which brought Jorgensen down, Stephensen projected himself on to the outlines of the Dane's career. Critical of Christianity, Jorgensen had been a student at the time of the French Revolution, just as Stephensen had been a schoolboy at the time of the Russian Revolution. An early member of the Australian Communist Party, Stephensen claimed Jorgensen as possibly 'the first writer in the Australian colonies to express "socialistic" ideas', and the Dane was also preoccupied with the evils of 'usury'. Most importantly, Jorgensen was 'a rare combination of a man of action and a man of letters'.[38] Yet, like Stephensen, he had been frustrated both in his political and literary ambitions.

The biography therefore contains a fragmentary and ghost-like autobiography, in which Jorgensen's attempt to liberate Iceland from colonial domination is shadowed closely by Stephensen's own struggle for Australian independence in the 1930s and early 1940s. 'The failure of his attempt to liberate the Icelanders from Danish rule was the immediate cause of his life's tragedy', Stephensen wrote, 'but history has vindicated him'[39]—just as Stephensen felt he had been vindicated by Australia's more independent role in foreign affairs during and after the war. Stephensen saw himself as an intellectual adventurer, a Viking out of his time, stamping his feet and shaking his hair 'in the great winds of the earth', as he had expressed his defiant, questing personality many years before as an Oxford student.[40] Now at fifty, and reflected in the image of Jorgensen, Stephensen confirmed this vision of himself:

> His life was one of frustrations, but also of many positive achievements. In some ways he was a Viking, born ten centuries too late: in other ways

he was an adventurer on seas of thought born too soon. Never was he a conventional man of his own times.⁴¹

Stephensen's self-image was ultimately as romantic as his assessment of Jorgensen, but there was also a recognition of the faults which had influenced both their stormy careers:

> He was impulsive, imaginative, and lacked the steadiness of thought and action which is a heritage of the Norse breed. His mind turned quickly to extremes. Living in a romantic and 'literary' atmosphere, which was partly the result of his education, partly an expression of his individuality, and partly a reaction to contemporary events, he was a poet in action—the most dangerous kind of poet, and more dangerous to himself than to others when he attempted to mould reality to conform with his capricious visions.⁴²

The failure to liberate Iceland/Australia was viewed quite philosophically and in terms of pragmatic political morality. 'It is well known that successful treason soon ceases to be viewed as treasonable', Stephensen commented. 'Jorgensen's principal offence in Iceland was in the *failure* of his revolutionary efforts'.⁴³ In another passage Stephensen, perhaps unconsciously, defended his own *Publicist* articles and criticized the secretive enemies who had exacted the same penalty as that dealt out to Jorgensen:

> The pen, in his hand, was the last resort of a man of action reduced to inactivity. He used it as a duellist uses a rapier—to defend himself and wound his enemies; but those against whom he fought used methods less valorous and more sure than his. By secret political influence, they bludgeoned him with incarceration and put him under the law's mean displeasure.⁴⁴

In a chapter entitled 'The Abyss', Stephensen gave some indication of the mental torment he had suffered since his political suppression in Sydney. The instability of character he discerned in Jorgensen applied equally to himself:

> If excuses are to be found for his conduct, they may be sought in the frustration of his ambitions and the disappointment of his ideals; or beyond that in some innate instability of his character. The humiliations he suffered were small compared with his mental agonies. His life for fifteen years had a nightmarish quality: often he must have wondered whether he was being tormented by the goblins of a hideous dream from which he would presently be awakened. At other times he would know the truth: that his life had become a catastrophe, and that his great talents were floundering in a morass of shame and disgrace.⁴⁵

Yet 'his buoyancy was such that he could not accept the defeat of his ambitions', and the 'creative frenzy of his Genius surged within him'. In literary imagination, at least, Stephensen still possessed those powers of defiant optimism which had sustained him since his days as a schoolboy prankster: 'In his mind great thoughts are soaring, resonant phrases are reverberating for the public weal. Never has he accepted defeat. He is as buoyant as cork. Pushed under again and again, he will forever rise'.[46]

Stephensen's 'Epilogue', reviewing Jorgensen's treatment at the hands of other historians and biographers as well as novelists like Marcus Clarke, includes both an epitaph to Stephensen's own autobiographical fragments and a challenge to Australian biographers and historians:

> His restless ghost has haunted writers again and again. Some have attempted to dismiss him with a sneer, others to summarize his life and character in the few words of a footnote or a flashing phrase. All such attempts must fail. Jorgensen's crowded life cannot be compressed to a tabloid. His own attempt at compression was, as he recognized, a mere 'shred of autobiography'. Will the present, by far the lengthiest biography ever attempted, at last lay his ghost?[47]

Like Jorgensen, Stephensen was never able to write more than a 'shred' of his own story. Perhaps realizing that he had already addressed the baffling puzzle of his own life through *The Viking of Van Diemen's Land*, Stephensen did make one attempt to begin his autobiography just after completing the Jorgensen manuscript. However, he got no further than half a dozen introductory pages, written in blue ink with a number of revisions. Entitled 'Experience Comes Too Late', this unpublished preface acknowledged little beyond Stephensen's pathological failure to anticipate the consequences of his actions. Internment had 'surprised me so greatly', he wrote, 'that even now I cannot grasp its full implications':

> My experiences, both happy and unhappy, have taught me, *always after the event*, what I ought to have done and what I ought to have avoided; but this knowledge is useless in retrospect, and equally useless when I am confronted with new situations.[48]

In 1952 the Stephensens purchased a house at Sandringham, Melbourne, and he made the first tentative return to metropolitan society after ten years of imprisonment and exile. At the prospect of re-entering an intellectual and literary community, Stephensen's confidence and enthusiasm began to rise once again. He was indeed buoyant as cork. 'There is no real future for me in your travel books', he informed Clune as he was packing to leave Bethanga. 'It's a waste of my valuable ability. I am an Australian, and I don't care if Europe sinks beneath the sun.' Instead he planned to re-issue his story collection, *Bushwhackers*, as well as *The Foundations of Culture in Australia* and possibly a selection of his 'prophetic writings' from the *Publicist*. He might even, he mused provocatively to Clune, start a small press to publish his autobiography and other works.[49]

None of these plans eventuated, of course, but when Clune heard that his tame ghost was emerging from solitude he was quick to respond. 'You're rushing out of Bethanga without a cracker', Clune wrote irritably.

> Just because a few of the rising generation scratch your back you want to get into the literary scene in Melbourne ... Your house will be

crowded with hobohemians bludging your wine and tucker, while you expound your views on sheep cockies, dingoes, commos, and other extroverts in the Australian scene.

More significantly, Clune feared Stephensen would fall behind in their work, at a time when sales from the Clune Industry were dropping and the future of writing was 'hazardous'. 'We have to watch our step', Clune warned.[50]

But Stephensen's spirit had been restrained for too long and he was becoming more independent again. 'I now intend to emerge from my hermit silence of ten years and to resume volcanic activity in Melbourne', he wrote to Mudie with some of the old exuberance. He was thinking of publishing a history of the Australia First internments, as part of his autobiography, or even re-starting the *Publicist*.[51] These schemes also came to nothing, but when he moved to Melbourne Stephensen did write his first signed article for ten years, a book review for the new magazine, *Austrovert*.[52] Then the bibliophile, Walter Stone, encouraged him to compose a short memoir of the Fanfrolico Press, *Kookaburras and Satyrs* (1954), which was the first book published by Stone at his Talkarra Press in Sydney.

The title of this memoir echoed that of an article Stephensen had written for the University of Queensland magazine thirty years before, 'Satyrs or Kookaburras?'.[53] Appropriately, the article had been part of a published debate with his fellow undergraduate, Jack Lindsay, on nationalism and literature. Though it contained a number of minor factual errors, *Kookaburras and Satyrs* faithfully outlined the history and significance of the Fanfrolico period. Stephensen wrote that it was the 'sunlit quality', the reaffirmation of vitality, which the Fanfrolican movement had attempted to project back at Europe. He stated emphatically that Norman Lindsay had been the founder of the movement, and that the impact of a 'brilliant father upon a brilliant son' had 'engendered, sustained, and ultimately killed, the Fanfrolico Press'.[54]

Although Stephensen also used the memoir to criticize Jack Lindsay and other expatriates as 'cultural careerists or opportunists',[55] *Kookaburras and Satyrs* confirmed Stephensen's acceptance of the Dionysian creed of the Lindsays, and located the roots of his contempt for liberalism and democracy in World War I:

> Like others of that generation, I was disillusioned with the bogus ideals of 'Democracy' and so on, that had been plugged in by the professional propagandists to stir up hatred against the Germans in the First World War. Being optimistic, I was hoping for a rebirth of the human spirit ... The rebelliousness that we might feel could be directed only against those who had caused the world-wide calamities.[56]

Reviewing *Kookaburras and Satyrs*, Jack Lindsay pointed out some of Stephensen's errors, adding his own more complex synthesis of 'Norman-Lindsayism'. He also accused his former partner of having been a Trotskyist, and dismissed Stephensen's claim about having discarded communism at Oxford in 1926 after discovering it to be 'only banditry disguised as a political philosophy'.[57] Lindsay's comments were finally published along with a testy rejoinder by Stephensen in Walter Stone's journal, *Biblionews*, in 1959.[58]

Hearing that Stephensen was litigiously inclined, Lindsay sent the proofs of his own memoir of the period, *Fanfrolico and After* (1962), to Australia before publication and was somewhat surprised to find that Stephensen heartily approved the work. Stephensen's long review of the book was one of his best pieces of literary criticism.[59] During their friendly correspondence about *Fanfrolico and After*, Inky ranged provocatively over his troubled past. He felt he had always lived on the margin:

> Mein Kampf in Australia since 1932 has been for Nationalism, which in the Australian scene was orthodox Leninism, although the silly Communist Party here was and still is unaware of it. I am opposed as equally to Soviet Imperialism as to Capitalist Imperialism. In literature as in politics I am for the genius loci and for the individual... if I must be classified I am a Nietzschean Bakuninite! Better say simply an Individualist, unregimentable. In literary evaluations, I stand on Croce's Aesthetic: the creative artist is always alone, cannot belong, must swim against the stream...[60]

It was in the wake of the Jorgensen biography, and his renewed participation in literary affairs signalled by *Kookaburras and Satyrs*, that Stephensen began actively seeking other literary work and collaborations. Yet he never broke away completely from Clune's employment, and their clashes became more bitter and weary as the years passed. 'Any carpenter, wharfie or shearer earns more than I do and gets it regular without having to beg for it', Stephensen complained in 1954. To which the other responded: 'You won't work at all when you have a bank account'.[61] As Clune well knew, his ghost never had any money put by, and would therefore continue to depend upon him.

Later in 1954, after Clune had accused Stephensen of another attack of the 'go slows' and general 'buggering around', each fired the other, Stephensen remarking sarcastically: 'Instead of the expected cheque, your letter of abuse has just arrived, the usual annual outburst I get every December, as Christmas draws nigh, the season of peace and goodwill'. Within a week, though, Clune had repented. 'I don't want to see you have to take up hard yakker at your age', he wrote from Sydney, in as humble a tone as he could manage. 'You'd die at the first swing of the pick.'[62]

In the meantime, however, Stephensen had rushed off letters to George Ferguson at Angus & Robertson and to BHP, offering to write a history of the Australian iron and steel industry.[63] Nothing came of this, but a few days later Stephensen signed a contract for the publication of a book of sailing ship memoirs he had written for Captain William H. S. Jones, *The Cape Horn Breed* (1956). This led to a lengthy collaboration with another retired seafarer, Sir James Bisset, for whom Stephensen compiled a three-decker autobiography, and he later wrote on commission other maritime books including *Sydney Sails* (1962) and the comprehensive *History and Description of Sydney Harbour* (1966).⁶⁴

In 1956, with his health beginning to break down after years of anxiety and overwork, Stephensen returned to Sydney after an absence of almost fifteen years. He and Winifred lived one more in Raglan Street, Mosman (where they had stayed in the early 1930s), and then at Cremorne. The last ten years of his life were therefore passed within sight of Sydney Harbour and he became involved with charting the maritime life and history of a place which had long ago symbolized for him the fresh, clean image of a new Australia. Now he was sustained by the brooding, timeless rhythms of a harbour which inspired so much of Kenneth Slessor's best poetry. Once again Stephensen was buoyed up, and tossed about, by the literary life of a city which had already deeply disappointed him, both as a publisher and as a political activist.

If he remained as impoverished as before, and was regarded suspiciously in some quarters and as pre-historic in others, his interests and activities became wider than perhaps they had ever been. He wrote or edited numerous entries for Angus & Robertson's ten-volume *Australian Encyclopaedia*, and proposed the toast to the editor of the encyclopaedia, A. H. Chisholm, at the lunch which launched this prodigious publication at the Hotel Metropole in 1958.⁶⁵ He began to work as a literary agent almost as soon as he moved to Sydney from Melbourne, and by 1960 he was handling the work of about twenty writers, though characteristically he was making barely enough to cover the expenses of his agency.

He also renewed contact with Laurence Pollinger, whom he had known as D. H. Lawrence's agent in London in the 1920s. Pollinger had since left Curtis Brown and set up on his own, taking the lucrative Lawrence estate business with him. Although Stephensen corresponded frequently and often at great length with Pollinger in the late 1950s and 1960s, they did not transact much business. With a few exceptions, Stephensen's stable of writers consisted of amateurs with little chance of publication, and he laboured in the vain hope of receiving a small percentage of their royalties.

One outcome of his experience as a publisher and literary agent, however, was his appointment to the staff of Angus & Robertson in August 1960 to develop paperback fiction. Unfortunately he was hired by Walter Burns, the new managing director of the parent company, without the consent of George Ferguson, the head of the publishing division. Burns regarded books as consumer merchandise like soap, and knew more about financial management than publishing. He represented new shareholding interests in the company, whereas Ferguson, a grandson of the founder George Robertson, stood for the old family interest and for the firm's traditional prestige as Australia's leading publisher. In just a few months Burns had sacked almost half the editorial staff, sold A & R's London publishing house, bought up rival booksellers, and then sold off slabs of the backlist including the encyclopaedia.⁶⁶

To make Stephensen's position even more difficult, he was appointed at a salary of £2500—higher in fact than that paid to the firm's senior editors, Beatrice Davis and Colin Roderick—and was answerable to Burns directly, not to the publisher, Ferguson. Burns had obviously sent Stephensen in as a shock trooper to shake up the publishing division of A & R and increase profitability with an aggressive programme of paperbacks. Stephensen claimed to be 'an innocent spectator or referee' in this 'donnybrook', but, as a literary agent, he had been lobbying Burns for several months, urging the publication of more popular titles.[67] He was confident that, with his experience and contacts, he could unearth two hundred titles a year, either from reprints or new manuscripts, and these would be printed in England or America for worldwide paperback distribution. Burns had discussed this arrangement with prospective overseas publishers, and he was depending on Stephensen to deliver the titles quickly.

Angus & Robertson, however, were not organized for the mass production of soap. In a series of memos to Burns, Stephensen complained of delays in assessment by the firm's editorial and sales staff, and suggested the establishment of a separate paperback division under his own control.[68] But despite the expenditure of much enthusiasm and hard work, Stephensen's stay was as brief as that of Burns, and they both became casualties in the 'A & R War'. The *Bulletin* report of the battle gave Ferguson's summary of his 'policy', while Burns's side was put by Stephensen who criticized the 'Old Regime' and commented that publishers everywhere had to cope with the 'paperback revolution'.[69]

When Burns was deposed as managing director, Stephensen's position at A & R was quickly terminated and he was left with an ambitious paperbacks scheme, but no publisher. After an unsuccessful attempt to interest Sir Frank Packer, Stephensen even thought of floating his own publishing company and offering shares to 'friends and to selected authors'. It was like a sad replay of his elusive 1930s dreams, except that he did not get as far as issuing prospectuses this time.[70] While George Ferguson and Beatrice Davis breathed a sigh of relief, Stephensen characterized the old firm as 'Anguish and Robberson', and took legal steps to recover his promised salary.[71]

With dispatches from the A & R war filling magazine columns in late 1960 and early 1961, Stephensen became embroiled in yet another public conflict—with Xavier Herbert over the editing and publication of *Capricornia*. The object of this deliberately stimulated controversy was to transfer the *Observer* readership to the *Bulletin* when the magazines merged early in 1961.[72] The controversy did generate the desired publicity, and it was reported in another magazine that Herbert was in training to punch Stephensen. Herbert's old hatred was revived, and in subsequent letters to the *Bulletin*, author and publisher hacked away at one another, Herbert stridently proclaiming that 'NO ONE EDITED "CAPRICORNIA" BUT MYSELF'.[73] The *Bulletin* editor, Peter Coleman, refused to publish one letter from Herbert describing Stephensen as the 'most discredited Australian who ever lived' and a 'poor inoffensive hack-writer' with dreams of becoming 'Fuhrer'.[74] Herbert then offered *Meanjin* a long and detailed article on the controversy, but this too was finally rejected as libellous.[75]

For his part, Stephensen thought the clash with Herbert 'amusing'. He was always ready to tilt with an inky lance, but said he preferred 'windmills (such as Xavier Herbert)'.[76] He was still constructing a Quixote legend about himself. As he had written to Miles Franklin in the early 1950s:

> My distinctive contribution (as compared with that of A.G.S., for example) was that I saw the necessity of linking Australian literature with political nationalism, the movement for political independence from Britain. As I got no support from Australian writers, I've retired from the unequal combat. For eleven years, 1931–1942, I was a Don Quixote, then I was unhorsed.[77]

The shock of that fall in 1942 had crippled his spirit, and he had not been as successful as one of the other Australia First internees who finally received a secret compensation settlement of £2500 from the federal government after years of persistent lobbying.[78]

Stephensen had long since given up protesting, but he did accidentally profit by his disaster. In a short article about Adela Pankhurst Walsh in May 1961, the Melbourne *Herald* described the AFM scheme for 'murdering national leaders and taking over Australia'.[79] Stephensen threatened the newspaper with a libel suit, but wrote to a friend that he did not want a public hearing as the 'raking over of old muck' would be too distressing. 'I have really suffered badly for sixteen years', he said, 'and I am just getting on my feet again when this blow comes'. Within a month, however, he had received a private, out-of-court settlement of £1000, and the paper also published a lengthy apology.[80]

Stephensen had become a confirmed white racist as well as an unrepentant anti-Semite and pro-fascist. Although he took little active part in any political movement after the war, he corresponded regularly with members of extreme right-wing organizations in Australia and overseas. He received material from the Australian League of Rights, and someone in America sent him *The Cross and the Flag* which he enjoyed. The Australian Nationalist Workers' Party, which later became the National Socialist Party of Australia, made contact with him, and he received letters from fascists who signed themselves proudly 'Heil Hitler'. Stephensen sometimes signed his own letters, half humorously and always provocatively, 'Sieg Heil!'[81]

In 1952 he had written to Ian Mudie that 'Hitler was right' about communism being Jewish, and that after the 'Third World War' Jerusalem would be 'the capital of the world'.[82] It was also in 1952 that the historian Manning Clark visited Stephensen at Bethanga to talk with him about *The Foundations of Culture in Australia* and about his stimulating survey of Australian history in the January 1938 *Publicist*. Clark was therefore prepared to take his views seriously, but found instead a 'wreck' of a man, obsessed with the Jews and with the events of his own life. Clark regarded him as a tragic and anachronistic figure, and an *artiste manqué*—a man with creative talent whose sense of failure and frustration had been twisted into violent, irrational fears and hatreds.[83]

'As there is a school of Semitic studies at Melbourne', Stephensen wrote to Manning Clark after the visit, 'I'm hoping that someday a school of anti-Semitic studies will also be established there, and in that case I might be offered a chair'. He could not resist adding another joke which he had no doubt shared with W. J. Miles years before: 'Incidentally, I am not "anti-Semitic", as I rather like Arabs'. His central political obsession now was racial purity and the need for a 'Teutonic federation' to preserve 'real civilisation' against the encroachment of Jews, Negroes, Slavs and Asians. 'I'm expecting that, before the end of this century, the white races everywhere will combine for self-preservation', he told Manning Clark. 'I'm *hoping* that Australia will be held by the whites as a national home.'[84]

To the fanatical anti-Semite, Tom Graham, Stephensen wrote the following year in even more unequivocal terms about his political fears and hopes:

> If the Americans and the British peoples take effective steps to rid themselves of the Jewish incubus, Australians would quickly follow suit. I am sure that Germany will rise again, perhaps in alliance with Britain, as Hitler wished. I hold myself in readiness for any genuine opportunity to be of service to the cause for which I have suffered in the past, but I am not going to be associated with any premature or ill-considered efforts, which would be doomed to failure. Experience is no use unless it teaches us what to avoid. As you know the Australia First Movement in 1941–42 attracted many weaklings, who failed at the first test. It also attracted various cranks ... and unbalanced types ... .[85]

Stephensen certainly had not yet learned the lesson of his own political experience. In 1954, the year of the Petrov Commission, at the height of anti-communist 'McCarthyism' in Australia, he wrote to another acquaintance that National Socialism would rise again, but 'with some combination of the political genius of a Hitler with the ethical intensity of a Gandhi'. Hitler and Mussolini, he considered, had been 'too exclusively "political"'.[86] Though Stephensen's own political thinking had petrified around his paranoia, he was a rebel no longer in the depths of the Cold War.

With Frank Clune, he helped lobby for the maintenance of the White Australia Policy and the restriction of 'coloured' immigration. Although he voted for the right-wing DLP, Stephensen was very critical of the party for failing to support the White Australia Policy. He met and corresponded with the former Labor immigration minister, Arthur Calwell, and supported his White Australia crusade. Stephensen wrote to the newspapers about white race superiority, and in 1959 once more contacted Calwell, then deputy opposition leader, with plans for a White Australia League.[87]

Stephensen relinquished none of his old obsessions, protesting whenever possible about such things as decadent modernism and homosexuality. Machiavelli's *The Prince* and the *Essay on Population* by Malthus were among his most closely studied texts,[88] and his polemical edge remained sharp. Continuing to imagine himself a revolutionary, he had in fact stood still while the world spun out of his grasp:

The Editor,
NATION, Sydney.   21st June, 1961
Sir,
                     O TEMPORA O MORES!

In a world in which art is the cult of ugliness and literature is obscurantist; in which music is discord, sculpture distorted, and architecture solely utilitarian; in which justice is an instrument of propaganda; in which universities are career factories; in which primary education is a personality-cult instead of an instrument for social discipline: in such a world, sir, in which mediocrity is paramount and equality is substituted for quality, to be a conservative is to be a revolutionary.
                                 P. R. STEPHENSEN[89]

Despite his status as a literary and political ghost whom few took seriously any more, Stephensen made two lecture tours for the Commonwealth Literary Fund, the first in 1959 to South Australia where he spoke alongside his old friend, Ian Mudie. Stephensen's lecture on factual writing in Australia, delivered at the University of Adelaide, was published in the *Bulletin*,[90] but even his ideas on literary nationalism were now rather stale. In an article for *Nation*, entitled 'The Years have Caught up with P. R. Stephensen', another nationalist, Geoffrey Dutton, commented that, paradoxically, it was 'thanks to Stephensen and pioneers like him that what he has to say seems more than twenty years out of date'.[91]

Earlier in 1959 *Nation* had run a two-part biographical feature on Stephensen, the first instalment of which was aptly titled 'Traveller's Ghost: The tempestuous and hitherto unlogged voyage of P. R. Stephensen'.[92] Although both this and the second instalment contained some minor errors, it was indeed the first really perceptive analysis of his career, and he was flattered to be in the public eye once more. No authorship was acknowledged, but the articles were written by *Nation*'s editor, T. M. Fitzgerald, who had met Stephensen at one of Walter Stone's gatherings. Though he disagreed with some aspects of Fitzgerald's 'leftish' journalism, Stephensen felt the articles had helped him—'chiefly by pointing out that I have written Frank Clune's books'.[93]

The response to the *Nation* profile was perhaps predictable. Judah Waten deplored Stephensen's anti-Semitism, and Clune immediately wrote to the editor that his collaboration with Stephensen was scarcely a secret. Clune, though, took pains to minimize Stephensen's role.[94] It was not until 1963 that the reluctant Clune signed a formal agreement with his ghost, assigning rights in their works. Under this agreement Stephensen waived all claims to the travel books, but was to receive a half share in any future revenues from twenty-one of their history titles. As well, Stephensen's name was to appear with Clune's in future editions of these twenty-one books. Yet Stephensen also signed away all but subsidiary rights in some of the most enduring Clune titles, including the major bushranging works *Wild Colonial Boys*, *Ben Hall the Bushranger*, and *The Kelly Hunters*, which would continue to appear under Clune's name only. Stephensen had wanted future co-authorship with Clune on these books, but was denied it when the contract was finally drawn up.[95]

Stephensen seemed destined to accept such disappointments. As Fitzgerald had written in defence of his *Nation* profile of the 'Traveller's Ghost', his articles had been 'an outline study of the nature of a man's deterioration'. Stephensen remained something of a puzzle, to others as well as to himself. One correspondent wrote to *Nation* that the magazine had still not found 'the precise chemical formula which brought about Stephensen's sell-out or reversal of liberal principles in a short two years'[96]—that is, between *The Foundations of Culture in Australia* (1936) and his *Publicist* pro-fascism. Fitzgerald rightly pointed to the influence of W. J. Miles, though the whole development of Stephensen's thought and ambition from schooldays, indeed the peculiar composition of his mercurial personality and attitudes, had been equally significant elements in his tragic ideological regression. Miles had been perhaps no more than a catalyst at a time of increased personal and political instability and crisis. The effect of the widely publicized Moscow Trials of 1936–38 had also hastened Stephensen's disillusionment with the left. 'It broke my heart when Old Bolsheviks such as Bukharin and Zinoviev were executed', he wrote to Jack Lindsay in 1961.[97]

Stephensen had always been an enthusiast, attracted to ideas, ideologies and gestures which stimulated his sense of fun and satisfied his romantic need for action and excitement. Yet for all his talk of revolution and fighting in the streets, he was essentially a naive idealist, eternally opposed to the financial, political or military establishment. He could swing wildly from one extreme to another, from elaborate and irrational optimism to sullen despair at times. His fear was that he would fail to make a mark on history, and in his literary as well as political escapades in the 1930s an increasing desperation was evident. His final resort to bizarre and sinister conspiracy theories was an attempt to convince himself that at last he had discovered the real basis of his enemy's power and influence.

All the time, of course, he was his own worst enemy, and in his wildness there was as much anger and verbal violence as there was panache. When he arrived in Brisbane for another series of CLF lectures in 1962, his first return visit to the scene of his undergraduate years, he described himself to the press as 'Australia's oldest angry young man'.[98] Yet however foolish, sad and even tragic he appeared at times, he was an immensely likeable character and a remarkably talented and accomplished man of letters. He was also, as Marcus Clarke said of Jorgen Jorgensen, 'one of the most interesting human comets recorded in history'.[99]

One of Stephensen's last literary tasks was to edit the multi-volume edition of the works of his friend, William Baylebridge. The wealthy Baylebridge had died during the war, appointing Stephensen one of the administrators of his will. This provided for the endowment of an annual poetry award, the Grace Leven prize, as well as for the publication of his own works which had appeared during his lifetime only in small, privately printed editions. It was Stephensen's idea that, in conjunction with Angus & Robertson, a uniform six-volume edition of Baylebridge's works should be issued, and R. G. Howarth of the University of Sydney was initially appointed editor. When Howarth left Australia, Stephensen took over as editor and organized the publication of the first four volumes: *This Vital Flesh* (1961), *An Anzac Muster* (1962), *The Growth of Love* (1963), and *Salvage* (1964).[1]

In his prefaces Stephensen provided useful biographical and critical details about the secretive Baylebridge, but could not resist unleashing a few tired and predictable broadsides against modernist writers and academics. Part of Stephensen's irritability stemmed from the disappointing response to the early volumes. In her review of *This Vital Flesh*, for example, Judith Wright described Baylebridge as 'emphatically' not a poet. His 'pomposity and emptiness' betrayed the 'confusion of thought behind the book'. Politically, she thought Baylebridge was also 'a long way behind his time', his work suggesting fascism and totalitarianism.[2] Although the original edition of *This Vital Flesh* had won the gold medal of the Australian Literature Society in 1939, Baylebridge was now regarded, like Stephensen, as something of a dinosaur.

Other critics were harsher than Judith Wright who had after all once described Baylebridge as potentially Australia's greatest writer.[3] Reviewing *The Growth of Love*, the Rockhampton *Morning Bulletin*'s book critic decided that Baylebridge was an anachronism, and 'far from being one of Australia's shining poetic lights', he was 'bathed only in the dim glow of mediocrity'. This led to a heated exchange in the letters column of the newspaper, which did little for the reputation of either Stephensen or Baylebridge.[4] Angus & Robertson's sales of the Baylebridge volumes were so poor that George Ferguson unsuccessfully tried to convince Stephensen and the Baylebridge estate to reduce the print runs from 2500 to 750 copies.[5]

The most damning Baylebridge review of all appeared in the *Sydney Morning Herald* after Stephensen's death. Under the title 'poet who never was', it was a review of *Salvage*, the last volume of the memorial edition which Stephensen edited. Remarking that Baylebridge remained the 'most shadowy figure in all Australian literature', the *Herald* critic commented that Stephensen's faith in the enduring quality of his work was 'touching', but that 'the sad fact is that these poems can outlive nothing, for there has never been the least spark of life in them'.[6] Baylebridge had been a friend to Stephensen, and a supporter of his publishing ventures in the 1930s, so his dedication to Baylebridge's memory and his misplaced faith in Baylebridge's poetry are understandable.

Of Inky's own life there was not much more to salvage from the 1960s, and he and Winifred continued to exist on the proceeds from Clune work and other writing commissions. His health declined further and his literary agency provided him only with anxiety and the illusion of literary activity. He was, however, one of the foundation members of the Australian Society of Authors, just as he had taken an active part in the Fellowship of Australian Writers in the 1930s.

It was at the time of his public argument with Xavier Herbert in 1961, and just after his involvement with the feud at Angus & Robertson, that Stephensen had his first heart attack. Despite the writing commissions and the £1000 libel settlement, he remained in debt, and it was financial anxiety, plus a lifetime of heavy smoking, which had weakened his heart. The doctor confided to Winifred that Inky might die at any time, and their last years together were the closest of their long relationship.[7]

'Our love affair blossomed till the end', Winifred wrote to a friend. 'We had a little ritual, when he left to go to town, I would open the verandah window and wave, and every few yards he would turn and wave to me until he reached the corner.'[8] He had never been an easy person to live with, yet for forty years Winifred had been an unshakeable ally who faced all their misfortunes with a tough, uncompromising spirit. The saddest irony was that although she had worried for half her life about their age difference, she outlived him by several years.

In May 1965 Colin Roderick invited Inky along to the annual Australian literature night at the Savage Club. This was held at the state ballroom in Market Street, and Stephensen spoke brilliantly about book censorship and his part in the secret London edition of *Lady Chatterley's Lover*. It was a 'spontaneous and polished' speech, Walter Stone remembered, 'filled with enthusiasm, gusto, reminiscence, challenge and flamboyance'.[9] The members of the Savage Club gave him a standing ovation, and the occasion was like an echo of a Jorgensen speech made in 1840, which Stephensen had described in *The Viking of Van Diemen's Land*:

> His appearance on the platform, to speak with fluency and lucidity, was loudly applauded ... Everyone in the audience knew him and was aware of his many faults, which he himself had so candidly avowed in print. As individuals they might avoid him or ignore him, pass him in the street with pity or amused contempt; but now, in a crowd, as he stood before them to express in clear words ideas of which they enthusiastically approved, they spontaneously cheered him for his good and great qualities, and forgot his faults. That tribute of a long and loud cheer for the dauntless old man cost them nothing; but it was none the less sincere for that ...
>
> As he sat down after his speech, then rose again to bow his acknowledgments of the prolonged applause, he felt that at last he had won, if only for that moment, a recognition that was overdue.[10]

After the applause from the members of the Savage Club had died away, Stephensen rose again, thanked them, and fell dead in his seat.

'Trust him to finish up flamboyantly!', Ian Mudie wrote to A. D. Hope.[11] The obituaries described him as a 'noted literary figure', a 'Sydney publisher' and 'The Man Called "Inky"', but it was his old antagonist and former ally, the *Bulletin*, which summed him up most succinctly: 'Few will ever be found to agree with his political ideas, even among those who considered his internment during World War II was unjust, but his literary achievements and his passion for Australian literature will be remembered when the Australia First affair is forgotten'.[12]

The funeral service was held at the Northern Suburbs Crematorium, a not inappropriate staging place for a restless spirit who had looked back with pride on his Nordic ancestry. In the panegyric address Walter Stone avoided the more controversial aspects of Stephensen's life, describing his departed friend as an 'unpredictable radical'.[13] Stone was also careful to keep his eye on the chapel clock. The crematorium staff allowed only a limited time for each funeral and seemed as anxious as Stephensen's enemies had always been to transform him quickly into ashes.

During the course of a life of intellectual and literary adventuring, Inky himself had carefully kept one eye on posterity. To the end he had been sustained by the hope that, Phoenix-like, his reputation and achievements might some day be resurrected.

Abbreviations

AA   Australian Archives, Canberra
FL   Fryer Library, Brisbane
ML   Mitchell Library, Sydney
NLA   National Library of Australia, Canberra
S   P. R. Stephensen
SP   Stephensen Papers (MSS 1284), Mitchell Library, Sydney. (An uncatalogued collection. Stephensen's own letters here are usually carbon copies.)
SPFL   Stephensen Papers, Fryer Library, Brisbane. Principally the Walter Stone Collection (MSS 55) and the Jack Lockyer Collection.

Notes

Unless otherwise noted, interviews cited were conducted by the author and are in the author's possession.

A question mark before a date indicates that the date is conjectural.

1: Wartime Rebel

[1] Unless otherwise noted, the sources for Stephensen's family history and childhood years are: Jules L. Tardent, *The Swiss-Australian Tardent Family History and Genealogy*; obituaries of Henry Tardent in *Queenslander*, 12 September 1929, p. 17, and *Queensland Agricultural Journal*, October 1929; S talking about Biggenden and his family, tape (1961), Box K164729, SP; interviews with Rosaline and Eric Stephensen (1977-81).
[2] See *The Bushwhackers: Sketches of Life in the Australian Outback*.
[3] Unless otherwise noted, the sources for Stephensen's time at M.B.G.S. are: S, 'The Maryborough Boys' Grammar School', *Palma* (school magazine), 1956, pp. 21-5; S. E. A. Walker, 'School Days with Percy', Fotheringham Papers (MSS 46), FL.
[4] School prospectus, Box Y2150, SP.
[5] Ibid. His academic record is in SPFL, and his athletic record in Box Y2150, SP.
[6] *Maryborough Chronicle*, 5 December 1918. See also Jim Allen, 'Aspects of V. Gordon Childe', *Labour History*, no. 12 (May 1967), pp. 52-9; and Bruce G. Trigger, *Gordon Childe: Revolutions in Archeology* (London, Thames & Hudson, 1980).
[7] Interview with Manning Clark (1981).
[8] *Maryborough Chronicle*, 5 December 1918.
[9] Raymond Evans, Loyalty and Disloyalty: Social and Ideological Conflict in Queensland during the Great War, p. 414.
[10] *Maryborough Chronicle*, 5 December 1918.

2: Students and Workers

[1] *Publicist*, January 1938, p. 23.
[2] Raymond Evans, Loyalty and Disloyalty: Social and Ideological Conflict in Queensland during the Great War, pp. 421-5.
[3] Interviews with Herbert Burton, Kathleen Campbell-Brown, and Lord Roberthall (1980-81).
[4] S to parents, 13 July 1919, Box Y2135, SP.
[5] Evans, pp. 444-78.
[6] For Jack Lindsay at university, see Lindsay, *Life Rarely Tells* (London, Bodley Head, 1958); and S, *Kookaburras and Satyrs: Some Recollections of the Fanfrolico Press*.
[7] WEA Queensland Central Council Minutes, 1919-25, John Oxley Library (OM 64), Brisbane.
[8] Jack Lindsay, *Life Rarely Tells*, pp. 132, 137.
[9] S to parents, 27 April 1919, Box Y2135, SP.
[10] *Queensland University Magazine*, June 1919, p. 9.

[11] Ibid., October 1919, p. 34.
[12] Ibid., August, 1919, pp. 14-16; Minutes of Senate Meeting, 10 October 1919, University of Queensland Archives (S2).
[13] Fred Paterson, 'The Early Years', *60 Years of Struggle*, vol. 1 (1980), pp. 7-15; and interview with Fred Paterson, Audio-Visual Library, University of Queensland.
[14] Vere Gordon Childe, *How Labour Governs: A Study of Workers' Representation in Australia* (1923. Melbourne, Melbourne University Press, 1964), p. xxi.
[15] *Daily Mail* (Brisbane), 13, 15, 16, 17 September 1919.
[16] Paterson, 'The Early Years', p. 11; Richard Fotheringham, 'Biographical Study of Percy Reginald Stephensen, 1901-32', p. 22; Minutes of Senate Meetings, 10 October and 14 November 1919, University of Queensland Archives (S2); and Mary Murnane, The Workers' Educational Association of Queensland 1913-1939.
[17] Frank Anstey, *Red Europe* (Melbourne, Frazer & Jenkinson, ? 1919). See also Paterson, 'The Early Years', p. 10.
[18] Anstey, *Red Europe*, p. 192.
[19] Evans, p. 512.
[20] Frank Anstey, *The Kingdom of Shylock* (Melbourne, Labor Call, rev. ed. 1917).
[21] S. E. A. Walker, 'Schooldays with Percy', p. 2, Fotheringham Papers (MSS 46), FL.
[22] See Evans, p. 512.
[23] Jules L. Tardent, *The Swiss-Australian Tardent Family History and Genealogy*, p. 216; Jack Lindsay, 'Nietzsche', *Queensland University Magazine*, October 1920, pp. 13-15.
[24] *Queensland University Magazine*, May and August 1920.
[25] Norman Lindsay, *Creative Effort* (London, Cecil Palmer, 1924). *Art in Australia* published the first small edition of this work in 1920, but Lindsay revised and expanded it for the 1924 London edition. Quotations are from this London edition. See also Craig Munro, 'Two Boys from Queensland: P. R. Stephensen and Jack Lindsay', in Bernard Smith (ed.), *Culture and History: Essays in Honour of Jack Lindsay*.
[26] Norman Lindsay, *Creative Effort*, p. 124. For a more detailed evaluation of Norman Lindsay's philosophy see John Docker, *Australian Cultural Elites* (Sydney, Angus & Robertson, 1974); and Vincent Buckley, 'Utopianism and Vitalism', *Quadrant*, vol. 3, no. 2 (1958-59).
[27] Norman Lindsay to Hugh McCrae, undated letter, *Letters of Norman Lindsay*, ed. R. G. Howarth and A. W. Barker, p. 153.
[28] *Queensland University Magazine*, May 1920, pp. 8-9.
[29] Ibid., August 1920, p. 16.
[30] Ibid., pp. 17-18.
[31] Ibid., October 1920, p. 42.
[32] S to Rosaline Stephensen, 25 November 1920 (letter in the possession of Rosaline Stephensen). See also *Brisbane Courier*, 22 November 1920, p. 7; and Minutes of Professorial Board Meeting, 24 November 1920, University of Queensland Archives.
[33] *Galmahra*, May 1921, p. 5. See also *Kookaburras and Satyrs*, p. 13.
[34] Fotheringham, pp. 27-8; Jack Lindsay, *Life Rarely Tells*, p. 223.
[35] *Galmahra*, August 1921, p. 81; letter to Registrar from S and others, 9 September 1921, University of Queensland Archives (130).
[36] S to Rosaline Stephensen, 6 June 1921 (letter in the possession of Rosaline Stephensen).
[37] *Galmahra*, May 1921, p. 57.
[38] *Argo*, July 1921, p. 10.
[39] *Advocate*, 10 February 1922.
[40] WEA Minutes 1919-1925, John Oxley Library, Brisbane.
[41] Interview with Herbert Burton (1981).
[42] 'Viewing an Eclipse', *New Statesman*, 18 June 1927, pp. 309-10.
[43] Lord Roberthall, 'Notes about P. R. Stephensen, 1918-1932', pp. 6-7, Fotheringham Papers (MSS 46), FL.
[44] *Galmahra*, May 1923, pp. 28, 31. The Fryer Library at the University of Queensland was named in memory of J. D. Fryer.
[45] S to Herbert Burton, 28 July 1923, Box K164720, SP.
[46] Paterson, 'The Early Years'; and interview, Audio-Visual Library, University of Queensland.
[47] S to Herbert Burton, 28 July 1923, Box K164720, SP.
[48] Ibid.
[49] Plan for a Soviet Queensland State is in SPFL. Also mentioned in S to B. H. Molesworth, 15 April 1925, Box Y2148, SP.
[50] S to Herbert Burton, 28 July 1923, Box K164720, SP.
[51] *Daily Standard*, 11 September 1923.
[52] Ibid., 15 October 1923.

⁵³ Application for Rhodes Scholarship, October 1923, University of Queensland Archives (135).
⁵⁴ Reference from L. D. Edwards, 17 October 1923, Box Y2149, SP.
⁵⁵ Interview with A. K. Thomson (1981).
⁵⁶ Interview with J. A. Hunt (1981).
⁵⁷ S to Burton and Hall, 26 December 1923, Box K164720, SP.
⁵⁸ Ibid. Also interview with Rosaline Stephensen (1981).
⁵⁹ S to Burton and Hall, 26 December 1923, Box K164720, SP.
⁶⁰ *Daily Standard*, 22 December 1923, p. 10, and 14 July 1924, p. 10. Richard Aldington's introduction to the Penguin editions of *Kangaroo* incorrectly states that Stephensen wrote one of the only two reviews the novel received in Australia, although Stephensen was certainly involved in the publication of the *Daily Standard* review.
⁶¹ *Daily Standard*, 31 March 1924, p. 10.
⁶² *Queensland Times*, ? July 1924; H. E. Roberts to S, 3 August 1924, Box Y2143, SP.
⁶³ S to Hall and Burton, 16 July 1924, Box K164720, SP.
⁶⁴ S to R. V. Smith, 27 August 1924, Box Y2149, SP.
⁶⁵ Watch now in the possession of Jack Lockyer.
⁶⁶ S to R. V. Smith, 27 August 1924, Box Y2149, SP.
⁶⁷ Ibid.
⁶⁸ S to R. V. Smith, 6 September 1924, Box Y2149, SP.
⁶⁹ Ibid.
⁷⁰ *Workers' Weekly* (Sydney), 22 August 1924.
⁷¹ S to R. V. Smith, 6 September 1924, Box Y2149, SP.
⁷² Ship newspaper is in Box Y2149, SP; also notes on his trip to England in Box K164720, SP.
⁷³ *Argo*, September 1924, p. 14.

3: A Bolshevik comes to Oxford

¹ Lord Roberthall, 'Notes about P. R. Stephensen 1918-1932', pp. 7-8, Fotheringham Papers (MSS 46), FL; also S to family, 13 October 1924, SPFL.
² S to family, 13 October 1924, SPFL; S to Joseph Maguire, 12 November, Box Y2144, SP.
³ *Daily Standard*, 26 November 1924.
⁴ S to family, 13 October 1924, SPFL.
⁵ *Cherwell* (Oxford), 11 October 1924, p. 3.
⁶ Queen's College Archives, Oxford.
⁷ Interview with A. J. P. Taylor (1980). See also Harold Acton, *Memoirs of an Aesthete* (London, Methuen, 1948); and Martin Green, *Children of the Sun: A Narrative of "Decadence" in England after 1918* (New York, Basic Books, 1976), especially p. 6. The character Blanche was based on Acton and his friend Brian Howard.
⁸ *Cherwell*, 11 October 1924, p. 4.
⁹ *Maryborough Chronicle*, 25 May 1926.
¹⁰ The address is in Box Y2135, SP.
¹¹ S to Joseph Maguire, 12 November 1924, Box Y2144, SP.
¹² A. J. P. Taylor interview. See also M. P. Ashley and C. T. Saunders, *Red Oxford: A History of the Growth of Socialism in the University of Oxford* (Oxford, Oxford University Labour Club, 1933).
¹³ *Daily Standard*, 9 December 1924.
¹⁴ Manuscripts of articles he submitted to English papers are in Box Y2135, SP.
¹⁵ *Cherwell*, 24 and 31 January 1925, 7 and 14 February 1925.
¹⁶ Ibid., 9 and 16 May 1925.
¹⁷ The balance sheet of the Biggenden shop is in Box Y2149, SP. See L. A. Crosby et al. (eds), *A Manual for Prospective Rhodes Scholars* (New York, Oxford University Press, 1927); and C. W. Carter, 'Expenses of a Rhodes Scholar', *American Oxonian*, vol. 11, no. 1 (January 1924), pp. 1-6.
¹⁸ S to Rosaline Stephensen, 28 April 1925 (letter in the possession of Rosaline Stephensen).
¹⁹ Ibid., also *Daily Standard*, 5 June 1925.
²⁰ *Daily Standard*, 22 June 1925.
²¹ Lord Roberthall, letter to author, 11 August 1981 (author's possession).
²² S to B. H. Molesworth, 15 April 1925, Box Y2148, SP.
²³ S to R. V. Smith, 15 April 1925, Box Y2148, SP.
²⁴ Novel manuscript 'Clean Earth' is in Box K164723, SP; *Biblionews*, vol. 12, no. 2 (February 1959), pp. 7-8.
²⁵ S to Rosaline Stephensen, 28 April 1925 (letter in the possession of Rosaline Stephensen).

[26] S to Winifred, 16 May 1925, Box K164719, SP.
[27] Interview with Jack Lockyer (1980).
[28] Interview with A. J. P. Taylor (1980). See also Chapman Pincher, *Their Trade is Treachery* (London, Sidgwick & Jackson, 1981), p. 96; Tom Driberg, *Ruling Passions*, chapters 5 and 6; and Graham Greene, *A Sort of Life* (London, Bodley Head, 1971), p. 132.
[29] Taylor interview. See also Henry Pelling, *The British Communist Party: A Historical Profile* (London, Adam & Charles Black, 1975).
[30] Thomas Bell to S and Thomas, 8 June 1925, Box Y2143, SP. Their report on Indians at Oxford is also in Box Y2143. It was subsequently published as Command Paper 2682, 'Communist Papers', *British Parliamentary Papers*, vol. 23 (1926), pp. 681-3.
[31] S to Joe Maguire, 17 June 1925, Box Y2139, SP. Copies of *The Searchlight* are in Box Y2146, SP.
[32] Tutors' reports, 28 July 1925, University of Queensland Archives; S to B. H. Molesworth, 15 April 1925, Box Y2148, SP.
[33] The manuscripts of these papers are in Boxes Y2123 and Y2135, SP.
[34] *Communist Review*, vol. 6, no. 9 (January 1926), pp. 412-18; Roberthall, 'Notes about P. R. Stephensen', p 13; Richard Fotheringham, 'Biographical Study of Percy Reginald Stephensen, 1901-32', p. 54, FL.
[35] D. H. Lawrence letter, 9 October 1925, in Harry T. Moore, *The Priest of Love: A Life of D. H. Lawrence*, p. 409.
[36] *The Times*, 15 and 16 October 1925, 26 November 1925.
[37] Communist Party to S, 16 November 1925, Box Y2143, SP.
[38] *Cherwell*, 14 November 1925, p. 105.
[39] *The Times*, 9 December 1925, p. 14; E. M. Walker to F. J. Wylie, 16 December 1925, Rhodes House records, Oxford.
[40] ? to S, 17 December 1925, Box Y2143, SP; *The Times*, 18 December 1925, p. 7.
[41] *The Times*, 11 January 1926, p. 9.
[42] All this correspondence between 15 and 17 January 1926 is in Box Y2143, SP.
[43] S to Winifred, 17 January 1926, Box K164719, SP: S to Communist Party secretary, 17 January 1926, Box Y 2143, SP.
[44] R. Stewart to S, 20 January 1926, Box Y2143, SP.
[45] S to F. J. Wylie, 18 January 1926, Box Y2143, SP; Warden's record book, 1924-25, and reports to the Rhodes Trust Selection Committee, Rhodes House records, Oxford.
[46] *Brisbane Courier*, 21 January 1926; *Daily Standard*, 23 January 1926; *Daily Mail*, 27 January 1926; (Brisbane) *Telegraph*, ? 27 January 1926.
[47] *Daily Standard*, 7 January 1927.
[48] *Daily Sketch* (London), 18 January 1926, p. 3. Knox's broadcast was later published in Ronald A. Knox, *Essays in Satire* (London, Sheed & Ward, 1928) as 'A Forgotten Interlude', pp. 279-87. Later in 1926 Knox became Catholic chaplain of Oxford.
[49] *The Times*, 16 February 1926, pp. 14, 15. See also *Cherwell*, 13 February 1926.
[50] *Communist Review*, vol. 6, no. 10 (February 1926), pp. 443-7; the Majlis dinner menu is in Box Y2143, SP.
[51] See Gabriel Gorodetsky, *The Precarious Truce: Anglo-Soviet Relations 1924-27* (Cambridge University Press, 1977).
[52] Jack Lindsay to S, ? April 1926, Box Y2121, SP.
[53] Jack Lindsay, *Fanfrolico and After* (London, Bodley Head, 1962), p. 23.
[54] Ibid., pp. 23-6; interview with Jack Lindsay (1980).
[55] Poetry manuscripts in Box Y2134, SP.
[56] *New Statesman*, 18 June 1927, pp. 309-10.
[57] For the background of the strike, see *British Gazette*, no. 6, 11 May 1926; Alfred F. Havighurst, *Twentieth-Century Britain* (New York, Harper & Row, 1966), and Gorodetsky, *Precarious Truce*.
[58] Taylor interview; John Parker, 'Oxford Politics in the Late Twenties', *Political Quarterly*, vol. 45, no. 2 (1974), pp. 216-31; Margaret Cole, *The Life of G. D. H. Cole* (London, Macmillan, 1971).
[59] S to Winifred, ? 4 May 1926, Box K164719, SP.
[60] Letter from Tom Inglis Moore, 9 May 1926, Tom Inglis Moore Papers, NLA.
[61] Box Y2135, SP.
[62] *British Gazette* and *British Worker*, issues for May 1926. Copies are held in the British Library, London.
[63] *Oxford Times*, 11 May 1926.
[64] *Oxford Workers' Strike Bulletin*, 7 May 1926. Copies of this *Bulletin* are in Box Y2146, SP.

Stephensen (right) with Frank Clune at a book signing in the late 1940s

Stephensen and Winifred with friends at Bethanga, 1950

Stephensen and Albert Namatjira, the artist; the photograph was taken during a trip with Frank Clune to Central Australia in the late 1950s

Inky and Winifred, with Jules Tardent, Sydney, 1961, not long after Inky's first heart attack

65 S to Winifred, ? 13 May 1926, Box K164719, SP; Attorney-General's Department, Investigation Branch Correspondence Files, CRS A369, Item D/480, AA. See also Richard Hall, *The Secret State: Australia's Spy Industry*, p. 31.
66 Oxford essays by S are in Box Y2134, SP.
67 His Communist Party Membership Card is in Box Y2143, SP.

4: Bloomsbury Fanfrolics

1 Jack Lindsay, 'Aids to Vision', *Southerly*, vol. 14, no. 3 (1953), pp. 204-5; A. G. Stephens: *Selected Writings*, ed. Leon Cantrell (Sydney, Angus & Robertson, 1978), p. 353.
2 Harry Chaplin, *The Fanfrolico Press: A Survey*, pp. 8-9. Chaplin has in his possession Kirtley's unpublished manuscript on the history of the Fanfrolico Press, but refused to make it available, even for research purposes. Unless otherwise noted, much of the background of this chapter is from Chaplin, *The Fanfrolico Press* and Jack Lindsay, *Fanfrolico and After* (London, Bodley Head, 1962).
3 Lindsay, *Fanfrolico and After*, pp. 21-2.
4 Ibid., p. 167; Jack Lindsay to S, ? June 1926, Box Y2121, SP. See also Craig Munro, 'Two Boys from Queensland: P. R. Stephensen and Jack Lindsay', in Bernard Smith (ed.), *Culture and History: Essays in Honour of Jack Lindsay*.
5 S to Winifred, ? 30 May 1926, Box K164719, SP; Jack Lindsay, *Fanfrolico and After*, p. 31.
6 Lindsay, *Fanfrolico and After*, p. 52.
7 S to Jack Lindsay, verse letter, ? May 1926, Box Y2120, SP. 'Rus Insula' is in Box Y2134, SP.
8 *Times Literary Supplement*, 16 September 1926, p. 607; Jack Kirtley to S, ? November 1926, Box Y2142, SP.
9 Jack Kirtley to S, 11 October 1926, Box Y2142, SP.
10 Various letters, Jack Kirtley to S, ? October and November 1926, Box Y2142, SP; Chaplin, p. 23.
11 Jack Kirtley to S, ? September 1926, Box Y2142, SP.
12 Various Letters Jack Lindsay to S, ? October 1926, Box Y2121, SP.
13 S to Winifred, 24 October 1926, Box K164719, SP.
14 Jack Kirtley to S, ? November 1926, Box Y2142, SP.
15 Jack Lindsay to S, ? November 1926, Box Y2121, SP.
16 *Cherwell*, 11 December 1926, p. 332.
17 A copy of the company registration is in the Fotheringham Papers (MSS 46), FL; Jack Kirtley to S, ? December 1926, Box Y2142, SP; S to Winifred, ? January 1927, Box K164719, SP.
18 S to Winifred, ? March 1927, and Winifred to S, 3 March 1927, Box K164719, SP.
19 Various letters Jack Lindsay to S, and draft agreements, in Box Y2121, SP.
20 S to family, 31 March 1927, SPFL; S to Rosaline Stephensen, 30 May 1927 (letter in the possession of Rosaline Stephensen).
21 Various undated letters Jack Lindsay to S, Box Y2121, SP. See also Lindsay, *Fanfrolico and After*, p. 102, which incorrectly suggests that Lindsay put Partridge off; Lord Roberthall, 'Expatriate Publishing', *Meanjin*, vol. 33, no. 2 (June 1974), pp. 170-6; and Eric Partridge, *The First Three Years: An Account and a Bibliography of the Scholartis Press*.
22 Tom Driberg, *Ruling Passions*, pp. 68-70; Jack Lindsay to S, ? March 1927, Box Y2121, SP.
23 The Harrington book was published by the Fanfrolico as *The Metamorphosis of Ajax* (1929). See also Lindsay, *Fanfrolico and After*, p. 73; and Cecil Gray, *Peter Warlock: A Memoir of Philip Heseltine*.
24 Full details, including sources, of Stephensen's WTM involvement, in Craig Munro, 'P. R. Stephensen and the Early Workers' Theatre Movement in London', *Australasian Drama Studies*, vol. 1, no. 2 (April 1983), pp. 124-54, which also includes the text of one of Stephensen's plays, *Blasting the Reds*.
25 The manuscript of *Stanley's Pipe Dream* is in Box Y2136, SP. The MI5 Reports are in Attorney-General's Department, Investigation Branch Correspondence Files, CRS A369, Item D/480, AA.
26 Examination results in *Oxford University Calendar* (1928), pp. 246-7; see also Lord Roberthall, 'Notes about P. R. Stephensen, 1918-1932', Fotheringham Papers (MSS 46), FL.
27 Jack Lindsay to S, ? June 1927, Box Y2121, SP. Lunachasky was the Soviet commissar for education.
28 Norman Lindsay to S, ? May 1927, Box Y2135, SP.
29 Jack Lindsay to S, ? April 1927, Box Y2121, SP.
30 Norman Lindsay to S, ? May 1927, Box Y2135, SP.

[31] Ibid.
[32] Original typescript letter, S to Norman Lindsay, on Fanfrolico Press letterhead, ? June 1927, Box Y2135, SP.
[33] S to Norman Lindsay, 6 November 1927, Box Y2135, SP. This letter mentions earlier attempts at writing to Lindsay.
[34] Jack Kirtley to S, ? November 1926, Box Y2142, SP.
[35] See, for example, *Times Literary Supplement*, 27 January 1927, p. 61; 24 March 1927, p. 216; and 17 November 1927, p. 838.
[36] Chaplin, p. 26; *The Fanfrolico Press: Catalogue & Announcements*, January 1928; and Lindsay, *Fanfrolico and After*, p. 71.
[37] Jack Lindsay to Bruce Muirden, ? May 1964 (letter in the possession of Bruce Muirden).
[38] The Blake lines are from the poem 'Human Abstract'. See also Roberthall, 'Notes about P. R. Stephensen', p. 11.
[39] Lindsay, *Fanfrolico and After*, p. 99. For details of O'Flaherty see P. A. Doyle, *Liam O'Flaherty* (New York, Twayne, 1971); and Patrick Sheeran, *The Novels of Liam O'Flaherty: A Study in Romantic Realism* (Dublin, Wolfhound Press, 1976).
[40] 'Plough Inn' is in Box Y2136, and 'To the Fitzroy Tavern' is in Box Y2135, SP; Lindsay, *Fanfrolico and After*, p. 98.
[41] Hugh McCrae, *Satyrs and Sunlight* (London, Fanfrolico Press, 1928).
[42] S to Rosaline Stephensen, 4 April 1928 (letter in the possession of Rosaline Stephensen).
[43] Bank receipt for the £200, 7 April 1928, Box Y2135, SP.
[44] Hal Collins to Fanfrolico Press, April 1928, Box Y2135, SP.
[45] Jack Lindsay to S, ? June 1928, Box Y2121, SP.
[46] *Fanfrolicana*, June 1928, pp. 5-7. Copy in SPFL.
[47] Manuscript is in Box Y2135, SP.
[48] Norman Lindsay to Jack Lindsay, ? August 1928, SPFL.
[49] S to Rosaline Stephensen, 30 May 1927 (letter in the possession of Rosaline Stephensen).
[50] *London Mercury*, August 1928, p. 348.
[51] *London Aphrodite*, no. 1 (August 1928), pp. 2, 64.
[52] *Times Literary Supplement*, 4 October 1928, p. 715.
[53] Roy Campbell, *The Collected Poems of Roy Campbell*, vol. 1 (1949. London, Bodley Head, 1955), p. 206.
[54] *Times Literary Supplement*, 26 July 1928, p. 555. For another highly critical review of Norman Lindsay's art, see Robert Hughes, *The Art of Australia* (1970. Ringwood, Penguin, 1981), pp. 83-5.
[55] Michael Wilding, introduction to *Life Rarely Tells*, by Jack Lindsay (Ringwood, Penguin, 1982), p. xiii. (This edition contains all three volumes of Jack Lindsay's autobiography.)
[56] Aldous Huxley, *Point Counter Point* (1928. London, Chatto & Windus, 1941), p. 178.
[57] Ibid., p. 168.
[58] *London Aphrodite*, no. 2 (October 1928), p. 160.
[59] Lindsay, *Fanfrolico and After*, p. 127.
[60] Ibid., pp. 109-10.
[61] Ibid., p. 107. Liam O'Flaherty also thought Jack Lindsay should 'stick to prose', O'Flaherty to S, 29 October 1928, Box Y2135, SP.
[62] Roberthall, 'Notes about P. R. Stephensen', p. 21.
[63] Walter Kaufman (ed.), *The Portable Nietzsche* (London, Chatto & Windus, 1971), p. 2.
[64] *The Antichrist of Nietzsche*, translated by P. R. Stephensen, Parts 24, 17. Further quotations from the *Antichrist* are from Stephensen's translation. For an account of how Nietzsche's philosophy was distorted and exploited by the Nazis see H. F. Peters, *Zarathustra's Sister: The Case of Elisabeth and Friedrich Nietzsche* (New York, Crown, 1977); and Michael Hamburger, 'A Craving for Hell: Nietzsche and the Nietzscheans', *Encounter*, vol. 19, no. 4 (October 1962), pp. 32-40.
[65] *Antichrist of Nietzsche*, Part 57.
[66] See Hermann Glaser, *The Cultural Roots of National Socialism*, translated by E. A. Menzc (London, Croom Helm, 1978), pp. 138-40.
[67] Jack Lindsay to author, March 1980 (letter in the possession of the author).
[68] Prospectus for the *Antichrist*, SPFL.
[69] *Antichrist of Nietzsche*, Final Part.
[70] This term—suggesting a folder of loose prints rather than a book—was first used by Lawrence himself on 2 April 1928 and then later by both Rhys Davies and Lawrence. In correspondence with the author in 1981, Jack Lindsay said he had never used the term. After Stephensen had visited Lawrence, however, the project was always referred to by Lawrence as a book.
[71] Liam O'Flaherty to S, 29 October 1928, Box Y2135, SP.

5: D. H. Lawrence and the Lord's Police

[1] Rhys Davies to S, 10 December 1928, Box Y2135, SP.
[2] *John Bull*, 20 October 1928, quoted in Edward Nehls (ed.), *D. H. Lawrence: A Composite Biography*, vol 3, pp. 262-3.
[3] See Vera Brittain, *Radclyffe Hall: A Case of Obscenity?*
[4] *London Aphrodite*, no. 2 (October 1928), pp. 86-92; Jack Lindsay, *Fanfrolico and After* (London, Bodley Head, 1962), p. 122; Nehls, *Lawrence*, vol 3, p. 301.
[5] Brittain, p. 95.
[6] Lindsay, p. 123.
[7] *Policeman of the Lord: A Political Satire*. The book is unpaginated.
[8] The pamphlet is in Box Y2119, SP.
[9] S, *Kookaburras and Satyrs: Some Recollections of the Fanfrolico Press*, p. 22.
[10] See Martin Green, *Children of the Sun: A Narrative of "Decadence" in England After 1918* (New York, Basic Books, 1976).
[11] See Eric Partridge, *The First Three Years: An Account and a Bibliography of the Scholartis Press*, pp. 24-6.
[12] Donald Thomas, *A Long Time Burning: A History of Literary Censorship in England* (London, Routledge & Kegan Paul, 1969), p. 314.
[13] D. H. Lawrence *Sex, Literature and Censorship*, ed. Harry T. Moore (London, Heinemann, 1955), pp. 202-3.
[14] Quoted in Nehls, vol. 3, p. 274.
[15] D. H. Lawrence to Jack Lindsay, 14 December 1928, in *Australian Literary Studies*, vol. 9, no. 2 (1979), pp. 242-3; D. H. Lawrence to S. S. Koteliansky, 14 December 1928, in *The Quest for Rananim: D. H. Lawrence's Letters to S. S. Koteliansky 1914-1930*, p. 369.
[16] French bill of sale for the Fanfrolico books, dated Nice 17 December 1928, is in Box Y2121, SP. Jack Lindsay, in *Fanfrolico and After*, p. 150, suggests Stephensen's trip was unsuccessful, but he may have confused this with a trip Kirtley and Stephensen made to Paris early in 1927.
[17] S to Winifred, ? 18 December 1928, Box K164719, SP.
[18] Recalled by Rhys Davies in a letter to Bruce Muirden, 22 March 1964 (letter in the possession of Bruce Muirden).
[19] D. H. Lawrence to Aldous Huxley, 23 December 1928, in *The Letters of D. H. Lawrence*, pp. 767-8; D. H. Lawrence to S. S. Koteliansky, 21 December 1928, in *Quest for Rananim*, pp. 370-1.
[20] Jack Lindsay to S, 19 December 1928, Box Y2121, SP. Details about Edward Goldston from interview with London bookseller, W. R. Fletcher (1980).
[21] D. H. Lawrence to S, ? 20 December 1928 (copy in the possession of the author).
[22] Ibid.
[23] Jack Lindsay rejected Lawrence's poems. See *Fanfrolico and After*, p. 152.
[24] S to D. H. Lawrence, ? 21 December 1928, Box Y2135, SP.
[25] D. H. Lawrence to S, 24 December 1928 (copy in the possession of the author).
[26] There are drafts or fragments of one or more letters from Stephensen to Jack Lindsay at this time, Box Y2121, SP.
[27] Jack Lindsay, ? December 1928, Box Y2121, SP.
[28] Various letters to S, ? December 1928, Box Y2121, SP.
[29] Liam O'Flaherty, *Shame the Devil*, p. 196; O'Flaherty to S, ? 29 December 1928, Box Y2135, SP.
[30] *London Aphrodite*, no. 3 (December 1928), p. 229.
[31] S to Winifred, 31 December 1928, Box K164719, SP.
[32] D. H. Lawrence to S, 2 January 1929 (incorrectly dated 1928 by Lawrence). Copy in the possession of the author.
[33] See Nehls, vol. 3, pp. 282-4, 294.
[34] D. H. Lawrence to Rhys Davies, 11 January 1929, in *Letters of D. H. Lawrence*, p. 780.
[35] D. H. Lawrence to Aldous Huxley, ? 23 December 1928, in *Letters of D. H. Lawrence*, pp. 767-8; D. H. Lawrence to Martin Secker, ? 23 December 1928, in *Letters from D. H. Lawrence to Martin Secker 1911-1930* (London, private, 1970), p. 113; D. H. Lawrence to S. S. Koteliansky, 21 December 1928, in *Quest for Rananim*, pp. 370-1; Nehls, vol. 3, p. 281.
[36] *Observer* (Sydney), 26 November 1960, p. 11. S gave the impression he brought all the Lawrence paintings back to England but the fact that he did bring three is verified by a list of paintings signed by Lawrence, copy in the possession of the author.
[37] D. H. Lawrence to S. S. Koteliansky, 11 January 1929, in *The Collected Letters of D. H. Lawrence*, vol. 2, p. 1118.

[38] Jack Lindsay to S, ? January 1929, Box Y2121, SP.
[39] S to Norman Lindsay, 20 June 1929, Box Y2135, SP. The Mandrake Press company registration is in the Fotheringham Papers (MSS 46), FL. Information about Goldston from interview with W. R. Fletcher (1980).
[40] See Michael Wilding, *Political Fictions* (London, Routledge & Kegan Paul, 1980), pp. 162-3; also D. H. Lawrence, *Lady Chatterley's Lover* (1928. Harmondsworth, Penguin, 1960), pp. 74, 202, 272.
[41] See Lawrence, *Lady Chatterley's Lover*, pp. 226-7.
[42] See Norman Cohn, *Warrant for Genocide: The Myth of the Jewish World-Conspiracy*.
[43] *London Aphrodite*, no. 4 (February 1929), p. 278.
[44] D. H. Lawrence to S, 15 February 1929 (copy in the possession of the author).
[45] Manuscript of a Preface for a possible reprint of *Bushwhackers*, 1945, in Box Y2153, SP.
[46] D. H. Lawrence to S, 15 February 1929 and 1 March 1929 (copies in the possession of the author).
[47] D. H. Lawrence to S, 7 June 1929 (copy in the possession of the author).
[48] D. H. Lawrence to S, ? 17 June 1929 (copy in the possession of the author).
[49] 'Brent of Bin Bin' to S, August 1932, SPFL.
[50] *Times Literary Supplement*, 5 September 1929, p. 686; *All About Books*, 20 September 1929.
[51] See S, *The Foundations of Culture in Australia*, p. 11.
[52] S to Rosaline Stephensen, 30 May 1927 (letter in the possession of Rosaline Stephensen).
[53] S, *The Bushwhackers: Sketches of Life in the Australian Outback*, p. 42.
[54] Ibid., pp. 120-2.
[55] Quoted in Harry Chaplin, *The Fanfrolico Press: A Survey*, p. 78.
[56] D. H. Lawrence to G. Orioli, 18 April 1929, in *Collected Letters of D. H. Lawrence*, vol. 2, p. 1142.
[57] For more details on this episode see Craig Munro, '*Lady Chatterley* in London: The Story of the Secret Third Edition', in Michael Squires and Dennis Jackson (eds), *D. H. Lawrence's 'Lady': A New Look at Lady Chatterley's Lover*.
[58] D. H. Lawrence to Charles Lahr, 18 April 1929, in *Collected Letters of D. H. Lawrence*, vol. 2, p. 1143; D. H. Lawrence to Orioli, ? 9 May 1929, in Harry T. Moore, *The Priest of Love: A life of D. H. Lawrence*, p. 470.
[59] See Craig Munro, '*Lady Chatterley* in London'. The third edition is listed as Item B.II, in Warren Roberts, *A Bibliography of D. H. Lawrence*, p. 368.
[60] *Manchester Guardian*, 16 August 1929. See also Roberts, *Bibliography of D. H. Lawrence*, pp. 114-16.
[61] *London Aphrodite*, no. 5 (April 1929), pp. 338-41.
[62] D. H. Lawrence signed some of his paintings 'Lorenzo'.
[63] D. H. Lawrence to S, 1 May 1929 (copy in the possession of the author).
[64] D. H. Lawrence to S, 3 May 1929, in *Collected Letters of D. H. Lawrence*, vol. 2, pp. 1145-6; D. H. Lawrence to S, 1 March 1929 (copy in the possession of the author).
[65] D. H. Lawrence to Aldous Huxley, 17 May 1929, and D. H. Lawrence to Max Mohr, 25 May 1929, in *Collected Letters of D. H. Lawrence*, vol. 2, pp. 1152-6.
[66] D. H. Lawrence to S, 25 May 1929, Humanities Research Center, University of Texas Library.
[67] S to D. H. Lawrence, ? 21 July 1929 (copy in the possession of the author).
[68] D. H. Lawrence to S, 7 and 12 June 1929 (copies in the possession of the author).
[69] S to Norman Lindsay, 20 June 1929, Box Y2135, SP.
[70] D. H. Lawrence to S, 7 June 1929 (copy in the possession of the author).
[71] D. H. Lawrence to S. S. Koteliansky, 21 December 1928, in *Quest for Rananim*, pp. 370-1.
[72] See Nehls, vol. 3, pp. 326-9, 342-6.
[73] Harry T. Moore, introduction to *Sex, Literature and Censorship* by D. H. Lawrence (London, Heinemann, 1955), p. 21.
[74] D. H. Lawrence to Dorothy Warren, 14 July 1929, in *Collected Letters of D. H. Lawrence*, vol. 2, pp. 1164-5.
[75] S to D. H. Lawrence, ? 21 July 1929 (copy in the possession of the author).
[76] Ibid.
[77] *The Times*, 9 August 1929; D. H. Lawrence to Dorothy Warren, 14 August 1929, in *Collected Letters of D. H. Lawrence*, vol. 2, pp. 1179-80.
[78] *London Aphrodite*, no. 6 (July 1929), pp. 421-32.
[79] D. H. Lawrence to Frieda's sister Else, 12 June 1929, in Frieda Lawrence, '*Not I—But the Wind...*' (1935. Cedric Chivers, 1973), p. 252.

6: Mandrake, Magic and Depression

[1] List of Mandrake contracts in Box Y2120, SP. Mandrake catalogues of Autumn 1929 and May 1930 in Boxes Y2123 and Y2120, SP.
[2] Jack Lindsay, *Fanfrolico and After* (London, Bodley Head, 1962), p. 167.
[3] *Observer* (London), ? November, 1929, a clipping in Box K164730, SP.
[4] For more details of Crowley see: John Symonds, *The Great Beast: the Life of Aleister Crowley*; Aleister Crowley, *The Spirit of Solitude: An Autohagiography*, 2 vols (London, Mandrake Press, 1929); S, *The Legend of Aleister Crowley*; and Israel Regardie, *The Eye in the Triangle: An Interpretation of Aleister Crowley*.
[5] *John Bull*, 24 March 1923, quoted in S, *Legend of Aleister Crowley*, p. 152.
[6] Crowley, vol. 1, p. 50.
[7] Ibid., p. 189.
[8] Ibid., p. 10.
[9] W. Somerset Maugham, *The Magician* (1908. London, Heinemann, 1956), pp. viii-xi.
[10] See Francis Dickie, 'Aleister "Black Magic" Crowley', *American Book Collector*, vol. 11 (1961), pp. 34-7.
[11] Symonds, p. 62.
[12] Lindsay, p. 173.
[13] Lord Roberthall, 'Notes about P. R. Stephensen, 1918-1932', p. 24, Fotheringham Papers (MSS 46), FL; Credit Report on the Mandrake Press, 9 September 1929, in Aleister Crowley Papers (G. J. Yorke Collection), Warburg Institute, London.
[14] D. H. Lawrence to Rhys Davies, 24 August 1929, in *The Letters of D. H. Lawrence*, pp. 818-19.
[15] D. H. Lawrence to S, 5 September 1929 (copy in the possession of the author).
[16] *Times Literary Supplement*, 21 November 1929, p. 938.
[17] See, for example, Patrick F. Sheeran, *The Novels of Liam O'Flaherty: A Study in Romantic Realism* (Dublin, Wolfhound Press, 1976); and Philip Lindsay, *I'd Live the Same Life Over*, p. 174.
[18] S, *Publicist*, September 1937.
[19] Gerald Griffin, *The Wild Geese: Pen Portraits of Famous Irish Exiles* (London, Jarrolds, 1938), p. 30; Mandrake Press, May 1930 Catalogue, p. 15, in Box Y2120, SP.
[20] *Nation* (Sydney), 31 January 1959, p. 11.
[21] Liam O'Flaherty to author, 24 March 1980 (letter in the possession of the author).
[22] Liam O'Flaherty to S, ? 1930, Box K164720, SP.
[23] See Lindsay, chapters 16 and 17; Philip Lindsay, *I'd Live the Same Life Over*; and Harry Chaplin, *The Fanfrolico Press: A Survey*.
[24] Philip Lindsay, p. 177.
[25] Ibid., pp. 174-5.
[26] S to Gerald Yorke, 12 December 1953, Box Y2110, SP.
[27] S to Edward Goldston, 21 January 1930, Box Y2120, SP.
[28] S to D. H. Lawrence, 31 October 1929 (copy in the possession of the author).
[29] D. H. Lawrence to S. S. Koteliansky, ? 27 November 1929, in *The Collected Letters of D. H. Lawrence*, vol. 2, p. 1217.
[30] The drafts, handwritten as well as typescript, are in Boxes Y2144 and K164723, SP. The typescript draft is 'Dedicated to the Memory of David Herbert Lawrence'. This indicates that it was typed during 1930 or later.
[31] Edward Nehls (ed.), *D. H. Lawrence: A Composite Biography*, vol. 3, p. 284.
[32] S to J. K. Moir, 6 June 1952, Box Y2116, SP.
[33] On 3 February 1954 Gerald Yorke sent S a copy of the suppressed dedication to *The Legend of Aleister Crowley*, Box Y2110, SP. Crowley himself mentioned the problem with the printer over libel in a letter to Karl Germer, 8 February 1930 (letter in the possession of Gerald Yorke).
[34] S, *The Legend of Aleister Crowley*, pp. 19-21, 30.
[35] S described this in a letter to J. K. Moir, 6 June 1952, Box Y2116, SP.
[36] Prospectus for the *Confessions of Aleister Crowley*, Box Y2117, SP.
[37] Aleister Crowley to Karl Germer, 31 August 1929 (letter in the possession of Gerald Yorke).
[38] Draft syndicate plan in Box Y2143, SP.
[39] *Evening News* to S, 14 February 1930, Box Y2135, SP.
[40] Note by Jack Lockyer on a letter from Robert Hall to S, ? 1929, Box K164720, SP.
[41] Undated typescript, Box K164720, SP.
[42] A copy of the banned lecture, as printed by S, is in Box Y2116, SP. See also Symonds, p. 271.

[43] D. H. Lawrence to Laurence Pollinger, 20 February 1930, in *Collected Letters*, vol. 2, p. 1244.
[44] Description by S of Mandrake Press history, Box Y2120, SP; Gerald Yorke to S, 24 December 1953, Box Y2110, SP; Note by S on *The Confessions of Aleister Crowley*, February 1956, Box Y2109, SP; and Mandrake Press, May 1930 Catalogue, Box Y2120, SP.
[45] Gerald Yorke, correspondence with author, August 1982 (letter in the possession of the author).
[46] S to Aleister Crowley, 3 May 1930, Box Y2143, SP.
[47] Aleister Crowley to S, ? 20 April 1930, SPFL; Aleister Crowley to S, 9 May 1930, Box K164724, SP; Aleister Crowley to S, ? May 1930, Box Y2143, SP.
[48] Lord Roberthall to author, 16 July 1982 (letter in the possession of the author).
[49] Roberthall, 'Notes about P. R. Stephensen', p. 27.
[50] Symonds, p. 275.
[51] Jack Lockyer to author, 30 April 1983 (letter in the possession of the author).
[52] Interview with Jack Lockyer (1980).
[53] Ibid.
[54] Liam O'Flaherty, *Shame the Devil*, p. 136. Mandrake Press did not publish O'Flaherty's book which appeared as *I Went to Russia* (London, Cape, 1931).
[55] O'Flaherty, *I Went to Russia*, pp. 52, 68, 72.
[56] O'Flaherty, *Shame the Devil*, pp. 135, 30.
[57] The pencilled prospectus is in Box K164724, SP.
[58] S to C. R. Bradish, 30 July 1930, Box Y2135, SP.
[59] Liam O'Flaherty to S, ? September 1930, Box Y2135, SP. The printer's quote is in Box K164726, and the sample issues in Boxes Y2135 and Y2146, SP.
[60] Lawrence had suggested Stephensen be involved in the 'Squib'. See Lawrence to Charles Lahr, ? 14 September and 7 October 1929, in *Collected Letters*, vol. 2, pp. 1196, 1206.
[61] R. Thynne to S, 30 November 1930, and note of shareholders meeting, 29 November 1930, in Box Y2120, SP.
[62] Gerald Yorke to S, 24 December 1953, and S to Gerald Yorke, 26 January 1954, in Box Y2110, SP. See also *John Bull* 27 December 1930, which accuses Thynne of fraud.
[63] Mandrake Press Balance Sheet at 31 December 1929, Box Y2120, SP; Roberthall, p. 23.
[64] The American cartoon strip by Lee Falk, drawn by Phil Davies, began on 11 June 1934. It seems likely that a copy of Crowley's *Confessions*, published by the Mandrake Press, suggested the name Mandrake to the originators of the cartoon. Aleister Crowley himself died in England in 1947, after living for some time in an old people's home. See Symonds, *The Great Beast*.
[65] S, telegram to family, 10 November 1930, Box Y2135, SP (original telegram in the possession of Rosaline Stephensen); interview with Jack Lockyer (1980).
[66] Lindsay, p. 179; Fanfrolico Press Balance Sheet as at 1 August 1930, Box Y2121, SP.
[67] Jack Lindsay to S, undated, and S to Jack Lindsay, 25 December 1930, Box Y2121, SP.
[68] Ditty in SPFL.
[69] Cecil Gray, *Peter Warlock: A Memoir of Philip Heseltine*, pp. 259-89.

7: Cutting Adrift

[1] Jack Lockyer to author, 23 May 1983 (letter in the possession of the author).
[2] S to Val Valentine, May 1931, Box Y2120, SP.
[3] Information supplied in interviews with Jack Lockyer and Rosaline Stephensen (1980).
[4] [S], *A Master of Hounds: Being the Life Story of Harry Buckland of Ashford*, pp. xviii, 89.
[5] S to Rosaline Stephensen, 21 July 1931 (letter in the possession of Rosaline Stephensen).
[6] Arthur Freeman to S, 22 September 1931, Box Y2120, SP. Background material on the greyhound guide from interviews with Jack Lockyer and Rosaline Stephensen (1980); and Lord Roberthall, 'Notes about P. R. Stephensen, 1918-1932', Fotheringham Papers (MSS 46), FL.
[7] C. W. Stewart to S, 13 January 1932, Box K164720, SP.
[8] Rosaline Stephensen to family, 18 October 1931 (letter in the possession of Rosaline Stephensen); interview with Rosaline Stephensen (1980). See also Jack McLaren, *My Civilised Adventure* (London, Peter Nevill, 1952), pp. 80-1.
[9] Roberthall, pp. 30-1.
[10] John Hetherington, *Norman Lindsay: The Embattled Olympian*, pp. 192-4. See also Ian Reid, 'Sheep Without a Fold: Publishing and Fiction-Writers in the 'Thirties', *Meanjin*, vol. 33, no. 2 (June 1974), p. 164.

11 Norman Lindsay to Godfrey Blunden, 6 February 1932, in *Letters of Norman Lindsay*, ed. R. G. Howarth and A. W. Barker, p. 313.
12 *Smith's Weekly*, March 1932.
13 Winifred, diary, 1 March and 6 July 1932, Boxes K164720 and K164722, SP. The list of shareholders in the new publishing company, as at December 1934, in Archives Office of New South Wales, R38127, Packet No. 14522.
14 Winifred, diary, 12 and 29 June 1932, Box K164722.
15 Norman Lindsay to Brian Penton, ? May 1932, in *Letters*, ed. Howarth and Barker, p. 315.
16 S to Norman Lindsay, 15 May 1932, Box Y2125, SP.
17 Draft proposal in SPFL.
18 S to Norman Lindsay, 1 June 1932, Box Y2125. SP.
19 Richardson's book, *The Bath*, was finally published late in 1933 by P. R. Stephensen & Co.
20 Winifred, diary, 17 July 1932, Box K164722, SP; *Miles Franklin: A Tribute by Some of Her Friends*, p. 37.
21 Miles Franklin to S, ? 19 July 1932, SPFL.
22 S to 'Brent of Bin Bin', 25 July 1932, Box Y2125, SP; *Miles Franklin: A Tribute*, pp. 35-6.
23 'Brent of Bin Bin' to S, August 1932, SPFL.
24 S to 'Brent of Bin Bin', 7 August 1932, SPFL; S to 'Brent of Bin Bin', 28 August 1932, Box K164720, SP. Stephensen did not publish the 'Brent of Bin Bin' stories.
25 S to Nettie Palmer, 20 July 1932, Palmer Papers (MSS 1174), NLA.
26 Nettie Palmer, diary, 28 August 1932, Palmer Papers (MSS 1174), Series 16, NLA.
27 Nettie Palmer to Frank Dalby Davison, 17 October 1932, in *Letters of Vance and Nettie Palmer, 1915-1963* (Canberra, National Library of Australia, 1977), pp. 76-8.
28 S to Katharine Susannah Prichard, 29 August 1932, Box K164720, SP.
29 Colin Roderick, *Miles Franklin: Her Brilliant Career*, p. 146.
30 S to Jack Lindsay, August 1932, in Lindsay Family Papers (MSS 1969), vol. 2, ML.
31 Sir Vernon Kell to Major Jones, 31 August 1932, Attorney-General's Department, Investigation Branch Correspondence Files, CRS A369, Item D/480, AA.

8: A New Endeavour

1 John Hetherington, *Norman Lindsay: The Embattled Olympian*, p. 198.
2 *Daily Mail* (Brisbane), 11 October 1932. Only the Miles Franklin book was published by the company.
3 Hetherington, p. 201.
4 Eric Stephensen, 'Further Recollections of P. R. Stephensen', 1979, p. 8, FL.
5 See Keith Amos, *The New Guard Movement, 1931-1935*. Eric Campbell's broadcasts were published as *The New Road* (Sydney, Briton Publications, 1934).
6 Inspector Longfield Lloyd to IB Director, Canberra, 26 October 1932, Attorney-General's Department, Investigation Branch Correspondence Files, CRS A369, Item D/480, AA.
7 S to Winifred, 17, 18 and 20 October 1932, Box K164720, SP.
8 S to Norman Lindsay, 26 October 1932, Box Y2125, SP; Nettie Palmer to Lucille Quinlem, 11 December 1932, in *Letters of Vance and Nettie Palmer, 1915-1963* (Canberra, National Library of Australia, 1977), p. 74; and Norman Lindsay to Louis Stone, 1932, in *Letters of Norman Lindsay*, ed. R. G. Howarth and A. W. Barker, p. 319.
9 *Bulletin* (Sydney), 2 November 1932, p. 17.
10 Various letters in November 1932, Box Y2117, SP.
11 *Bulletin*, 9 November 1932, pp. 2-5.
12 The text of this FAW address is in Box Y2134, SP. Another copy is in the Palmer Papers (MSS 1174), 30/187, NLA.
13 See Drusilla Modjeska, *Exiles at Home: Australian Women Writers 1925-1945*, especially p. 72.
14 Ken Slessor to S, 11 November 1932, Box Y2144, SP.
15 In correspondence, Baylebridge invariably used a Post Office box number. For more information about Baylebridge see Stephensen's Prefaces to the Memorial Edition of his Collected Works in 4 volumes (Sydney, Angus & Robertson, 1961-64); special Baylebridge number of *Southerly*, vol. 16, no. 3 (1955); and Noel Macainsh, *Nietzsche in Australia: A Literary Inquiry into a Nationalistic Ideology*.
16 S to Norman Lindsay, 14 November 1932, Box Y2125, SP.
17 Judith Wright. 'Australian Poetry', Commonwealth Literary Fund Lecture, University of New England, Armidale, 1955, p. 31.
18 S to Norman Lindsay, 17 November 1932, Box Y2125, SP; S, memo, 12 December 1932, Box Y2117, SP.

[19] Norman Lindsay to S, November 1932, Box Y2125, SP.
[20] Norman Lindsay to Ken Prior, 26 November 1932, Box Y2125, SP.
[21] Nettie Palmer to Winifred, 29 November 1932, SPFL; S to Norman Lindsay, 3 December 1932, Box Y2125, SP.
[22] Company documents including list of shareholders, in Archives Office of New South Wales, R3812, Packet No. 14522.
[23] S to A. G. Stephens, 13 December 1932, A. G. Stephens Collection, FL.
[24] Leon Cantrell, Introduction to *A. G. Stephens: Selected Writings*, ed. Leon Cantrell (Sydney, Angus & Robertson, 1978), p. 25. See also John Docker, Literature and Social Thought: Australia in an International Context, 1890-1925.
[25] Quoted in S, *The Life and Works of A. G. Stephens ("The Bookfellow"): A Lecture, Delivered to the Fellowship of Australian Writers, Sydney, 10 March 1940*, p. 1.
[26] See Ian Reid, 'Sheep Without a Fold: Publishing and Fiction-Writers in the 'Thirties', *Meanjin*, vol. 33, no. 2 (June 1974), pp. 164-5.
[27] Memos, December 1932, Box Y2117, SP. For a list of Endeavour Press publications, see Eric Stephensen, *Bibliography of Percy Reginald Stephensen*, pp. 34-6.
[28] There are various drafts, handwritten and typescript, of 'The Settlers', in Box Y2135, SP.
[29] Carl Täuber, *Entwicklung der Menschheit von den Ur-Australiern bis Europa, auf Grund der neuesten Forschungen über die Wanderungen der Ozeanier* ['The Development of the Human Race from the Proto-Australians to Europe, based on the most recent research on migrations of the peoples of Oceania'] (Zurich, 1932). *Sydney Morning Herald*, 2 April 1938, p. 13.
[30] Typescript copy of novel, pp. 115-16, Box Y2135, SP.
[31] Ibid., p. 117.
[32] S to Nettie Palmer, 3 January 1933, Palmer Papers (MSS 1174), 1/4182, NLA.
[33] Ibid.
[34] Norman Lindsay to Frank Morley, 1 January 1933, in *Letters*, ed. Howarth and Barker, p. 321.
[35] Norman Lindsay to Hal Porter, 17 January 1933, ibid., p. 322. Hal Porter's first story collection was not published till 1942.
[36] Norman Lindsay to S, 2 January 1933, Box Y2138, SP and January 1933, Box Y2155, SP.
[37] January 1933, Box Y2155, SP.
[38] Quoted in Rosaline Stephensen to family, 27 January 1933 (letter in the possession of Rosaline Stephensen).
[39] Background on the Endeavour Press provided by Jack Lockyer and Eric Stephensen, interviews (1977-79).
[40] Eric Stephensen, 'Further Recollections of P. R. Stephensen', 1979, pp. 6-7, FL.
[41] *Sydney Morning Herald*, 24 February 1933, p. 8.
[42] *Publicist*, November-December 1936, p. 17. The rejected printing of *The Animals Noah Forgot* was later bound up and sold as the third edition. See Eric Stephensen, 'Some Comments on *The Puzzled Patriots* by Bruce Muirden', pp. 4-5, FL.
[43] S, memo to S. H. and H. K. Prior, 27 February 1933, SPFL.
[44] Eric Stephensen, 'Comments on *The Puzzled Patriots*', p. 5.
[45] Ibid., p. 6.
[46] S to Norman Lindsay, 11 March 1933, Box Y2125, SP.
[47] Winifred, diary, 25 February 1933, Box K164721, SP. Letter from Jane Lindsay to S, May 1933, in Box K164720, SP.
[48] Her novel *No Escape* (London, Butterworth, 1932) had been a *Bulletin* prize winner.
[49] Winifred, diary, 4 March 1933, Box K164721, SP.
[50] Rose Lindsay to S, ? March 1933, Box Y2125, SP.
[51] See John Hetherington, *Norman Lindsay: The Embattled Olympian*, p. 204; and Rose Lindsay, *Model Wife: My Life with Norman Lindsay*, p. 267.
[52] Norman Lindsay to L. L. Politzer, 23 March 1933, Politzer Papers, La Trobe Library, State Library of Victoria, Melbourne.
[53] Miles Franklin to Hartley Grattan, 29 March 1933, Miles Franklin Papers (MSS 364), vol. 23, ML.
[54] Norman Lindsay to Peter Hopegood, ? April 1933 in *Letters*, ed. Howarth and Barker, p. 324.
[55] *Bulletin*, 15 March 1933, pp. 2-5.
[56] Miles Franklin, *Bring the Monkey: a Light Novel* (Sydney, Endeavour Press, 1933), p. 15.
[57] Sales figures in Manager's Report to 25 June 1933, Box Y2124, SP.
[58] Text of FAW address in Box Y2109, SP. Report also in *All About Books*, 13 July 1933, p. 108.
[59] S to Vance Palmer, 22 June 1933, Palmer Papers (MSS 1174), 1/4275, NLA.

60 Manager's Report to 25 June 1933, Box Y2124, SP.
61 Norman Lindsay, 'Have We Reached Maturity?', *Age*, 16 July 1966. See also Hetherington, pp. 202-3.
62 S to Norman Lindsay, 12 July 1933, Box Y2125, SP. Compare with Hetherington, p. 203; Douglas Stewart, *Writers of the Bulletin* (Sydney, ABC, 1977), pp. 74-7.
63 See Marianne Ehrhardt and Lurline Stewart, 'Xavier Herbert: A Checklist', *Australian Literary Studies*, vol. 8, no. 4 (October 1978), pp. 499-511. For more details of Herbert's relationship with S, see Craig Munro, 'Some Facts About a Long Fiction: The Publication of *Capricornia*', *Southerly*, no. 1 (1981), pp. 82-104.
64 S to Xavier Herbert, 14 July 1933, Box Y2141, SP.
65 Letters and telegrams, July 1933, Box Y2122, SP.
66 Theo Price to S, 14 August 1933, Box Y2122, SP.
67 H. K. Prior to S, 22 July 1933, in Harry F. Chaplin, *Norman Lindsay: His Books, Manuscripts and Autographed Letters*, p. 36; fragment [possibly letter, S to H. K. Prior, 24 July 1933], Box Y2124, SP.
68 Agreements of 28 July 1933 in Archives Office of New South Wales R38127, Packet No. 14522.
69 S to George Robertson, ? August 1933, Box Y2117, SP, and S to H. K. Prior, 16 August 1933, Box Y2124, SP.
70 Proposal for P. R. Stephensen & Co., Box Y2119, SP; telegram, Miles Franklin to S, 29 August 1933, Box Y2124, SP.
71 S to H. K. Prior, 16 September 1933, Box Y2124, SP.
72 Hetherington, p. 202.
73 S to William Baylebridge, 16 September 1933, SPFL.
74 Henry Kendall, 'In Memoriam: Marcus Clarke'; Nettie Palmer to Frank Dalby Davison, 17 October 1932, in *Letters of Vance and Nettie Palmer*, ed. Smith, pp. 76-8.
75 Bruce Muirden, *The Puzzled Patriots: The Story of the Australia First Movement*, p. 27.

9: Xavier Herbert, P. R. Stephensen & Co.

1 S to Norman Lindsay, 20 September 1933, Box Y2125, SP.
2 Much of the background for this chapter was provided by interviews with Jack Lockyer (1977), Arthur Dibley (1977) and Rosaline Stephensen (1980); also Eric Stephensen, 'Further Recollections of P. R. Stephensen', pp. 9-11, FL; and Eric Stephensen, *Bibliography of Percy Reginald Stephensen*, pp. 37-8.
3 Prospectus in Box Y2116, SP.
4 Frank Dalby Davison to Nettie Palmer, 2 November 1933, Palmer Papers (MSS 1174), NLA.
5 Xavier Herbert, telegram to S, 23 December 1933, Box K164720, SP. For more detail on Herbert's relationship with S, see Craig Munro, 'Some Facts about a Long Fiction: The Publication of *Capricornia*', *Southerly*, no. 1 (1981), pp. 82-104; also Craig Munro, 'Inky Stephensen, Xavier Herbert, and *Capricornia*: The Facts about a Long Fiction'.
6 Contracts for P. R. Stephensen & Co. Ltd. (copy in the possession of author).
7 *Sunday Sun and Guardian*, 28 January 1934.
8 Kirtley's introductions, and his note to Rosaline Stephensen, January 1934, Box Y2144, SP. P. R. Stephensen & Co. accounts to 14 December 1933, in Box Y2125, SP.
9 S to E. C. Lemont, 14 January 1934, Box Y2109, SP (copy also in SPFL).
10 Contract with E. H. Coote, 10 November 1933, and other correspondence, January 1934, Box Y2109, SP. Coote's *Hell's Airport* was subsequently published in 1934 (Peterman Press edition, April 1934; and NSW Bookstore Co. edition, May 1934).
11 P. R. Stephensen & Co. Ltd. documents in Archives Office of New South Wales, R38135, Packet No. 15212.
12 Arthur Dibley to S, 8 February 1934, Box K164720, SP.
13 List of shareholders in P. R. Stephensen & Co. Ltd. as at 16 May 1934 and July 1934, Boxes Y2117 and Y2125, SP.
14 Interview with Jack Lockyer (1977). See also Craig Munro, 'Some Facts about a Long Fiction', pp. 84-5. In a letter from Xavier Herbert to S, 3 October 1936 (Box Y2141, SP), Herbert said: 'Remember those all night sittings when I used to unfold the plot? [of *Capricornia*] Remember those days and nights at Narrabeen when you used to read the typescript—rape it with avid eyes as it lay prone and blushing and submissive fresh from the machine?'
15 *Stephensen's Circular*, no. 1, 26 January 1934, p. 4: *Stephensen's Circular*, no. 2, May 1934, p. 4. Copies in SPFL.

[16] See *Australian Journal*, 1 September 1928, p. 1144, and 1 April 1933, pp. 486-7. See also Craig Munro, 'Xavier Herbert: A Disturbing Element', *This Australia*, vol. 2, no. 2 (1983), pp. 11-16.
[17] *Stephensen's Circular*, 26 January 1934, p. 3.
[18] 'Book-Publishing in Australia', *Australian Rhodes Review* (March 1934), p. 47.
[19] See Xavier Herbert, 'The Writing of *Capricornia*', *Australian Literary Studies*, vol. 4, no. 3 (1970), pp. 207-14; Xavier Herbert, 'The Facts of the Publication of *Capricornia*: For the Historical Record', Herbert Papers (MSS 758), Series ii, NLA; also Craig Munro, Inky Stephensen, Xavier Herbert and *Capricornia*.
[20] See Margriet R. Bonnin, A Study of Australian Descriptive and Travel Writing, 1929-45. The Jindyworobak movement was also involved in this. See Brian Elliott (ed.), *The Jindyworobaks*.
[21] Herbert, 'The Facts of the Publication of *Capricornia*', pp. 15-18, NLA.
[22] See chapter 11.
[23] Xavier Herbert to S, ? April 1934, SPFL.
[24] Herbert's receipt for the advance is in Box K164727, SP.
[25] Nettie Palmer to Frank Dalby Davison, 7 March 1934, Davison Papers (MSS 764), NLA.
[26] S to Nettie Palmer, 8 March 1934, Palmer Papers (MSS 1174), NLA.
[27] Nettie Palmer to Leslie Rees, 10 March 1934, and Vance Palmer to Leslie Rees, 26 March [1934], in *Letters of Vance and Nettie Palmer*, ed. Vivian Smith, pp. 104, 84-5.
[28] Marjorie Barnard to Nettie Palmer, 17 April 1934, Palmer Papers (MSS 1174), NLA.
[29] Contracts for P. R. Stephensen & Co. Ltd. (copy in the possession of the author); list of shareholders, Box Y2117, SP.
[30] Miles Franklin to Nettie Palmer, 22 May 1934, Palmer Papers (MSS 1174), NLA.
[31] *Stephensen's Circular*, no. 2, March 1934, p. 1.
[32] *Sun* (Melbourne), 2 April 1934; *Labor Daily*, 19 May 1934; *Townsville Bulletin*, 21 April 1934.
[33] Although Eleanor Dark had published her first novel *Slow Dawning* in 1932, it was published in England (London, Longman). *Prelude to Christopher* (Sydney, P. R. Stephensen & Co., 1934) began establishing her reputation as a novelist. S was always proud that he had 'discovered' Dark and Herbert. S to Bruce Muirden, 5 May 1952 (letter in the possession of Bruce Muirden).
[34] S to Kate Baker, 16 April 1934, Palmer Papers (MSS 1174), NLA.
[35] B. Barker to S, 18 April 1934, Box Y2153, SP.
[36] Copies of the address to shareholders, 28 May 1934, in Boxes Y2116 and Y2119, SP; lists of creditors, 31 May and 30 June 1934, Box Y2117, SP.
[37] Telegrams to and from S. B. Snow, June 1934, Box Y2144, SP.
[38] Notice of share allotment, 2 July 1934, Box Y2125; S to W. T. Baker, 6 July 1934, Box Y2144, SP.
[39] Ruth White to S, 11 February 1935, Box Y2144, SP. See also Leon Cantrell, 'Patrick White's First Book', *Australian Literary Studies*, vol. 6, no. 4 (October 1974), pp. 434-6.
[40] Patrick White to S, 21 October 1934, Box Y2144, SP.
[41] See *Bulletin*, 11 August 1962, p. 32. It is possible that 'Finding Heaven' was one of the early novels White refers to in *Flaws in the Glass* (London, Cape, 1980), p. 49. The mid-section of his novel *The Twyborn Affair* (London, Cape, 1979), based on his jackerooing experience in Australia in the early 1930s, may also derive to some extent from 'Finding Heaven'.
[42] Contract in Box Y2109, SP.
[43] *The Ploughman* was published by Beacon Press, 1935. It is very likely that Ruth White paid The Beacon Press to issue the volume.
[44] Nettie Palmer to Miles Franklin, 9 July 1934, in *Letters of Vance and Nettie Palmer*, ed. Smith, p. 99.
[45] Nettie Palmer to S, 23 July 1934, Box Y2142, SP.
[46] *Telegraph* (Brisbane), 27 July 1934.
[47] Proof copy of prospectus for Stephensen's National Book-Publishing House, July 1934 (copy in the possession of the author).
[48] Registrar of Companies, Canberra, to S, 6 April 1938, Box K164720, SP.
[49] S to Winifred, ? 10 August 1934, and various other letters July/August, Box K164724, SP.
[50] See Craig Munro, 'Some Facts About a Long Fiction: The Publication of *Capricornia*', *Southerly*, no. 1 (1981), pp. 88-9; and Xavier Herbert, 'The Facts of the Publication of *Capricornia*', NLA.
[51] S to Xavier Herbert, ? September 1934, Box Y2142, SP.
[52] See Munro, 'Some Facts About a Long Fiction', pp. 89-91.
[53] Most of Herbert's letters to Arthur Dibley are undated and are in the Herbert Papers (MSS 758), NLA.

[54] Undated note [S to Winifred], on letterhead P. R. Stephensen, ? October 1934 (copy in the possession of the author); J. J. Mulligan to S, 20 September 1934, Box Y2144, SP; and *Bulletin*, 4 November 1936, p. 5.
[55] Xavier Herbert to Arthur Dibley, 'Saturday' [? 13 October 1934], Herbert Papers (MSS 758), NLA; Stephensen Book Agency Agreement (copy in the possession of the author).
[56] Xavier Herbert to Arthur Dibley, 'Sunday' [? 21 October 1934], Herbert Papers (MSS 758), NLA.
[57] Herbert, 'Facts of the Publication of *Capricornia*', p. 22, NLA.
[58] Randolph Hughes, *C. J. Brennan: an Essay in Values* (Sydney, P. R. Stephensen, 1934), pp. 52-75.
[59] *Bulletin*, 10 October 1934, pp. 2-5. See chapters 10 and 11 for court cases involving Crockett and S.
[60] C. P. Greenwood to S, 11 October 1934, Box Y2124; and P. R. Stephensen & Co. Ltd. Financial Statement at 30 November 1934, Box Y2119, SP.
[61] Xavier Herbert to Arthur Dibley, 'New Year's Eve' [31 December 1934], Herbert Papers, NLA.
[62] S to Ken Prior, 5 December 1934, quoted in *Publicist*, November-December, p. 18.
[63] P. R. Stephensen & Co. Ltd. catalogue, ? September 1934, Box Y2155, SP. Hughes's book may have been published as *Crusts and Crusades* (Sydney, Angus & Robertson, 1947). W. M. Hughes to S, 13 December 1934, Box Y2144, SP.
[64] S to W. M. Hughes, 17 December 1934, Box Y2144, SP.
[65] Bailiff's notice, re public auction, 17 December 1934, Box Y2125, SP.
[66] S to William Baylebridge, 21 December 1934, Box Y2114, SP.
[67] S to William Baylebridge, 6 December 1934, Box Y2114, SP.
[68] *Sydney Morning Herald*, 19 January 1935, pp. 10, 15-16.
[69] Miles Franklin to Hartley Grattan, 25 October 1933, Franklin Papers (MSS 364), vol. 23, ML. See also E. M. Andrews, *Isolationism and Appeasement in Australia: Reactions to the European Crises, 1935-39*.
[70] Nettie Palmer to Miles Franklin, 5 January 1935, in *Letters of Vance and Nettie Palmer*, ed. Smith, pp. 107-8.
[71] S to L. Anthony, 8 January 1935, Box Y2144, SP.
[72] The *Capricornia* jacket artwork is in Box Y2122, SP along with similar designs for other P. R. Stephensen & Co. books.
[73] See Herbert, 'Facts of the Publication of *Capricornia*', NLA. In 'How I Edited "Capricornia"', *Bulletin*, 15 March 1961, pp. 33-4, S claimed he offered Herbert's novel to Angus & Robertson.
[74] Resolution to wind up Australian Book Publishing Ltd, 20 May 1935, Archives Office of New South Wales, R38127, Packet No. 14522.

10: Mercurial Nationalism

[1] Margriet R. Bonnin, A Study of Australian Descriptive and Travel Writing, 1929-45, pp. 329-30; Miles Franklin to Nettie Palmer, 15 February 1935, Palmer Papers (MSS 1174), NLA.
[2] For more details on this episode see: Egon Erwin Kisch, *Australian Landfall*; 'Julian Smith' [Tom Fitzgerald], *On the Pacific Front: The Adventures of Egon Kisch in Australia*; Katharine Susannah Prichard, *Straight Left*, ed. Ric Throssell (Sydney, Wild and Woolley, 1982), pp. 70-81; also Drusilla Modjeska, *Exiles at Home: Australian Women Writers 1925-1945*, chapter 5.
[3] Marjorie Barnard to Nettie Palmer, 23 December 1934, Palmer Papers, NLA.
[4] 'Julian Smith', p. 118.
[5] *Age*, 9 February 1935, p. 6, and 16 February 1935, p. 6.
[6] Ibid., 23 February 1935, p. 4.
[7] Miles Franklin to Hartley Grattan, 14 March 1935, Franklin Papers (MSS 364), vol. 23, ML.
[8] *Age*, 23 February 1935, p. 4.
[9] This was issued as Pamphlet no. 1, June 1935. This and other Cultural Defence Committee material, in Box Y2148, SP.
[10] Draft prospectus for the Literary Guild, SPFL.
[11] S to mother, 25 February 1935, SPFL.
[12] S to Packer, 4 April 1935, Box Y2122, SP.
[13] There were at least three numbers of *The Opinion*: in May, June-July, July-August 1935. Possibly also an October number. Copies in FL.

Notes (pages 153–62)

14 The 'Cooee' material is in Box Y2117, SP.
15 Proposal for *Australian Mercury*, SPFL; list of shareholders in the *Australian Mercury* establishment fund, Box Y2138, SP.
16 S to F. W. Robinson, 22 May 1935, SPFL.
17 F. W. Robinson to S, 2 July 1935, Box Y2125, SP.
18 See Bonnin, p. 326.
19 See Kay Dreyfus and Janice Whiteside, 'Percy Grainger and Australia', *Meanjin*, vol. 41, no. 2 (June 1982), pp. 155-70. See especially pp. 168-9.
20 S, *The Foundations of Culture in Australia: An Essay Towards National Self-Respect*, p. 35. All quotations are from the book version of the essay.
21 Ibid., p. 21.
22 The narrator in Joseph Conrad's *Heart of Darkness* (1902) makes a similar point. See Penguin edition, 1981, pp. 8-10.
23 *Foundations of Culture*, p. 22.
24 Ibid., pp. 19, 32, 55.
25 Though Mackworth Praed was related by marriage to the Australian Rosa Campbell Praed.
26 *Foundations of Culture*, pp. 36-7.
27 Ibid., p. 52
28 Ibid., pp. 57, 65.
29 Ibid., pp. 68-70.
30 Ibid., p. 132; also pp. 25, 126.
31 Ibid., pp. 130-3.
32 Ibid., p. 132.
33 Ibid., pp. 127-8.
34 Ibid., p. 25.
35 Xavier Herbert to S, 'Tuesday' [? August 1935], Box K164727, SP; W. M. Hughes to S, 15 July 1935, Box Y2144, SP; and Randolph Hughes to S, 17 August 1935, Box Y2123, SP.
36 F. Wilmot to S, 26 June 1935, Box Y2141, SP.
37 Ken Slessor to S, 18 July 1935, Box Y2144, SP.
38 Summary of *Australian Mercury* distribution in Boxes Y2117 and Y2138, SP. Financial liabilities of the magazine given in S to R. E. G. Cunningham, 17 October 1935, Box Y2140, SP.
39 Details of the action in Box Y2117, SP.
40 *Truth* (Sydney), 23 June 1935.
41 The £20 000 figure mentioned in Marjorie Barnard to Nettie Palmer, 15 September 1935, Palmer Papers, NLA. See Chapter 11 for the hearing of Stephensen's action.
42 The manuscripts and proofs for the August number of the *Australian Mercury* in SPFL; S to Ernest Watt, August 1935, SPFL. For more details on the history of the *Australian Mercury*, see Craig Munro, 'P. R. Stephensen and the *Australian Mercury*', in Bruce Bennett (ed.), *Crosscurrents: Magazines and Newspapers in Australian Literature*, pp. 103-14.
43 Electricity Department to S, 11 September 1935, Box K164720, SP.
44 C. W. Sedgwick to S, 20 September 1935, Box K164720, SP.
45 Miles Franklin to Nettie Palmer, 13 August 1935, Palmer Papers, NLA.
46 See *Sydney Morning Herald*, 20 July 1935, p. 16; Peter Coleman, *Obscenity, Blasphemy, Sedition: 100 Years of Censorship in Australia*, pp. 84-6.
47 This was eventually published as a Frank Clune book, ghosted by S, as *D'Air Devil*.
48 A copy of *Trade Without Money!* is in Box Y2134, SP. The agreement with Trans-Continental Airlines is in Box K164720, SP.
49 S to Winifred, 'Sunday' [? 13 October 1935], Box K164724, SP.
50 Winifred, diary, ? September 1935, Box K164720, SP.
51 S to Kathleen Watson, 22 October 1935, Box Y2142, SP.
52 Nettie Palmer to William Baylebridge, 17 October 1935, Box Y2113, SP.
53 Jack Kirtley to Winifred, ? September 1935, Box K164720, SP.
54 *Independent Sydney Secularist*, no. 1 (July 1935), p. 3. Copies of this very rare magazine are in SP.
55 W. J. Miles to S, 21 August 1935, Box Y2153, SP.
56 *Publicist*, February 1942, p. 3.
57 For material on W. J. Miles see: Bruce Muirden, *The Puzzled Patriots: The Story of the Australia First Movement*; *Nation* (Sydney), 31 January 1959, pp. 10-12, and 14 February 1959, pp. 8-10; *Publicist*, February 1942, pp. 2-4; William John Miles, Valedictory Address by S, 11 January 1942 (privately printed), copy in Box Y2114, SP; correspondence between Edward Masey and Bruce Muirden (in the possession of Bruce Muirden).

58 W. J. Miles to Kate Baker, 9 January 1920, Box Y2144, SP. Frank Dalby Davison's father began the *Australian Post*. See Owen Webster, *The Outward Journey* (Canberra, Australian National University Press, 1978), p. 199.
59 W. J. Miles to S, 13 November 1935, Box Y2117, SP. The Australia First Party Plan is in Box Y2122, SP.
60 Winifred, diary, 14 January 1936, Box K164720, SP.
61 W. J. Miles to S, 16 January 1936, Box Y2140; and W. J. Miles to Hector Ross, 31 January 1936, Box Y2146, SP.
62 Coleman, p. 87.
63 *Foundations of Culture*, pp. 139-42.
64 Ibid., p. 154.
65 This had been the loyal pledge of Australia's Prime Minister to Britain during World War I.
66 *Foundations of Culture*, pp. 158, 162-5.
67 Ibid., p. 190.
68 This inscribed copy of *Foundations of Culture* is copy 12 in FL.
69 Royalties account, as at 27 April 1936, in Box Y2114, SP. The first printing of *The Foundations of Culture in Australia* was 1500 copies in paperback, published in February or March 1936. Another 2000 copies were printed about the middle of the year, most again in paperback, but some copies bound in orange cloth. The paperback edition sold for 2s and the cloth edition for 3s 6d. The two printings can be identified as follows: the first printing has the printing details on the imprint page set in four lines; whereas the second printing has them in three lines.
70 Muirden, p. 13; Edward Masey Notes (in the possession of Bruce Muirden).
71 B. N. Fryer to S, 4 April 1936; E. J. Brady to S, 6 April 1936; and J. Kirtley to S, ? April 1936, all in Box Y2138, SP.
72 E. Morris Miller to S, 17 April 1936, Box Y2144, SP.
73 Nettie Palmer to Leslie and Coralie Rees, 6 July 1936, in *Letters of Vance and Nettie Palmer*, ed. Smith, pp. 134-5.
74 *Australian Quarterly*, no. 29 (March 1936), pp. 106-9. The manuscript of this review is in SPFL.
75 *Melbourne Herald*, 8 April 1936, p. 36; text of review on radio station 3LO, Melbourne, 16 April 1936, Box Y2138, SP.
76 *All About Books*, 12 May 1936, pp. 69-70.
77 Text of talk by S on radio station 2KY, Sydney, 14 May 1936, Box Y2138, SP.
78 S to W. J. Miles, 24 April 1936, Box K164720, SP.
79 Muirden, p. 13.
80 Miles Franklin, *Laughter, Not for a Cage*, p. 215. Since the 1960s, however, *The Foundations of Culture in Australia* has been quoted extensively in many books of Australian political, cultural and literary history and extracts from it have been published in John Barnes (ed.), *The Writer in Australia: A Collection of Literary Documents 1856-1964* (Melbourne, Oxford University Press, 1969); and in Brian Elliott (ed.), *the Jindyworobaks*, pp. 223-6.
81 *Nineteenth Century and After*, vol. 120, no. 717 (November 1936), pp. 614, 616, 618.
82 Xavier Herbert to S, ? June 1936, Box Y2142, SP.
83 *Publicist*, July 1938, p. 3.

11: War of Words

1 S to Xavier Herbert, 5 December 1936, Box Y2117, SP. The background for this chapter supplied by Bruce Muirden, *The Puzzled Patriots: The Story of the Australia First Movement*; and interview with Jack Lockyer (1980). There is an index to the *Publicist* in the June 1941 issue, pp. 8-16. It was compiled by S.
2 *Publicist*, July 1936, p. 4.
3 Ibid., pp. 4-7. Spengler's *Decline of the West* originally appeared in Germany between 1918 and 1922 and was translated into English, 1926-28. T. S. Eliot's *The Waste Land* was published in 1922, Evelyn Waugh's *Decline and Fall* in 1928, and Aldous Huxley's *Those Barren Leaves* in 1925.
4 *Publicist*, July 1936, p. 8.
5 Muirden, p. 3.
6 W. J. Miles to G. Dohler, 16 February 1939, Box Y2112, SP.
7 *Publicist*, August 1937, p. 10.
8 Correspondence between Edward Masey and Bruce Muirden (in the possession of Bruce Muirden).

[9] *Bulletin*, 8 March 1975, p. 49.
[10] Foreword by S, 1937, Box Y2134, SP.
[11] See Margriet R. Bonnin, Study of Australian Descriptive and Travel Writing, 1929-45, pp. 31-4. See also Eric Stephensen, *Bibliography of Percy Reginald Stephensen*, pp. 11-14. Eric Stephensen incorrectly attributes to Stephensen the editing of the following books: *Rolling Down the Lachlan* (1935), *Roaming Round the Darling* (1936), *Tobruk to Turkey* (1943), and *Search for the Golden Fleece* (1965). See Section B2 of the Bibliography. See also Bartlett Adamson, *Frank Clune: Author and Ethnological Anachronism* (Melbourne, Hawthorn Press, 1943).
[12] S to Murphy and Maloney, 2 December 1962, Box K164725, SP.
[13] *Publicist*, October 1936, pp. 9-10.
[14] Yabber Club Invitation Card (copy in the possession of the author). For other material on the Club see Muirden, p. 45; Edward Masey Notes (in the possession of Bruce Muirden); transcript of the Clyne Inquiry, p. 531, Attorney-General's Department, Special Files 1906-1951, Series CRS A467, Bundle 96, File 43, Item 1, AA (hereafter referred to as Clyne transcript).
[15] *Bulletin*, 26 May 1937, p. 8, and 9 June 1937, p. 2.
[16] *Publicist*, July 1937, p. 8, and August 1937, p. 9.
[17] Prospectuses in Boxes Y2149 and K164720, SP.
[18] *Bulletin*, 4 November 1936, p. 5; *Publicist*, November-December 1936, pp. 20-2.
[19] Miles Franklin to Nettie Palmer, 18 October 1936, Palmer Papers (MSS 1174), NLA.
[20] S to Xavier Herbert, 7 November 1936, Box Y2139, SP. (In a number of letters, S addressed Herbert as 'Fred'.)
[21] S to Xavier Herbert, 27 November 1926, SPFL.
[22] Deed of arrangement, 24 November 1936, and other material, NSW Bankruptcy Registry, no. 179 of 1936 XII.
[23] Xavier Herbert to Arthur Dibley, 'Tuesday' [? 19 January 1937], Herbert Papers (MSS 758), NLA.
[24] S to Xavier Herbert, 14 January 1937, Box Y2125, SP.
[25] Muirden, p. 41.
[26] Text of broadcast, 18 January 1937, Box Y2125, SP.
[27] July 1939, p. 14. In *Literature and the Aborigine in Australia, 1770-1975* (St. Lucia, University of Queensland Press, 1978), pp. 268-9, J. J. Healy has commented:
> ... although Stephensen possessed a strident ego and an opportunism tempered periodically by genuine emotion, he did, more than anyone else, wade into the debate of Australian culture. In doing so, especially in his *Foundations of Culture in Australia*, and the *Publicist*, he made that debate acrimonious, visible and through his extreme opinions, a matter of oppositions. The *Publicist* has a place in Australian history as a forcer of definitions which might otherwise have been less prominent.

[28] S to W. J. Miles, 26 January 1937, Box K164720, SP.
[29] S to Xavier Herbert, 18 December 1936, SPFL.
[30] *Publicist*, January 1938, pp. 8-24.
[31] Ibid., April 1938, p. 5.
[32] Ibid., November 1939, p. 5.
[33] Ibid., August 1936, p. 3.
[34] Winifred, diary, 25 December 1937, Box Y2143. For more on the APA see Jack Horner, *Vote Ferguson for Aboriginal Freedom*.
[35] S to Ian Mudie, 14 July 1938, Mudie Papers (PRG 27), State Library of South Australia (Archives) Adelaide. (There is another copy of this letter in Boxes Y2142 and Y2146, SP.)
[36] S to Helen Baillie, 14 December 1937, Box Y2142, SP.
[37] Miles Franklin to Xavier Herbert, 30 December 1937, Franklin Papers (MSS 364), vol. 28, ML.
[38] W. J. Miles to Winifred Stephensen, 22 December 1937, Box K164720, SP.
[39] *Publicist*, January 1938, p. 2.
[40] 'Without Semitism, there could be no Anti-Semitism', Stephensen wrote, *Publicist*, January 1939, p. 7. He also wrote that anti-Semitism was 'abhorrent . . . to all decent-minded men'.
[41] See Horner, pp. 56-8, p. 177, n2; also Clyne transcript, p. 751.
[42] Text of interview with Jack Patten, ? January 1938, Box Y2109, SP. Copy of poster for APA day of mourning and protest (in author's possession). See also Horner, chapter 5.
[43] Horner, pp. 60-1.
[44] *Sydney Morning Herald*, 4 March 1938, p. 11.
[45] Ibid., 5 March 1938, p. 11.
[46] Text of radio broadcast, 7 March 1938, Box Y2143, SP.
[47] *Sydney Morning Herald*, 21 April 1938, p. 12, and 22 April 1938, p. 14.

48 Xavier Herbert to Miles Franklin, 5 April 1938, Franklin Papers, ML.
49 Eleanor Dark to S, 1 April 1938, Box Y2140, SP.
50 Ian Mudie to S, 2 April 1938, Box Y2139, SP.
51 Correspondence between W. J. Miles and R. D. FitzGerald, April 1938, Box Y2112.
52 *Sydney Morning Herald*, 18 April 1938, p. 17.
53 For the collapse of the APA see Horner. A notice of meeting to disband the APA dated 21 April 1939 (copy in the possession of the author).
54 Richard Griffiths, *Fellow Travellers of the Right: British Enthusiasts for Nazi Germany*, p. 292.
55 The title of Muirden's book, *The Puzzled Patriots*, suggests this. See Muirden, p. 28. In *From Deserts the Prophets Come: The Creative Spirit in Australia, 1788-1972* (Melbourne, Heinemann, 1973), p. 131, Geoffrey Serle calls S a 'tragic' figure, but makes no attempt to account for his sudden switch to extreme right-wing politics.
56 See E. A. Mann, *Arrows in the Air: A Selection from Broadcasts by "The Watchman"* (Melbourne, S. John Bacon, 1944).
57 E. M. Andrews, *Isolationism and Appeasement in Australia: Reactions to the European Crises 1935-1939*, p. 5.
58 Alastair Hamilton, *The Appeal of Fascism: A Study of Intellectuals and Fascism 1919-1945*, p. 268.
59 Rhodes House Warden, report to Lord Elton, 30 October 1942, Rhodes House Records, Oxford. There was a reply to Stephensen's article in the *Australian Rhodes Review*, no. 4 (1939).
60 Hamilton, pp. 272-82. See David Heymann, *Ezra Pound: The Last Rower: A Political Profile*.
61 David Walker, 'The Palmer Abridgement of *Such is Life*', *Australian Literary Studies*, vol. 8, no. 4 (October 1978), pp. 491-8. 'I am a Nietzschean Bakuninite!' S wrote to Jack Lindsay, 25 August 1961 (letter in the possession of Jack Lindsay; copy in the possession of the author).
62 *Publicist*, April 1938.
63 Hamilton, xxii. See also Eric Bentley, *A Century of Hero-Worship*, especially p. 195 on the myth of Armageddon attracting Heroic Vitalists such as Carlyle, Nietzsche, Spengler and D. H. Lawrence. S clearly had much in common with all these figures.
64 *Publicist*, January 1938, p. 24.
65 S to C. Brown, 4 July 1941, Box Y2140, SP.
66 S described the 'sordid executions' in Russia, *Publicist*, April 1938, p. 5.
67 He was not the only one. In *Homage to Catalonia* (1938. Harmondsworth, Penguin, 1977), p. 229, George Orwell wrote: 'Part of the price we paid for the systematic lying of 1914-17 was the exaggerated pro-German reaction which followed. During the years 1918-33 you were hooted at in left-wing circles if you suggested that Germany bore even a fraction of responsibility for the war'.
68 *Publicist*, January 1939, p. 14.
69 *Sydney Morning Herald*, 9 February 1939, p. 11.
70 Text of radio broadcast, 21 March 1938, Box Y2134, SP.
71 *Publicist*, April 1938, pp. 10-14, and May 1938, pp. 3-8; (*New York Times Book Review*, 15 August 1937, pp. 8, 20).
72 *Publicist*, April 1938, p. 11.
73 Ibid., May 1938, pp. 3-8.
74 Ibid., June 1938, p. 7.
75 Ibid., pp. 6-8, 13.
76 Ibid., July 1938, pp. 7-8.
77 Brian Elliott (ed.), *The Jindyworobaks*, p. xxxiii.
78 S to Ian Mudie, 14 July 1938, Mudie Papers, State Library of South Australia.
79 Ian Mudie to S, 31 August 1938, Box Y2139, SP.
80 Elliott, pp. xlv-xlvii.
81 Ibid., p. 65. Mudie's poem, 'As are the Gums', *Publicist*, October 1938.
82 *Publicist*, August 1938, pp. 5-7.
83 *Publicist*, October 1938, p. 14; text of radio interview with Herbert, 26 September 1938, Box Y2146, SP.
84 S to W. J. Miles, 3 October 1938, Box K164720, SP.
85 Ibid.
86 Muirden, p. 29.
87 See Robert Skidelsky, *Oswald Mosley*, chapter 13.
88 S to W. J. Miles, 3 October 1938, Box K164720, SP.
89 *Australian National Review*, 1 October 1938, p. 2; S to Warren Denning, 7 October 1938, Box Y2113, SP.

[90] *Publicist*, November 1938, p. 9. For more details on the *Publicist*'s attitude to women, see Craig Munro, 'Australia First—Women Last: Pro-Fascism and Anti-Feminism in the 1930s', *Hecate*, vol. 9, double issue (1983).
[91] Herbert Burton to S, 5 November 1938, Box Y2134; E. P. Dark to S, 15 December 1938, Box Y2140; and Herbert Burton to S, 25 March 1939, Box K164720, SP.
[92] *Publicist*, December 1938, pp. 2-7.
[93] Geoffrey Blainey, *Blainey View*, television series.
[94] *Publicist*, March 1939, p. 7.
[95] Ibid., July 1939, p. 10.
[96] Ibid., May 1939, p. 8; S, *The Foundations of Culture in Australia: An Essay Towards National Self-Respect*, p. 132.
[97] W. J. Miles to NSW Commissioner of Police, 4 September 1939, Box K164719, SP.

12: Fascism and Australia First

[1] IB reports of 2 and 3 August 1939, Attorney-General's Department, Investigation Branch Correspondence Files, CRS A369, Item D/480, AA. See also Bruce Muirden, *The Puzzled Patriots: The Story of the Australia First Movement*, p. 55. Muirden's book provides general background for this chapter.
[2] *Publicist*, May 1940, p. 7.
[3] Muirden, p. 46. See also Richard Hall, *The Secret State: Australia's Spy Industry*, chapter 4.
[4] Transcript of Clyne Inquiry, p. 533, Attorney-General's Department, Special Files 1906-1951, Series A467, Bundle 96, File 43, Item 1, AA (hereafter referred to as Clyne transcript).
[5] *Publicist*, November 1939, p. 6.
[6] Ibid., February 1940, p. 1.
[7] *Australian Quarterly*, March 1940, pp. 53, 58, 62.
[8] See Martin Gilbert, *Auschwitz and the Allies* (London, Michael Joseph/Rainbird, 1981).
[9] I. N. Steinberg, *Australia: The Unpromised Land*, p. 96.
[10] Miles Franklin to W. J. Miles, 28 March 1939, SPFL; Miles Franklin to Nettie Palmer, 31 May 1940, Franklin Papers (MSS 364), vol. 24, ML.
[11] Drusilla Modjeska, *Exiles at Home: Australian Women Writers 1925-1945*, p. 186.
[12] *Publicist*, October 1939, p. 2.
[13] W. J. Miles to Ian Mudie, 6 February 1939, Mudie Papers (PRG 27), State Library of South Australia (Archives), Adelaide.
[14] *Publicist*, June 1940, p. 2.
[15] Ibid., February 1940, pp. 4-7.
[16] Interim report, 14 August 1940, of the A. G. Stephens Memorial Committee, in S, *The Life and Works of A. G. Stephens*. Copy in FL. The bust of Stephens never got beyond the plaster stage, though it was intended to cast it in bronze.
[17] J. St Clair Street to S, 3 April 1940, Box Y2142, SP.
[18] S, *A. G. Stephens*, p. 6.
[19] W. J. Miles to Ian Mudie, 2 April 1940, Mudie Papers, State Library of South Australia.
[20] Correspondence with Censor, April 1940, Box Y2146, SP. See also Paul Hasluck, *The Government and the People 1939-1941* (Canberra, Australian War Memorial, 1952), vol. 1, pp. 39-41, 178-81.
[21] W. J. Miles to M. L. O'Loughlin, 1 July 1940, SPFL.
[22] W. J. Miles to Ian Mudie, 12 September 1940, Mudie Papers, State Library of South Australia.
[23] *Publicist*, May 1940, p. 20.
[24] Ibid.
[25] Ibid., August 1940, p. 11; George Berrie to S, 12 July 1940, Box Y2142, SP.
[26] *Daily News* (Sydney), 9 May 1940.
[27] *Publicist*, July 1940, p. 12, July 1941, p. 5; S to Xavier Herbert, 26 May 1941, Box K164720, SP. See also Modjeska, p. 103.
[28] W. J. Miles to S, 21 June 1940, Box Y2148, SP.
[29] S to Winifred, 21 June 1940, Box K164719, SP.
[30] S to W. J. Miles, 21 June 1940, Box Y2140, SP.
[31] *Publicist*, July 1940, p. 5.
[32] S to Ian Mudie, 13 July 1940, Mudie Papers, State Library of South Australia.
[33] E. A. Mann, *Arrows in the Air: A Selection from Broadcasts by "The Watchman"* (Melbourne, John Bacon, 1944), p. 69.

[34] 'The last temptation is the greatest treason/To do the right deed for the wrong reason', T. S. Eliot, *Murder in the Cathedral*, Part I.
[35] S to Frank Clune, 22 December 1954, Clune Papers (MSS 4951), NLA; Hartley Grattan to S, 11 July 1937, Box K164730, SP. See also *Publicist*, March 1937, p. 3, and July 1938, p. 16.
[36] S to H. V. Evatt, 22 August 1940, Box K164730, SP; *Publicist*, October 1940, p. 3.
[37] *Publicist*, January 1941, pp. 7-8.
[38] W. J. Miles to S. J. Ingwersen, 5 May 1941, Box Y2139, SP.
[39] See, for example, Xavier Herbert to Miles Franklin, 3 January 1938 [incorrectly dated 1937 by Herbert], Miles Franklin Papers, ML.
[40] S to Xavier Herbert, 26 May 1941, Box K164720, SP.
[41] Xavier Herbert to Ian Mudie, 21 July 1941, Mudie Papers, State Library of South Australia.
[42] Xavier Herbert, *Poor Fellow My Country* (Sydney, Collins, 1975), pp. 1032-42.
[43] W. Flexmore Hudson to Ian Mudie, 10 December 1940; and Victor Kennedy to Ian Mudie, 7 June 1941, Mudie Papers, State Library of South Australia.
[44] Typescript dated June 1941, Box Y2136. It remained unpublished.
[45] MPI Report, 12 November 1941, Attorney-General's Department, CRS A467, Special File 43, Bundle 97, Item 1, AA (hereafter referred to as Special File). See also Muirden, on Cahill.
[46] S. J. Ingwersen to W. J. Miles, 1 May 1941, Box Y2139, SP; Ian Mudie to W. J. Miles, 30 June 1941, SPFL; S to S. J. Ingwersen, 1 July 1941, Box Y2144, SP.
[47] Ian Mudie to S, 24 June 1941, Box Y2116, SP; S to Rex Ingamells, 4 July 1941, SPFL; S to Ian Mudie, 4 July 1941, Mudie Papers, State Library of South Australia.
[48] Ian Mudie to S, 7 July 1941, Box Y2116, SP; Rex Ingamells to S, 7 July 1941, Box Y2140, SP.
[49] S to Rex Ingamells, 14 July 1941, Box Y2140, SP.
[50] S to Ian Mudie, 16 July 1941, Box Y2116, SP.
[51] On the haphazard aspect of Fascist ideology, see Maria-Antonietta Macciocchi, 'Female Sexuality in Fascist Ideology', *Feminist Review*, no. 1 (1979), pp. 67-82.
[52] *Sydney Morning Herald*, 8 August 1941, p. 5.
[53] *Publicist*, August 1941, p. 8.
[54] S to Rex Ingamells, 14 August 1941, Box Y2140, SP.
[55] S to Rex Ingamells, 3 September 1941, Ingamells Papers, La Trobe Library, State Library of Victoria, Melbourne.
[56] S to H. V. Evatt, ? December 1941, Box Y2116, SP. Confirmed by S to Frank Clune, 22 December 1954, Clune Papers (MSS 4951), NLA.
[57] In the early 1930s the term 'dictator' did not have the same seriousness and was almost a jargon word. The English publisher Methuen, in fact, began a series of books entitled 'If I Were Dictator'. See Richard Griffiths, *Fellow Travellers of the Right: British Enthusiasts for Nazi Germany, 1933-39*.
[58] The Glossary was published as a separate booklet by the *Publicist* Publishing Company, 1941.
[59] For more details about Adela Pankhurst Walsh, see: Muirden, p. 60; and Elizabeth Windschuttle (ed.), *Women, Class and History: Feminist Perspectives on Australia 1788-1978* (Sydney, Fontana, 1980), which has a chapter on Walsh herself and another on the Australian Women's Guild of Empire.
[60] Muirden, pp. 59-60.
[61] Edward Masey Notes (in the possession of Bruce Muirden).
[62] Ibid.; Eric Stephensen, 'Some Comments on the *Puzzled Patriots* by Bruce Muirden', 1979, p. 10, FL; interview with Jack Lockyer (1980).
[63] Announcement of Australians Progress Movement, Mudie Papers (PRG 27) Series 1, State Library of South Australia.
[64] Clyne transcript, pp. 680-2, 748.
[65] *Publicist*, November 1941, p. 5. A copy of the AFM Constitution and Rules, in Box Y2145, SP.
[66] *Publicist*, November 1941, p. 5.
[67] *Meanjin*, vol. 1, no. 6 (November 1941), pp. 3, 7-9, 29-30. 'Brian Vrepont' was the pseudonym of Benjamin Truebridge.
[68] *Publicist*, December 1941, p. 7. See also *Meanjin*, vol. 1, no. 7 (January 1942), p. 14.
[69] S to S. B. Hooper and V. Crowley, 1 November 1941, Box Y2144, SP.
[70] The agreement, dated 25 November 1941, is in Box K164720, SP.
[71] See Clyne transcript; also Special File.
[72] MPI Report, 6 November 1941, Special File.

294   Notes (pages 212–19)

[73] IB Report of 5 November 1941 meeting, Special File.
[74] *Publicist*, December 1941, pp. 14-15. See Muirden, pp. 62-3.
[75] W. J. McKell to Prime Minister Curtin, 26 November 1941, Special File.
[76] MPI Report, 21 November 1941, Special File.
[77] Paul Hasluck, *The Government and the People, 1942-1945*, pp. 723-4.
[78] *Progress*, 21 November 1941, p. 4. See also Special File.
[79] *Publicist*, January 1942, p. 15.
[80] Most secret cablegram from Secretary of State for Dominion Affairs, London, to Prime Minister Curtin, 30 November 1941, H. V. Evatt Papers, Flinders University of South Australia Library, Adelaide.
[81] Rex Ingamells to Ian Mudie, 11 December 1941, Mudie Papers, State Library of South Australia.
[82] IB Report of 10 December 1941 meeting, Special File.
[83] AFM Circular, 30 December 1941, Box Y2139, SP; Clyne transcript, p. 579; Muirden, p. 64.
[84] IB Report of 17 December 1941, Special File.
[85] H. E. Jones (IB Director) to Secretary, Attorney-General's Department, 23 December 1941 and 22 January 1942, Special File; Clyne transcript, pp. 1087, 1928-30.
[86] *Publicist*, January 1942, p. 1.
[87] S to Rex Ingamells, 3 January 1942, Ingamells Papers, La Trobe Library, State Library of Victoria, Melbourne.
[88] IB Report of 7 January 1942 meeting, Special File. See also *Publicist*, February 1942, pp. 1-2.
[89] W. J. Miles died on 10 January 1942. A copy of Stephensen's Valedictory Address, 11 January 1942, is in Box Y2114, SP.
[90] S to W. D. Cookes, ? 23 January 1942, Clyne transcript, p. 618; *Inquiry into Matters Relating to the Detention of Certain Members of the "Australia First Movement" Group: Report of Commissioner Clyne*, Parliament of Commonwealth of Australia, 1945-46, pp. 17-18.
[91] IB Report by L. S. Fisher, 27 January 1942, Special File; notes by Edward Masey in the possession of Bruce Muirden.
[92] AFM Pamphlet, dated 29 January 1942, in Box Y2139, SP.
[93] IB Report by L. S. Fisher, 27 January 1942; and H. E. Jones (IB Director) to Secretary, Attorney-General's Department, 3 February 1942, Special File.
[94] MPI Report, 11 February 1942, Special File.
[95] Graham's pamphlet is with a letter from George A. Watson (Deputy Crown Solicitor) to Crown Solicitor, 12 February 1942, Attorney-General's Department, Correspondence File, W Series, CRS A472, Item W5932, AA.
[96] Hardy Wilson to S, 30 January 1942, SPFL.
[97] Hasluck, p. 724; MPI Report, 12 February 1942, Special File.
[98] W. J. MacKay to Chief Secretary's Department, 17 February 1942, Special File.
[99] AFM Circular of 14 February 1942, in Box Y2146, SP.
[1] F. K. Crowley (ed.), *A New History of Australia* (Melbourne, Heinemann, 1974), p. 465. See also Xavier Herbert's story, 'Day of Shame', in *Larger Than Life* (Angus & Robertson, 1963). Herbert later expanded this as a chapter of *Poor Fellow My Country* (Sydney, Collins, 1975).
[2] L. F. Bullock to S, 16 February 1942, Box Y2147, SP. (S obtained this copy from the Clyne Commission and it has a note by his solicitor on it.)
[3] See Richard Hall, *The Secret State: Australia's Spy Industry*, p. 34.
[4] See Muirden, chapter 8, and Hall, chapter 4.
[5] MPI and IB Reports of 19 February 1942 meeting, Special File; Eric Stephensen, 'Some Comments on the *Puzzled Patriots*', pp. 11-15; Clyne transcript, pp. 588-9; *Sydney Morning Herald*, 5 March 1942.
[6] See chapter 13 for more discussion of this.
[7] *Daily Telegraph* (Sydney), 26 February 1942, AFM Circulars of 26 and 28 February 1942, Box Y2145, SP.
[8] AFM Leaflet, 2 March 1942, Box Y2147, SP.
[9] See, for example, *Railway Advocate*, 20 February 1942, p. 1; see also *Publicist*, March 1942, pp. 5, 14.
[10] Muirden, p. 69; Clyne transcript, pp. 591-3.
[11] W. J. MacKay to Sir George Knowles (Commonwealth Solicitor-General), 7 March 1942, Special File (this includes Evatt's signed direction of 5 March 1942).
[12] See Hall, p. 36. The CSS was the forerunner of ASIO.

¹³ AFM Circular to MPs, 6 March 1942 (copy in the possession of the author); Muirden, p. 70.
¹⁴ For slightly differing versions of this telegram see: Clyne transcript, p. 5; Muirden, p. 87; and *Nation* (Sydney), 9 February 1963.

13: Behind Barbed Wire: High Treason or Low Comedy

¹ Winifred, diary note, about 10 March 1942, Box K16472, SP; S, Notes for Clyne Inquiry, Box Y2142, SP; 'In Re Habeas Corpus, Ex Parte P. R. Stephensen', sworn oath by S, 21 July 1942, Box Y2142, SP (hereafter referred to as 'Habeas Corpus Oath by S'); Bruce Muirden, *The Puzzled Patriots: The Story of the Australia First Movement*, p. 104; Attorney-General's Department, Special Files 1906-1951, Series CRS A467, File 43, Bundle 96, Item 1 (hereafter referred to as Clyne transcript), p. 594, AA. Unless otherwise noted the background for this chapter was provided by Clyne transcript; Muirden; Paul Hasluck, *The Government and the People, 1942-1945*, pp. 718-42. See also Richard Hall, *The Secret State: Australia's Spy Industry*, chapter 4.
² MPI Report of search, 10 March 1942, Box Y2147, SP; Clyne transcript, pp. 594-5.
³ Ibid.
⁴ Clyne transcript, p. 596.
⁵ Muirden, pp. 97, 106; Clyne transcript, pp. 918, 1087-8. Harley Matthews and Keith Bath were not AFM members either. See Muirden, p. 152.
⁶ Ian Mudie to Miles Franklin, 19 March and 8 April 1942, Franklin Papers (MSS 364), vol. 36, ML; Paul Grano to Ian Mudie, 3 April 1942, and Victor Kennedy to Ian Mudie, 15 May 1942, Mudie Papers (PRG 27), Series 1, State Library of South Australia. Ian Mudie's poem 'Australian Dream' won the 1943 W. J. Miles Memorial Prize for Poetry, a £50 prize donated by Val Crowley and other friends. See Miles Franklin to Dymphna Cusack, 13 October 1943, Cusack Papers (MSS 4621), NLA; and Rex Ingamells Papers (PRG 76), State Library of South Australia.
⁷ Eric Stephensen, 'Recollections mainly about P. R. Stephensen during the period of his internment 1942-45', 1979, pp. 1-2, FL.
⁸ Ibid.
⁹ S to Winifred, 16 March 1942, Box K164719, SP.
¹⁰ S to Winifred, ? 18 and 22 March 1942, Box K164719, SP.
¹¹ Miles Franklin to Ian Mudie, 17 March 1942, Mudie Papers. State Library of South Australia.
¹² Ian Mudie to Miles Franklin, 19 March 1942, Franklin Papers, ML.
¹³ See Muirden, pp. 119-23. A copy of National Security Regulation 26 is in Box Y2142, SP.
¹⁴ *Commonwealth Parliamentary Debates*, vol. 170, pp. 417-29.
¹⁵ This figure was arrived at by adding the three men and one woman involved in the Western Australian conspiracy to the sixteen Australia First men interned in New South Wales.
¹⁶ *Parliamentary Debates*, vol. 170, p. 462.
¹⁷ Gavin Long, *Macarthur as Military Commander* (Sydney, Angus & Robertson, 1969), pp. 87-90; Notes by Frank Forde (copy in the possession of the author; from material kindly made available by Elizabeth Ferrier).
¹⁸ *Parliamentary Debates*, vol. 170, p. 517.
¹⁹ Ibid., p. 522.
²⁰ Ibid., pp. 528-63.
²¹ *Sydney Morning Herald*, 27 March 1942.
²² Winifred to S, telegram, 27 March 1942, and letter, 30 March 1942, Box Y2143, SP.
²³ *Sunday Telegraph* (Sydney), 29 March 1942.
²⁴ *Tribune*, 29 April 1942, pp. 2-3.
²⁵ Miles Franklin to Ian Mudie, 21 April 1942 and ? May 1942, Mudie Papers, State Library of South Australia.
²⁶ *Bulletin*, 1 April 1942, pp. 6-7; Paul Grano to Ian Mudie, 3 April 1942, Mudie Papers, State Library of South Australia; Ian Mudie to Miles Franklin, 8 April 1942, Franklin Papers, ML.
²⁷ Mudie's poem was first published in *Their Seven Stars* (Adelaide, Jindyworobak, 1943), and subsequently reprinted in *Poems 1934-44* (Melbourne, Georgian House, 1945) and in *The Jindyworobaks*, ed. Brian Elliott, p. 75. 'If This Be Treason' is also the title of an edition of Ezra Pound's wartime radio talks in Italy. See C. David Heymann, *Ezra Pound: The Last Rower: A Political Profile*, p. 115.
²⁸ Muirden, p. 115.
²⁹ Eric Stephensen, 'Some Comments on *The Puzzled Patriots* by Bruce Muirden', 1979, p. 2, FL.

[30] Eric Stephensen, 'Recollections about Stephensen during Internment', p. 4; *Nation* (Sydney), 9 February 1963, p. 14; S to Winifred, 7 May 1942, Box K164719, SP.
[31] *War Cabinet Minutes*, vol. 11, 31 March 1942.
[32] H. F. Whitlam to Secretary, Attorney-General's Department, 16 April 1942, Attorney-General's Department, Series CRS A467, Special File 43, Bundle 97, Item 2, AA.
[33] Handwritten memo, George Knowles (Solicitor-General) to Beasley (Acting Attorney-General), 22 April 1942, in ibid., Item 3.
[34] S to Winifred, 22 April 1942, Box K164719, SP.
[35] Winifred, diary, 14 June 1942, Box K164722, SP.
[36] Winifred to S, 24 April and 27 May 1942, Box Y2143, SP.
[37] Muirden, pp. 117, 119.
[38] Flexmore Hudson to Ian Mudie, 28 June and 18 July 1942, Mudie Papers, State Library of South Australia.
[39] In Attorney-General's Department, CRS A467, Special File 43, Bundle 97, Item 3, 7, AA.
[40] Rhodes House Warden to J. C. Behan, 27 May 1942; Behan to Warden, 28 July 1942; Warden to Behan, 29 October 1942; and Warden's Report to Lord Elton, 30 October 1942, Rhodes House Records, Oxford. The *London Daily Telegraph* report was on 26 May 1942.
[41] Paul Grano to Ian Mudie, 3 April 1942, Mudie Papers, State Library of South Australia; Miles Franklin to Hartley Grattan, 8 June 1942, Franklin Papers, ML.
[42] Hartley Grattan to Miles Franklin, April 1942, Miles Franklin Papers, vol. 23, ML.
[43] Frank Clune to Army Headquarters, Victoria Barracks, 17 June 1942, and Frank Clune to C. R. McKerihan, 18 June 1942, Clune Papers (MSS 4951) Box 23, Folder 133, NLA.
[44] S, 'Habeas Corpus Oath', 21 July 1942, Box Y2142, SP. See also Muirden, p. 89.
[45] Note of address to the jury by Hughes, 11 June 1942, in Attorney-General's Department, CRS A467, Special File 43, Bundle 97, Item 6, AA. See also Muirden, chapter 8.
[46] This was the conclusion drawn by Paul Hasluck who probably had fullest access to Intelligence and other records when writing his official history of the war. See Hasluck, pp. 718-42.
[47] P. and L. Gillman, *"Collar the Lot!": How Britain Interned and Expelled its Wartime Refugees* (London, Quartet, 1980), pp. 115-29. See also Robert Skidelsky, *Oswald Mosley*.
[48] Muirden, pp. 81-4.
[49] See Clyne transcript, especially p. 1797. Copy of the 8 March 1942 Proclamation is in Attorney-General's Department, CRS A467, Special File 43, Bundle 97, Item 4, AA.
[50] A 'negotiated peace' suggests collaboration, whereas a 'separate peace' was an assertion of Australia's independence in foreign affairs. In 1939, for example, Menzies had considered that Australia was at war with Germany as soon as Britain declared war, whereas the Labor Government had declared war on Japan independently, in 1941.
[51] 8 March 1942 Proclamation, AA. See also Craig Munro, 'Australia First—Women Last: Pro-Fascism and Anti-Feminism in the 1930s', *Hecate*, vol. 9, double issue (1983).
[52] Muirden, p. 98; and Hall, p. 38.
[53] S to Chairman of Internment Advisory Committee, 8 May 1942, quoted in 'Habeas Corpus Oath by S', 21 July 1942, Box Y2142, SP; *Truth* (Sydney), 2 August 1942; and *Sun* (Sydney), 3 September 1942.
[54] *Parliamentary Debates*, vol. 172, p. 155.
[55] Ibid., p. 156.
[56] Hasluck, p. 733.
[57] S to Official Camp Visitor, 14 October 1942, Box Y2142, SP.
[58] Gianfranco Cresciani, *Fascism, Anti-Fascism and Italians in Australia 1922-1945* (Canberra, Australian National University Press, 1980), pp. 176-9.
[59] Clyne transcript, pp. 769-70; Muirden, p. 127.
[60] See Muirden, p. 126.
[61] S to Winifred, 21 December 1942, Box K164719, SP.
[62] Skidelsky, p. 468.
[63] Goethe, *Faust*. Trans. by John Prudhoe (Manchester University Press, 1974).
[64] S to Winifred, 11 October and 11 December 1942, 20 January 1943, Box K164719, SP; Frank Clune to S, 16 January 1943, Clune Papers (MSS 4951), NLA.
[65] Frank Clune to C. R. McKerihan, 12 February 1943, Clune Papers (MSS 4951), NLA.
[66] S to Winifred, 11 and 12 February 1943, 8 May 1943, Box K164719, SP. See also Charles Willyan, *Behind Barbed Wire in Australia: The Amazing Experiences of an Australian Citizen* (Victoria, private, 1948), pp. 15-16.
[67] Winifred to S, 26 May, 2 July and 19 August 1943, Box Y2143, SP.
[68] Miles Franklin to Dymphna Cusack, 30 June 1943, Cusack Papers (MSS 4621), NLA.
[69] Winifred to S, 26 August 1943, Box Y2143, SP.
[70] S to Winifred, 10 July 1943, Box K164719, SP.

[71] W. H. Downing to S, 27 July 1943 and 3 December 1943, Box Y2142, SP.
[72] S to Solicitors for the Estate of W. J. Miles, ? July 1943, Box Y2149, SP; Winifred to S, 1 September 1943, Box Y2143, SP.
[73] S to W. H. Downing, 20 September 1943, Box Y2142, SP.
[74] S to W. H. Downing, 30 December 1943; and S to Winifred, 5 February 1944, Box Y2142, SP.
[75] S to Winifred, 9 March 1944, Box K164719, SP.
[76] S to Winifred, 19 April 1944, ibid.
[77] S to Ian Mudie, 10 March 1944, Mudie Papers, State Library of South Australia.
[78] Miles Franklin to Ian Mudie, 2 April 1945, Franklin Papers, ML; Ian Mudie to S, 10 April 1945, Box Y2142, SP. A possible Preface for a reprint of *Bushwhackers* is in Box Y2153, SP.
[79] *Sydney Morning Herald*, 1 April 1944; W. H. Downing to Commonwealth Attorney-General, 3 May 1944, Box Y2142, SP.
[80] *Truth* (Sydney), 2 April 1944.
[81] *Herald* (Melbourne), 2 May 1944; Muirden, p. 133.
[82] S to W. H. Downing, 4 May 1944, Box Y2142, SP.
[83] Allan Dalziel, *Evatt the Enigma* (Melbourne, Lansdowne, 1967), p. 27.
[84] S to Winifred, 8 June 1944, Box K164719; Winifred to S, 23 June 1944, Box Y2143, SP.
[85] Eric Stephensen, 'Recollections about Stephensen during Internment', p. 6; Eric Stephensen, 'Some Reminiscences of P. R. Stephensen, 1945-1956', 1969, p. 13, FL.
[86] *Inquiry into Matters Relating to the Detention of Certain Members of the "Australia First Movement" Group: Report of Commissioner Clyne* (Parliament of Commonwealth of Australia, 1946).
[87] Hall, p. 38. See also Muirden, chapter 12; and Clyne transcript.
[88] Muirden, pp. 144-5.
[89] Clyne transcript, pp. 604, 608, 610.
[90] Ibid., p. 618A.
[91] Ibid., p. 713.
[92] It was actually published in March 1939; see *Publicist*, March 1939, p. 5.
[93] Clyne transcript, p. 640.
[94] Ibid., pp. 640, 669.
[95] Ibid., pp. 646-7.
[96] Ibid., p. 650.
[97] Ian Mudie to S, 22 October 1944, Box Y2142, SP. Winifred to Jack Lockyer, 22 October 1944 (letter in the possession of Jack Lockyer).
[98] S to Winifred, 13 June 1945, Box K164719, SP.
[99] S to Winifred, 21 June 1945, ibid.
[1] Order revoking detention, 15 August 1945, Box Y2147, SP; S to Commandant, Camp No. 3, Tatura, 15 and 16 August 1945, Box Y2141, SP.

14: Ghost in Exile

[1] S to Keith Bath, 30 December 1945 (letter in the possession of Bruce Muirden).
[2] S to Frank Clune, 23 August 1945, Box Y2142, SP; S to Bernard H. Corser, 13 September 1945, Box Y2144, SP.
[3] *Inquiry into Matters Relating to the Detention of Certain Members of the "Australia First Movement" Group: Report of Commissioner Clyne* (Parliament of Commonwealth of Australia, 1946), pp. 17-18.
[4] W. H. Downing to S, 1 June 1948, and notes by Downing on the Australia First cases, Box Y2147, SP; S to A. Rud Mills, 20 February 1950, Box Y2142, SP.
[5] S to Keith Bath, 2 July 1946 (letter in the possession of Bruce Muirden; copy also in Box Y2142, SP).
[6] S to W. H. Downing, 28 October 1945, Box Y2142, SP.
[7] Eric Stephensen, 'Some Reminiscences of P. R. Stephensen at East Warburton, Bethanga, Sandringham, Victoria, 1945-1956', 1969, pp. 3-5, FL.
[8] S to Ian Mudie, 17 March 1946, Box Y2142, SP.
[9] S to Denison Deasey, 14 August 1946, Box Y2139; Bruce Muirden, *The Puzzled Patriots: The Story of the Australia First Movement*, p. 177. For more on Kirtley see Muirden. Kirtley's internment correspondence is in the Frank Johnson Papers (MSS 1214/35), Item 1, ML. See also Clyne transcript, pp. 1457ff. After a serious illness in 1953 Kirtley was left with a weakened heart and died in 1967.
[10] S to A. Rud Mills, 13 February 1947, Box Y2141, SP; Eric Stephensen, 'Reminiscences of Stephensen, 1945-56', p. 15.

[11] Marriage Certificate in the possession of Jack Lockyer.
[12] Marjorie Barnard to Nettie Palmer, 19 May 1935, Palmer Papers (MSS 1174), NLA.
[13] Margriet R. Bonnin, A study of Australian Descriptive and Travel Writing, 1929-45, p. 33.
[14] Frank Clune to S, ? February 1945, Box Y2130, SP.
[15] Winifred to S, 6 December 1943, Box Y2143, SP.
[16] S to Frank Clune, 12 September 1959, Box Y2114; Frank Clune to S, 19 September, 1945, Box Y2142, SP; Frank Clune to Rex Ingamells, October 1952, Box Y2127, SP.
[17] S to W. H. Downing, 28 October 1945, Box Y2142, SP.
[18] Frank Clune to S, 21 September 1945, Box Y2142, SP.
[19] Frank Clune to S, 24 August 1946, Box Y2141, SP.
[20] Interview with Jack Lockyer (1980).
[21] Frank Clune to S, October 1947, SPFL.
[22] S to Frank Clune, 14 October 1947, SPFL.
[23] Frank Clune to S, 16 December 1954, Box Y2132, SP.
[24] S to Frank Clune, 14 October 1961, Box Y2124, SP. One of the few books Clune wrote on his own, *Search for the Golden Fleece: The Story of the Peppin Merino* (Sydney, Angus & Robertson, 1965), is a good example of how important Stephensen's work for Clune was. *Search for the Golden Fleece* is very badly written and constructed.
[25] See, for example, review of *Wild Colonial Boys*, in *Sydney Morning Herald*, 2 April 1948. For a list of some Clune reviews, see Bonnin, pp. 424-7.
[26] S to Frank Clune, 23 August 1945, Box Y2142, SP.
[27] Rex Ingamells to Frank Clune, 18 September 1952; S to Frank Clune, 28 October 1952, Box Y2127, SP. Also Rex Ingamells to S, 17 December 1952, Box Y2139, SP.
[28] S to Frank Clune, 29 November 1949, Box Y2150, SP.
[29] S to Frank Clune, 23 August 1945, Box Y2142, SP.
[30] S to Ian Mudie, 18 July 1952, Box Y2124, SP.
[31] The other book co-authored with Clune was *The Pirates of the Brig Cyprus*.
[32] Frank Clune and P. R. Stephensen, *The Viking of Van Diemen's Land: The Stormy Life of Jorgen Jorgenson*, p. 216.
[33] George Ferguson to S, November 1953, Box Y2112, SP; George Ferguson to Frank Clune, 3 April 1952, Box Y2126, SP.
[34] Frank Clune to S, 16 February 1953, Box Y2126, SP.
[35] S to Frank Clune, 13 October 1953, Clune Papers (MSS 4951), NLA.
[36] S to E. Morris Miller, 16 February 1954, Box Y2110, SP.
[37] E. Morris Miller to S, 8 February 1954, Box Y2110, SP.
[38] *Viking of Van Diemen's Land*, pp. 408, 414, 462.
[39] Ibid., p. 476.
[40] S to Winifred, 24 October 1926, Box K164719, SP.
[41] *Viking of Van Diemen's Land*, p. 476.
[42] Ibid., p. 11.
[43] Ibid., p. 466.
[44] Ibid., p. 241.
[45] Ibid., p. 270.
[46] Ibid., pp. 232, 406.
[47] Ibid., p. 465.
[48] A fragment of autobiography is in Box Y2136, SP.
[49] S to Frank Clune, 4 July 1952, Box Y2124, SP. The name S proposed for his new press was the Kookaburra Press. The *Publicist* masthead used to feature a kookaburra and Miles and S used to delight in thinking up satirical titles such as K.S.K. ('King of the Sydney Kookaburras').
[50] Frank Clune to S, 17 July 1952, Box Y2133, SP.
[51] S to Ian Mudie, 18 July 1952, Box Y2124, SP.
[52] He reviewed *The Ridge and the River* by Tom Hungerford and *The Shades Will Not Vanish* by Helen Fowler, *Austrovert*, no. 7 (1952), pp. 4-5. Bruce Muirden, later the historian of the Australia First Movement, edited *Austrovert*.
[53] *Queensland University Magazine*, August 1920, pp. 16-17.
[54] S, *Kookaburras and Satyrs: Some Recollections of the Fanfrolico Press*, pp. 11-12, 21.
[55] Ibid., p. 13.
[56] Ibid., pp. 21-2.
[57] Ibid., p. 21.
[58] *Biblionews*, vol. 12, no. 2 (February 1959).
[59] 'Fanfrolico Fantasia', *Australian Book Review*, August 1962, pp. 132-4.
[60] S to Jack Lindsay, 25 August 1961 (letter in the possession of Jack Lindsay; copy also in box K164724, SP).

[61] Frank Clune to S, 13 July 1954, Box Y2142, SP.
[62] Frank Clune to S, 'Dawn Tuesday' [? December 1954], and 16 December 1954; S to Frank Clune, 9 December 1954, Box Y2132, SP.
[63] S to George Ferguson, 14 December 1954, Box Y2132, SP. He may have been beaten to the gun on this project by Geoffrey Blainey, whose book *The Peaks of Lyell* was published by Melbourne University Press in 1954.
[64] For details of all these books see Bibliography, Section B.1; for details of various editions and translations, see Eric Stephensen, *Bibliography of Percy Reginald Stephensen*, pp. 6-10.
[65] A copy of the souvenir menu for the luncheon, 18 June 1958, is in Box Y2118, SP.
[66] *Bulletin*, 14 December 1960, p. 6; S to Laurence Pollinger, 20 September 1960, Box Y2124, SP.
[67] S to Laurence Pollinger, 20 September 1960, Box Y2124, SP. See also S to Molly Lawrence, 31 March 1960, Box Y2113, SP; and S to W. V. Burns, 14 June 1960, Box Y2110, SP.
[68] Memos, S to W. V. Burns, 3, 10 and 14 September 1960, Box Y2112, SP.
[69] *Bulletin*, 14 December 1960, p. 7.
[70] S to George Lauri, 27 December 1960, Box Y2113, SP; S to W. V. Burns, 14 February 1961, Box Y2109, SP.
[71] S to Rolf Hennequel, 30 September 1961, Hennequel Papers (MSS 2923), NLA; Solicitors for S to Angus & Robertson, 1 November 1960, Box Y2139, SP.
[72] For more detail on this episode see Craig Munro, 'Inky Stephensen, Xavier Herbert and *Capricornia*: the Facts About a Long Fiction', pp. 55-7.
[73] *Bulletin*, 29 March 1961, p. 52.
[74] Xavier Herbert, draft letter to editor [*Bulletin*?], ? April 1961, Herbert Papers (MSS 83), Box 20, FL.
[75] Xavier Herbert to Clem Christesen, 21 March 1961; and Christesen to Herbert, 26 June 1961, Herbert Papers, Box 27, FL.
[76] S to Rolf Hennequel, 15 March 1961, Hennequel Papers, NLA; S to Geoffrey Dutton, 24 October 1961, Box Y2123, SP.
[77] S to Miles Franklin, 30 May 1952, SPFL. The years S spent in Sydney were 1932-42. In *Kookaburras and Satyrs*, p. 34, he made the same mistake of thinking he had returned from England in 1931, when in fact it was 1932.
[78] See Muirden, p. 173.
[79] *Herald* (Melbourne), 24 May 1961, p. 4.
[80] S to A. Rud Mills, 27 May 1961; Solicitor to S, 19 June 1961; and S to Solicitor, 26 June 1961, Box Y2113, SP.
[81] David Wilson to S, ? 1958, Box Y2109, SP; S to A. Rud Mills, 12 December 1958, Box Y2150, SP.
[82] S to Ian Mudie, 6 June 1952, Box Y2124.
[83] Interview with Manning Clark (1981). See also Stephen Holt, *Manning Clark and Australian History* (St Lucia, University of Queensland Press, 1982), pp. 33, 94-5, 97, 108.
[84] S to Manning Clark, 19 August 1952, Box Y2153, SP.
[85] S to Tom Graham, 23 November 1953, Box Y2145, SP.
[86] S to A. Rud Mills, 1 July 1954, SPFL.
[87] S to A. A. Calwell, 9 December 1959, SPFL; S to Charles Willyan, 7 April 1960, Box Y2125, SP.
[88] S to A. P. Sachs, 18 November 1964, Box Y2113, SP.
[89] A copy of the letter is in SPFL.
[90] *Bulletin*, 23 December 1959, pp. 2, 58-9.
[91] *Nation*, 10 October 1959, p. 22.
[92] *Nation*, 31 January 1959, pp. 10-12; and 14 February 1959, pp. 8-10. Bruce Muirden used this as the basis for much of his material on Stephensen's life in *The Puzzled Patriots*.
[93] S to E. Dimmock, 22 March 1959, Box Y2123, SP.
[94] *Nation*, 28 February 1959, pp. 17-18.
[95] S to Frank Clune, 10 November 1962, Box K164725, SP; S to George Ferguson, 29 November 1962, Box Y2124, SP; Agreement between S and Clune, 19 February 1963, Box K164720, SP.
[96] Letter from M. R. A. Warren, *Nation*, 28 February 1959, p. 17.
[97] S to Jack Lindsay, 25 August 1961 (letter in the possession of Jack Lindsay; copy also in Box K164724, SP).
[98] *Telegraph* (Brisbane), 4 June 1962. One of his lectures 'Colonialism in Our Literature', was published in the *Bulletin*, 16 June 1962, pp. 27-9.
[99] *Viking of Van Diemen's Land*, p. vii.

[1] S to Ida Leeson, 17 March 1953, Box Y2110, SP; S to A. D. Hope, 7 November 1956, Box Y2117, SP. It is possible that the remaining volumes of the Baylebridge Memorial Edition will be edited by Noel Macainsh.
[2] *Nation*, 24 February 1960, p. 23. S replied in *Nation*, 10 March 1962, p. 16.
[3] Judith Wright, *Australian Poetry*. Commonwealth Literary Fund Lecture, University of New England, Armidale, 1955, p. 31.
[4] *Morning Bulletin* (Rockhampton), 11 February 1964, p. 7; 19 and 27 February 1964.
[5] George Ferguson to S, 26 January 1965, Box Y2150, SP. The first three volumes of the Baylebridge Memorial Edition had sold only between 200 and 750 copies each.
[6] Review by Gustav Cross, *Sydney Morning Herald*, 21 August 1965.
[7] Winifred, diary, 9 March 1961 and ? 1965, Box Y2144, SP.
[8] Winifred to Herbert Burton, 15 August 1965 (letter in the possession of Professor Burton).
[9] Walter Stone, 'The Death of P. R. Stephensen' (draft copy in the possession of Bruce Muirden).
[10] *Viking of Van Diemen's Land*, p. 452.
[11] Ian Mudie to A. D. Hope, 22 June 1965, Hope Papers, correspondence about publications, in II, Folder 7, NLA.
[12] *Daily Telegraph* (Sydney), 29 May 1965; *Sydney Morning Herald*, 31 May and 3 June 1965; *Bulletin*, 5 June 1965, p. 11.
[13] Stone, 'The Death of P. R. Stephensen'.

Bibliography

A. UNPUBLISHED SOURCES

A.1 Manuscript Collections and Items

Australian Archives, Canberra: Attorney-General's Department, Series CRS A467, File 43, Bundle 96, item 1 (Clyne transcript); and Bundle 97, item 1 (MPI & IB reports).
Australian Encyclopaedia. Papers (MSS 1144/1, items 2–3). Mitchell Library, Sydney.
Australian Mercury. Papers (MSS 1727, vols 1-3). Mitchell Library, Sydney.
Clune, Frank. Papers (MSS 4951). National Library of Australia, Canberra.
———. Diaries. Mitchell Library, Sydney.
Crowley, Aleister, Papers (G. J. Yorke Collection). Warburg Institute, London.
———. Papers (in the possession of G. J. Yorke).
Cusack, Dymphna. Papers (MSS 4621). National Library of Australia, Canberra.
Evatt, H. V. Papers. Flinders University of South Australia Library, Adelaide.
Fotheringham, Richard. Papers (MSS 46). Fryer Library, University of Queensland, Brisbane.
———. 'Biographical Study of Percy Reginald Stephensen, 1901-32'. Fryer Library, University of Queensland, Brisbane.
Franklin, Miles. Papers (MSS 364). Mitchell Library, Sydney.
Green, H. M. Papers (MSS 3925). National Library of Australia, Canberra.
Hennequel, Rolf. Papers (MSS 2923). National Library of Australia, Canberra.
Herbert, Xavier. Papers (MSS 758). National Library of Australia, Canberra.
———. Papers (Sadie Herbert Collection, MSS 83). Fryer Library, University of Queensland, Brisbane.

——. 'The Facts of the Publication of *Capricornia*: For the Historical Record'. Herbert Papers (MSS 758, Series II). National Library of Australia, Canberra.
Ingamells, Rex. Papers (PRG 76). State Library of South Australia (Archives), Adelaide.
——. Papers. La Trobe Library, State Library of Victoria, Melbourne.
Kennedy, Victor. Papers, La Trobe Library, State Library of Victoria, Melbourne.
Lawrence, D. H. Calendar of Letters (1928-30). Computer print-out for the Cambridge University Press edition of the letters of D. H. Lawrence (copy in the author's possession).
——. Letters to P. R. Stephensen (copies in the possession of the author).
Mackaness, George. Papers (MSS 534). National Library of Australia, Canberra.
Miller, E. Morris. Papers (MSS 87). National Library of Australia, Canberra.
Mudie, Ian. Papers (PRG 27). State Library of South Australia (Archives), Adelaide.
Muirden, Bruce. Papers (in the possession of Bruce Muirden; may be available later in Fryer Library, Brisbane).
Palmer, Vance and Nettie. Papers (MSS 1174). National Library of Australia, Canberra.
Politzer, L. L. Papers. La Trobe Library, State Library of Victoria, Melbourne.
Queen's College Records, Oxford.
Rhodes House Records, Oxford.
Roberthall, Robert Lowe Hall, baron. 'Notes about P. R. Stephensen 1918-1932'. Fotheringham Papers (MSS 46), Fryer Library, University of Queensland, Brisbane.
Stephensen, Eric. 'Recollections of P. R. Stephensen'. Fryer Library, University of Queensland, Brisbane.
Stephensen, P. R. Papers (MSS 1284). Mitchell Library, Sydney.
——. Papers (Walter Stone Collection, MSS 55, and Jack Lockyer Collection). Fryer Library, University of Queensland, Brisbane.
——. Papers (in the possession of Rosaline Stephensen).
Stone, Walter. Papers (MSS 1674). Mitchell Library, Sydney.
——. Papers. John Oxley Library, Brisbane.
University of Queensland Archives, Brisbane.
Walker, S. E. A. 'School Days with Percy'. Fotheringham Papers (MSS 46), Fryer Library, University of Queensland, Brisbane.
WEA Queensland Central Council Minutes, 1919-25 (OM 64). John Oxley Library, Brisbane.

A.2 Interviews

NOTE: Unless otherwise stated, these were usually tape recorded and transcribed by the author. Copies in the author's possession.

Ayerst, David (1980) Burford, England.
Burton, Herbert (1981) Canberra.

Campbell-Brown, Kathleen (1981) Brisbane.
Clark, Colin (1980) Brisbane.
Clark, Manning (1981) Canberra.
Clune, Thelma (1980) Sydney.
Davis, Beatrice (1980) Sydney.
Dibley, Arthur (1977) Sydney.
Downing, W. A. J. (1980) Melbourne.
Elliott, Brian (1982) Adelaide.
Fletcher, W. R. (1980) London.
Herbert, Sadie (1976) Audio Visual Library, University of Queensland, Brisbane.
Herbert, Xavier. Canberra interview 1975. Transcript copy in the Sadie Herbert Collection (MSS 83). Fryer Library, University of Queensland, Brisbane.
Hunt, J. A. (1981) Brisbane.
Lindsay, Jack (1980) Castle Hedingham, England.
Lockyer, Jack (1977-80) Sydney.
Paterson, Fred. Audio Visual Library, University of Queensland, Brisbane.
Reissner, A. (1980) London.
Roberthall, Robert Lowe Hall, baron (1980) London.
Ruhen, Olaf (1977) Sydney.
Stephensen, Eric (1979) Melbourne.
Stephensen, Rosaline (1977-81) Brisbane.
Stone, Walter, (1977) Sydney.
Taylor, A. J. P. (1980) London.
Thomson, A. K. (1981) Brisbane.
Ward, Russel (1982) Brisbane.

A.3 Theses

Bonnin, Margriet R. A Study of Australian Descriptive and Travel Writing, 1929-45. Ph.D., English, University of Queensland, 1980.
Bryson, David B. C. Hartley Grattan: An American Intellectual and Reformer 1925-1945—An Evaluation. B.A. Hons, Flinders University, 1974.
Docker, John. Literature and Social Thought: Australia in an International Context 1890-1925. Ph.D., English, Australian National University. 1980.
Evans, Raymond. Loyalty and Disloyalty: Social and Ideological Conflict in Queensland During the Great War. Ph.D., History, University of Queensland, 1981.
Fotheringham, Richard. The Life of P. R. Stephensen, Australian Publisher, parts 4 & 5: 1927-32. B.A. Hons, English, University of Queensland, 1970.
Linton, Gary H. An Approach to P. R. Stephensen. B.A. Hons, History, University of Melbourne, 1974.
McDougall, Russell J. Xavier Herbert's *Capricornia*: Ironic Structure and Imaginative Vision. M.A., English, University of Adelaide, 1981.

Munro, Craig. Inky Stephensen, Xavier Herbert and *Capricornia*: The Facts about a Long Fiction. M.A. qual., English, University of Queensland, 1977.

Murnane, Mary. The Workers' Educational Association of Queensland 1913-1939. M.A. qual., History, University of Queensland, 1969.

B. PUBLISHED WORKS BY P. R. STEPHENSEN
(details of first editions only)

B.1 Books (including translations and collaborations)

Imperialism. By V. I. Lenin (trans.). London, Communist Party of Great Britain, 1925.

On the Road to Insurrection. By V. I. Lenin (trans.). London, Communist Party of Great Britain, 1926.

The Antichrist of Nietzsche (trans.). London, Fanfrolico Press, 1928.

The Sink of Solitude. London, Hermes Press, 1928.

Policeman of the Lord: A Political Satire. London, Sophistocles Press, [?1929].

The Well of Sleevelessness: A Tale for the Least of These Little Ones. London, Scholartis Press, 1929.

The Bushwhackers: Sketches of Life in the Australian Outback. London, Mandrake Press, 1929.

The Legend of Aleister Crowley. London, Mandrake Press, 1930.

Pavlova (ghosted for Walford Hyden). London, Constable, 1931.

A Master of Hounds: Being the Life Story of Harry Buckland of Ashford (anon). London, Faber, 1931.

Trade Without Money! An Examination of the German Barter System (anon). Sydney, Australian Book Services Ltd., 1935.

The Foundations of Culture in Australia: An Essay Towards National Self Respect. Sydney, W. J. Miles, 1936.

The Life and Works of A. G. Stephens ("The Bookfellow"): A Lecture, Delivered to the Fellowship of Australian Writers, Sydney, 10 March 1940. Sydney, private, 1940.

Glossary to "Bio-Politics". Sydney, Publicist Publishing Co., 1941.

Fifty Points for Australia: An Exposition of a Policy for an Australia-First Party After the War. Sydney, Publicist Publishing Co., 1941.

Kookaburras and Satyrs: Some Recollections of the Fanfrolico Press. Sydney, Talkarra Press, 1954.

The Viking of Van Diemen's Land: The Stormy Life of Jorgen Jorgensen (with Frank Clune). Sydney, Angus & Robertson, 1954.

Flynn's Flying Doctors (with Harry Hudson). London, Heinemann, 1956.

The Cape Horn Breed (with Captain William H. S. Jones). London, Melrose, 1956.

Philip Dimmock: A Memoir of a Poet. Sydney, Talkarra Press, 1958.

Sail Ho! (with Sir James Bisset). Sydney, Angus & Robertson, 1958.

Tramps and Ladies (with Sir James Bisset). Sydney, Angus & Robertson, 1959.

Commodore (with Sir James Bisset). Sydney, Angus & Robertson, 1961.

Sydney Sails: The Story of the Royal Sydney Yacht Squadron's First 100 Years (1862-1962). Sydney, Angus & Robertson, 1962.
The Pirates of the Brig Cyprus (with Frank Clune). London, Hart-Davis, 1962.
The History and Description of Sydney Harbour. Adelaide, Rigby, 1966.

B.2 **Books Written for Frank Clune** (published under Clune's name)

NOTE: Unless otherwise stated, the publisher is Angus & Robertson, Sydney.

Dig. 1937.
Free and Easy Land. 1938.
Sky High to Shanghai. 1939.
Isles of Spice. 1940.
All Aboard for Singapore. 1941.
Chinese Morrison. Melbourne, Bread & Cheese Club, 1941.
D'Air Devil. Sydney, Allied Authors & Artists, 1941.
Prowling through Papua. 1942.
Last of the Australian Explorers. 1942.
The Red Heart. Melbourne, Hawthorn, 1944.
Dark Outlaw. Sydney, Invincible, 1945. (Reprinted as *Gunman Gardiner.* Melbourne, Cheshire, 1952; and as *King of the Road.* 1967.)
Pacific Parade. Melbourne, Hawthorn, 1945.
Captain Starlight. Melbourne, Hawthorn, 1945.
The Greatest Liar on Earth. Melbourne, Hawthorn, 1945.
The Forlorn Hope. Melbourne, Hawthorn, 1945.
Golden Goliath. Melbourne, Hawthorn, 1946.
Song of India. Sydney, Invincible, 1946.
Try Nothing Twice. 1946.
Roaming Around Australia. Melbourne, Hawthorn, 1947.
Ben Hall the Bushranger. 1947.
Wild Colonial Boys. 1948.
High-Ho to London. 1948.
"The Demon" Killer. Sydney, Invincible, 1948.
Noose for Ned. Melbourne, Hawthorn, 1949.
Land of My Birth. Sydney, Invincible, 1949.
Land of Hope and Glory. 1949.
Ashes of Hiroshima. 1950.
All Roads Lead to Rome. Sydney, Invincible, 1950.
Hands Across the Pacific. 1951.
Somewhere in New Guinea. 1951.
Castles in Spain. 1952.
Flying Dutchmen. 1953.
Land of Australia. Melbourne, Hawthorn, 1953.
Roaming Round Europe. 1954.
The Kelly Hunters. 1954.
Martin Cash. 1955.
Overland Telegraph. 1955.
Korean Diary. 1955.
Captain Melville. 1956.
Roaming Round New Zealand. 1956.
The Fortune Hunters. 1957.
Scandals of Sydney Town. 1957.
A Tale of Tahiti. 1958.
Flight to Formosa. 1958.
Murders on Maunga-tapu. 1959.
The Blue Mountains Murderer. Sydney, Horwitz, 1959.
Jimmy Governor. Sydney, Horwitz, 1959.
Journey to Canberra. 1960.
Saga of Sydney. 1961.
Across the Snowy Mountains. 1961.
Ned Kelly's Last Stand. 1962.
Bound for Botany Bay. 1964.
Journey to Kosciusko. 1964.
Journey to Pitcairn. 1966.
Norfolk Island Story. 1967.
Captain Bully Hayes. 1970.

C. SELECTED BOOKS AND ARTICLES

Amos, Keith. *The New Guard Movement 1931-1935*. Melbourne, Melbourne University Press, 1976.

Andrews, E. M. *Isolationism and Appeasement in Australia: Reactions to the European Crises 1935-1939*. Canberra, Australian National University Press, 1970.

Barnard, Marjorie. *Miles Franklin*. Melbourne, Hill of Content, 1967.

Bentley, Eric. *A Century of Hero-Worship*. 1944. Boston, Beacon Hill, 1957.

Brittain, Vera. *Radclyffe Hall: A Case of Obscenity?* London, Femina, 1968.

Buckley, Vincent. 'Utopianism and Vitalism'. *Quadrant*, vol. 3, no. 2 (1958-59), pp. 39-51.

Cave, Roderick. *The Private Press*. London, Faber & Faber, 1971.

Chaplin, Harry F. *The Fanfrolico Press: A Survey*. Sydney, Wentworth Press, 1976.

——. *Norman Lindsay: His Books, Manuscripts and Autograph Letters*. Sydney, Wentworth Press, 1969.

Cohn, Norman. *Warrant for Genocide: The Myth of the Jewish World-Conspiracy and the Protocols of the Elders of Zion*. London, Eyre & Spottiswoode, 1967.

Coleman, Peter. *Obscenity, Blasphemy, Sedition: 100 years of Censorship in Australia*. Sydney, Angus & Robertson, 1974.

Coleman, Verna. *Miles Franklin in America: Her Unknown (Brilliant) Career*. Sydney, Angus & Robertson, 1981.

Davidson, Alastair. *The Communist Party of Australia: A Short History*. Stanford, Hoover, 1969.

Day, A. Grove. *Eleanor Dark*. Boston, Twayne, 1976.

Driberg, Tom. *Ruling Passions*. London, Cape, 1977.

Elliott, Brian, ed. *The Jindyworobaks*. St Lucia, University of Queensland Press, 1979.

Ellis, M. H. *The Garden Path: The Story of the Saturation of the Australian Labour Movement by Communism*. Sydney, The Land Newspaper Ltd, 1949.

[Fitzgerald, Tom] 'Julian Smith'. *On the Pacific Front: The Adventures of Egon Kisch in Australia*. Sydney, Australian Book Services Ltd., 1936.

[Fitzgerald, T. M.]. 'Traveller's Ghost: The Tempestuous and Hitherto Unlogged Voyage of P. R. Stephensen'. *Nation*, 31 January 1959, pp. 10-12, and 14 February 1959, pp. 8-10.

Fotheringham, Richard. 'Expatriate Publishing: Jack Lindsay and the Fanfrolico Press'. *Meanjin*, vol. 31, no. 1 (March 1972), pp. 55-61.

——. 'Expatriate Publishing: P. R. Stephensen and the Mandrake Press'. *Meanjin*, vol. 31, no. 2 (June 1972), pp. 183-8.

Franklin, Miles. *Laughter, Not for a Cage*. Sydney, Angus & Robertson, 1956.

Fromm, Erich. *The Fear of Freedom*. London, Routledge & Kegan Paul, 1942.

Gibson, Ralph. *My Years in the Communist Party*. Melbourne, International Bookshop, 1966.

——. *Stop This Fascist Propaganda*. Melbourne [? 1942].

Grattan, C. Hartley. 'A Garrulity about Australian Literature Since 1927'. *Meanjin*, vol. 24, no. 4 (1965), pp. 405-16.
Gray, Cecil. *Peter Warlock: A Memoir of Philip Heseltine*. London, Cape, 1934.
Griffiths, Richard. *Fellow Travellers of the Right: British Enthusiasts for Nazi Germany 1933-39*. London, Constable, 1980.
Hall, Richard. *The Secret State: Australia's Spy Industry*. Sydney, Cassell, 1978.
Hamilton, Alastair. *The Appeal of Fascism: A Study of Intellectuals and Fascism 1919-1945*. London, Anthony Blond, 1971.
Hasluck, Paul. *The Government and the People 1942-1945*. Canberra, Australian War Memorial, 1970.
Herbert, Xavier. 'How "Capricornia" was Made'. *Bulletin*, 8 March 1961, pp. 51-2.
Hetherington, John. *Norman Lindsay: The Embattled Olympian*. Melbourne, Oxford University Press, 1973.
Heymann, C. David. *Ezra Pound: The Last Rower: A Political Profile*. New York, Viking, 1976.
Horner, Jack. *Vote Ferguson for Aboriginal Freedom*. Sydney, ANZ Book Co., 1974.
Ingamells, Rex. *Conditional Culture*. Adelaide, F. W. Preece, 1938.
Inquiry into Matters Relating to the Detention of Certain Members of the 'Australia First Movement' Group: Report of Commissioner Clyne. Canberra, 1946.
Kisch, Egon Erwin. *Australian Landfall*. Trans. from German by John Fisher and Irene and Kevin Fitzgerald. Sydney, Australasian Book Society, 1969.
Lawrence, D. H. *The Collected Letters of D. H. Lawrence*, ed. Harry T. Moore. Vol. 2. London, Heinemann, 1962.
———. *The Letters of D. H. Lawrence*, ed. Aldous Huxley. London, Heinemann, 1932.
———. *The Quest for Rananim: D. H. Lawrence's Letters to S. S. Koteliansky 1914-1930*, ed. George J. Zytaruk. Montreal, McGill-Queens University Press, 1970.
Lindsay, Jack. 'Expatriate Publishing (Part II).' *Meanjin*, vol. 33, no. 2 (June 1974), pp. 176-9.
———. *Life Rarely Tells: An Autobiography in Three Volumes*. (Includes *Life Rarely Tells* [1958], *The Roaring Twenties* [1960], and *Fanfrolico and After* [1962]). Ringwood, Penguin, 1982.
———. '*Vision* and *London Aphrodite*'. In Bruce Bennett, ed., *Cross Currents: Magazines and Newspapers in Australian Literature*. Melbourne, Longman Cheshire, 1981.
Lindsay, Norman. *Letters of Norman Lindsay*, ed. R. G. Howarth and A. W. Barker. Sydney, Angus & Robertson, 1979.
Lindsay, Philip. *I'd Live the Same Life Over*. London, Hutchinson, 1941.
Lindsay, Rose. *Model Wife: My Life with Norman Lindsay*. Sydney, Ure Smith, 1967.
Macainsh, Noel. *Nietzsche in Australia: A Literary Inquiry into a Nationalistic Ideology*. Munich, Verlag Für Dokumentation und Werbung, 1975.

Miles Franklin: A Tribute by Some of Her Friends. Melbourne, Bread & Cheese Club, 1955.

Modjeska, Drusilla. *Exiles at Home: Australian Women Writers 1925-1945*. Sydney, Angus & Robertson, 1981.

Moore, Harry T. *The Priest of Love: A Life of D. H. Lawrence*. London, Heinemann, rev. ed., 1974.

Mudie, Ian. *This is Australia*. Adelaide, Frank E. Cork, [1941].

Muirden, Bruce. *The Puzzled Patriots: The Story of the Australia First Movement*. Melbourne, Melbourne University Press, 1968.

Munro, Craig. 'Australia First—Women Last: Pro-fascism and anti-feminism in the 1930s'. *Hecate*, vol. 9, double issue (1983), pp. 25-34.

———. '*Lady Chatterley* in London: The Story of the Secret Third Edition'. In Michael Squires and Dennis Jackson, eds, *D. H. Lawrence's 'Lady': A New Look at Lady Chatterley's Lover*. University of Georgia Press, forthcoming, 1985.

———. 'P. R. Stephensen and the *Australian Mercury*'. In Bruce Bennett, ed., *Cross Currents: Magazines and Newspapers in Australian Literature*. Melbourne, Longman Cheshire, 1981, pp. 103-14.

———. 'P. R. Stephensen and the Early Workers' Theatre Movement in London'. *Australasian Drama Studies*, vol. 1, no. 2 (1983), pp. 124-54.

———. 'Some Facts About a Long Fiction: The Publication of *Capricornia*'. *Southerly*, vol. 41, no. 1 (1981), pp. 82-104.

———. 'Two Boys from Queensland: P. R. Stephensen and Jack Lindsay'. In Bernard Smith, ed., *Culture and History*. Sydney, Hale & Iremonger, 1984.

———. 'Xavier Herbert: A Disturbing Element'. *This Australia*, vol. 2, no. 2 (1983), pp. 11-16.

Nehls, Edward, ed. *D. H. Lawrence: A Composite Biography*, vol. 3, 1925-30. Madison, University of Wisconsin Press, 1959.

O'Flaherty, Liam. *Shame the Devil*. London, Grayson & Grayson, 1934.

Palmer, Nettie. *Fourteen Years: Extracts from a Private Journal 1925-1939*. Melbourne, Meanjin Press, 1948.

Palmer, Vance and Nettie. *Letters of Vance and Nettie Palmer 1915-1963*, ed. Vivian Smith. Canberra, National Library of Australia, 1977.

Parker, John. 'Oxford Politics in the Late Twenties'. *Political Quarterly*, vol. 45, no. 2 (April-June 1974), pp. 216-31.

Partridge, Eric. *The First Three Years: An Account and a Bibliography of the Scholartis Press*. London, Scholartis, 1930.

Paterson, Fred. 'The Early Years'. *Sixty Years of Struggle*, vol. 1 (1980).

Regardie, Israel. *The Eye in the Triangle: An Interpretation of Aleister Crowley*. St Paul, Minneapolis, Llewellyn, 1970.

Reid, Ian. *Fiction and the Great Depression: Australia and New Zealand 1930-1950*. Melbourne, Edward Arnold, 1979.

———. 'Sheep Without a Fold: Publishing and Fiction-writers in the 'Thirties'. *Meanjin*, vol. 33, no. 2 (1974), pp. 163-9.

———. 'A Splendid Bubble: Publishing and Fiction-Writing in the 'Thirties'. *Meanjin*, vol. 33, no. 3 (1974), pp. 266-71.

Roberthall, Robert Lowe Hall, baron. 'Expatriate Publishing'. *Meanjin*, vol. 33, no. 2 (June 1974), pp. 170-6.

Roberts, Warren. *A Bibliography of D. H. Lawrence*. London, Rupert Hart-Davis, 1963.
Roderick, Colin. *Miles Franklin: Her Brilliant Career*. Adelaide, Rigby, 1982.
Roe, Michael. 'P. R. Stephensen & Aleister Crowley'. *Meanjin*, vol. 33, no. 2 (June 1974), p. 180.
Sagar, Keith. *The Life of D. H. Lawrence*. New York, Pantheon, 1980.
Skidelsky, Robert. *Oswald Mosley*. London, Macmillan, 1975.
Spearritt, Peter and Walker, David, eds. *Australian Popular Culture*. Sydney, Allen & Unwin, 1979.
Steinberg, I. N. *Australia: The Unpromised Land*. London, Gollancz, 1948.
Stephensen, Eric. *Bibliography of Percy Reginald Stephensen*. Eltham, private, rev. ed., 1981.
——. *Brief Biographical Memorandum of Percy Reginald ("Inky") Stephensen*. Eltham, private, rev. ed., 1981.
Stone, Walter W. 'Collecting Books and Manuscripts for Australia's Libraries'. University of Queensland, *Alumni News*, vol. 3, no. 3 (December 1971).
Symonds, John. *The Great Beast: The Life of Aleister Crowley*. London, Rider, 1981.
Tardent, Jules L. *The Swiss-Australian Tardent Family History and Genealogy*. Southport, private, 1982.
Tregenza, John. *Australian Little Magazines 1923-1954: Their Role in Forming and Reflecting Literary Trends*. Adelaide, Libraries Board of South Australia, 1964.
Walker, David. *Dream and Disillusion: A Search for Australian Cultural Identity*. Canberra, Australian National University Press, 1976.
——. 'The Palmer Abridgement of *Such is Life*'. *Australian Literary Studies*, vol. 8, no. 4 (October 1978), pp. 491-8.

Index

Abo Call, 180
Aboriginal Day of Mourning and Protest (1938), 183, 211
Aboriginal Fellowship Group (AFG), 181
Aborigines, Australian, 19, 21, 122, 140, 155, 165, 178, 179-80, 183-4, 206, 207; culture of, 125, 139, 144, 192, 208; extermination of, 6, 80-1, 123, 139, 173, 179, 188; guilt about, 6, 123, 124; protest groups of, 181-2
Aborigines Progressive Association (APA), 180-5, 215
Action, 194
Acton, Harold, 32-3, 34-5, 71-2
Adamson, Bartlett, 159, 160, 172, 202
Addled Art, 188
Advance Australia League, 163
Advocate, 21
Adyar Hall, 184, 215, 218
aestheticism, 32-3, 34, 71-2
Age (Melbourne), 151-2
All Aboard for Singapore, 254
All About Books, 132, 168
Amorous Fiammetta, 88
Andrews, E. M., 186
Angus & Robertson: publishing of, 119, 121-2, 132, 136, 141, 142, 149, 254, 257, 263, 269; Stephensen and, 133, 142, 262, 263-4, 269, 270
Animals Noah Forgot, 122, 127, 129
Anstey, Frank, 16-17, 77
Antichrist, 57, 65-7
anti-Christianity, *see* Christianity
anti-intellectualism, 75, 176, 208, 269
anti-modernism, *see* modernism
anti-Semitism: Australia-First Movement and, 212, 217, 219; D. H. Lawrence and, 77; Ezra Pound and, 186; Hardy Wilson and, 246; in Germany, 161, 179, 188; Liam O'Flaherty and, 100-1; Miles Franklin and, 198-9; Nietzsche and, 66; Norman Lindsay and, 18, 54, 66, 78, 188; *Publicist* and, 198, 200-1, 205, 240-1; Stephensen and, 15, 17-18, 25, 77-8, 187-8, 189, 192, 195, 198, 201, 205, 206-7, 211, 215, 240-1, 252, 265-6, 267; Thomas Graham and, 217; W. J. Miles and, 181-3, 187-8, 192, 195, 196, 198, 201, 202; *see also* communism, Jews and
Anzac Muster, An, 119, 120, 269
A Propos of Lady Chatterley's Lover, 98
Aquila Press, 98
Archibald, J. F., 157
Argo (St John's College), 20, 28
Art in Australia, 27, 46
atheism, *see* Christianity
Australasia, 156, 173
Australia First, 163, 166, 170, 177-8, 188, 194, 199, 205, 206, 208
Australia-First Movement (AFM), 205, 210-19, 265, 266, 271; in Western Australia, 224, 231, 233-5, 245, 246; internment and, 223, 224, 226-7, 228, 229, 231-2, 234, 236, 240-1, 243-4, 245, 246, 252, 261, 265, 271
Australia First party plan, 163-4, 194-5, 199, 201, 202, 205, 217
Australian Book Publishing Company Ltd, 117, 120-1; *see also* Endeavour Press
Australian Book Services Limited, 152, 160, 164
Australian Encyclopaedia, 263
Australian Journal, 138, 140
Australian Mercury, 153-4, 155, 157-9,160, 161-2, 163, 169, 174, 192; *see also Foundations of Culture in Australia*
Australian National Review, 194
Australian Post, 163
Australian Quarterly, 166-7, 198

311

Australian Railways Union, 21
Australian Rhodes Review, 139, 186
Australian Society of Authors, 270
Australian Trans-Continental Airways Ltd, 160-1
Australian Workers' and Farmers' Socialist Republic, 23, 36, 42
Australians Progress Movement, 210
Austrovert, 261
authoritarianism, 9, 10, 201, 205, 209

Baillie, Helen, 181
Baker, Kate, 142, 175
Baker, W. T. & Co., *see* W. T. Baker & Co.
Bakunin, Michael, 54, 84, 86-7, 92, 144, 148, 158, 186, 204, 262
Barnard, Marjorie, 122, 141, 150, 151, 184, 253
Barrachi, Guido, 28
Bath, 136, 142
Baylebridge, William: life of, 119-20, 150, 173, 200, 241; politics and, 148, 192, 199, 269; Stephensen and, 120, 132, 133, 135, 162, 208; works of, 119-20, 148, 153, 171, 269
Bean, C. E. W., 200
Beasley, J. A., 226, 228, 231
Bed of Feathers, 88
Ben Hall the Bushranger, 254, 268
Berrie, George, 137, 142
Bethanga, 256-7, 260, 265
Bibliography of D. H. Lawrence, 82
Biblionews, 262
Biggenden, 4-6, 24-5, 122, 231
Bio-Politics, 199, 210
Birkenhead, Lord, 39, 40, 42, 52
Bissett, Sir James, 262-3
Blackburn, Maurice, 226, 227-8, 231
Blainey, Geoffrey, 195
Blamey, General Thomas, 227, 238
Blood, Captain, 215
Bolshevism, 9, 11, 12, 13-14, 15, 17, 22, 40, 42, 51, 54-5, 58, 73-4, 78-9, 158, 268; *see also* communism
Bombelli, G. L., 121, 126, 127, 130, 133, 175
Bombelli, Ron, 126
Bonnin, Margriet, 154-5
Book Censorship Abolition League, 160
Boynton, A. S. R., 152, 159, 160
Brady, E. J., 142, 166
Brave New World, 156
Brecht, Bertolt, 53
Bréhat, Ile de, 47-8, 49, 50
Brent of Bin Bin (pseud.), *see* Franklin, Miles
Brereton, R. Le Gay, 193
Brideshead Revisited, 33

Bring the Monkey, 127, 129, 132
Brisbane Courier, 14
Britain, 17, 18, 110, 188, 189, 193, 195, 265, 266; imperialism of, 22-3, 28, 32, 41-2, 105, 106, 116-17, 155-6, 162, 165, 186, 187, 201, 204, 207; World War II and, 202, 204, 209-10, 216, 246-7, 251
British Gazette, 45
British Worker, 45
Buckland, Harry, 104, 105
Bulletin (Sydney), 101, 121, 128, 157, 161, 264-5; contributors to, 115, 117-19, 175, 267; Endeavour Press and, 107, 115-16, 117, 120-1, 122, 124-6, 127, 128-34, 135, 160; internment and, 229, 232; litigation against, 147, 153, 159, 175-6
Bullock, L. F., 234-5
Burke, Thomas, 47, 88
Burns, Walter,. 263-4
Burton, Herbert, 13, 21, 22, 23, 24, 25, 31, 32, 33, 35, 36, 37, 185, 195, 253
Bushwhackers, 79-81, 84, 88, 109, 119, 122, 243, 260

Cahill, L. K., 205, 207-8, 210-11, 212, 213, 235-6, 241, 251
Calwell, Arthur, 266
Cameron, Archie, 228
Campbell, David, 173, 192
Campbell, Eric, 116, 148
Campbell, Roy, 62-4, 186
Cape, Jonathan, 69, 141
Cape Horn Breed, 262
capitalism, 173, 177; anti-Semitism and, 54, 78; criticism of, 17, 18, 23, 25, 26, 38, 39, 262
Capricornia, 131, 184, 264-5; at P. R. Stephensen & Co., 136, 137-8, 140, 145, 146, 149; *Publicist* edition, 177, 178, 181, 182, 183, 185
Catholic Advocate, 25
censorship: D. H. Lawrence and, 68, 72, 85-6, 90, 270; Kisch episode and, 150-1, 152; Stephensen and, 67, 69-72, 73, 74, 89, 94, 98, 157, 160, 164, 168, 192, 270; World War II and, 200, 212, 231-2, 233
Chauvel, Charles, 122, 129
Cherwell, 32, 33, 34-5, 39-40, 50
Chesleigh, Commander, 144
chess, 8, 35, 39, 94, 101, 115, 133, 161, 162, 239
Childe, Vere Gordon, 9, 14, 15, 16, 25, 34
Chisholm, A. H., 263
Chiswick Press, 48, 57
Christianity, 15, 20, 24-5, 26, 27, 66-7, 71, 103, 123, 162-3, 170, 181, 258
Churchill, Winston, 52, 165, 207, 234, 245

C. J. Brennan: An Essay in Values, 147
Clarke, Marcus, 157, 265-6, 268
'Clean Earth', 94
Clune, Frank, 171, 233, 253; FAW and, 151, 152; Stephensen and, 172-3, 178, 193, 197, 202, 253-6, 257-61, 262, 266, 267-8, 270; Stephensen's internment and, 238-9, 240, 244
Clyne Commission, 3-4, 243-7, 251, 252; *see also* internment
Cole, G. D. H., 44
Cole, Margaret, 44
Coleman, Peter, 264
Collins, Hal, 59, 72
Colonial Club, 33
Commonwealth Investigation Branch (IB), 112, 117, 197, 212, 215, 216, 217, 235, 245
Commonwealth Literary Fund, 267, 268
Commonwealth Pictures Ltd, 175
Commonwealth Security Service (CSS), 219, 238
communism, 177, 200, 201, 207; Fred Paterson and, 16-17, 22; French, 35-6; General Strike and, 44-5; Jack Lindsay and, 53; Jews and, 54; Oxford and, 34, 37-8; Stephensen and, 32, 39, 40-1, 43, 45, 53, 54, 82-4, 87, 92, 104, 117, 163, 169, 187, 188, 208-9, 210, 261-2, 268; *see also* Bolshevism
Communist Association (Ipswich), 22
Communist Party (French), 39
Communist Party of Australia, 20, 22, 28, 36, 164, 165, 202, 207, 210, 215, 236, 258, 262
Communist Party of Great Britain, 3, 36, 37-8, 39, 40, 41, 42-3, 45, 87, 104; Colonial Department of, 38; Oxford branch of, 34, 35, 37
Communist Review, 39, 42
Conditional Culture, 192
Confessions of Aleister Crowley, 89-90, 96, 99
Connolly, Captain L. A., 152, 153
conscription, 8, 9, 163, 165, 170, 213
Contract Bridge, 127, 129
Cookes, W. D., 216
Coonardoo, 122
Cousins, Walter, 132, 149
Cowling, Prof. G. H., 151-2, 153, 155
Creative Effort, 18, 53-4
Crockett, Vivian, 147, 150, 153, 159, 173, 175-6
Cross and the Flag, 265
Crowley, Aleister, 87, 89-91, 93, 94-100, 102, 103, 224
Crowley, Valentine, 211, 224

Crypt House Press, 88
culture, Australian, 5, 153, 154-6, 158-9, 164, 165, 171, 177-8, 193, 194, 199-200, 201, 239
Cummings, E. E., 62
Curtin, John, 212, 213, 216, 232
Cusack, Dymphna, 205

Daily Mail (Brisbane), 14, 16, 41
Daily Mail (London), 34, 70
Daily News (Sydney), 201-2
Daily Standard (Brisbane), 14, 23, 24, 25, 26, 31, 32, 34, 35, 36, 42
Dalley, John, 129
Dark, Eleanor, 136, 142, 150, 159, 173, 181, 184-5, 195, 200
Davies, Rhys, 64, 65, 68, 72, 76, 88, 91
Davis, Beatrice, 264
Davison, Frank Dalby, 110, 121, 135-6, 140, 150, 159, 160, 173, 184
de Groot, Francis, 116
de Locre, Elza, 47, 48, 49, 59, 65, 75, 92, 103, 111
de Miramar, Marie, 90-1, 99
Deamer, Dulcie, 160, 173, 232
Decline of the West, 62, 170
democracy, 5, 10, 20, 148, 164, 186, 189-92, 204, 205, 261
Devanny, Jean 157, 160
Dibley, Arthur, 137, 143, 146, 147
Dickson, Lovat, 146-7
dictatorship, 195, 203, 208, 209, 210
Dig, 172
Dimmock, Edmund, 13
Dionysos: Nietzsche Contra Nietzsche, 65
Direct Air Transport Ltd, 175
Doughman, 130-1
Douglas, James, 62, 69, 73, 94
Douglas, Norman, 55, 76, 84
Dovey, W. R., 244, 245
Downing, W. H., 240, 243, 244, 245, 251-2
Driberg, Tom, 37, 45, 50, 51-2
drinking, 21, 24, 31, 35, 50, 53, 58, 64, 65, 73, 74, 88, 93, 103
Duhig, Archbishop, 15
Dujardin, Edouard, 91-2
Dutton, Geoffrey, 267

Earp, Thomas, 59
Earth-Visitors, 48
Egan, Beresford, 69
Eldershaw, Flora, 122, 184
Eliot, T. S., 55, 62, 186, 204, 207
Elliott, Brian, 192, 193
Ellis, Havelock, 69, 110
Ellis, Lionel, 100, 101, 106
Elton, Godfrey, 33

Endeavour Press, 115-34, 135, 136, 141, 144, 147, 149, 243
eugenics, theories of, 4, 6, 17, 26, 121, 188
Evatt, Clive, 160
Evatt, H. V., 204-5, 209-10, 213, 215, 216, 218, 226, 235-6, 241, 243-4, 246, 252

Fadden, Arthur, 209, 227, 231
Falstein, S. M., 213
Fanfrolicana, 59-61
Fanfrolico and After, 262
Fanfrolico Press, 46-67, 69, 75, 77, 81, 85, 88, 92, 93, 102-3, 127, 176, 262; see also *Kookaburras and Satyrs*; *London Aphrodite*
Farrow, Will, 65
fascism: Australia First and, 163, 164, 199; Australia and, 116, 148, 157-8, 169, 177, 269; French, 35; German, 150-1, 161, 178; *Publicist* and, 202, 206, 207; Stephensen critical of, 3, 24, 157-8, 189; Stephensen sympathetic to, 3, 39, 161, 186-7, 189, 192, 194-6, 201, 202, 203-4, 206, 207, 208-9, 236, 255, 265; W. J. Miles and, 181, 185, 192, 201, 202
Fauns and Ladies, 46
Faust, 238
Fellowship of Australian Writers (FAW), 119, 124, 126, 130, 136, 150-2, 155, 172, 200, 202, 232, 270; Cultural Defence Committee, 152, 172, 178
Ferguson, George, 262, 264, 269
Ferguson, William, 180, 181, 183, 184, 185
Fifty Points for Australia, 209, 211
'Finding Heaven', 143
Finey, George, 173, 229, 230
Fisher, Andrew, 5
FitzGerald, R. D., 185
Fitzgerald, T. M., 267, 268
Fitzgerald, Tom, 164
Fitzroy Tavern, 58
Flesh in Armour, 122
Forde, F. M., 223, 224, 226-7, 228, 231, 235
Forward Press, 164, 165
Foundations of Culture in Australia, 154, 155-9, 164-9, 171, 178, 185, 192, 193, 195, 204, 260, 265, 268; see also *Australian Mercury*
Fox, Sir Frank, 107
Franklin, Miles, 124, 153, 173; as Brent of Bin Bin, 80, 109, 116; books by, 109-10, 116, 127, 132, 142, 171; letters by, 80, 109, 128-9, 141-2, 148, 150, 152, 175, 176, 181, 198-9, 243; Stephensen and, 108-9, 110, 111, 122, 133, 157, 159, 160, 176, 181, 186, 200, 243; war and, 226, 229, 233, 239, 243; see also anti-Semitism, Miles Franklin and

Free Oxford, 34
Fryer, Benjamin, 166
Fryer, Dennis ('Chut'), 13, 22, 157
Furphy, Joseph, 142, 156, 175

Galmahra, 19-20, 21, 22, 43, 101; see also *Queensland University Magazine*
Game, Sir Philip, 116
Garden, Jock, 28
General Strike (1926), 39-40, 42, 44-5, 52, 69
Gentleman Never Tells, A, 141, 142
Georgiad, 62
Germany, 17, 148, 202, 247; Stephensen and, 3, 39, 66, 158, 161, 188, 189, 195, 198, 203, 216, 261, 266
Gibb, Helen, 105, 106
Gibbs, Pearl, 183, 184
Gilbert, Stuart, 91-2
Gilmore, Mary, 126, 166, 184
God in the Sand, 142
Goethe, Johann Wolfgang von, 238
Goldston, Edward, 73, 75, 77, 86, 88, 90, 93, 96, 101, 102
Gordon and Gotch, 127
Graham, Thomas, 217, 266
Grainger, Percy, 155
Grano, Paul, 224, 229, 233
Grattan, C. Hartley, 128, 148, 152, 188-9, 204, 233
Green, H. M., 200
Greene, Graham, 34-5, 37
Greyhound Form Guide, 105-6, 107, 111
Griffiths, Richard, 185
Growth of Love, 269

Hall, Radclyffe, 68-71, 72, 94, 99, 175
Hall, Robert (Lord Roberthall), 13, 21, 24, 25, 31, 32, 33, 35, 36, 39, 40, 43, 53, 65, 100, 102, 106, 111, 185, 195
Hamilton, Alastair, 186-7
Hanchant, W. L., 99
Harrington, Sir John, 52
Harrison, E. J., 228
Heathcote, 180
Herald (Melbourne), 265
Herbert, Sadie, 136, 138, 140, 145, 205
Herbert, Xavier, 173; Aborigines and, 81, 139; sesquicentenary prize and, 181, 184, 185, 193; Stephensen and, 81, 131-2, 136, 139-40, 142, 145-7, 159, 166, 169, 176-7, 178, 205-6, 264-5, 270; see also *Capricornia*
Heseltine, Philip, 52, 59, 64, 72, 88, 103
Higgins, Esmonde, 22, 109
High Ho to London, 255
Hirtzel, Sir Arthur, 40
History and Description of Sydney Harbour, 263

Hitler, Adolf, 148, 158, 189, 194, 224, 245; Australia First and, 206; Stephensen and, 3, 157, 161, 165, 169, 187, 188, 189, 190, 192, 195, 196, 202, 203, 208, 216, 229, 245, 265, 266
Homage to Sappho, 59
Hooper, S. B., 166, 173, 211, 224, 225, 251
Hopegood, Peter, 129
House is Built, A, 122, 141
Howarth, R. G., 269
Hudson, Flexmore, 206, 232
Hudson, G. Inglis, 145
Hughes, Randolph, 147, 159, 169
Hughes, T. J., 233-4
Hughes, W. M., 137, 147-8, 159, 227-8, 231
Hulbert. Madalen, 19
Huxham, John, 14, 31-2
Huxley, Aldous, 3, 64, 69, 73, 75-6, 79, 85, 156
Hyden, Walford, 104

imperialism, 4, 38-9, 183, 189, 262; *see also* Britain, imperialism of
In the Wake of the 'Bounty', 122, 129
Independent Sydney Secularist, 162, 194, 200
Ingamells, Rex, 192, 193, 208, 209, 211, 213, 215, 224, 256
Ingwersen, S. J., 208
intelligence services, *see* Commonwealth Investigation Branch (IB); Commonwealth Security Service (CSS); MI5; Military Intelligence (MI); Military Police Intelligence (MPI)
International Workers of the World (IWW), 12, 44, 163
internment, 3, 224-47, 260, 271; conditions, 224-5, 232, 236-8, 239; press reports of, 227, 228-9, 243; *Publicist* and, 193; tribunal, 226, 235; *see also* Australia-First Movement, internment and; Clyne Commission
Ipswich Boys' Grammar School, 13, 21, 22, 23, 24
isolationism, 80, 116, 153, 187, 189, 217

James, Nora, 72, 94
Japan, 208, 213, 233; AFM and, 226; collaboration with, 204, 216, 217, 219, 223, 227, 228, 229, 234, 235, 245-6, 251; Stephensen and, 3, 6, 165, 188, 189, 195, 197, 215, 216, 223, 246, 251; Adela Walsh and, 210, 212, 213
Jindyworobak poetry movement, 192, 206, 208, 224
John Bull, 68
Johnson, Frank, 27

Jonah, 110, 117, 122, 129, 132
Jones, Captain William H. S., 262
Jorgensen, Jorgen, 257-60, 268
Joyce, James, 61, 62, 89, 91-2
Joynson-Hicks, Sir William (Jix), 39, 40, 42-3, 52, 69-71, 72, 73, 82

Kanga Creek, 110
Kangaroo, 25, 73, 77, 79, 84, 124, 192, 203, 204
Kell, Colonel Sir Vernon, 112
Kelly Hunters, 268
Kennedy, Victor, 206
Kerr, R. A., 21
Kingdom of Shylock, 17
Kirtley, John (Jack): Fanfrolico Press and, 46, 47, 48-51, 53, 55-7, 59, 85; internment and, 224, 230-1, 235-6, 241, 251; Stephensen and, 48, 49-50, 85, 135, 136, 137, 143, 145, 162, 166, 253
Kisch, Egon, 150-1, 152, 155, 159, 164, 173
Knockholt (Kent), 65, 85, 93, 94, 96
Knowles, Sir George, 231
Knox, Ronald, 42, 98
Kookaburras and Satyrs, 261-2
Koteliansky, S. S., 72, 73, 85, 89, 94

Labor Party, Australian, 5, 6, 9, 11, 12, 21, 22, 23, 31, 40, 213, 216, 232, 236, 240
Labour Club (Oxford), 33-4, 42, 44
Labour Party, British, 40
Lady Chatterley's Lover, 68, 72, 76, 77, 78-9, 81-2, 84, 87, 156, 176, 270
Lahr, Charles, 64, 65, 81-2
Lancaster, G. B. (pseud.), 129-30, 132, 142
Landor, Robert Eyres, 51
Landtakers, 107, 134, 144, 150, 157
Lang, Jack, 108, 116-17
Lawrence, D. H., 39, 64, 87, 101, 263; censorship and, 68, 73, 74, 90; paintings of, 67, 68, 72, 73, 74, 76, 82, 84-6, 88, 89, 176; Stephensen and, 3, 25, 61, 72-4, 76, 78-80, 81-2, 84, 87, 91, 94, 98, 104, 110, 111, 122, 124, 128, 176; works of, 64, 73, 76, 156, 192
Lawrence, Frieda, 68, 72, 76, 80, 82, 84, 85
Lawson, Henry, 80, 147, 156
League of Rights, 265
Lee, Frank, 42
Legend of Aleister Crowley, 94-6
Lemont, E. C., 136-7, 142
Lemont, Ruby, 136, 137, 142
Lenin, V. I., 22, 39, 262
Lewis, Wyndham, 168, 186
Life and Works of A. G. Stephens, 200
Lindsay, Jack, 43, 69, 72, 90-1, 111-12, 268; D. H. Lawrence and, 76, 84; Fanfrolico

Press and, 46-9, 50-1, 52, 53, 54, 55, 58, 59, 61, 62, 64, 65, 67, 81, 85, 92, 102-3, 127, 261-2; in Sydney, 27, 46; Mandrake Press and, 73, 75, 77, 88, 89; University of Queensland and, 14, 15, 18-19, 20, 261
Lindsay, Lionel, 173, 188
Lindsay, Norman: family life, 14, 47, 125, 128; Fanfrolico Press and, 46-7, 49, 50, 51, 58-9, 64, 66, 71, 75, 77, 85, 261; Jack Lindsay and, 18, 20, 27, 46, 47, 61, 111, 112, 261; Mandrake Press and, 73, 89; publishing and journalism of, 106-8, 109, 115, 116, 117, 120, 121, 124-5, 134; Stephensen and, 53-5, 61, 71, 74, 77, 82, 85, 104, 107-8, 109, 110, 111, 117, 120, 122, 124, 125, 127-8, 130-1, 133, 138, 160; writing and philosophy of, 18, 46-7, 49, 53-5, 66, 78, 106, 110, 122, 127, 129; *see also* anti-Semitism, Norman Lindsay and
Lindsay, Philip, 14, 27, 54, 64, 81, 92, 112
Lindsay, Ray, 14
Lindsay, Rose, 107, 117, 125, 128, 135
Literary Guild of Australia, 152
literature, Australian, 151-2, 154-5; Endeavour Press and, 109-10, 111, 117-19, 120, 121, 125; Miles Franklin and, 80; Norman Lindsay and, 107; Stephensen and, 15, 18-19, 80, 108, 130, 140-1, 154, 156-8, 160, 165, 178, 243, 261, 265, 267, 271; Vance Palmer and, 151-2
Liverpool internment camp, 224-6, 229-31, 232, 236
Lockyer, Jack, 40, 47, 100, 101, 105, 106, 111, 116, 126, 135, 171, 225, 240, 254
London Aphrodite, 61-5, 68, 69, 74, 75, 76, 78-9, 82-4, 86-7, 101, 103, 144, 176, 206
London Mercury, 47, 62, 69, 133, 154
Lone Hand, 116, 129
Love Redeemed, 148
Loveday internment camp, 236-8
Lysistrata, 46, 48, 50, 51, 55, 58, 59, 64

Macarthur, General Douglas, 227
Macartney, Frederick, 152, 168
McCrae, Hugh, 18, 58-9, 64, 126
Mack, Louise, 136
Mackaness, George, 151, 152
MacKay, Police Commissioner, 217, 218-19
McLaren, Jack, 28, 32, 34, 47, 88, 109, 116
Macquarie Head Press, 122
Magician, 90
Magrath, Rev., 42
Maguire, Joe, 26
Maguire, Mona, 26
Majlis Club, 38, 42
Makala Farm, 136
Mandrake Press, 73, 75, 76, 77, 81, 88-9, 92, 98-9, 101, 102-3; Aleister Crowley and, 90-1, 93-4, 98-9, 102; D. H. Lawrence and, 73, 77, 86, 87, 88, 91, 98
Manifold, John 173
Mann, Cecil, 130, 133
Mann, Leonard, 122
Mannix, Daniel, 177, 207
Man-Shy, 121
Marino Faliero, 48, 51
Marx, Karl, 20, 22, 26, 33, 38, 67, 206
Maryborough, 4, 6, 7-8, 10, 122
Maryborough Boys' Grammar School, 6-11, 12
Maryborough Chronicle, 5, 10
Masefield, John, 151
Massey, Edward, 166-7, 171, 173, 212, 213, 216, 218, 251
Master of Hounds, 104, 105
Matthews, Harley, 225, 229, 251
Maugham, Somerset, 90
Meanjin, 211, 265
Memoirs of a Fox-Hunting Man, 104
Mencken, H. L., 61, 168, 172
Mental Rubbish from Overseas, 152
Menzies, R. G., 209, 240
Mercantile Gazette, 25
Mezzomorto, 147, 150, 153, 159, 175, 176
MI5, 3, 37, 112, 117, 234
Miles, 'Bee', 171-2
Miles, J. B., 200
Miles, W. J., 162-3, 177, 295n6; Aborigines and, 180, 181, 183, 185; business sense of, 173, 185, 187, 199, 200; health of, 200, 207, 209, 216; personality and philosophy of, 171, 185, 199, 200, 207, 210, 211-12, 216; *Publicist* and, 166, 170-1, 181-3, 194, 199, 200, 209, 211-12, 240; Stephensen and, 162, 164, 165, 168, 178, 192, 193, 194, 201-2, 266, 268; *see also* anti-Semitism, W. J. Miles and; nationalism, W. J. Miles and
Military Intelligence (MI), 197, 215, 223, 224, 226-7, 234, 235, 239, 245
Military Police Intelligence (MPI), 197, 212-13, 216, 217, 223-4, 226, 231
Miller, E. Morris, 154, 166, 257-8
modernism, 18, 34, 48, 59, 61, 62, 105, 154, 188, 206-7, 267, 269
Modjeska, Drusilla, 199
Mohr, Max, 85
Moir, J. K., 253
Molesworth, Bevil, 36, 38
Moonchild, 90
Moore, Tom Inglis, 32, 36, 44, 57-8, 151, 173
Moseley, Colonel, 234, 235
Mosley, Oswald, 194, 234, 238
Mountainside Press, 253

Mudie, Ian: Australia-First Movement and, 211; internment and, 224, 226, 230, 231, 243, 247; *Publicist* and, 173, 175, 193, 200; Stephensen and, 185, 192-3, 203-4, 206, 208, 209, 213, 267, 271; works by, 160, 171, 173, 175, 200; Xavier Herbert and, 206
Muirden, Bruce, 134, 194, 245
Mulligan, J. J., 137, 141, 142, 146
Muskett, Herbert G., 86
Mustar, Captain Ernest, 161

Nation, 267, 268
National Security Act, 226, 231, 236, 240
National Socialist Party of Australia, 265
nationalism, 4, 5, 155, 163; cultural, 117, 128, 155-6, 158-9, 165; Lindsays and, 58-9; Stephensen and, 39, 106, 110-17, 119, 126, 140, 148, 158, 168, 173, 183, 186-7, 188-9, 199-200, 205, 206, 207, 208, 216, 245, 265; W. J. Miles and, 162, 163, 173, 178, 183, 189; Xavier Herbert and, 139, 140; *see also* Australia-First Movement; *Australian Mercury*; literature, Australian; *Publicist*
Nazism, *see* fascism
New Guard, 116, 148, 151, 157, 163, 209, 210, 255
New South Wales Bookstall Company, 122, 142
New Statesman, 21, 43, 151
Nietzsche, Friedrich Wilhelm, 65-6, 103, 120, 172, 187; Lindsays and, 18, 19, 46; Stephensen and, 45, 65-6, 67, 75, 78, 82, 84, 89, 120, 186, 208, 262
Nineteenth Century, 169
Norman Lindsay Does Not Care, 71

Observer (Sydney), 264
O'Ferrall, Ernest, 129
O'Flaherty, Liam, 58, 64, 65, 67, 75, 80, 88, 91, 92, 99, 100-1, 193
Old Blastus of Bandicoot, 142
On the Pacific Front, 164
One Big Union, 12, 14
Opinion, 153
Orioli, Pino, 67, 68, 72, 81, 82
Oxford Union, 42
Oxford University, 32-5, 105; communism and, 37-8, 40-2; General Strike and, 45; PPE course at, 33, 53; *see also* Queen's College
Oxford University Poetry Society, 98
Oxford Workers' Strike Bulletin, 44, 45

P. R. Stephensen & Co. Ltd, 135-44, 145-9, 150, 152, 175; *see also* Stephensen's National Book-Publishing House Ltd

Packer, Sir Frank, 153, 264
Packsaddle, 183-4
Pageant, 129-30, 132
Pailthorpe, Grace, 98
Paintings of D. H. Lawrence, 84-5, 86, 88, 160
Palmer, Nettie, 119, 150; letters from, 162, 166; Stephensen and, 80, 110, 134, 135, 140-1, 142, 144, 148, 166
Palmer, Vance, 110, 116, 117, 119, 126, 130, 141, 150, 151, 153, 175
Pansies, 74, 81, 82, 86
Paris, 35-6, 39, 43-4, 69
Parlement of Pratlers, 59
Partridge, Eric, 20, 51, 72
Paterson, A. B., 122, 127, 129, 147, 156
Paterson, Fred, 16-17, 22, 23, 157
patriotism, 8, 15, 16, 45, 121, 156, 162, 251
Patten, Jack, 180, 181, 183, 184, 185
Pavlova, 104
Pearl, Cyril, 229
Penton, Brian, 92, 107, 134, 144, 157, 229; Fanfrolico Press and, 81, 85; litigation and, 147, 150, 153, 159, 175-6
Pétain, Marshal, 203, 204
Petrov case, 217, 266
Piddington, A. B., 159, 176
Piscator, Erwin, 53
Plough Inn, 58, 77, 92, 95
Ploughman, 143, 144
Point Counter Point, 64, 69, 75
Policeman of the Lord, 69-71
Pollinger, Laurence, 263
Poor Fellow My Country, 206
Porter, Hal, 125
Pound, Ezra, 61, 186, 295n27
Praed, W. Mackworth, 156
Pratt, Ambrose, 137, 159
Prelude to Christopher, 136
press propaganda, 17, 158, 179, 187, 198, 261
Price, Theo, 125, 132, 142
Prichard, Katharine Susannah, 111, 116, 122, 151, 152, 157, 173
Prior, Ken, 115, 120, 121, 127, 130, 132, 133, 135, 147
Prior, S. H., 115, 116, 117, 120, 121, 127, 130

propaganda, *see* press propaganda
Propertius in Love, 55-7, 59
Protocols of the Elders of Zion, 66, 77-8, 183, 188, 198, 215
Publicist, 166, 168, 185, 194, 204, 214, 268; 'Brief Survey of Australian History', 178-9, 181; Adela Walsh and, 210; contributions for, 170-1, 173-5, 176, 179-80, 181-3, 187, 188, 189-92, 193, 195, 196, 209, 211, 212, 215, 251, 259, 265; intern-

ment and, 232, 239, 240-1, 244, 245, 246, 251; radio talks, 177-8, 183, 184, 188; revival of, 232, 252, 260, 261; war and, 197-8, 199, 202, 217; see also anti-Semitism, *Publicist* and; fascism, *Publicist* and
Publicist Publishing Company, 205
publishing, Australian, 106-11, 115, 119, 121-2, 124-5, 130, 134, 141, 144, 155, 160, 162, 239, 243

Queen's College (Oxford), 32, 33, 38-9, 40, 42
Queensland University Magazine, 15, 18; see also *Galmahra*
Quicke, Edward Cunningham, 238

racism, 6, 17-18, 21, 39, 45, 54, 165, 179, 181-4, 265, 266; see also Aborigines, Australian; anti-Semitism; White Australia Policy
Radio 2SM (Sydney), 177
railway workers, 21, 22, 26, 38, 44
Rainbow, 86
Rais, Gilles de, 98
rationalism, 162, 163
Rationalist Association, 25
Rationalist Press Association, 162-3
Red Europe, 16-17
Redheap, 106, 110
Rees, Leslie, 141
Regardie, Israel, 94, 104, 105
Return of the Brute, 91
revolution, 12, 16, 17, 39, 42, 45, 116; Liam O'Flaherty and, 58; Stephensen and, 17, 18, 21, 23, 24, 26, 27, 28, 36, 38, 41, 44, 45, 52, 54, 87, 207, 267, 268
Rhodes Scholarship, 3, 21, 23-4, 28, 33, 35, 40, 41-2, 44, 52, 110, 232-3, 251
Rice, Gordon, 229-31
Richards, Detective Sergeant G. R., 217, 234-5, 236, 245
Richardson, Henry Handel, 108, 110, 115-16, 126, 133, 136
Rickety Kate (pseud.), 168
Rickword, Edgell, 88
riots, red flag, 13-14, 16
Roberthall, Lord, see Hall, Robert
Roberts, Morley, 199, 210
Robertson, George, 133
Robertson and Mullens, 122, 142
Robinson, F. W., 154
Roderick, Colin, 264, 270
Rosenberg, Alfred, 188
Ross, Hector, 165
Rudd, Steele (pseud.), 80, 126, 157
Russell, Bertrand, 34

Russia, 36, 37, 38, 100, 216, 246
Russian Association (Brisbane), 14
Ryan, T. J., 6

St John's College (University of Queensland), 13
Salier, C. W., 166, 173, 210
Salvage, 269
Sane Democracy League, 178
'Saturdee', 122, 125, 127, 129
Satyricon, 59
Satyrs and Sunlight, 58-9, 64
Savage Club, 270
Sawtell, Michael, 185
Schindler, Charles, 14
Scholartis Press, 51, 72
Searchlight, 38
Sedgwick, Cecil, 144, 145, 149, 152, 160
sesquicentenary celebrations, 178, 180, 181, 183, 184
'Settlers', 122-4, 139
sexism, 15, 18, 58, 72, 89, 172, 181-3, 195, 199, 202, 235
Sexual Inversion, 69
sexuality, 15, 19, 25, 27, 31, 34, 48, 64, 67; see also censorship
Shalimar Cafe, 151, 160, 173, 193, 197, 211
Shame the Devil, 100
Shand, J. W., 244, 245, 246
Shaw, Bernard, 84, 186
Sink of Solitude, 69
Sitwell, Sacheverell, 64
Sky High to Shanghai, 254
Sleeveless Errand, 72
Slessor, Kenneth, 27, 48, 64, 119, 159, 263
Smith, Victor, 26-7, 28, 36, 41
Smith's Weekly, 119, 254
Sons of Men, 142
Squire, J. C., 47, 61-2, 69
Stanley's Pipe Dream, 52-3
Stead, Christina, 122, 153
Stein, Gertrude, 61, 62, 207
Steinberg, I. N., 198
Stephens, A. G., 46, 116, 121, 154, 157, 199-200, 265
Stephensen, Christian Julius, 4, 5, 20, 25, 27, 35
Stephensen, Cyril Edward (Ted), 247
Stephensen, Eric, 116, 126, 135, 224, 229-31
Stephensen, Jens Christian Julius, 4, 5, 81
Stephensen, Marie-Louise, 5, 20, 25, 27, 35
Stephensen, P. R. ('Inky'): academic record, 6, 8, 13, 38, 53; bankruptcy action, 168, 175, 176, 177; childhood and schooling, 5-11; death, 270-1; family, 4-5, 26-7, 81, 84; income, 35, 51, 59, 77, 88, 96, 102, 104, 117, 121, 135, 147, 164, 166, 168,

172, 178, 197, 254, 255, 258, 262, 264, 265; lifestyle, 19, 47, 65, 73, 126; literary agency, 263, 264; literary style, 43-4, 69-71, 76; marriage, 53, 105, 253; personal characteristics, 3, 32, 43, 93, 128, 133, 176, 223, 229, 232, 249; personal finances, 50, 96, 102, 104, 106, 107, 111, 119, 145, 146, 159, 160-1, 164, 177, 210, 240, 251-2, 260, 263, 265, 270; personality, 3-4, 8-9, 11, 13, 17, 19, 22, 24, 26, 36, 43, 44, 51-2, 53-4, 58, 64, 72, 89, 92-3, 99, 103, 128, 133, 136, 139, 162, 258-60, 266, 268; pseudonyms, 52, 170, 171, 193, 194, 198, 203, 205; psychological state, 49, 102, 103, 106, 210, 241, 251, 253, 265-6; Quixote figure, 13, 134, 265; racial pride, 4, 17, 121, 123, 271; self-image, 24, 104, 171, 245, 258-60, 268; sport and recreation, 6, 8, 13, 15, 24, 32, 34, 105, 106, 133 (*see also* chess; drinking); **work as:** autobiographer, 94, 258-60; book editor, 125, 131-2, 138 (*see also* Clune, Frank); businessman, 20, 59, 76, 80, 93, 98, 99, 102, 111, 119, 130, 132-3, 134, 135, 136-7, 142-3, 145, 146, 147, 149, 153-4, 160-1, 162, 175, 176, 200; fiction writer, 65, 76, 79-81, 122, 203; ghost writer, 104, 105, 172, 197, 253, 262-3, 267 (*see also* Clune, Frank); journalist, 23, 25, 53, 117 (*see also* Daily Standard; Galmahra; Worker's Weekly); periodical editor, 19-20, 62, 64-5, 101, 108, 153-9, 160, 161-2, 168; playwright, 52-3; poet, 43, 78; publisher, 64, 88, 107, 111, 117, 121, 127, 131, 142, 144, 200, 203 (*see also* Endeavour Press; Fanfrolico Press; Mandrake Press; P. R. Stephensen & Co. Ltd); reviewer and critic, 25, 173, 185, 199; satirist, 43, 70-1, 72, 75, 173; social critic, 15, 61, 82-3, 86-7; speaker, 10, 16, 20, 22, 24, 25, 33, 38, 40, 44, 200, 213, 215-16, 218, 270; translator, 39, 65, 66-7
Stephensen, P. R. & Co. Ltd, *see* P. R. Stephensen & Co. Ltd
Stephensen, Rosaline, 8, 20, 35, 51, 104, 105, 106, 107, 111, 126, 135, 136, 137, 140
Stephensen, Winifred, 47, 100, 104, 111, 116, 137, 146, 150, 254, 256; age of, 37, 43, 49; as dancer, 32, 37; diary of, 95, 107, 108, 128, 161, 164, 180, 232; illnesses, 49, 168, 209, 232, 238, 239-40, 241; internment and, 225, 226, 228-30, 232, 238, 239-40, 241, 244, 247, 252; pregnancy, 96, 105; relationship with P. R. Stephensen, 32, 34, 36-7, 40, 41, 43, 50-1, 53, 58, 65, 84, 94, 95, 128, 270

Stephensen's Circular, 138, 139, 142
Stephensen's National Book-Publishing House Ltd, 135, 144-5, 147
Stivens, Dal, 160
Stone, Louis, 117, 122, 132
Stone, Walter, 261, 262, 267, 270, 271
Such is Life, 142, 152, 163, 175
Sunday Express, 62, 69, 94
Sunday Worker, 52, 53
Sydney Harbour, 116, 119, 134, 233, 263
Sydney Morning Herald, 148, 183-4, 228, 232, 269
Sydney Sails, 263

Talkarra Press, 261
Tardent, Henry, 4-5, 18, 23, 26, 41, 77, 164
Tate, Robert, 130-1
Tatura internment camp, 238-47, 252
Täuber, Prof. Carl, 123
Taylor, A. J. P., 33, 34, 37, 44
Teens Triumphant, 136
Telegraph (Brisbane), 41
Theodore, E. G., 10, 21, 28
Thirteen Poems, 143
This Vital Flesh, 119-20, 199, 269
Thomas, F. J., 234, 245
Thomas, Ieuan, 37, 38, 40, 44
Thompson, Piers Gilchrist, 146
Threebrooks, 137, 142
Thynne, Major Robin, 98, 99, 102
Times, The, 40, 42
Times Literary Supplement, 48, 62, 64, 80, 91
Tourist's Guide to Ireland, 88
Toys Hill (Ailsa Lodge), 100, 101, 104, 105, 106, 107
'Toys Hill Bible' plan, 101, 103
Trade Without Money, 161
Trades Union Congress (TUC), 44, 45
Transport and General Workers' Union (Oxford), 44
Try Anything Once, 151
Tunning of Elynour Rumming, 59
Turner, W. J., 89

unemployment, 1, 12, 38, 39, 104, 116, 136
United States, 105, 189, 193, 195, 206, 210, 212, 216, 217, 246, 266
University Labour Federation, 40
University of Queensland, 12, 15, 16, 105, 108; *see also* St John's College

Valentyne, Val, 104
Viking of Van Diemen's Land, 257-60, 270
Vision, 27, 46
Voice, 101-2
Vrepont, Brian, 211

W. T. Baker & Co., 143, 144
Waite, George, 178
Waite and Bull, 160
Walker, Rev. E. M., 40
Wallace, J. T. Noble, 6, 9-11
Walsh, Adela Pankhurst, 210-11, 212, 213, 224, 234, 235, 265
Walsh, Tom, 210
Warburton, 252-3
Warlock, Peter (pseud.), see Heseltine, Philip
Warren, Dorothy, 73, 76, 85-6
Waten, Judah, 267
Watts, Martin, 225
Waugh, Evelyn, 33, 72
Weekley, Barbara, 76, 80
Welles, Orson, 42
Well of Loneliness, 68-71, 72, 94, 175
Well of Sleevelessness, 72
Wells, Dr Joseph, 40-1, 42, 45
Welsby, Albert, 22, 23, 166
Wentworth, W. C., 156, 173
Weston, Nancy, 104
White, A. G., 137, 175
White, Patrick, 137, 143-4
White, Ruth, 143
White, V. M., 137, 143
White Australia League, 266
White Australia Policy, 6, 21, 81, 163, 165, 179, 182, 195, 201, 266
Whitlam, H. F. E., 231
Wickham, Anna, 65
Wild Colonial Boys, 239, 255, 258, 268
Wilmot, Frank, 159
Wilson, Hardy, 217, 246
Witherby, T. C., 14-15, 16, 17, 19
'Wobblies', see International Workers of the World (IWW)
Woman's Mirror, 125-6, 130, 133
Women's Guild of Empire, 210, 211
Workers' Educational Association (WEA), 14, 15, 16, 21, 22, 23
Workers' Theatre Movement (WTM), 52-3, 80
Workers' Weekly (London), 34
Workers' Weekly (Sydney), 28, 196
World War I, 4, 8, 12, 157, 187, 207, 213, 261; see also conscription
Wright, Judith, 120, 192, 269
Writers' League, 152
Wylie, F. J., 42

Yabber Club, 173, 193, 197, 199, 205, 209, 211, 229, 245
Yorke, G. J., 99

Zipine, Michael, 36, 39, 43